THE HOUGHTON LIBRARY
1942-1967

THE HOUGHTON LIBRARY

1942-1967

*A Selection of Books and Manuscripts
in Harvard Collections*

CAMBRIDGE
The Harvard College Library
MCMLXVII

COPYRIGHT © 1967
BY THE PRESIDENT AND FELLOWS OF HARVARD COLLEGE
LIBRARY OF CONGRESS CATALOGUE CARD NUMBER 67-14051
DISTRIBUTED FOR THE HARVARD COLLEGE LIBRARY
BY THE HARVARD UNIVERSITY PRESS

CONTENTS

Introduction	xi
John Harvard	1
Thomas Hollis of Lincoln's Inn	4
Friends of the Library	7
Medieval Text Manuscripts	9
Incunabula	16
Early Maps	23
The Reformation	26
Erasmus	32
The William King Richardson Library	35
S.T.C.	47
English Literature	51

John Keats	73
Lewis Carroll	76
T. E. Lawrence	81
The Amy Lowell Collection	82
American History	91
American Literature	103
Emily Dickinson	117
Thomas Wolfe	119
Canadiana	120
Russian Literature and History	125
German Literature	130
Heinrich Heine	143
Rainer Maria Rilke	144

French Literature	146
Italian Literature	154
Camoẽs and Cervantes	158
The History of Science	161
Music	162
The Theatre Collection	164
Printing and Graphic Arts	177
Index	251

COLOR PLATES

The De Buz Book of Hours	*facing page* 38
Book of Common Prayer and Bible	43
William Blake's The Judgment of Adam and Eve	62
The Calderini Pontifical	182
The Hours of Juana la Loca	187
Hours written by Bartolomeo San Vito	187
Portrait of Mary, Queen of Scots	*after page* 200
Portrait of François II of France	*after page* 200
Jean Desmarets de St. Sorlin: *Clovis ou la France Chrestienne*	*facing page* 214
Guillaume Apollinare: *Si Je Mourais La-Bas*	244

The end-papers reproduce a paste paper designed by Rudolph Ruzicka and executed by Veronica Ruzicka for Rosamond Bowditch Loring. The Incipit and Explicit inscriptions on slate by John Howard Benson were commissioned in 1950 by Philip Hofer, H 1921, and presented to the library in 1966. The Harvard arms embossed on the cover were drawn by Rudolph Ruzicka in 1963.

The original dimensions are given for those illustrations that have been reduced in scale; all other illustrations are full size.

Introduction

THE earliest published description of the Harvard College Library occurs in *New Englands First Fruits* (1643), where John Eliot writes of 'a large Library with some Bookes to it, the gifts of diverse of our friends.' Today more than ninety libraries totalling some 7,500,000 volumes make up the vast complex of the Harvard University Library, and four of these—Widener, Houghton, Lamont, and the Fine Arts Library—comprise what is known as the Harvard College Library, the central collection of the Faculty of Arts and Sciences, containing more than 3,000,000 volumes. Although most book selection has long been in the hands of a professional staff, 'the gifts of diverse of our friends' are still responsible for providing most of the wealth of books and manuscripts available to scholars at Harvard. They have been acquired through gift and bequest, and through purchase with the income of endowed funds established by alumni and other supporters of the university.

Such a library does not initially set out to collect what are usually called 'rare books,' but in its normal development it accumulates books and manuscripts that obviously deserve special measures for their better preservation. They may or may not have been expensive to acquire, but they would be difficult or impossible to replace, their absence from a scholarly library would be unthinkable, and their artistic or historical values are susceptible to attrition through ordinary handling. They constitute the basic raw material and the evidence that must be handed on, intact if possible, from one generation of scholars to all those that follow. Moreover, perspectives change; the current publications of one century often become the rare books of the next.

Libraries respond according to their stage of development and the resources available to them. During the eighteenth century the librarians of Harvard began to mark their treasures for special care by inserting a bookplate printed in carmine, instead of the usual one printed in black. In 1841 Gore Hall (the pride of Cambridge, still featured on the official seal of the city) was opened to house the library, and such books were marked 'Closet' or 'Cl' and locked up in bookcases with wire mesh doors. In 1913 Gore Hall, by then much too small despite the construction of an annex and the adoption of various awkward expedients, was pulled down. Two years later the Widener Library opened on the site, providing for the first time a separate Treasure Room with its own reading room, offices, and stacks. Meantime the libraries of the other faculties had become separate entities, each with its own shelves of special books and manuscripts, which have since grown into the modern Treasure Rooms of the libraries of Law, Medicine, Divinity, and Business Administration.

At first the Widener building had room to spare. Its lower stack levels were empty and were not even provided with shelving. But the central collections grew more rapidly than anticipated. After an interval of only twenty-five years the Treasure Room stacks were bulging, and so were the open stacks; their juxtaposition made further expansion almost impossible. Even worse, the simplest needs of conservation could not be met without air conditioning, which seemed forbiddingly difficult and costly to install in the Widener building.

In 1940 Arthur Amory Houghton, Jr., H 1929, himself a book collector and acutely aware of the urgency of the problem and its magnitude, offered to enable the university to build a wholly new library building specifically designed to provide the best possible facilities for the preservation, cataloguing, consultation and exhibition of rare books and manuscripts. The Treasure Room at that time was headed by the young, enthusiastic, and formidably expert team of William A. Jackson and Philip Hofer, while the Director of the University Library was Keyes D. Metcalf, an international authority on library planning. The architects, Perry, Shaw & Hepburn, threw themselves into the task with all the skill at their command.

With Europe at war and the United States on the verge of the conflict, the planners pushed forward at top speed, but with the most careful attention to detail. The building was designed to take advantage of the latest technological advances in air conditioning and lighting. Many of its innovations have since become standard in the planning of other libraries. Ground was broken late in 1940, and the Houghton Library was opened in a formal ceremony on the evening of February 28, 1942.

The opening of the Houghton Library did much more than provide an ideal environment for the preservation and study of books and manuscripts. It brought to a focus the efforts of friends of the library who sought to support it, and it provided a powerful impetus for the strengthening of its collections, an impetus that still prevails. The Houghton Library was built with a capacity of 250,000 volumes, and when it opened in 1942 it was half full. By 1949, when the Lamont Library opened next door, Houghton was nearly full. Its available space was thereupon doubled by connecting it with the upper level of Lamont's underground stack. Today that too is nearing its combined capacity of 500,000 volumes, posing anew the old problem and at the same time providing a concrete measure of growth.

But the story is not merely one of piling book on book and gathering in more material year by year. The process of selection became increasingly sophisticated in answer to the needs of scholars and often in anticipation of them. The systematic building of the collections and the steady enlargement and refinement of the catalogues in turn increased the use of the library—the true test of its value. The Houghton Library now serves three times as many readers as the old Treasure Room recorded in its last year, and the capacity of the reading room is frequently strained by the number of those needing to use it. In addition to faculty members and graduate students, the library reaches a widening segment of the university family as the current emphasis on the honors program brings more undergraduates to consult primary sources in their research.

The influence of the library is by no means restricted to the Harvard community. President James B. Conant remarked on the occasion of the opening,

> One of the functions of a university is to act as a guardian of the cultural riches of the past. Our libraries and museums serve only in part our own students and our staff. To a large measure they are of benefit to the much greater world of scholars. As trustees pledged to the continuation and loving care of such enterprise, we are the servants of a community that extends far beyond these academic walls—our responsibilities transcend both the immediate aims of this institution of learning and the days in which we live.

Without question the Houghton Library is fulfilling Mr. Conant's pledge to international scholarship. Half of its readers have no official connection with Harvard, and they come from all over the world. Many who cannot visit Cambridge in person send a mounting flood of requests for information and orders for photographic copies. Books, editions, dissertations, monographs, and papers in great profusion and bewildering variety acknowledge their indebtedness. The collections are freely available to all serious students within a framework of rules designed to protect scholarly work in progress, to prevent improper exploitation of materials, and to assure the preservation of literary, artistic, and historical evidence for future generations of scholars.

A library such as this has a further obligation, and to a still wider public. Most of its collections are necessarily stored out of sight, including many books and manuscripts that are world-renowned as monuments of art and literature. They would speedily deteriorate or be altogether destroyed if they were put into the hands of everyone who might profit from seeing them. Exhibitions, both permanent and changing, serve to display our cultural heritage without subjecting it to such hazards. Exhibition catalogues providing both a guide and a permanent record can now occasionally be published through the recently established Houghton Development Fund.

Exhibitions are often tied to the university curriculum, for the educational and indeed the emotional impact of seeing works in their original form while they are being discussed in the classroom cannot be denied. But the application need not be immediate and obvious. Exposure to books and manuscripts at any time may bring no less tangible benefits. As W. A. Jackson wrote in his classic paper, *The Importance of Rare Books and Manuscripts in a University Library*,

> At any moment, the sight of any one of them may be the spark which will kindle in some young scholar the desire to unravel the complex which makes them important for mankind and set forth on a scholarly adventure which may result in one more solid addition to the structure of man's understanding of his past.

The pages that follow present an exhibition on paper, rather than under glass, to mark the twenty-fifth anniversary of the Houghton Library by displaying something of the range, scope, and richness of its holdings of books and manuscripts, some of them the property of Harvard for more than three centuries. Any selection of three hundred and seventy individual pieces out of some hundreds of thousands of books and several million manuscripts is necessarily arbitrary and only partially representative, but specialists on the staff of the library have chosen these to suggest as broad a spectrum as possible of scholarly and cultural values. Each item depicted represents a numerous class on the shelves of Houghton, and each is made more valuable to scholarship through being a part of the vast resources of a great university library.

The library of Harvard University is the creation of the devoted labor of generations of librarians and scholars in all the branches of learning touched upon by its faculties, and, as these pages show, the disinterested generosity of many donors in every period of its history. It occupies a central position in the existence of the university. As such, it must be as dynamic as the body it serves. This volume is intended not merely to celebrate the achievement of the past, but also to suggest the exciting vistas of the future.

W. H. BOND

INCIPIT

John Harvard

JOHN HARVARD, B.A. and M.A. of Emmanuel College, Cambridge, came to Charlestown in 1637 and died there a year later, leaving all his books and half his estate to the newly founded and as yet unnamed College. Some six months later the Great and General Court of the Massachusetts Bay Colony ordered 'that the colledge agreed vpon formerly to bee built at Cambridg shalbee called Harvard Colledge,' and so the first important donor to the Library also gave his name to the College.

No inventory of John Harvard's effects is known to exist, but about 1667 a list of his books was copied into the College Records, some 329 titles representing about 400 volumes. Two titles on this list have survived among the books in the library of the Hollis Professor of Divinity, and they may have come from the Harvard Bequest. But they are less likely candidates for this post of honor than one of the 404 volumes to have survived the disastrous fire of 1764 that destroyed most of the College Library: John Downame's *Christian Warfare*, which must be *primus inter pares* in any account of the Harvard College Library.

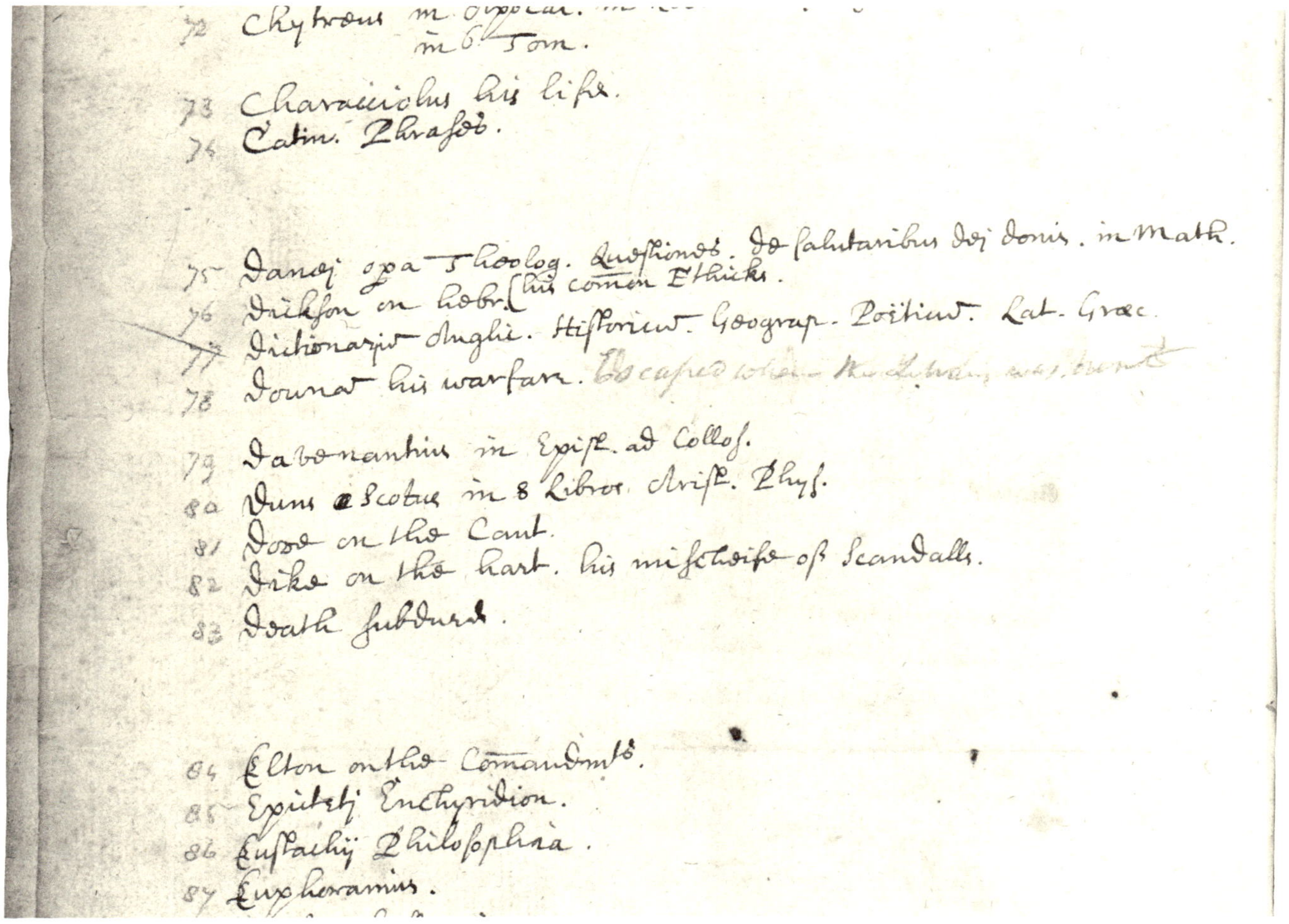

MS. CATALOGUE OF JOHN HARVARD'S LIBRARY
College Book No. 1

יְהוָֹה אֱלֹהִים

Omnia hæc tibi dabo. *State, vigilate et orate.* *Resistite diabolo et fugiet.*

Mundus Adulans

Saltem visi non dolo. *Vetus homo.*

THE
CHRISTIAN
warfare
Against the Deuill
World and Flesh
Wherein is described their
nature, the maner of
their fight and meanes
to obtaine victorye
By Iohn Downame
Bachelar in Divinity and
preacher of Gods word.

LONDON
Printed by William Stansby

Mundus sæviens. *Deponite veterem hominem.*

Certamen præclarum decertavi

Ia: Payne sculp.

An Account of the Fire at *Harvard-College*,

in *Cambridge*; with the Loss sustained thereby.

CAMBRIDGE, JAN. 25. 1764.

LAST night HARVARD COLLEGE, suffered the most ruinous loss it ever met with since its foundation. In the middle of a very tempestuous night, a severe cold storm of snow attended with high wind, we were awaked by the alarm of fire. *Harvard*-Hall, the only one of our ancient buildings which still remained,[*] and the repository of our most valuable treasures, the public LIBRARY and Philosophical APPARATUS, was seen in flames. As it was a time of vacation, in which the students were all dispersed, not a single person was left in any of the Colleges, except two or three in that part of *Massachusetts* most distant from *Harvard*, where the fire could not be perceived till the whole surrounding air began to be illuminated by it : When it was discovered from the town, it had risen to a degree of violence that defied all opposition. It is conjectured to have begun in a beam under the hearth in the library, where a fire had been kept for the use of the General Court, now residing and sitting here, by reason of the Small-Pox at Boston : from thence it burst out into the Library. The books easily submitted to the fury of the flame, which with a rapid and irresistable progress made its way into the Apparatus-Chamber, and spread thro' the whole building. In a very short time, this venerable Monument of the Piety of our Ancestors was turn'd into an heap of ruins. The other Colleges, *Stoughton*-Hall and *Massachusetts*-Hall, were in the utmost hazard of sharing the same fate. The wind driving the flaming cinders directly upon their roofs, they blazed out several times in different places ; nor could they have been saved by all the help the Town could afford, had it not been for the assistance of the Gentlemen of the General Court, among whom his Excellency the Governor was very active ; who, notwithstanding the extreme rigor of the season, exerted themselves in supplying the town Engine with water, which they were obliged to fetch at last from a distance, two of the College pumps being then rendered useless. Even the new and beautiful *Hollis*-Hall, though it was on the windward side, hardly escaped. It stood so near to *Harvard*, that the flames actually seized it, and, if they had not been immediately suppressed, must have carried it.

But by the Blessing of God on the vigorous efforts of the assistants, the ruin was confined to *Harvard*-Hall ; and there, besides the destruction of the private property of those who had chambers in it, the public loss is very great ; perhaps, irreparable. The Library and the Apparatus, which for many years had been growing, and were now judged to be the best furnished in America, are annihilated. But to give the public a more distinct idea of the loss, we shall exhibit a summary view of the general contents of each, as far as we can, on a sudden, recollect them.

Of the LIBRARY.

IT contained—The Holy Scriptures in almost all languages, with the most valuable Expositors and Commentators, ancient and modern :—The whole Library of the late learned Dr. Lightfoot, which at his death he bequeathed to this College, and contained the Targums, Talmuds, Rabbins, Polyglot, and other valuable tracts relative to oriental literature, which is taught here : The library of the late eminent Dr. Theophilus Gale : —

---

[*] *Harvard*-Hall, 42 feet broad, 97 long, and four stories high, was founded A. D. 1672.

—All the Fathers, Greek and Latin, in their best editions. — A great number of tracts in defence of revealed religion, wrote by the most masterly hands, in the last and present century.— Sermons of the most celebrated English divines, both of the established national church and protestant dissenters :—Tracts upon all the branches of polemic divinity :—The donation of the venerable Society for propagating the Gospel in foreign parts, consisting of a great many volumes of tracts against Popery, published in the Reigns of Charles II. and James II. the Boylean lectures, and other the most esteemed English sermons :—A valuable collection of modern theological treatises, presented by the Right Rev. Dr. Sherlock, late Lord Bishop of London, the Rev. Dr. Hales, F. R. S. and Dr. Wilson of London :—A vast number of philological tracts, containing the rudiments of almost all languages, ancient and modern :—The Hebrew, Greek and Roman antiquities.—The Greek and Roman Classics, presented by the late excellent and catholic-spirited Bishop Berkeley ; most of them the best editions :—A large Collection of History and biographical tracts, ancient and modern.—Dissertations on various Political subjects —The Transactions of the Royal Society, Academy of Sciences in France, Acta Eruditorum, Miscellanea curiosa, the works of Boyle and Newton, with a great variety of other mathematical and philosophical treatises.—A collection of the most approved Medical Authors, chiefly presented by Mr. James, of the island of Jamaica ; to which Dr. Mead and other Gentlemen made very considerable additions : Also Anatomical cuts and two compleat Skeletons of different sexes. This collection would have been very serviceable to a Professor of Physic and Anatomy, when the revenues of the College should have been sufficient to subsist a gentleman in this character.—A few ancient and valuable Manuscripts in different languages.—A pair of excellent new Globes of the largest size, presented by Andrew Oliver, jun. Esq;—A variety of Curiosities natural and artificial, both of American and foreign produce.—A font of Greek types (which, as we had not yet a printing-office, was reposited in the library) presented by our great benefactor the late worthy Thomas Hollis, Esq; of London ; whose picture, as large as the life, and institutions for two Professorships and ten Scholarships, perished in the flames.——Some of the most considerable additions that had been made of late years to the library, came from other branches of this generous Family.

The library contained above five thousand volumes, all which were consumed, except a few books in the hands of the members of the house ; and two donations, one made by our late honorable Lieutenant Governor Dummer, to the value of 50 l. sterling ; the other of 56 volumes, by the present worthy Thomas Hollis, Esq; F. R. S. of London, to whom we have been annually obliged for valuable additions to our late library : Which donations, being but lately received, had not the proper boxes prepared for them ; and so escaped the general ruin.

As the library records are burnt, no doubt some valuable benefactions have been omitted in this account, which was drawn up only by memory.

Of the APPARATUS.

WHEN the late worthy THOMAS HOLLIS, Esq; of London founded a Professorship of Mathematics and Philosophy in Harvard-College, he sent a fine Apparatus for Experimental Philosophy in its several Branches.

Under the head of *Mechanics*, there were machines for experiments of falling bodies, of the centre of gravity, and of centrifugal forces ;—the several mechanical powers, balances of different sorts, levers, pullies, axes in peritrochio, wedges, compound engines ; with curious models of each in brass.

In *Hydrostatics*, very nice balances, jars and bottles of various sizes fitted with brass caps, vessels for proving the grand hydrostatic Paradox, siphons, glass models of pumps, hydrostatic balance, &c.

In *Pneumatics*, there was a number of different tubes for the Torricellian experiment, a large double-barrell'd Air-pump, with a great variety of receivers of different sizes and shapes ; syringes, exhausting and condensing ; Barometer, Thermometer ;—with many other articles.

In *Optics*, there were several sorts of mirrors, concave, convex, cylindric ; Lenses of different foci ; instruments for proving the fundamental law of refraction ; Prisms, with the whole apparatus for the Newtonian theory of light and colors; the camera obscura, &c.

And a variety of instruments for miscellaneous purposes.

THE following articles were afterwards sent us by Mr. Thomas Hollis, Nephew to that generous Gentleman, viz. an Orrery, an armillary Sphere, and a box of Microscopes ; all of exquisite workmanship.

For *Astronomy*, we had before been supplied with Telescopes of different lengths ; one of 24 feet ; and a brass Quadrant of 2 feet radius, carrying a Telescope of a greater length ; which formerly belonged to the celebrated Dr. Halley. We had also the most useful instruments for *Dialling* ;— and for *Surveying*, a brass semicircle, with plain sights and magnetic needle. Also, a curious Telescope, with a complete apparatus for taking the difference of Level ; lately presented by Christopher Kilby, Esq;

Many very valuable additions have of late years been made to this apparatus by several generous benefactors, whom it would be ingratitude not to commemorate here, as no vestiges of their donations remain. We are under obligation to mention particularly, the late Sir Peter Warren, Knt. Sir Henry Frankland, Bart. Hon. Jonathan Belcher, Esq; Lt. Governor of Nova-Scotia ; Thomas Hancock, Esq; James Bowdoin, Esq; Ezekiel Goldthwait, Esq; John Hancock, A. M. of Boston, and Mr. Gilbert Harrison of London, Merchant. From these Gentlemen we received fine reflecting Telescopes of different magnifying powers ; and adapted to different observations ; Microscopes of the several sorts now in use ; Hadley's Quadrant fitted in a new manner ; a nice Variation Compass, and Dipping needle ; with instruments for the several magnetical and electrical experiments—all new, and of excellent workmanship.——ALL DESTROYED !

Cambridge, Jan. 26. 1764. As the General Assembly have this day chearfully and unanimously voted to rebuild *Harvard*-Hall, it encourages us to hope, that the LIBRARY and APPARATUS will also be repaired by the private munificence of those who wish well to America, have a regard for New-England, and know the importance of literature to the Church and State.

BOSTON: PRINTED BY R. AND S. DRAPER.

1764.

Thomas Hollis of Lincoln's Inn

THE fire in 1764 summoned forth a new John Harvard in the somewhat eccentric person of Thomas Hollis of Lincoln's Inn. He was the third Thomas Hollis to support the college and its library, and he had already sent numerous books to Cambridge, many of which survived the fire merely because no one had yet unpacked them. He had also given or was to give books to other libraries, notably at Leipzig, Zurich, and Berne, not to mention parcels of worthy tracts that he was in the habit of sending anonymously to no doubt bewildered recipients throughout the kingdom. But his greatest benefactions were reserved for Harvard.

Hollis had his intended gifts handsomely bound and ornamented with a variety of emblematic tools, cut especially for him by J. B. Cipriani and intended to represent what he was pleased to call his 'republican' tendencies. An entry from his diaries tells of the melancholy loss by fire in London of a '*very fine* collection of books, relating chiefly to Government, which were . . . intended to be sent to Harvard College'; they were at the moment in the hands of the binder, preparatory to shipment. Many of Hollis's gifts were enlivened by characteristically moral or hortatory inscriptions from the donor. The fund of £500 that he bequeathed still buys books, and is the oldest such fund at the service of the Library.

A HOLLIS BINDING ON TWO AMERICAN SERMONS BY ANDREW ELIOT AND JONATHAN MAYHEW, 1765–1766   8 × 5⅛ inches

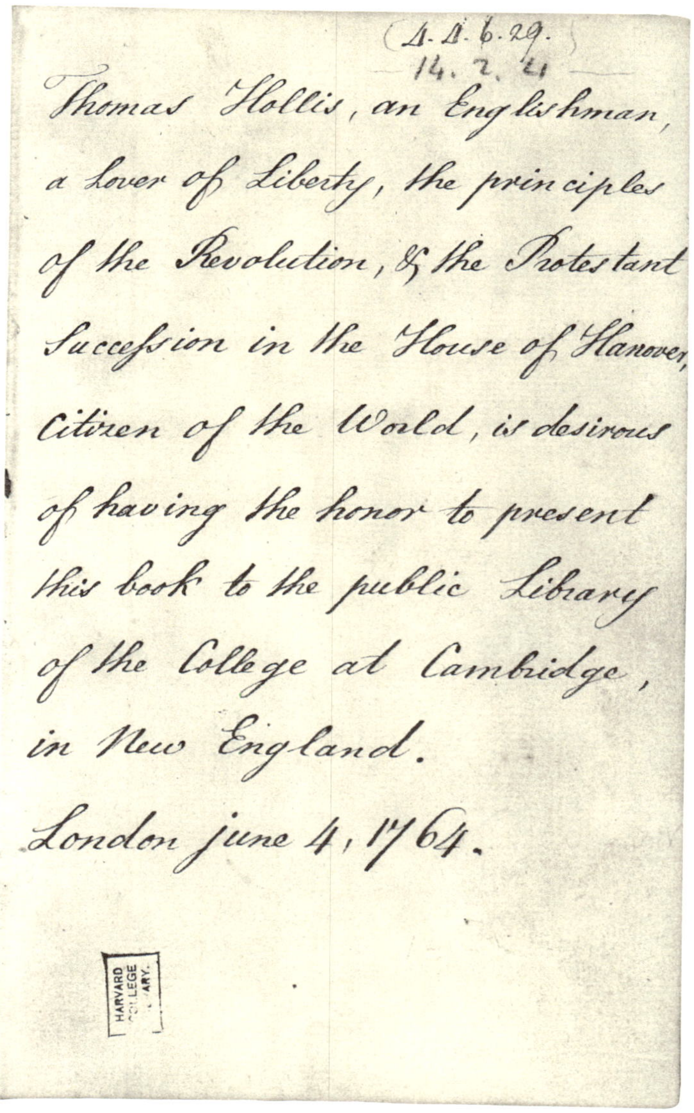

AN INSCRIPTION BY THOMAS HOLLIS IN FRANCIS HOME, *THE PRINCIPLES OF AGRICULTURE AND VEGETATION*, LONDON, 1762   7⅞ × 4⅞ inches

31. there for binding & were intended to be sent to Harvard College in N.E.; besides much time & thinking. I will not be discouraged however, but begin collecting a finer parcel for that College; and I thank God, that it was not my own house that was consumed; a calamity that would have masterd my poor Philosophy!

june 5,
30. Dispersed several copies of Locke's "Two Treatises," by Shove. Busied the whole day in preparing other copies to go abroad. Ned Buxton with me in the evening to take those copies on board of Ship. Dined at home alone.

6. Mathewman with me, to acquaint me, "that very early yesterday morning his House was burnt down, by what accident he could not say, tho' he suspected, from the carelessness of a maid servant, & all the things in it utterly consumed: That Himself, Mr. Bailey, his Wife, & their Servants had escaped, with difficulty, naked, from the Flames; and that the Fire had destroyed nine other Houses."

Lamented this misfortune on many accounts; but cheered Mathewman all I could.

I have lost by it a large & very fine collection of books, relating chiefly to Government, which were the parcel of ... writing a Note alone. At ... er Antiquarie. At Baker's the Rev. Mr. ... street. At ...an's lodgings,

TWO PAGES FROM
HOLLIS'S DIARY
Given in 1962 by
Arthur A. Houghton, Jr., H 1929

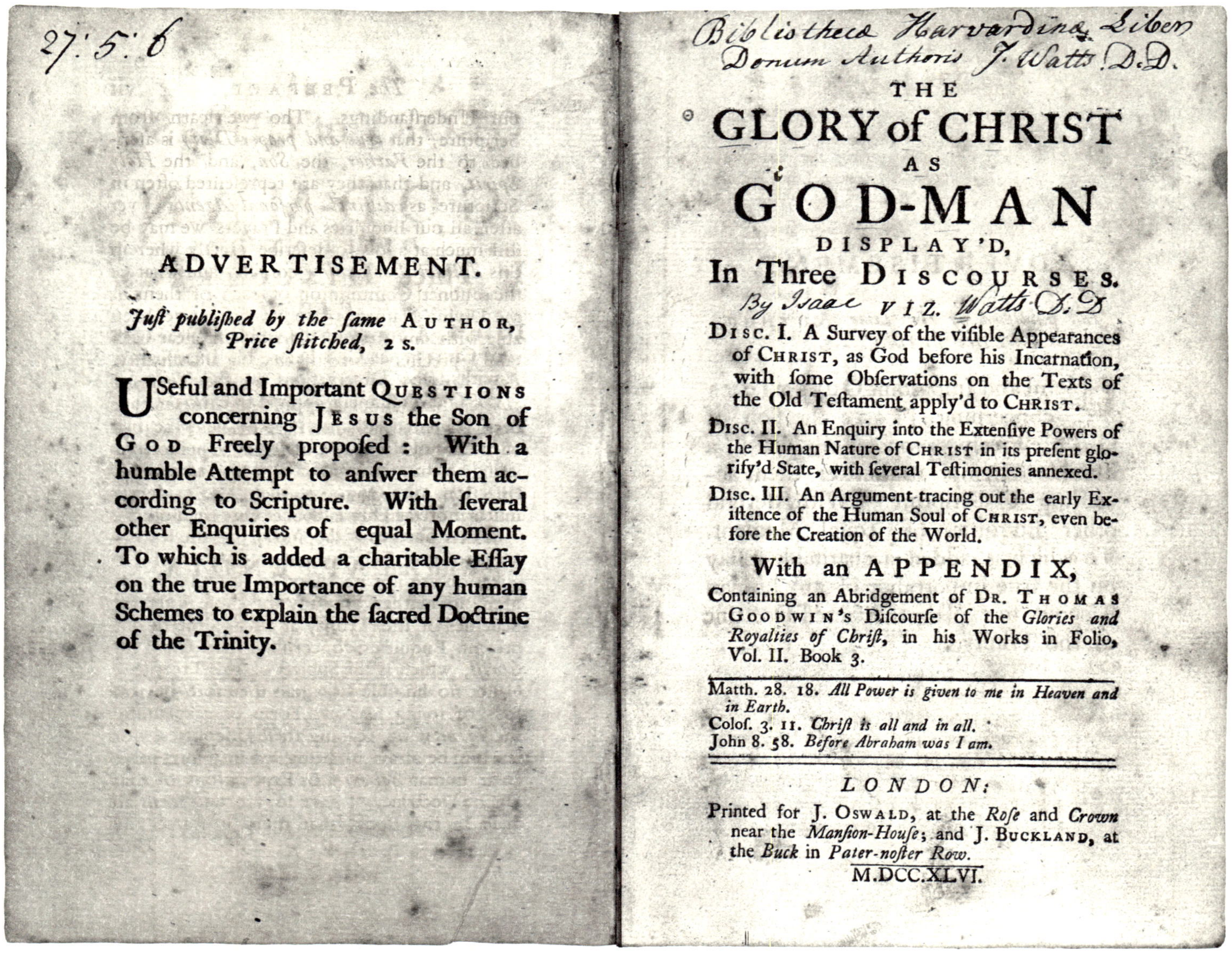

ISAAC WATTS: *THE GLORY OF CHRIST AS GOD-MAN*, LONDON, 1746   7⅞ × 9⅞ inches
Given by the author (date not recorded)

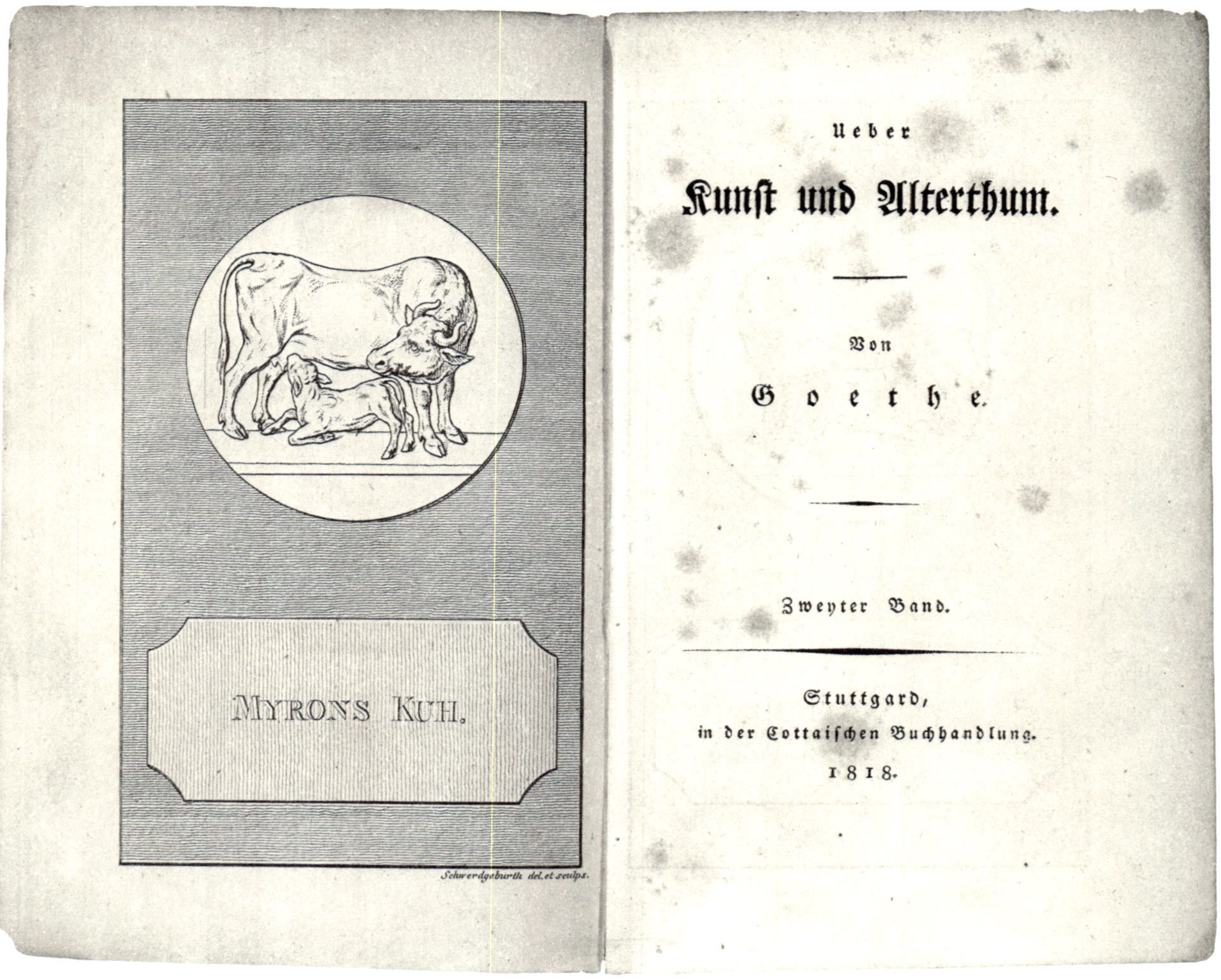

GOETHE: *UEBER KUNST UND ALTERTHUM*, STUTTGART, 1818   6¾ × 8¼ inches
Given in 1819 by the author

Friends of the Library

THE Friends of the Harvard College Library is an organization with a long and honorable history. As it is presently constituted, its members pay annual dues with a fixed minimum, though many contribute larger sums. In return for their support and interest, Friends are invited to special events and receive certain publications, including the *Harvard Library Bulletin*.

But the Library had friends long before it had Friends: in the truest sense, it owes its existence to private benevolence. What books and manuscripts have not been given or bequeathed have been purchased, almost entirely, with the income from endowed funds. Many Harvard men have been benefactors of the Library, but many notable benefactions besides those of John Harvard and the Hollises have come from persons with no previous Harvard connection.

A few eminent names may exemplify such disinterested support, otherwise memorialized in bookplates and inscriptions. Isaac Watts presented copies of his own works to the college overseas, and some happily survived the library fire of 1764. Another survivor is the copy of John Baskerville's *Virgil* (1757), given in 1758 by Benjamin Franklin, who said that many thought it to be 'the most curiously printed of any book hitherto done in the world.' At other times Franklin presented various mathematical and scientific works.

In 1819 a correspondence initiated by Edward Everett and Joseph C. Cogswell culminated in the receipt of some thirty-five volumes that were straightway bookplated 'The Gift of the Author, John W. von Goethe, of Germany.' In 1869 Thomas Carlyle wrote to his old friend Ralph Waldo Emerson of his intention 'of testifying my gratitude to New England (New England, acting mainly through one of her sons called Waldo Emerson), by *bequeathing to it my poor Falstaff Regiment, latterly two Falstaff Regiments of Books*'—gathered and used in writing his own two works on Cromwell and Frederick the Great. He carried out his intention by bequest, and some 325 volumes, many thickly annotated, came to Harvard in 1881.

Beyond such examples, the pages that follow testify over and over to the loyalty and generosity of those who have supported the Harvard College Library, and whose contributions to Harvard and to learning are in some measure acknowledged and commemorated here.

CARLYLE'S MARGINALIA IN SÉGUR'S *HISTORY...*
OF FREDERIC WILLIAM II, LONDON, 1801   8⅝ × 5½ inches
Bequeathed in 1873 by Thomas Carlyle (received 1881)

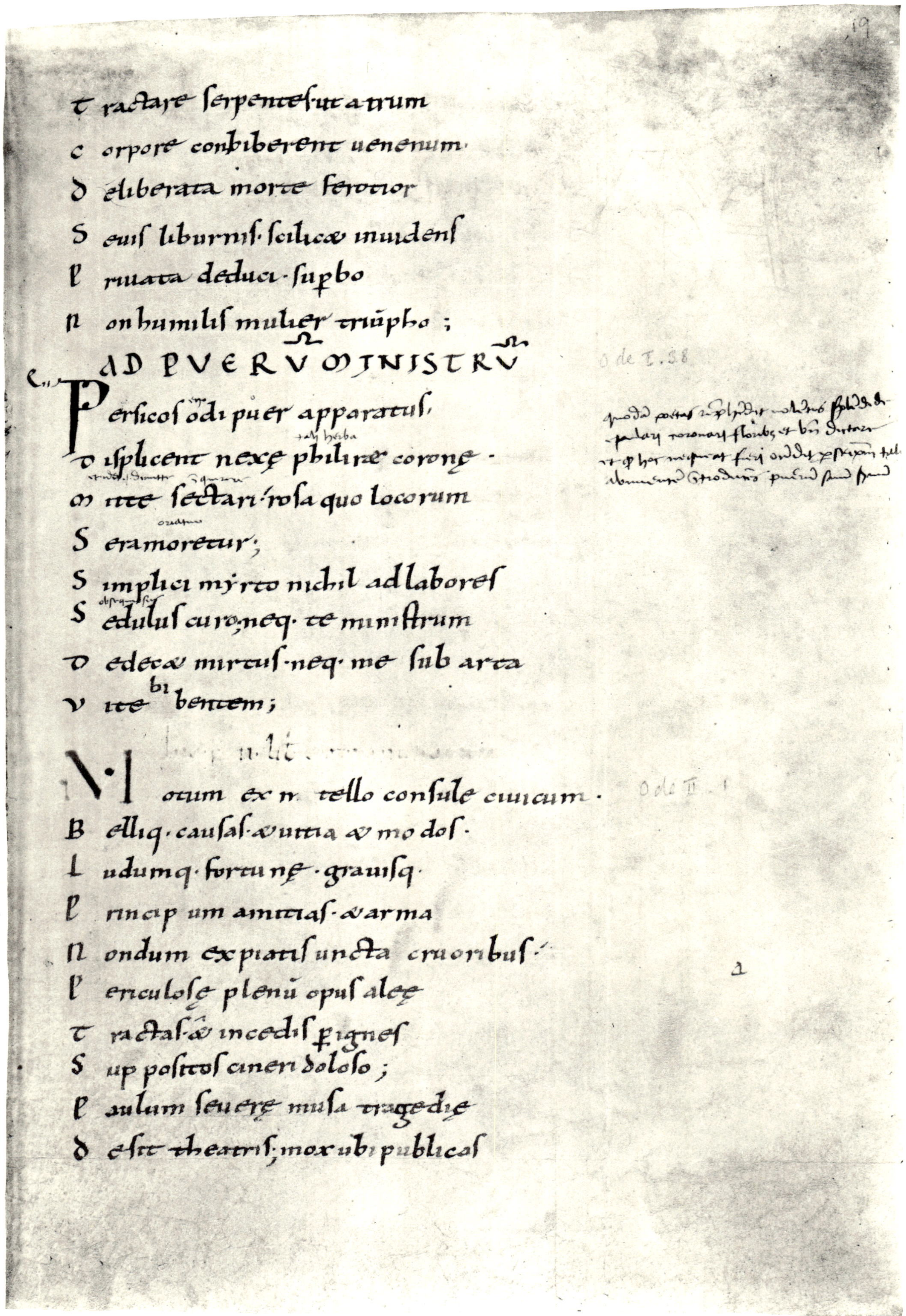

tractare serpentes ut atrum
corpore conbiberent uenenum
deliberata morte ferocior
seuis liburnis scilicet inuidens
priuata deduci supbo
non humilis mulier triumpho;

AD PUERU MINISTRU

Persicos odi puer apparatus,
displicent nexę philirae coronę·
mitte sectari rosa quo locorum
seramoretur;
simplici myrto nichil adlabores
sedulus curo neq. te ministrum
dedecet mirtus·neq; me sub arta
uite bibentem;

Motum ex mtello consule ciuicum·
Belliq; causas et uitia et modos·
ludumq. fortunę· grauisq;
principum amicias et arma
nondum expiatis uncta cruoribus·
periculose plenu opus aleę
tractas et incedis ignes
suppositos cineri doloso;
paulum seuerę musa tragedię
desit theatris; mox ubi publicas

HORACE MS. (SAEC. X–XI): ODES I, 38
Given in 1950 by Stephen W. Phillips, H 1895

Medieval Text Manuscripts

ALTHOUGH the pre-fire library had contained 'a few ancient and valuable Manuscripts in different languages,' the collection of such books may be said to have begun with a lot of seven Greek manuscripts purchased by Edward Everett (later President of Harvard) in Constantinople in 1819. Since Everett's gift, the collection has grown to considerable size with the acquisition of single manuscripts and such significant groups as the Riant manuscripts (mainly dealing with the history of the Crusades) and those in the library of William King Richardson '80.

Perhaps the most important Latin manuscript is the Horace, which some scholars ascribe to Italy and the tenth century, and some to France and the eleventh century. As important textually is the tenth-century Byzantine manuscript of Gregorius Nyssenus and Nemesius of Emesa, in its beautiful minute script. After them come numerous literary and historical texts, many acquired to meet the immediate needs of Harvard scholars. All but the most recent accessions are described in Seymour de Ricci's *Census* and its *Supplement*.

CHAUCER: *TREATISE ON THE ASTROLABE* (CA. 1410)
Given in 1953 by David P. Wheatland, H 1922

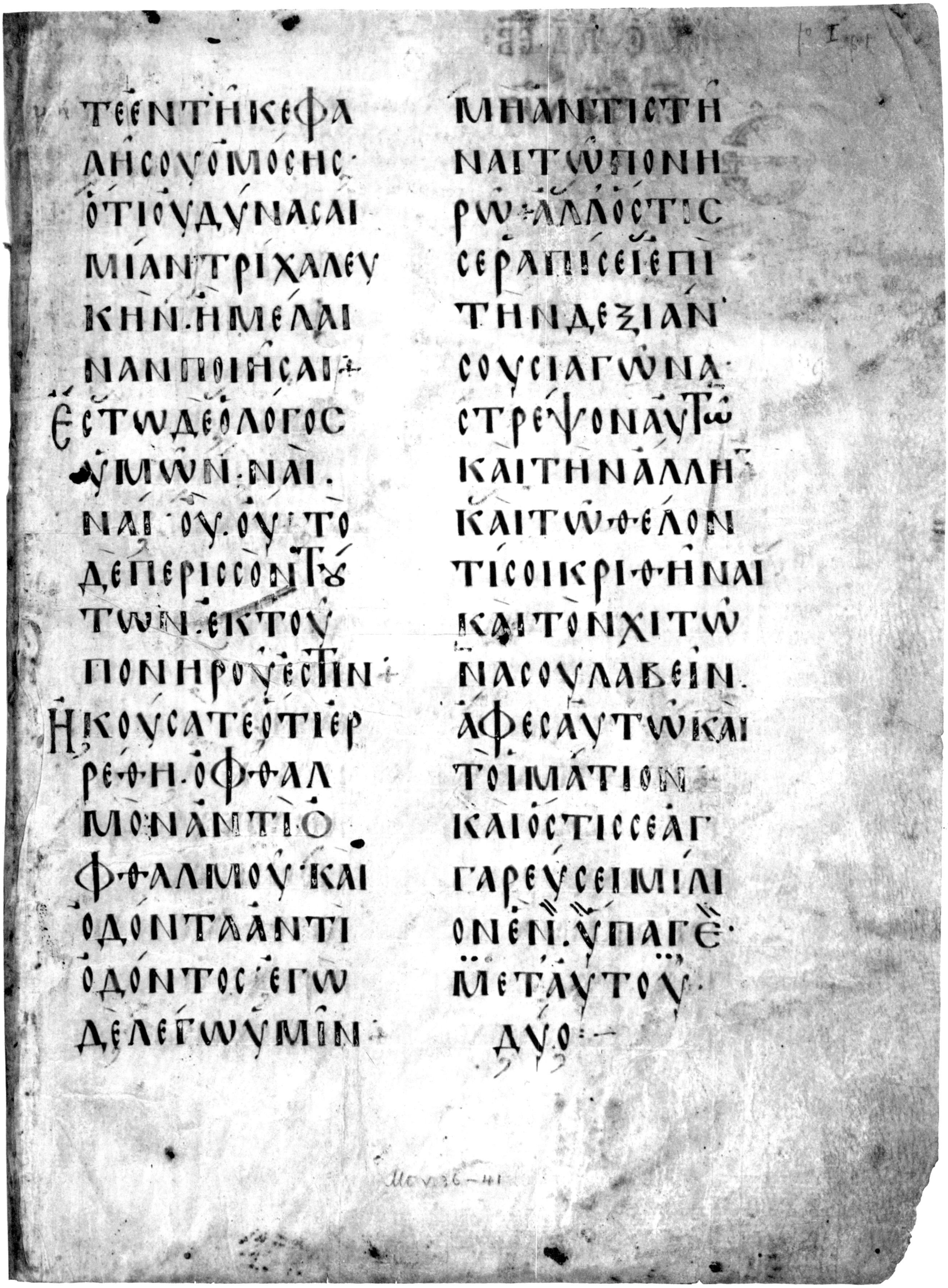

τε εν τη κεφα
λη σου ομοσης·
οτι ου δυνασαι
μιαν τριχα λευ
κην η μελαι
ναν ποιησαι·
εστω δε ο λογος
υμων ναι
ναι ου ου· το
δε περισσον τυ-
των εκ του
πονηρου εστιν·
Ηκουσατε οτι ερ-
ρεθη· οφθαλ-
μον αντι ο-
φθαλμου και
οδοντα αντι
οδοντος· εγω
δε λεγω υμιν

μη αντιστη-
ναι τω πονη-
ρω· αλλ ὁστις
σε ραπισει επι
την δεξιαν
σου σιαγονα
στρεψον αυτω
και την αλλην·
και τω θελον-
τι σοι κριθηναι
και τον χιτω-
νασου λαβειν
αφες αυτω και
το ιματιον·
και ὁστις σε αγ-
γαρευσει μιλι-
ον εν υπαγε
μετ αυτου
δυο·

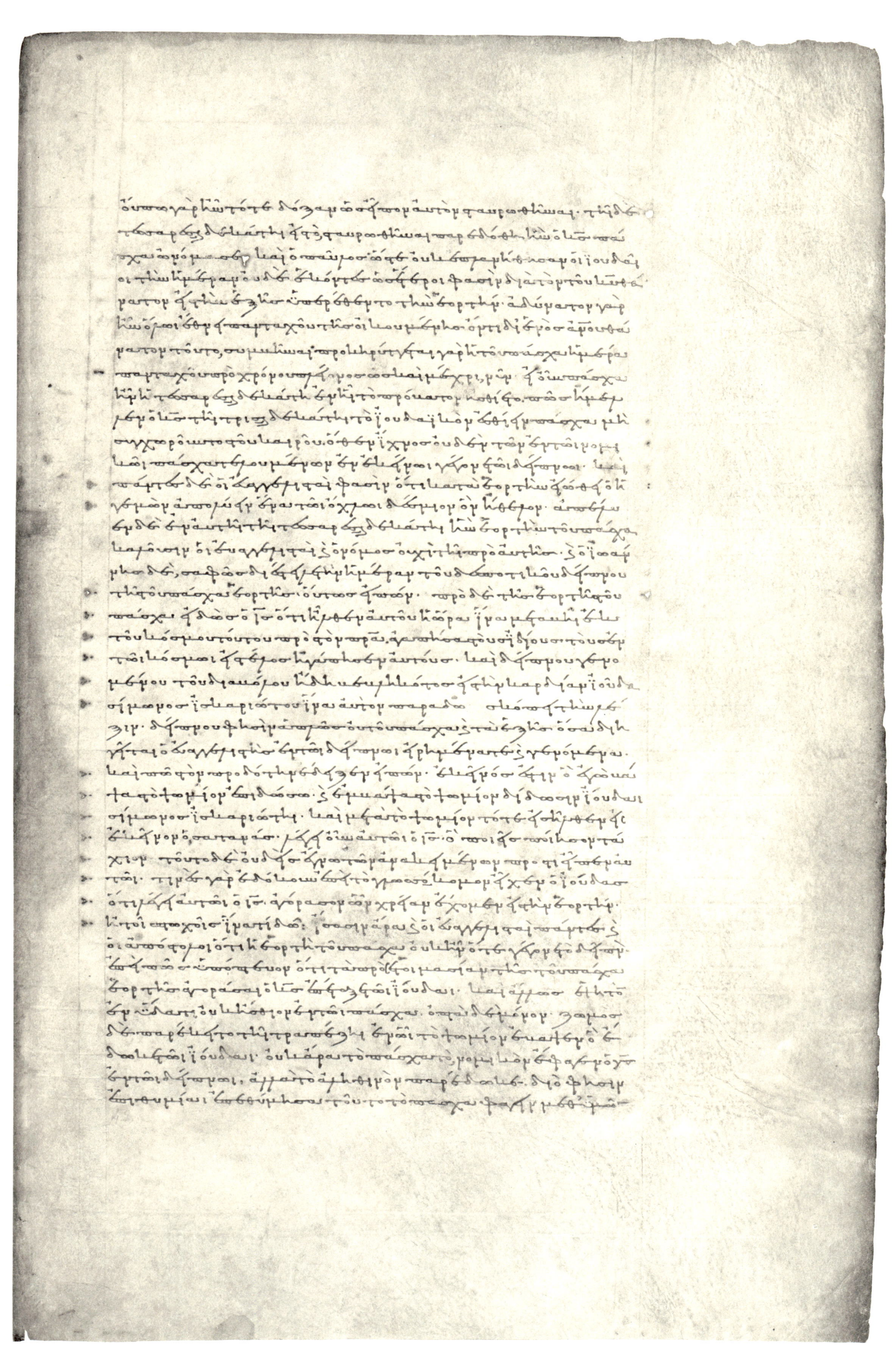

GREGORIUS NYSSENUS (ASCRIBED): *DE MYSTICA CENA* (SAEC. X)
Acquired in 1949 with the Treat and Hofer Funds

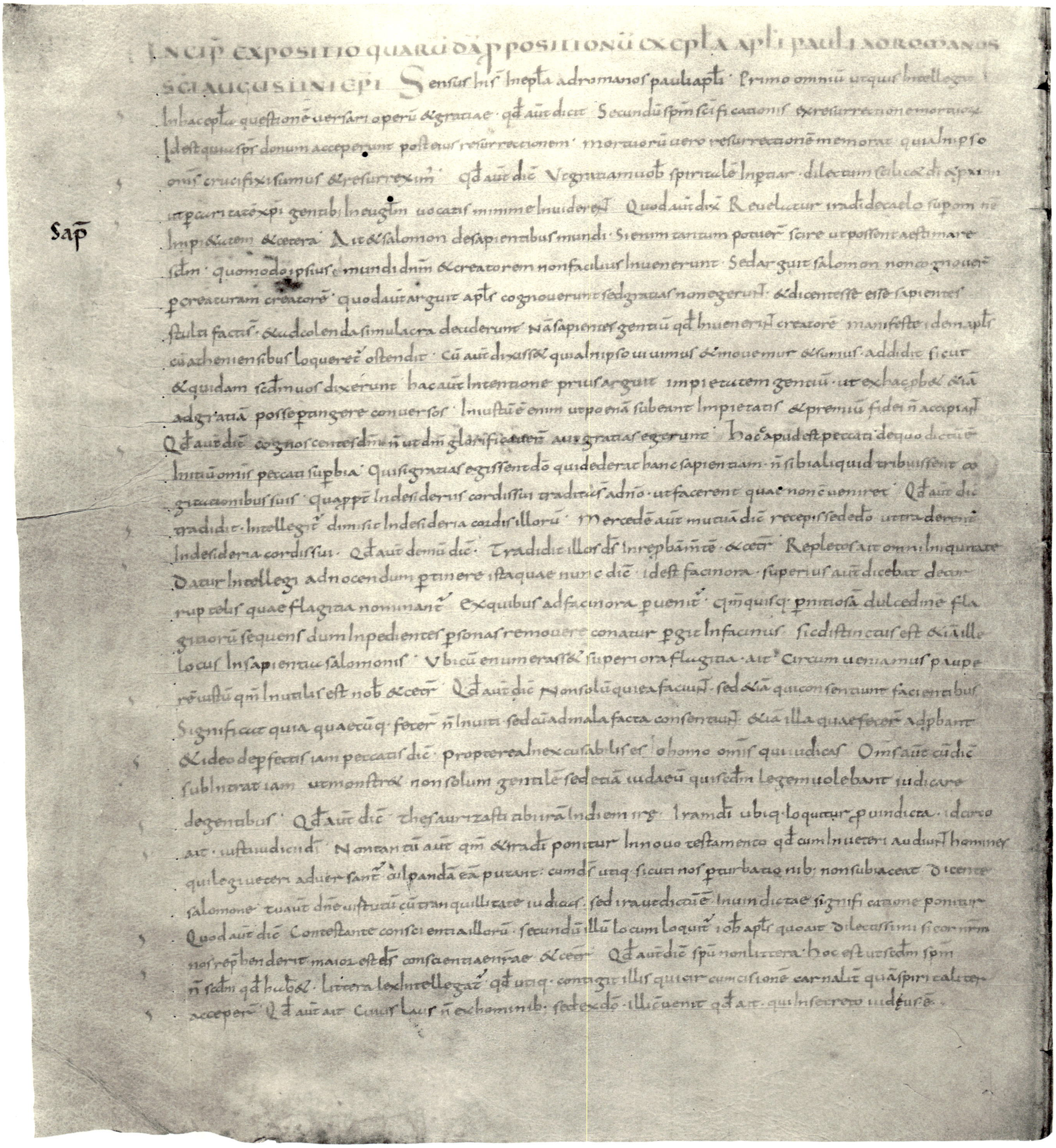

ST. AUGUSTINE: *EXPOSITIO QUARUNDAM PROPOSITIONUM EX EPISTOLA PAULI AD ROMANOS* (SAEC. IX)
Given in 1961 by Harrison D. Horblit, H 1933

EADMER: *VITA SANCTI ODILONIS* (SAEC. XII)
Given in 1862 by Dr. Winslow Lewis, H 1819

ECCLESIASTICUS, WITH COMMENTARY (SAEC. XIII) 16¼ × 11½ inches
Transferred in 1912 from the Harvard Divinity School

DANTE: *DIVINA COMMEDIA*, WITH COMMENTARY
WRITTEN IN 1457 BY BARTOLOMEUS FILIUS ANDREAE MAÇÇONIS 16⅞ × 11 inches
Acquired in 1906 with the collection of Charles Eliot Norton, H 1846

Incunabula

THE Harvard Library contains more than 3,600 incunabula, ranking third in numbers among American libraries. This does not reflect a striving for numerical strength; particularly in the last fifty years, the library has been highly selective in its acquisitions of early printed books. Many books printed before 1501 have little beyond the accident of chronology to recommend them to anyone's attention.

Harvard is well found in early books important in the history of printing and typography, from the forty-two line Bible to the *Hypnerotomachia Poliphili*. The library includes monuments of vernacular literature, such as the first editions of Wolfram von Eschenbach's *Parsival* and *Titurel* (1477); landmarks in the history of learning and science, such as Brunetto Latini, *Il tesoro* (1474), the first scientific book printed in any modern language; and *editiones principes* of the classics, such as the first Homer (1488–89). Already strong collections are improved when possible. Occasionally one of the few missing Aldines can be acquired for a series crowned by a manuscript actually used by compositors in Aldus's shop; and W. K. Richardson's bequest (discussed elsewhere) brought among its incunabula a magnificent copy of the first *Imitatio Christi* (1473), to head the great collection formed by W. A. Copinger and presented in 1921 by James Byrne '77.

Harvard's future acquisitions in this field are unlikely to be numerous, but when the library can add to strength it will try to do so.

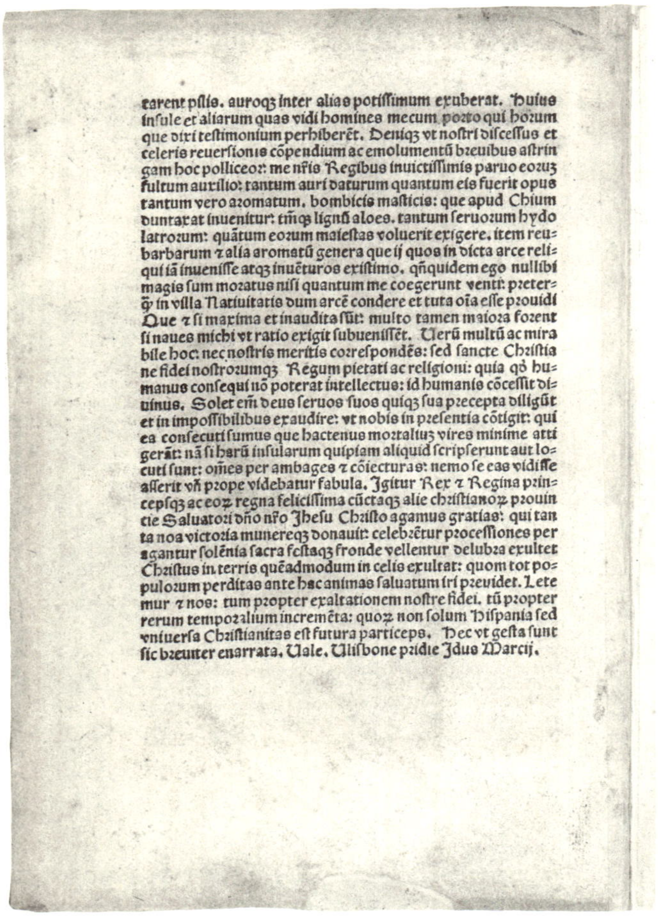

THIS COPY OF CHRISTOPHER COLUMBUS'S LETTER TO SANXIS, TREASURER OF ARAGON, ENTITLED 'EPISTOLA DE INSULIS NOVITER REPERTIS' AND PRINTED AT PARIS BY GUIOT MARCHANT ABOUT 1493, WAS PRESENTED TO THE UNIVERSITY OF HARVARD BY THE CURATORS OF THE BODLEIAN LIBRARY, OXFORD, IN SEPTEMBER 1936, ON THE OCCASION OF THE THREE HUNDREDTH ANNIVERSARY OF THE FOUNDATION OF HARVARD COLLEGE. THE BOOK, OF WHICH ANOTHER COPY REMAINS IN THE BODLEIAN, FORMED PART OF THE BEQUEST OF FRANCIS DOUCE

COLUMBUS: *EPISTOLA DE INSULIS NOVITER REPERTIS*
PARIS: [GUY MARCHANT, 1493]   8⅛ × 11 inches
Given in 1936 by the Curators of the Bodleian Library

EDITIO PRINCEPS OF HOMER
FLORENCE: BERNARDUS NERLIUS ET AL. [1488–89]
Bequeathed in 1951 by William King Richardson, H 1880

ΙΛΙΑΔΟΣ Ι ΟΜΗΡΟΥ ΡΑΨΩΔΙΑΣ

ἔξεσιν ἡ Ἀχιλῆος ἄπο θέος ἐσὶν ἰῶτα.

ὣς οἱ μὲν Τρῶες φυλακὰς ἔ-
χον· αὐτὰρ Ἀχαιοὺς
θεσπεσίη ἔχε φύζα, φόβου
κρυόεντος ἑταίρη·
πένθεϊ δ' ἀτλήτῳ βεβολήατο
πάντες ἄριστοι·
ὡς δ' ἄνεμοι δύο πόντον ὀ-
ρίνετον ἰχθυόεντα
βορέης καὶ ζέφυρος τώ τε θρῄ-
κηθεν ἄητον

ἐλθόντ' ἐξαπίνης· ἄμυδις δέ τε κῦμα κελαινὸν
κορθύεται· πολλὸν δὲ παρὲξ ἅλα φῦκος ἔχευαν,
ὣς ἐδαΐζετο θυμὸς ἐνὶ στήθεσιν ἀχαιῶν.
ἀτρείδης δ' ἄχεϊ μεγάλῳ βεβολημένος ἦτορ
φοίτα κηρύκεσσι λιγυφθόγγοισι κελεύων
κλήδην εἰς ἀγορὴν κικλήσκειν ἄνδρα ἕκαστον,
μὴ δὲ βοᾶν· αὐτὸς δὲ μετὰ πρώτοισι πονεῖτο.
ἷζον δ' ἀγορῇ τετιηότες· ἂν δ' Ἀγαμέμνων
ἵστατο δακρυχέων ὥστε κρήνη μελάνυδρος,
ἥτε κατ' αἰγίλιπος πέτρης δνοφερὸν χέει ὕδωρ,
ὣς ὁ βαρυστενάχων ἔπε' ἀργείοισι μετηύδα.
ὦ φίλοι ἀργείων ἡγήτορες ἠδὲ μέδοντες.
ζεύς με μέγα κρονίδης ἄτῃ ἐνέδησε βαρείῃ.
σχέτλιος· ὅς πρὶν μέν μοι ὑπέσχετο καὶ κατένευσεν
ἴλιον ἐκπέρσαντ' εὐτείχεον ἀπονέεσθαι.
νῦν δὲ κακὴν ἀπάτην βουλεύσατο, καί με κελεύει
δυσκλέα ἄργος ἱκέσθαι, ἐπεὶ πολὺν ὤλεσα λαόν.
οὕτω που Διὶ μέλλει ὑπερμενέϊ φίλον εἶναι.
ὃς δὴ πολλάων πολίων κατέλυσε κάρηνα,
ἠδ' ἔτι καὶ λύσει· τοῦ γὰρ κράτος ἐστὶ μέγιστον.
ἀλλ' ἄγεθ' ὡς ἂν ἐγὼ εἴπω πειθώμεθα πάντες·
φεύγωμεν σὺν νηυσὶ φίλην ἐς πατρίδα γαῖαν.
οὐ γὰρ ἔτι τροίην αἱρήσομεν εὐρυάγυιαν.
ὣς ἔφαθ'· οἱ δ' ἄρα πάντες ἀκὴν ἐγένοντο σιωπῇ.
δὴν δ' ἄνεῳ ἦσαν τετιηότες υἷες ἀχαιῶν.
ὀψὲ δὲ δὴ μετέειπε βοὴν ἀγαθὸς διομήδης.
ἀτρεΐδη σοὶ πρῶτα μαχήσομαι ἀφραδέοντι,

Darumb lasse ich euch wol so vil
Nun merckent wes ich üch bitten wil
Gefragent nymmer wer ich sie
So mag ich üch bleiben hie
Bin ich an euwer frage erkorn
So habt ir minne an mir verlorn
Ob ir nicht seit gewarnet des
So warnt mich got ich weis wol wes
Sy satte weibes sicherhait
Die seit durch liebe wencke lait
Sy wolte zu seinem gebotte ston
Vnd nymmer übergon
Was er sy laisten hieß
Ob sy got bei sinnen ließ
Bei nacht ir leib minne entpfant
Do ward er fürst in probant
Die hochgezeit reilich ergieng
Manig herr vö seiner hend entpfieng
Ir leben die das solten han
Gut richter ward der selbe man
Er thet auch dicke ritterschafft
Das er den preiß behielt mit krafft
Sy gewunnen schöne kint
Vil leüt im probant noch sint
Die wol wissent von in baiden
Ir entpbaben sin dan schaiden
Vn das ir frage in dan vertreib
Vn wie lang er do beleib
Er schied vngerne dan
Nun bracht im sein fründ des swan
Ein kleine gefüge seities
Seins klenotes er do lies
Ein schwert ein horn ein vingerlin
Hin für lohelangrin
w   Ellen wir dem mere recht thun
    So was es herr partzifals sun
Do für er wasser vn wege
Vntz wider in der grales pflege
Doch was verlassen das güte weib
Von fründen minnigliches leib

Er widerziet ir fragen ee
Do er zü ir gieng von dem see
Die solt man sprechen
Der kund mit rede sich rechen
Ab von troys maister kristian
Disem mer vnrecht hat getan
Des mag wol zürnen kyot
Der vnß die rechten mere enbot
Endehafft gicht der prouenzal
Wie hertzeloyden kint den gral
Erwarb als er geordent was
Do in verworchte anfortas
Von profantz in teütsche lant
Die rechten mere vns seint gesant
v   No diser auenteüre endes zil
    Nicht me do von sprechen wil
Ich wolffram von eschenbach
Wan als dort der maister sprach
Sein kint sein hoch geschlechte
Han ich benennet rechte
Herr partzifal den ich han bracht
Dar sein doch selde hat gedacht
Wes leben sich so verendet
Das got nit wirt gepfendet
Der selen durch des leibes schulde
Vn der doch der welte hulde
Behalten kan mit wirdikeit
Das ist ein nütze erbeit
Gute weib hont den sin
Desterwerder ich in bin
Ob mir keine gütes gan
Seit ich dise mer volsprochen han
Ist das durch ein weib beschehen
Die mus mir süsser worte iehen

M·CCCC·LXXVII·

WOLFRAM VON ESCHENBACH: *PARSIVAL* [STRASSBURG: JOHANN MENTELIN] 1477
Given in 1947 by Curt H. Reisinger, H 1921

Incipit libellus consolatorius ad instructo; devoto;
Cuius primū capitulū est de imitacōe xp̄i ꞇ ꝯtemptu
damni vanitatum mundi. Et q̄dam totū libellum
sic appellant scilicet libellum de imitatione xp̄i. sicut
euangelium Mathei appellatur liber generacōis iħu
xp̄i Eo ꝙ in primo capit̾o fit mentio de generacōne
xp̄i scdm carnem   Incipit primum capitulum

Ui sequit̄ me nō ambulat in tenebris dic
dn̄s. Hec sunt verba xp̄i q̄b; admonem̄
q̄tenus vitam eius et mores imitemur si
velim̄s veraciter illusari et ab oi cecitate
cordis liβari Summū igit̄ studiū nr̄m sit i
vita iħu meditari. Doctrina xp̄i. oēs doctrinas sctō;
precellit. et qui sp̄m dei habent. ibi manna abscōditū
inuenient. Sed ꝯtingit ꝙ multi ex frequenti auditu
euangelij paruum desiderium senciunt. quia spiritū
dei non habent. Qui autem vult plene et sapide xp̄i
verba intelligere. oportet vt totam vitam suam illi
studeat ꝯformare. Quid prodest tibi alta de trinitate
discutere. si careas humilitate vnde displiceas sancte
trinitati. Vere alta verba non faciunt sanctum et
iustum. sed virtuosa vita efficit hominem deo carum
Opto magis sentire conpunctionem q̄m scire eius
diffinitionem. Si scires totam bibliam exterius et
omnium philosopho; dicta. qd totum prodesset. sine
caritate et gratia dei. Vanitas vanitatum ꞇ omnia
vanitas p̄ter amare deū et illi soli seruire. Ista ē sūma
sapientia per contemptum mundi tendere ad celestia.
Vanitas igitur est diuitias pituras querere et in
illis sperare. Vanitas q̄ est honores mundi ambire
et in altum se extollere. Vanitas est carnis desideria
sequi et illa desiderare. Vnde post mortem oportet
grauiter puniri. Vanitas est longam vitam optare
et de bona vita non curare. Vanitas est presentem
vitam solum attendere. et q̄ futura sunt non preuidere.

EDITIO PRINCEPS OF *IMITATIO CHRISTI* [AUGSBURG:] GÜNTHER ZAINER [1473]
Bequeathed in 1951 by William King Richardson, H 1880

Qui inchomincia el tesoro di s̄ Brunetto latino di Firenze. E parla del nascimēto e della natura di tute le cose. caplō pīmo

SI come el signiore che vuole i vno luogo amassa re cose di grādissimo valore: non solamēte per suo viletto: ma p crescere il suo podere. e p assichurare lo suo stato. i guerra. e i pacie. vimette le piu care e le piu pciose gioie: che puote secodo la sua bona itenzione. Cosi e il chorpo di q̄esto libro copilato di sapiēzia. sichome q̄ello che istratto di tutti li mēbri di filosofia ī vna summa brieuemēte. E la pima parte di q̄esto tesoro: e come danari cōtāti: per dispēdere tutto giorno i chose bisogniose. cioe adire chegli tratte del chomīciamēto del mōdo. e delle vechie istorie. E dello stabiliment del mōdo. E della natura di tutte le cose ī summa. E cio aptiene alla pīma sciēzia della filosofia. cioe teorica. secōdo cio chel libro parla q̄appsso. E sichome senza danari nō aurebbe veruno mezzo tra lopere dele giēti: che dirizassẹ luno cōtra laltro. Altressi nō porrebbe luomo auere dellaltre cose pienamente: se nō sapesse q̄esta pīma parte del libro. La secōda parte che tratta de vizii e dele virtudi: sie de pciose pietre: che vanno altrui diletto e virtudi. Cioe adire. che chose dee luomo fare: e che no. E vicio mostra la ragione pche. E q̄esto aptiene alla secōda e alla terza parte della filosofia. cioe a pratica: et a logica. La terza pte del libro del tesoro sie de oro fino. Cioe adire: chella ī segnia parlare a luomo secōdo la dottrīa della Rettorica. Come el signiore dee ghouernare la giēte che a sotto lui. e specialmēte secōdo lusanzza dytalia. E tutto cio aptiene alla secōda sciēza della filosofia

cioe a p̄atica. Che sichome lo ro trascie de tutte maniere di metallo: cosi lasciēzza di benparlare: e di gouernare la giēte che luomo a sotto di se: e piu nobile che nulla ltra sciēza del mōdo. E po chel tesoro che qi: nō dee esser dato: se nō a p̄sona sufficiente a si alta richezza: lo daro io atte bel dolcie amico. che tu ne se ben degnio secōdo lo mio giudicamēto. Et nō dicho io niēte che q̄esto libro sia tratto del mio poue ro seno: ne della mia igniuda isciēzza. āzi e come vna arme dimele: tratta di diuersi fiori. Che q̄esto libro e copilato solamēte dimarauigliosi detti de li autori: che dinā zi al nostro tēpo anno trattato di filosofia. ciaschuno della parte della filosofia: di che ssintēdeua: che tutta nō la puo sapere buomo terreno. percio che la filosofia: e la radice: dichui creschono tutte le sciēze che buomo puote sapere. Cosi chome vna fontana: onde eschono molti riui: e corrono q̄a e la. siche luno bee duno: e laltro be dunaltro. e cioe in diuerso modo. che luno ebee piu: e laltro meno: sanza stagniare la fontana. percio che dice boezio nel libro della cōsolazione: che elli la vide ī sembiā za di donna: i tal habito e isi marauigli osa potēzia: che cresceua q̄ādo le piacie uā tanto: chel suo capo agiugnieua disopra alle stelle. e sopra il cielo: Et puedeua aimōti et alle valli secōdo viritura. Che appsso al buono comiciamēto: sinnescie bo na fine. El nostro ipadore disse in vno libro di logica. Lo comīciamento: e la magiōr parte della cosa. E se alchuno domā dasse. pche q̄esto libro e scritto ī linghua frācieska: poi che noi siamo di ytalia? Io li risōderei che cio e per due cose. Luna: pche noi siamo ī frācia. E laltra pciò: che la parlatura frācieska e piu delettēole e piu chomuna: che tutti lialtri ligua ggi

Come la materia di tutte le cose e diuisa ī tre maniere secōdo teorica. .ii.
FIlosofia e veracie cognoscimēto de

BRUNETTO LATINI: *IL TESORO*, TREVISO: GERARDUS DE LISA, 1474 Given in 1954 by Harrison D. Horblit, H 1933

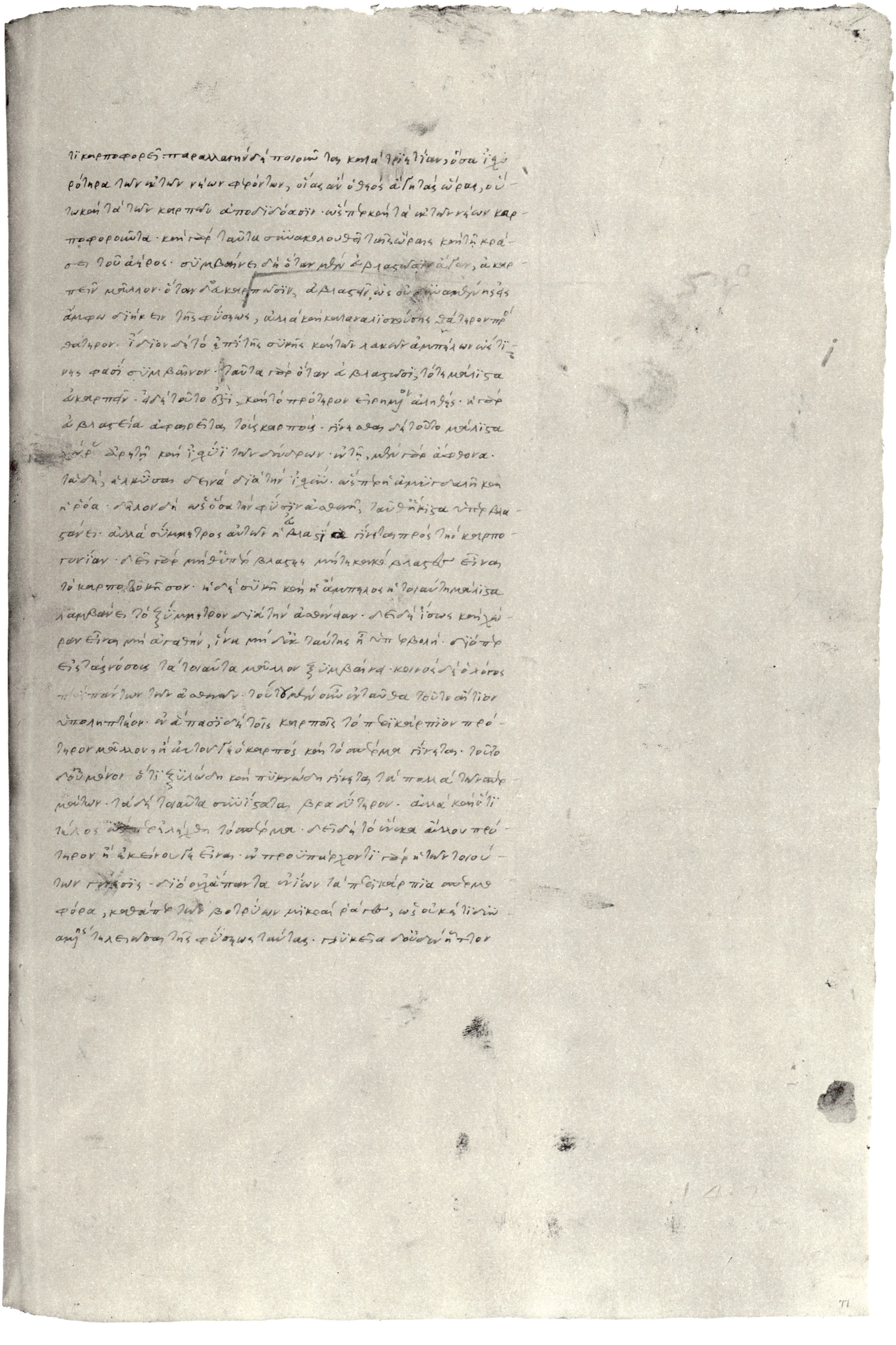

MS. OF THEOPHRASTUS USED BY ALDUS Given in 1938 by H. T. White, H 1897,
Lucius Wilmerding, H 1901, A. H. Parker, H 1897, and W. K. Richardson, H 1880

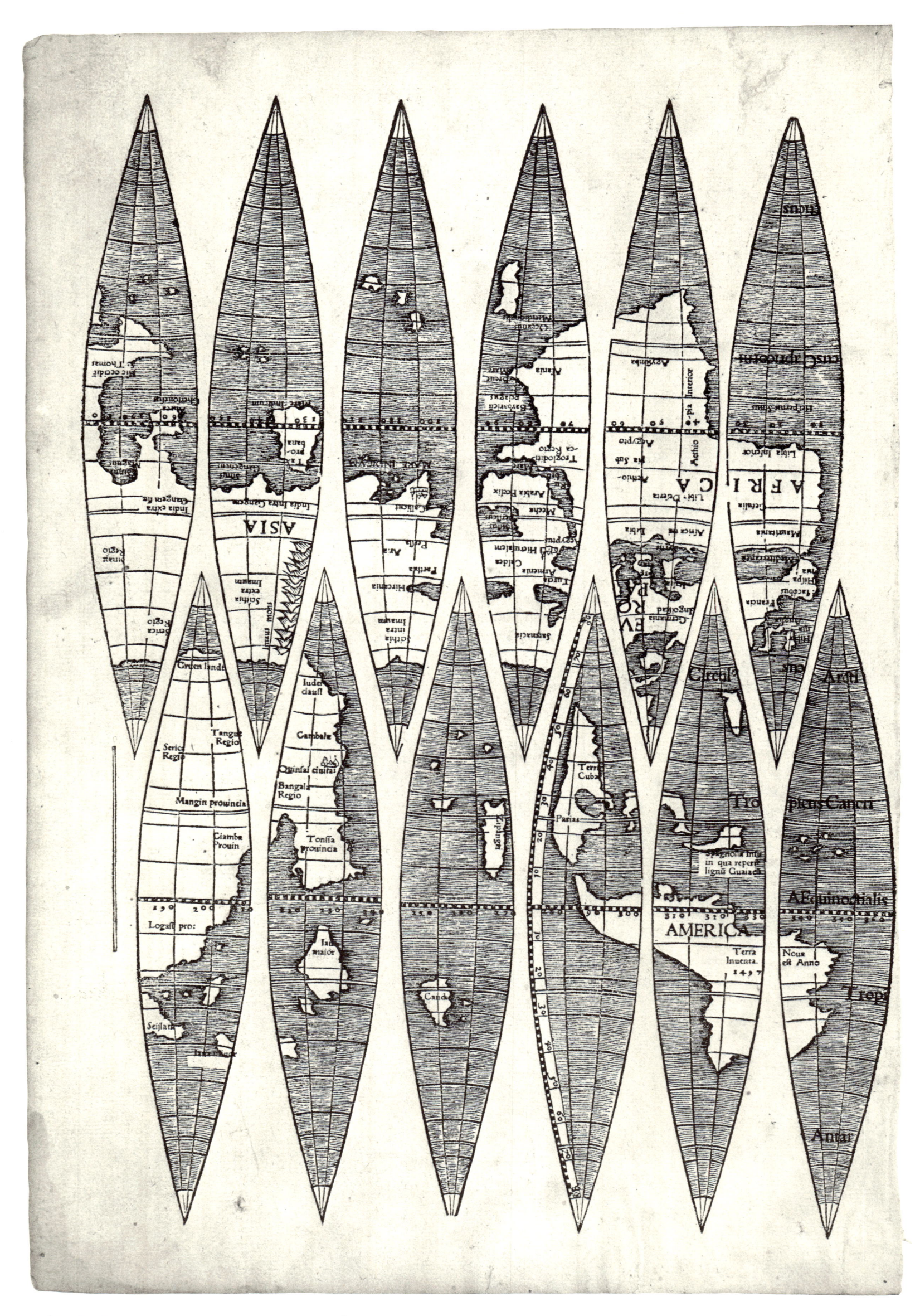

GORES FOR WORLD MAP, INGOLSTADT [CA.1518]
Given in 1951 by Stephen W. Phillips, H 1895, and Curt H. Reisinger, H 1912

Early Maps

IN 1951 Stephen W. Phillips, H 1895, and Curt H. Reisinger, H 1912, joined forces to present to Harvard the Hauslab-Liechtenstein Collection of Renaissance maps, consisting of more than 150 wall and sheet maps, a number of them unique. They gave new strength to a traditional field of Harvard collecting, as W. A. Jackson pointed out when announcing the gift:

'The Harvard Map Collection was founded early in the nineteenth century upon the Ebeling and Warren collections, which were particularly strong in American maps, and under the guidance of Justin Winsor most of the fundamental atlases of the early geographers were acquired. In recent years . . . from the Matt B. Jones collection and other sources notable items have been received.'

Acquisitions have continued from time to time: for example, in 1955 Mr. Reisinger added to his former gift the Bagrow collection of early Russian maps.

GERHARD MERCATOR: TERRESTRIAL GLOBE, 1541 20 inches high
Given in 1936 by Philip H. Rosenwald

NICHOLAS COMBERFORD: MS. MAP OF THE CENTRAL AND NORTH AMERICAN COAST, 1659 22¾ × 17 inches
Given in 1951 by Stephen W. Phillips, H 1895, and Curt H. Reisinger, H 1912

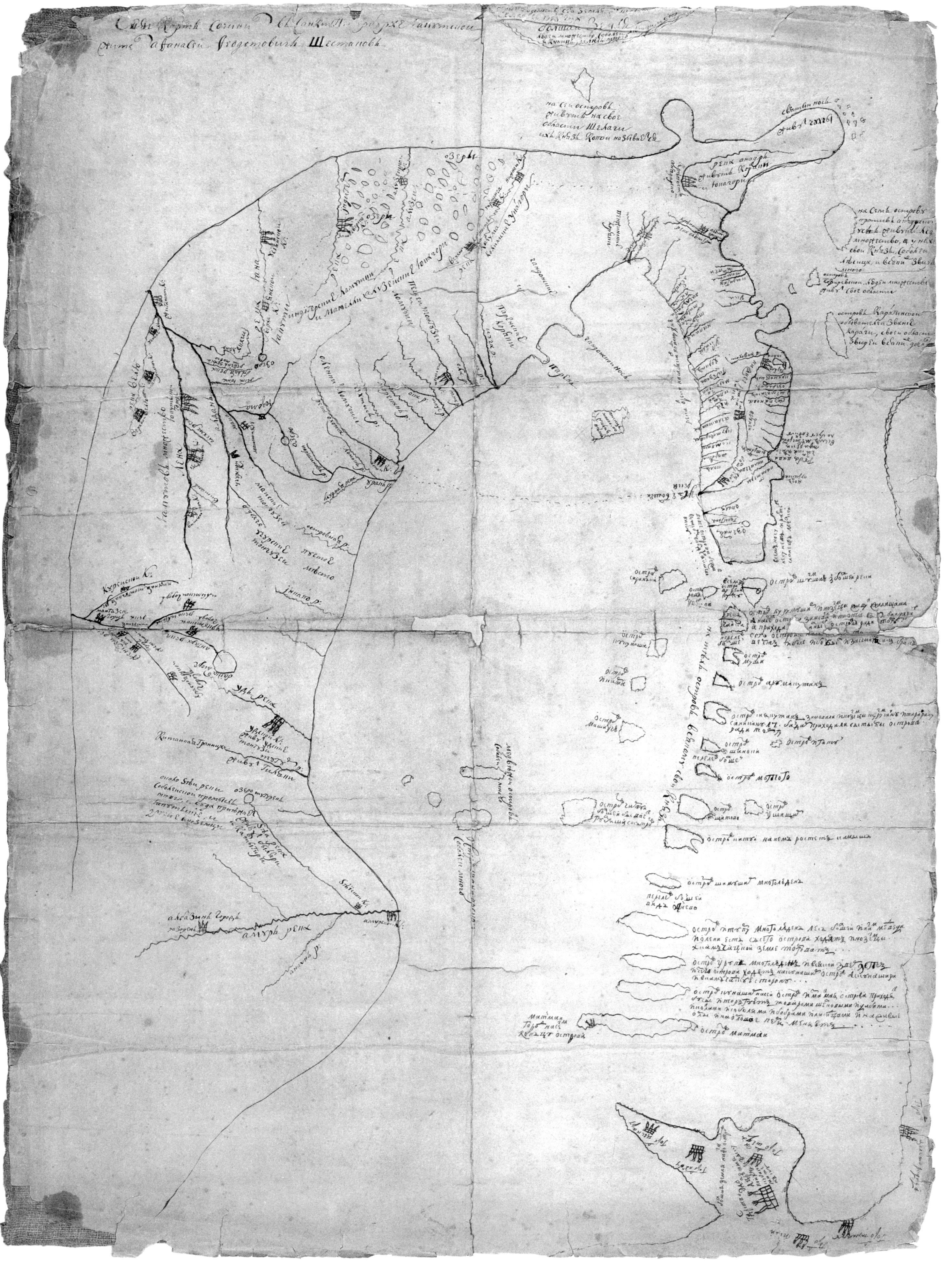

A. SHESTAKOV: MS. MAP OF KAMCHATKA, 1726   29 × 21 inches
Given in 1955 by Curt H. Reisinger, H 1912

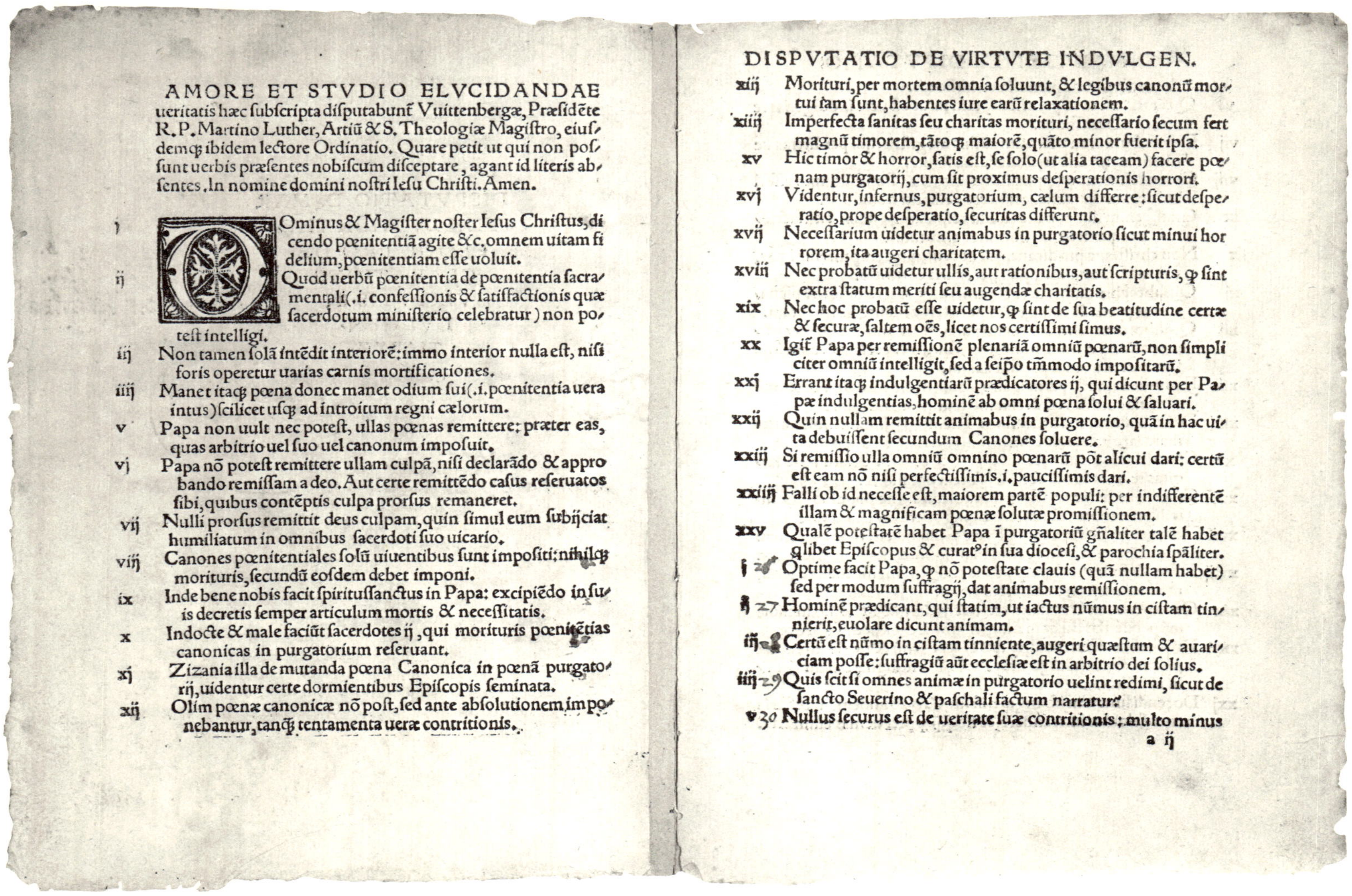

MARTIN LUTHER: *DISPUTATIO... PRO DECLARATIONE VIRTUTIS INDULGENTIARUM*, 1517   8⅜ × 12⅜ inches
The Ninety-Five Theses   Given in 1949 by Curt H. Reisinger, H 1912

The Reformation

FEW intellectual movements in the history of civilization have had such profound, far-reaching, and long-lasting effects as the one that began (so at least the story goes) with the nailing of ninety-five theses to a church door in Wittenberg in 1517. The Reformation is remarkably well documented at Harvard by contemporary publications, beginning with pre-Reformation grumblings during the first decades of the sixteenth century, culminating in what is undoubtedly the finest Luther collection in the Western hemisphere (Harvard is the only American library whose holdings are recorded in Josef Benzing's monumental Luther bibliography), and continuing through the later phases of the movement with good collections of such figures as Calvin, Cochlaeus, and Brenz, as well as, on the other side, representatives of the Counter-Reformation.

Only a few of the more important early documents can be shown here, but behind each of them stand strong supporting collections that make possible sustained research in this highly significant period of the intellectual and spiritual development of man.

PHILIPP MELANCHTHON: HOLOGRAPH OF
VON DEN FRON DIENSTEN, 1549   13⅜ × 8⅛ inches
Acquired in 1955 with the Amy Lowell Fund

6a.

6

leben, halt dise sach
wol verdamt, Ich weiss wol
das die besitz disputiren
von einem solchen fall, so
ledige person, und ledig
unzuchtig person, unzucht
treiben, das es die richter
nit straffen soll.
darumb were nutz zu reden,
Aber dieser Bader hatt auch
die sacramenta veracht,
~~und so ist ein oberkeit~~
und ein recht oberkeit schuldig
recht darum, so sie solche
verachter von sich weg weise,
dieses ist die recht excommunicatio
der warhafftig excommunication,
davon ich E. Gnaden nit schreiben
will so es zu ein disputation
kommen wolt, Philippus Melanthon

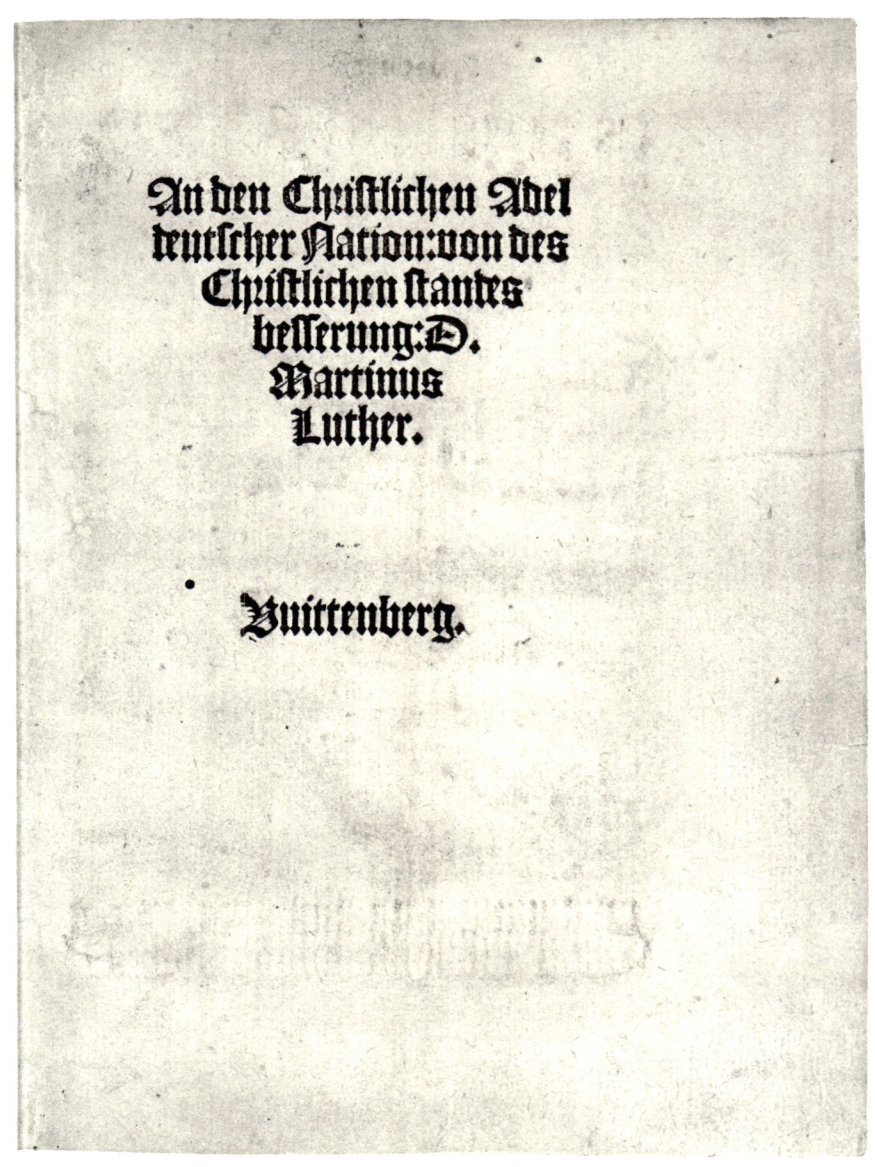

MARTIN LUTHER: *AN DEN CHRISTLICHEN ADEL DEUTSCHER NATION*, 1520   8⅛ × 5⅞ inches   Acquired in 1948 with the Coolidge Fund

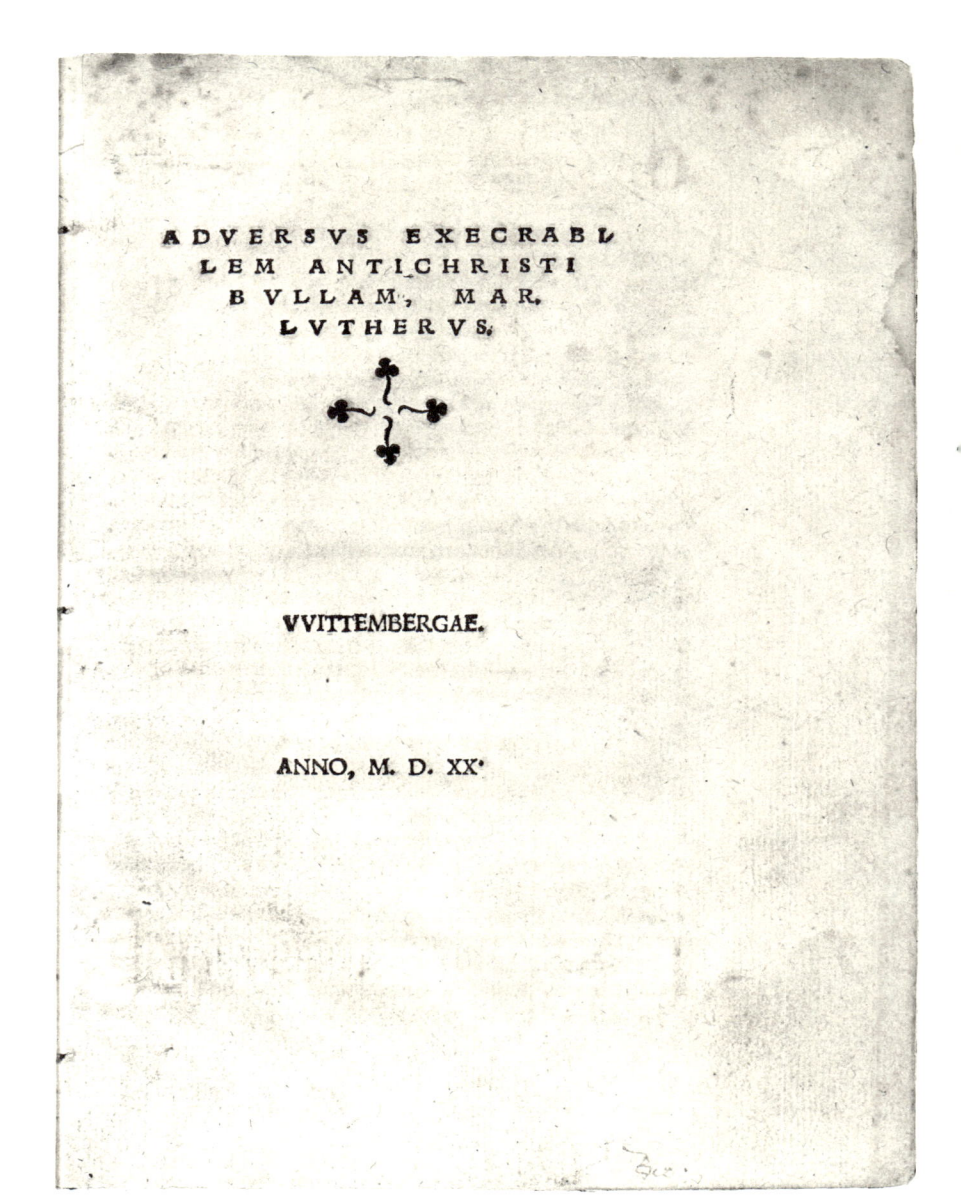

MARTIN LUTHER: *ADVERSUS EXECRABILEM ANTICHRISTI BULLAM*, 1520   8 × 6 inches   Given in 1964 by Curt H. Reisinger, H 1912

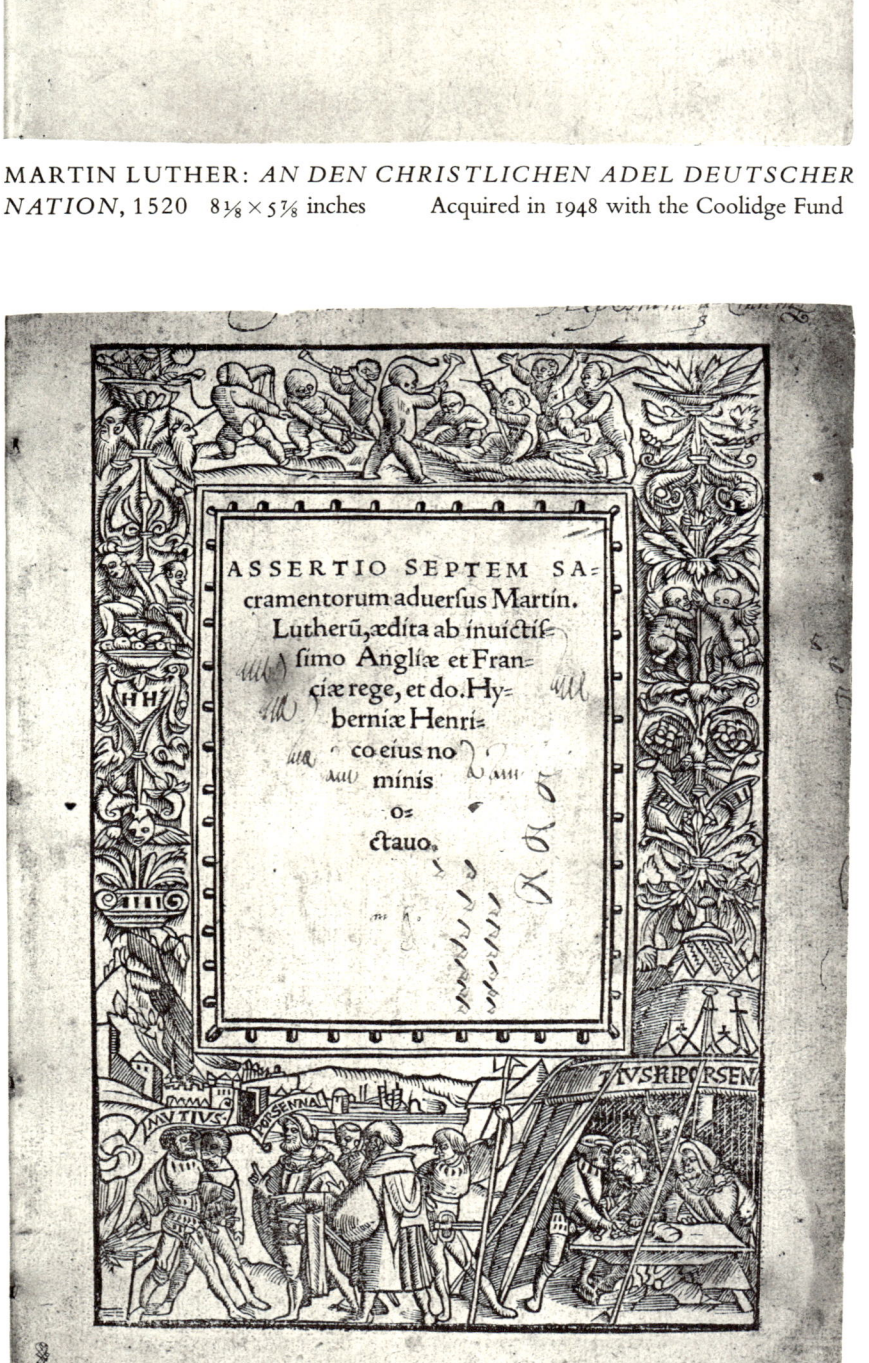

HENRY VIII: *ASSERTIO SEPTEM SACRAMENTORUM*, 1521 (*STC* 13078)   8 × 5¾ inches
Given in 1941 by Philip Hofer, H 1921

MARTIN LUTHER: *ANTWORTT... AUFF KÖNIG HENRICHS VON ENGELLAND BUCH*, 1522   7⅝ × 5⅝ inches
Acquired in 1966 with the fund bequeathed by George L. Lincoln, H 1895

PHILIPP MELANCHTHON: *DIDYMI FAVENTINI ADVERSUS THOMAM PLACENTINUM* [1521] 7½ × 5¼ inches
Acquired in 1966 with the fund bequeathed by George L. Lincoln, H 1895

PHILIPP MELANCHTHON: *APOLOGIA DER CONFESSION* [1531] 7¾ × 5¼ inches   Given in 1964 by Curt H. Reisinger, H 1912

BODENSTEIN VON CARLSTADT: *VON VORMUGEN DES ABLAS. WIDER BRUDER FRANCISCUS SEYLER*, 1520 7¾ × 5¾ inches
Given in 1964 by Curt H. Reisinger, H 1912

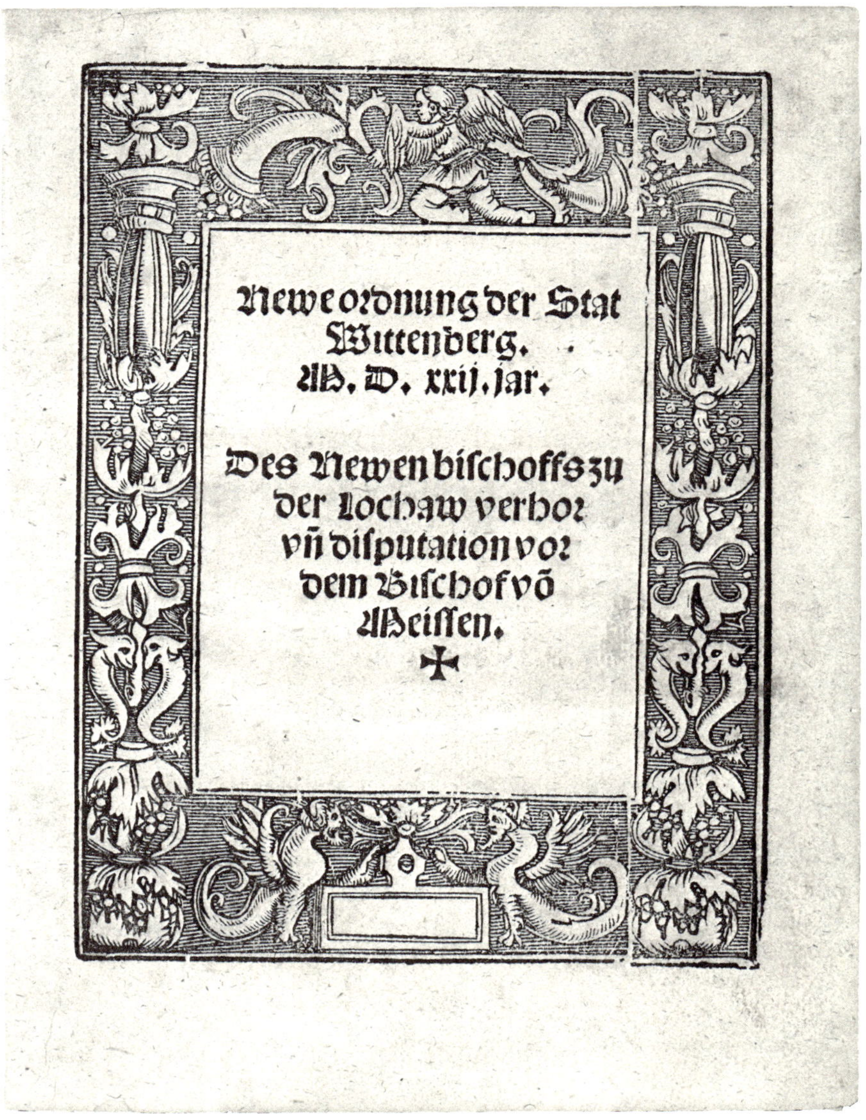

WITTENBERG *KIRCHENORDNUNG*, 1522 7⅜ × 5⅝ inches
Given in 1964 by Curt H. Reisinger, H 1912

The Reformation   29

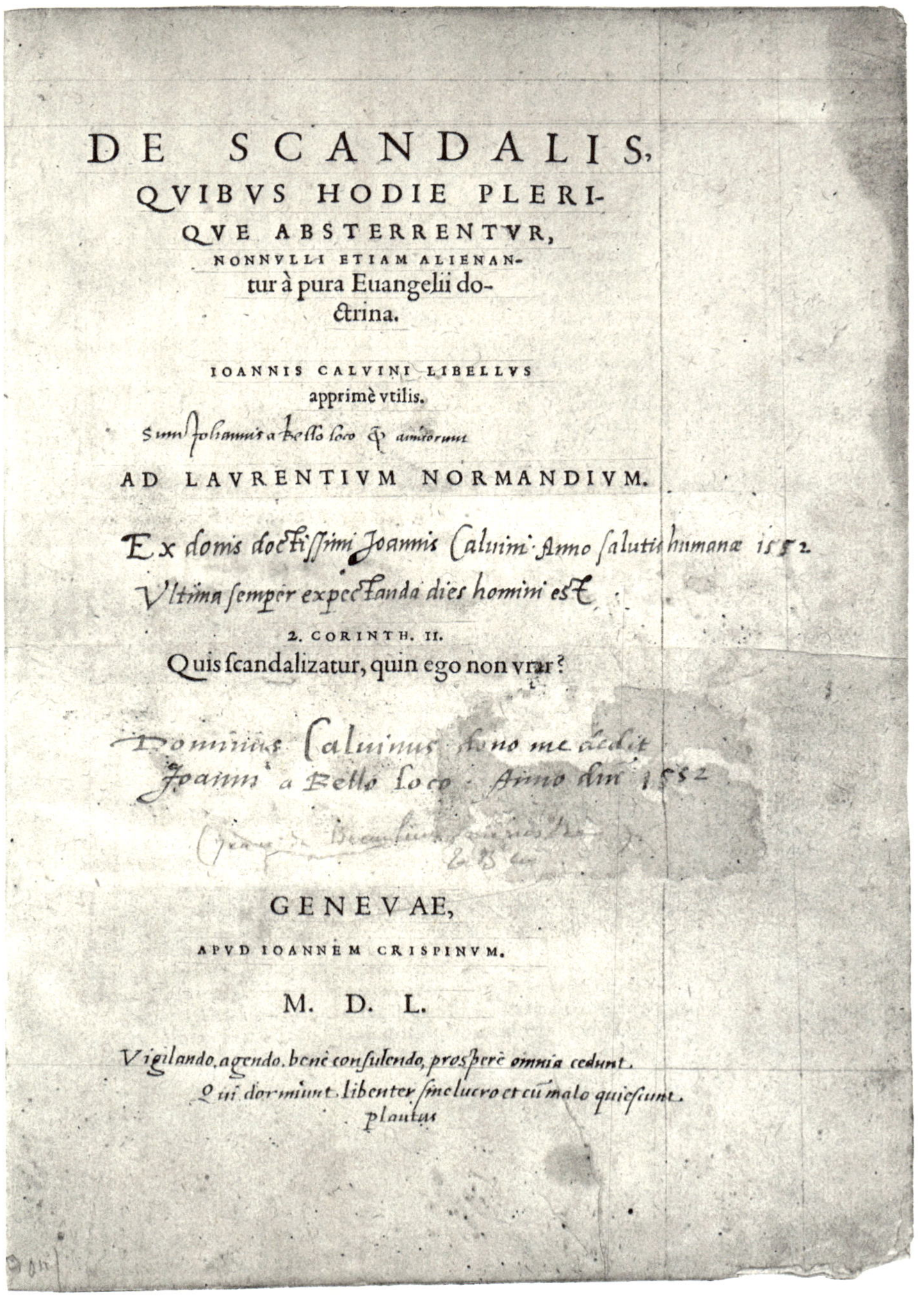

JEAN CALVIN: *DE SCANDALIS*, 1550   9¾ × 6¾ inches
Acquired in 1959 with the Henry Saltonstall Howe Fund

JEAN CALVIN: *DEFENSIO ORTHODOXAE FIDEI DE SACRA TRINITATE*, 1554   7¼ × 4¾ inches
Acquired in 1953 with the Susan A. E. Morse Fund

MICHAEL SERVETUS: *DE TRINITATIS ERRORIBUS*, 1531   6⅛ × 4 inches
Given in 1948 by William King Richardson, H 1880

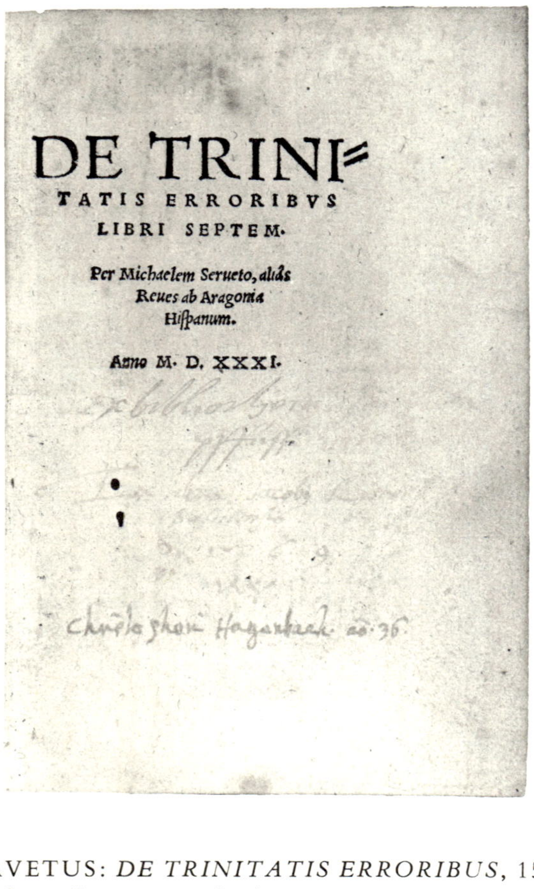

JOHANN ECK: *DISPUTATIO ET EXCUSATIO*, 1519
7¾ × 5⅞ inches   Acquired in 1956 with the Treat Fund

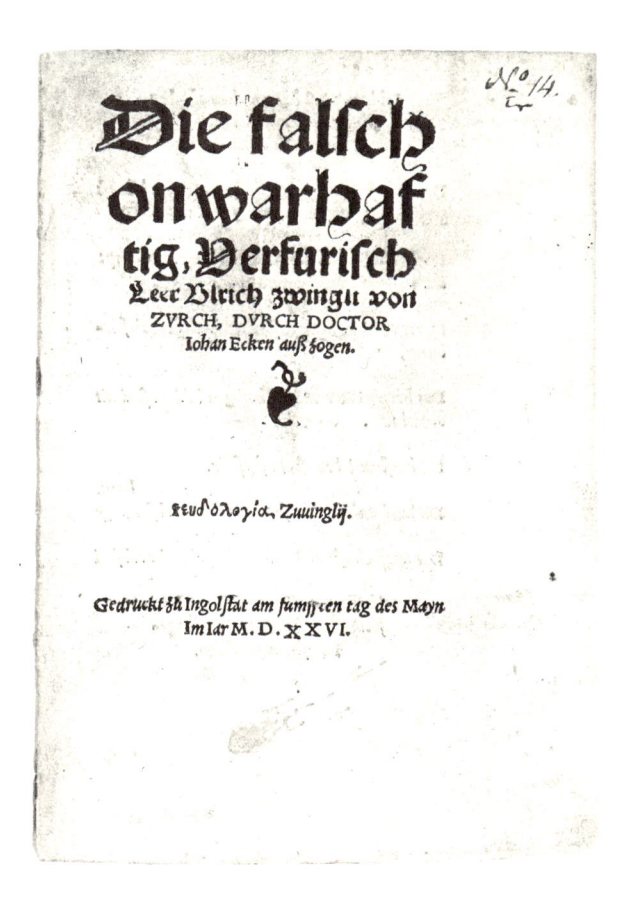

JOHANN ECK: *DIE FALSCH ONWAHRHAFTIG
... ULRICH ZWINGLI*, 1526   5⅞ × 3⅞ inches
Acquired in 1965 with the fund bequeathed by
George L. Lincoln, H 1895

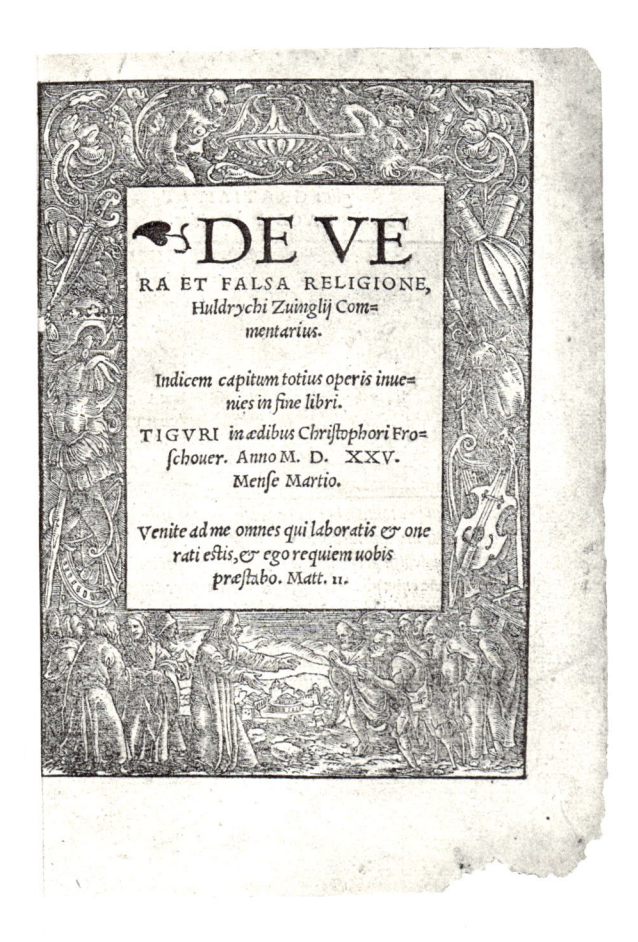

ULRICH ZWINGLI: *DE VERA ET FALSA
RELIGIONE*, 1525   6⅛ × 3⅞ inches
Acquired in 1957 with the Keller Fund

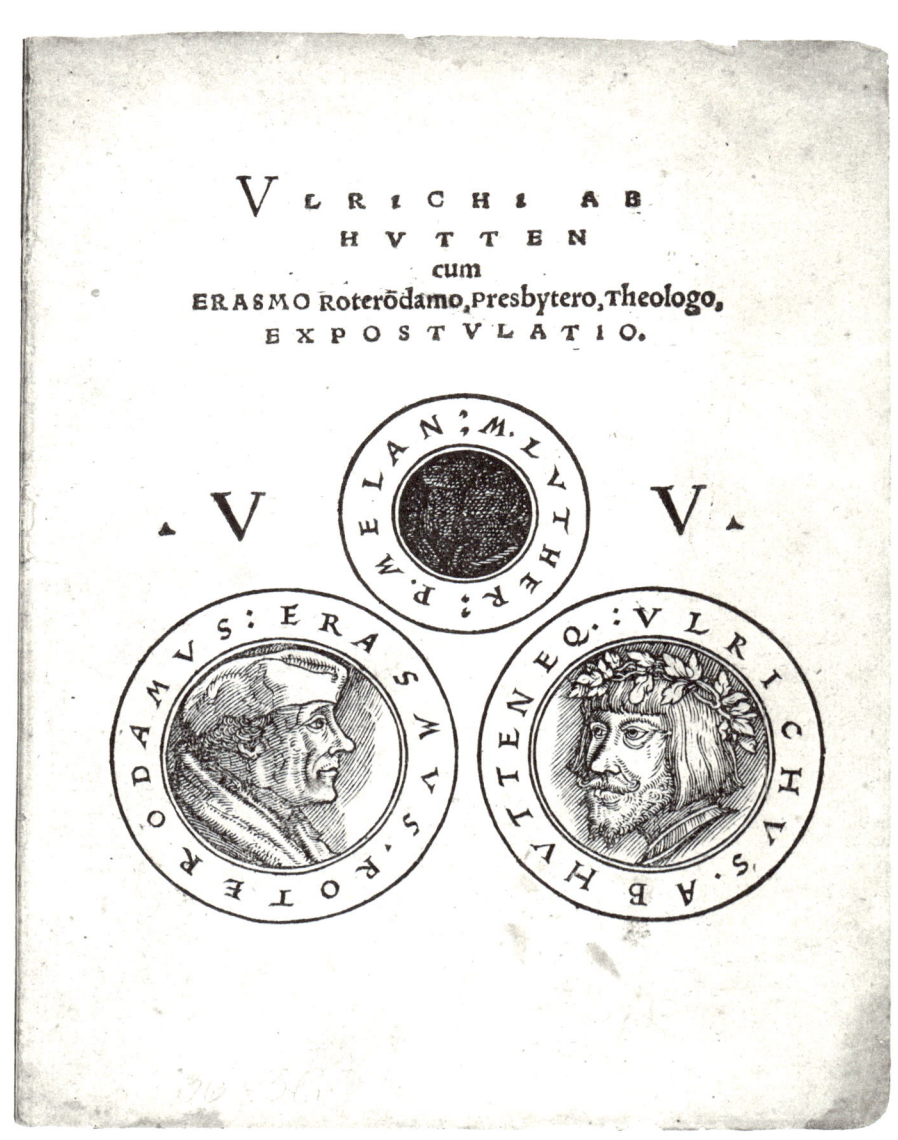

ULRICH HUTTEN: *EXPOSTULATIO*, 1523   7⅞ × 6 inches
Acquired in 1941 with the Treat Fund

The Reformation   31

Erasmus

ERASMUS: *ADAGIA*, 1500
The first edition
> Acquired in 1952 with funds from the sale of duplicates

ERASMUS: AUTOGRAPH LETTER TO BRUNO AMERBACH
[4 NOVEMBER 1517?]
> Given in 1951 by Carleton R. Richmond, H 1909

It is not often given to a single man to be at once the culmination of one great intellectual movement and a powerful force in the beginnings of another. Erasmus of Rotterdam can be said to have brought to a noble climax all that is implied in the term Renaissance to describe the unfettering of man's mind from the bonds of medieval scholasticism and the opening of his spirit to the liberating influence of the great Greek and Latin writers of the ancient world; he was also caught up in the midst of that spiritual storm called the Reformation which began to rage in the early years of the sixteenth century. Translations and editions of the text of ancient authors, many of them newly brought to light by his efforts, flowed from his pen in a constant stream, while his own creative writings had a strong influence on all levels of society. His religious works were all the more effective for his refusal to take sides with either the reformers or the established church.

The Harvard collection of Erasmus is distinguished both for extent and for quality, having had the devoted attention of the late William A. Jackson during his entire tenure as librarian of the Houghton Library. Almost all of Erasmus's main works are present not only in first edition but also in the revised and enlarged editions he himself was constantly issuing during his lifetime.

ERASMUS: *KINDER ZÜCHT*, 1531
The first edition of the first German version
Acquired in 1966 through gifts of the Friends of the Harvard College Library

ERASMUS: *A LYTLE TREATISE OF THE MANER AND FORME OF CONFESSION* [CA. 1535] (*STC* 10498) Given in 1961 by Christian A. Zabriskie in memory of Edward Powis Jones, H 1901

PRIMAE DECADIS LIBER PRIMVS

M. ANTONII SABELLICI RERVM VENETARVM AB VRBE CONDITA AD MARCVM BARBADICVM SERENISS. VENETIARVM PRINCIPEM ET SENATVM LIBER PRIMVS PRIMAE DECADIS FOELICITER INCIPIT.

QVONIAM IGITVR SATIS CONstat priscos Venetos & urbis & Imperii de quo hæc scripturi sumus conditores fuisse. nihil ab re fore existimaui quando de origine gentis inter ueteres auctores parum constare uideo: priusq̃ urbis primordia aperiantur: de illorum uetustate aliquid breuiter referre. Fuerunt itaq; prisci Veneti non Italiæ indigenæ: sed ut quidam tradiderunt a Venetis Gallis oceani accolis oriundi. Neq; hi nomen tantum secuti uidentur: Sed quia rei maritimæ studium & gloriam: qui Adriatici sinus oram tenuerunt: ut illi nunq̃ neglexerint: Essentq; iis qui in Gallia sunt si non lingua: moribus tamen & ornatu corporis: ut Polybius ait per q̃similes: Alii uero eos e Paphlagonia profectos affirmant: in quibus est Liuius: Is Pylæmene Duce ad Troiam amisso: cum Antenore in Italiam uenisse tradit: quod ipsum secutus Cato Troiana stirpe Venetos procreatos credidit: Cornelius nepos & ipse ex Henetis qui Cromnam oppidum circa Paphlagoniam tenuerunt: Venetos eorum cognomines in Italia ortos existimauit: Quidam Cappadocibus eam gentem finitimam tradiderunt: ac cum Cimeriis militasse: posteaq; Adriam peruenisse: Alii uicum non longe ab Amastri tenuisse arbitrati sunt: Requirebantq; interim tota regione Henetos quasi nusq̃ ostenderentur. Sed inter omnes fere constat hanc de qua loquimur Paphlagonum esse gentem: quod Xenodotus non solum credidit: sed Amysum quoq; oppidum id esse existimauit: quod in ea terra postea Henetia dicta sit: Cæterum qui ita esse autumant: præcipuam utriusq; gentis in equis mulisq; alendis industriam in argumentum adducunt Homeri usi testimonio cuius illud est: Mularum genus ex Henetis quæ robore præstent: quum de Asiaticis interim summus poeta loqueretur. Strabo uetustatis auctor diligentissimus nobilissimam equarum progeniem usq; ferme ad sua tempora in his Venetis qui Adriatici maris partem accolunt peruenisse scribit: quarum fama ob eximiam pernicitatem ualde celebris fuisset. Hæc certe atq; alia multa faciunt ut eorum sim sententiæ: qui cum Antenore Henetos in Italiam uenisse tradunt: ac mutata littera de inde Venetos appellatos. Antenoris aduentum in intimum maris Adriatici sinum non solum Veneti testantur qui eius comites fuere: Sed q̃ locus in quem primum egressi sunt Troia est dicta: quodq; Troiano deinde Pago nomen mansit. Ii primo pulsis suis sedibus Euganeis qui eius terræ oram: quæ est inter mare & alpes incolebant: Patauium condiderunt: Procedente deinde

Vet°de Venetoȝ origine opinio

Vera Venetoȝ origo

Troia Pagus in Venetis

a iii

The William King Richardson Library

ONE of the most magnificent bequests that have come to the Houghton Library is the collection of books and manuscripts formed by the late William King Richardson of Boston, received a few months after his death in 1951 and housed in a special room designed to his order.

Mr. Richardson's taste was catholic but discriminating, and among his books there were very few that could not be described as being in fine condition. Incunabula were one of his prime interests; of the 109 he owned, fifty-three were printed before 1480, and many are special copies, like the 1487 edition of Marco Sabellico's *Rerum Venetarum ab urbe condita decades*, printed in Venice by Andrea Torresano de Asola. It is one of four known copies on vellum and is the one presented to Marco Barbarigo, Doge of Venice, the dedicatee, whose arms are painted in the lower margin of the first page of text.

A case of fifty-six early manuscripts begins with three dating from the twelfth century and goes on to include fine specimens of French and Italian illumination of the fourteenth and fifteenth centuries. Productions of the Aldine press were another of Mr. Richardson's interests, and of the nearly 140 he collected, many are distinguished for rarity, condition, or provenance.

Bindings were another specialty, and some of the best examples at Harvard are in this collection. Finally Mr. Richardson gathered a small but choice selection of the great French illustrated books of the eighteenth century.

Several of Mr. Richardson's books are reproduced in other contexts in the present volume.

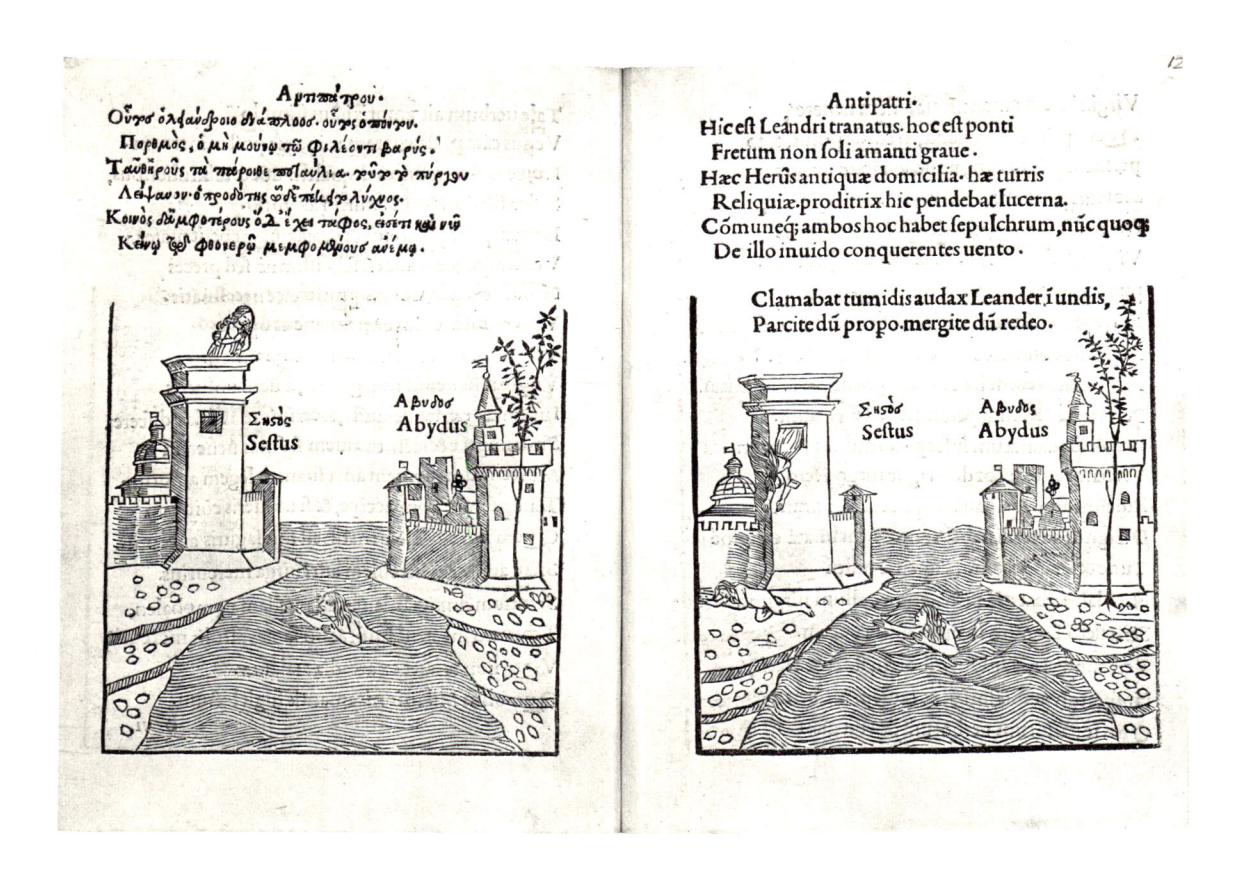

MUSAEUS: *DE HERONE & LEANDRO* [VENICE: ALDUS MANUTIUS, 1495–97] 7 × 10 inches
Bequeathed in 1951 by William King Richardson, H 1880

SABELLICO: *RERUM VENETARUM AB URBE CONDITA DECADES*
VENICE: ANDREA TORRESANO DE ASOLA, 1487, ON VELLUM
Bequeathed in 1951 by William King Richardson, H 1880

UNDECORATED BURY ST. EDMUNDS BINDING ON MS. OPERA OF ST. AUGUSTINE
(SAEC. XII)   12½ × 8½ inches   Bequeathed in 1951 by William King Richardson, H 1880

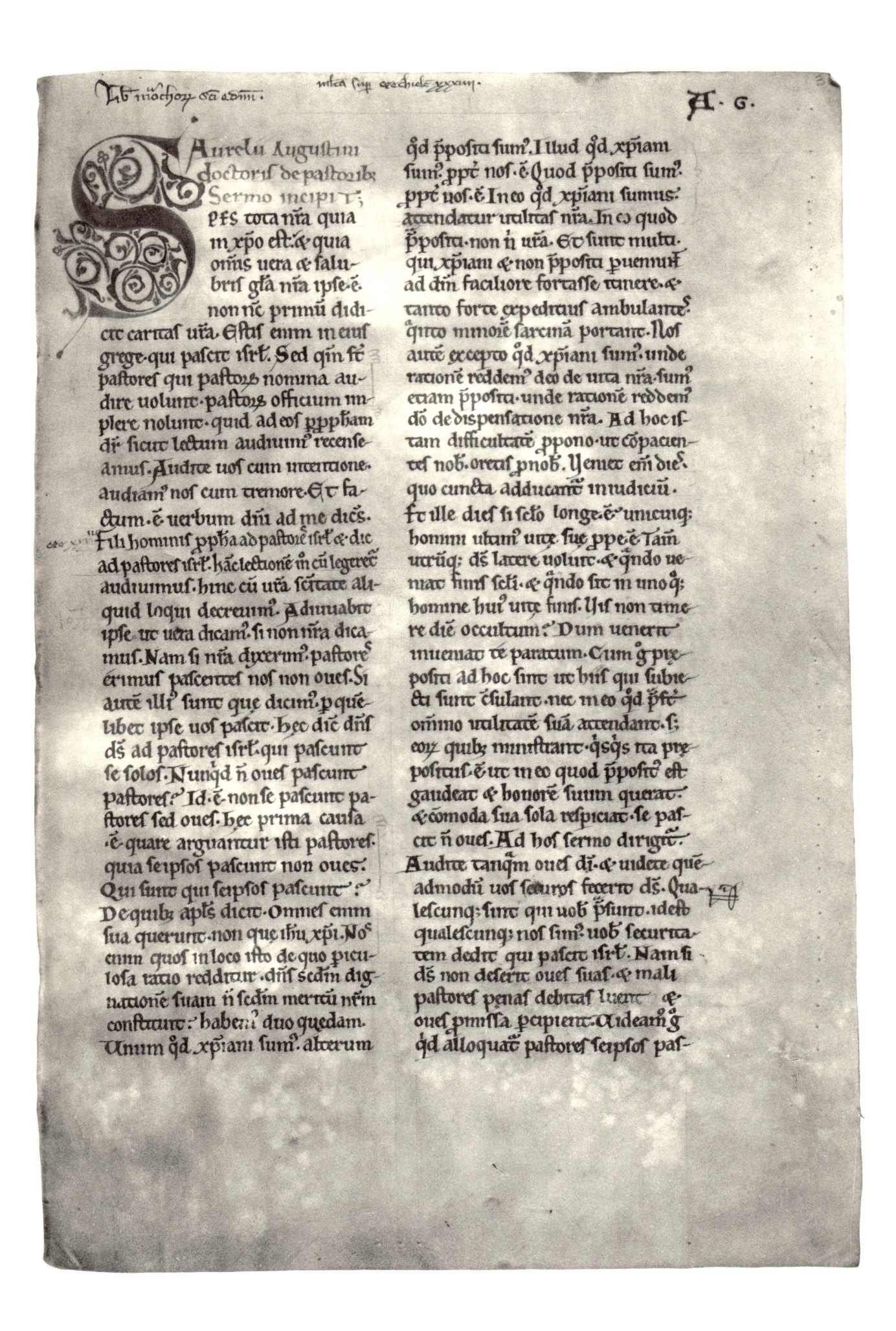

BURY ST. EDMUNDS MS., OPERA OF ST. AUGUSTINE (SAEC. XII) 12½ × 8½ inches
Bequeathed in 1951 by William King Richardson, H 1880

BOCCACCIO: *LE DECAMERON* (TR. LAURENT DE PREMIERFAIT) MS. WRITTEN CA. 1460 FOR ÉTIENNE CHEVALIER
Bequeathed in 1951 by William King Richardson, H 1880

eus in adiutorium
meum intende.
Domine ad

THE DE BUZ BOOK OF HOURS
    Executed in the Rohan atelier, ca. 1425, for Antoine de Buz,
seigneur de Villemareule
    Bequeathed in 1951 by William King Richardson, H 1880

LIVY: *LES DECADES* (TR. PIERRE BERÇEURE) MS. WRITTEN AT PARIS, CA. 1425   16¾ × 11½ inches
Bequeathed in 1951 by William King Richardson, H 1880

The Richardson Library   39

Lybya ut uetustissimi uolunt auctores epaphi egiptiorum regi fuit filia ex cassiopa iunge eaque nupsit neptuno .i. cetero atque potenti uiro cuius proprium nomen ad nos usque non uenit. Et ex eo peperit busyridem immanem postea superioris egipti tirannum. Huius magnifica opera ab aliis creduntur consumpta. Sed ea fuisse primaria satis argumenti prestat eam tante apud suos fuisse auctoritatis ut eius affrice pars cui imperauit lybia omnis de suo nomine apellata sit.

unde libia pars affrice dicta sit.

De Marpesia et Lampedone reginis Amaçonum.

Marpesia seu marthesia et lampedo sorores fuere amaçonum inuicem regine. Et ob illustrem bellorum gloriam sese martis uocauere filias. Quarum quoniam pro regina sit hystoria paulo altius assumenda est. Esct itaque ea tempestate siluestri et fere inaccessa extreris regione et sub arthoo se in oceanum usque ab eusino sinu protendente Sylisios et Scolopitas ut aiunt regii iuuenes factione maiorum pulsi cum parte populorum iuxta thermodohonte capadocie amnie deuenere et cinis occupatis armis raptu uiuere et incolas latrociniis infestare cepere. A quibus tractu temporis per insidias fere omnes trucidati sunt homines. Quod cum egre ferrent uiduate coniuges et maiorem uindicte deuenissent feruore cum paucis qui superuixerant uiris arma prorupere et primo impetu facto hostes a suis amouere finibus. Inde ultro circumstantibus intulere bellum demum arbitrantes seruitute potius quam iugum si ceteris adhererent hominibus et feminas solas posse sufficere bellis et armis. Ne mitiores uiderentur habuisse de cos ceteris hec quibus uiros a cede finitimo

rum fortuna seruasset comuni consilio uirtutes in eos omnes interimere. Inde in hostes furore conuerso quasi uirorum neces ultrice illos adeo contriuere ut ab eis facile pacem impetrarent. Qua suscepta ad successionem consequendam uicissim finitimis adherebant. et cum concepissent euestigio reuertebantur in sedes. Tandem qui nascebantur mares occidebantur illico. uirgines ad miliciam cum diligencia seruabantur tenellis igne seu medicamine alio sublato incremento mammille dextere. ne sagittandi exercicium impediretur adultis. sinistra linquebatur intacta ut ex illa nutrimenta porrigerent nascituris. ex quo amaçonum uocabulum sortite sunt. Nec eis malendis uirginibus fuit ea cura que nostris. Nam colo calatis ue aliisque muliebribus abiectis officiis uenationibus discursionibus domationibus equorum laboribus armorum assiduis sagittationibus et huiusmodi exerciciis maturiores puellulas durabant in aptitudine et uirile robur. Quibus artibus non solum cyrios tenuere campos a suis olim maioribus occupatos quin imo europe ingenti parte bellorum iure quesita plurimum asye occupauere formidabilesque deuenere omnibus. Sane ne uiribus deesset regimen ante alias marpesiam et lampedonem sibi post ceses uiros instituere reginas. sub quarum auspiciis ut prius ostratum est suum plurimum imperium auxere. He quidem cum militari disciplina insignes essent. partitis intra se prouinciis. ut puta cum una in regni tutelam subsisteret. reliqua parte copiarum sumpta ad subiciendos finitimos earum impe[rium] incedebat et sic uicissim maximis partitis prouinciis accepere aliquandiu rem publicam. Verum cum lampedo ad ultimum in hostes duxisset exercitum repentino barbarorum circumadiacencium incursu marpesia nimium sui fidens relictis aliquibus filiabus cum parte copiarum cesa est. quid autem ex lampedone secutum sit legisse non memini.

De Tisbe babilonia uirgine.

UNFINISHED MS. OF BOCCACCIO: *DE CLARIS MULIERIBUS*
(FLORENCE, SAEC. XV) 13 × 9¾ inches
   Bequeathed in 1951 by William King Richardson, H 1880

C. J. DORAT: *LES BAISERS*, ILLUSTRATED BY CHARLES EISEN, LA HAYE, 1770 9 × 10½ inches
   Bequeathed in 1951 by William King Richardson, H 1880

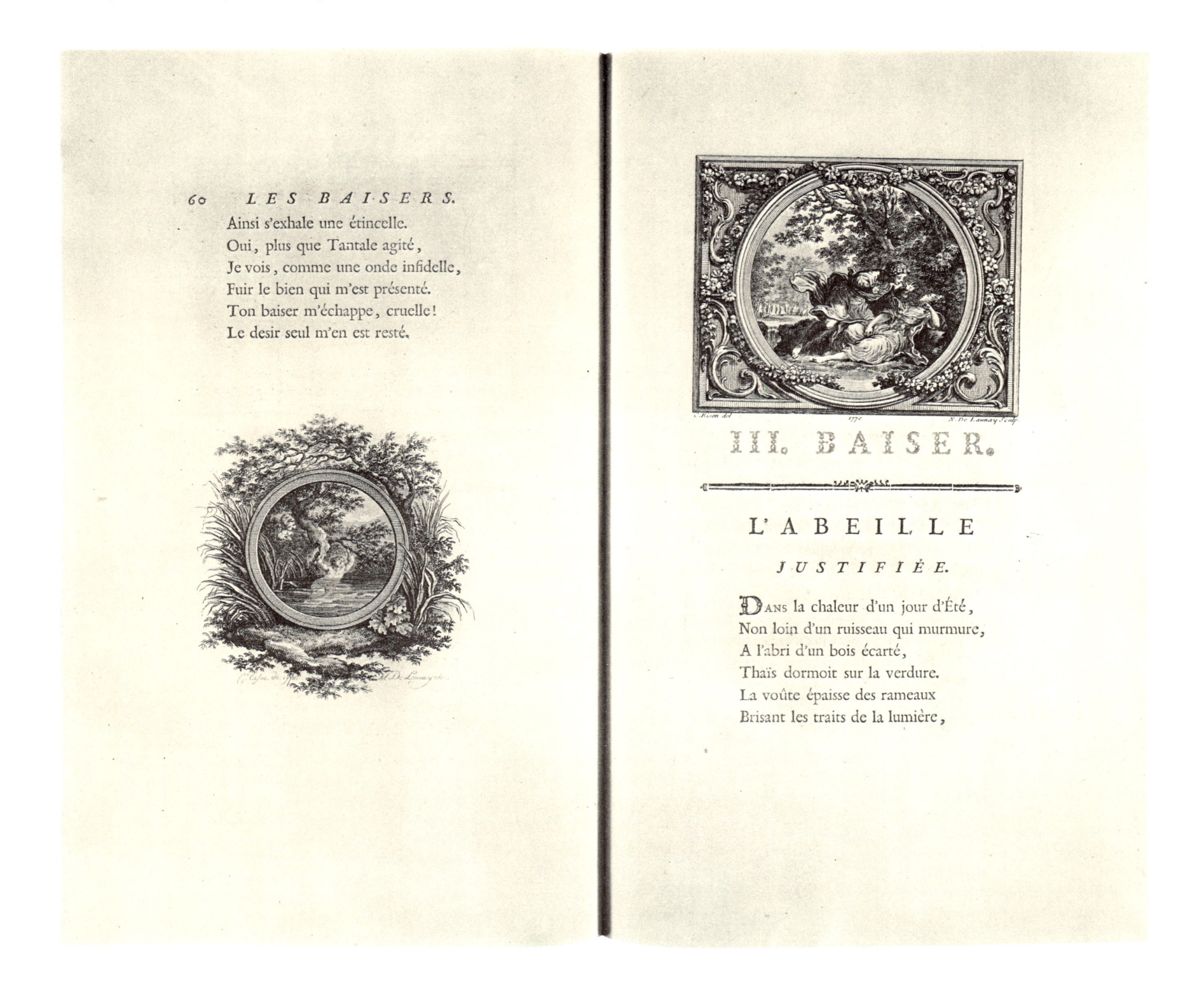

The Richardson Library 41

BINDING BY QUEEN'S BINDER B ON
RICHARD ALLESTREE: *THE LIVELY ORACLES
GIVEN US*, OXFORD, 1678
Bequeathed in 1951 by William King Richardson, H 1880

INLAID BINDING ASCRIBED TO PADELOUP
ON *NOUVEAU TESTAMENT*, PARIS, 1707
Bequeathed in 1951 by William King Richardson, H 1880

42

BOOK OF COMMON PRAYER AND BIBLE, LONDON, 1638
Contemporary morocco overlay binding with fore-edge painting;
repaired in 1791 by Roger Payne, with his bill laid in
Bequeathed in 1951 by William King Richardson, H 1880

13 3/8 × 10 3/4 inches

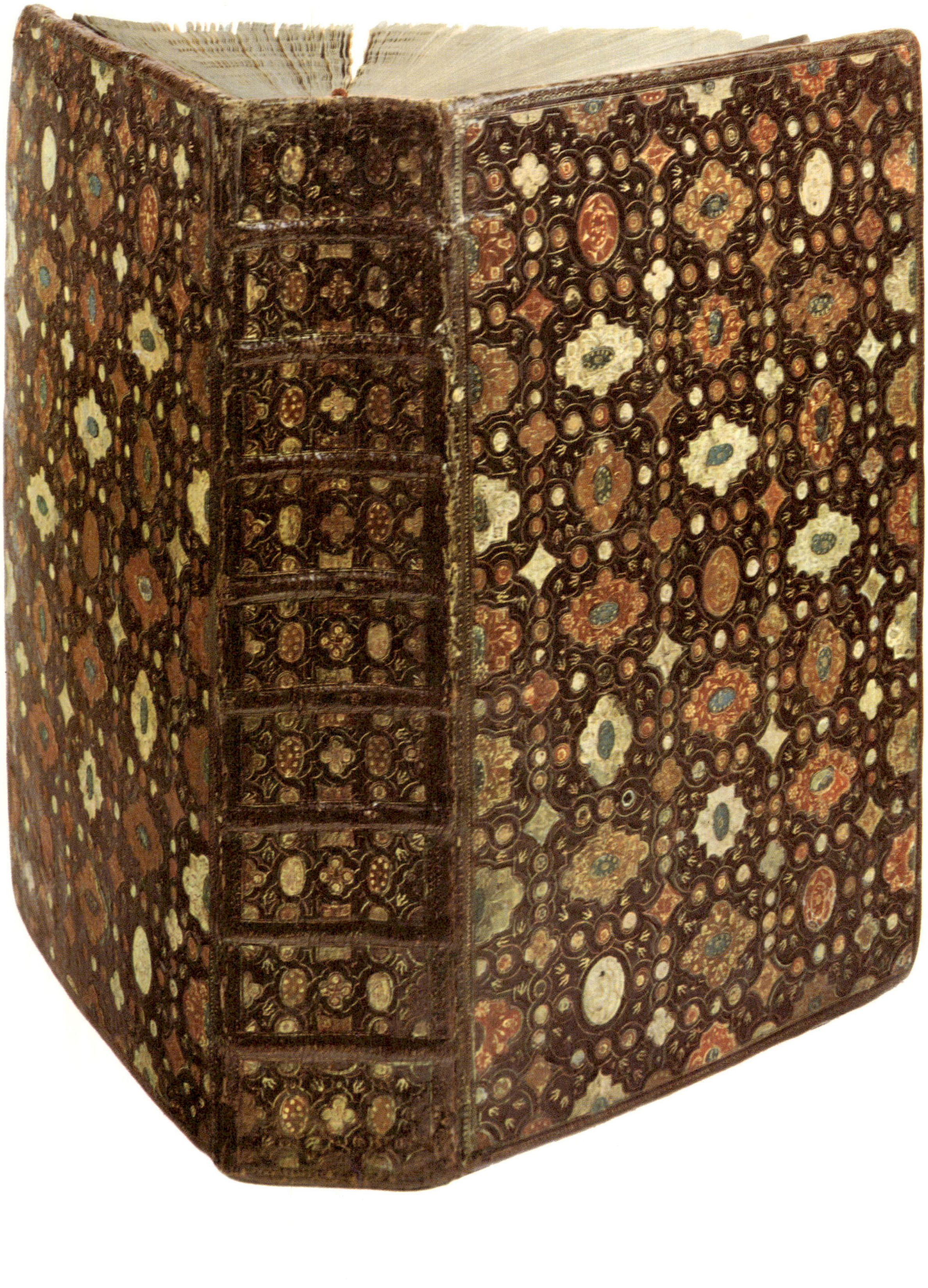

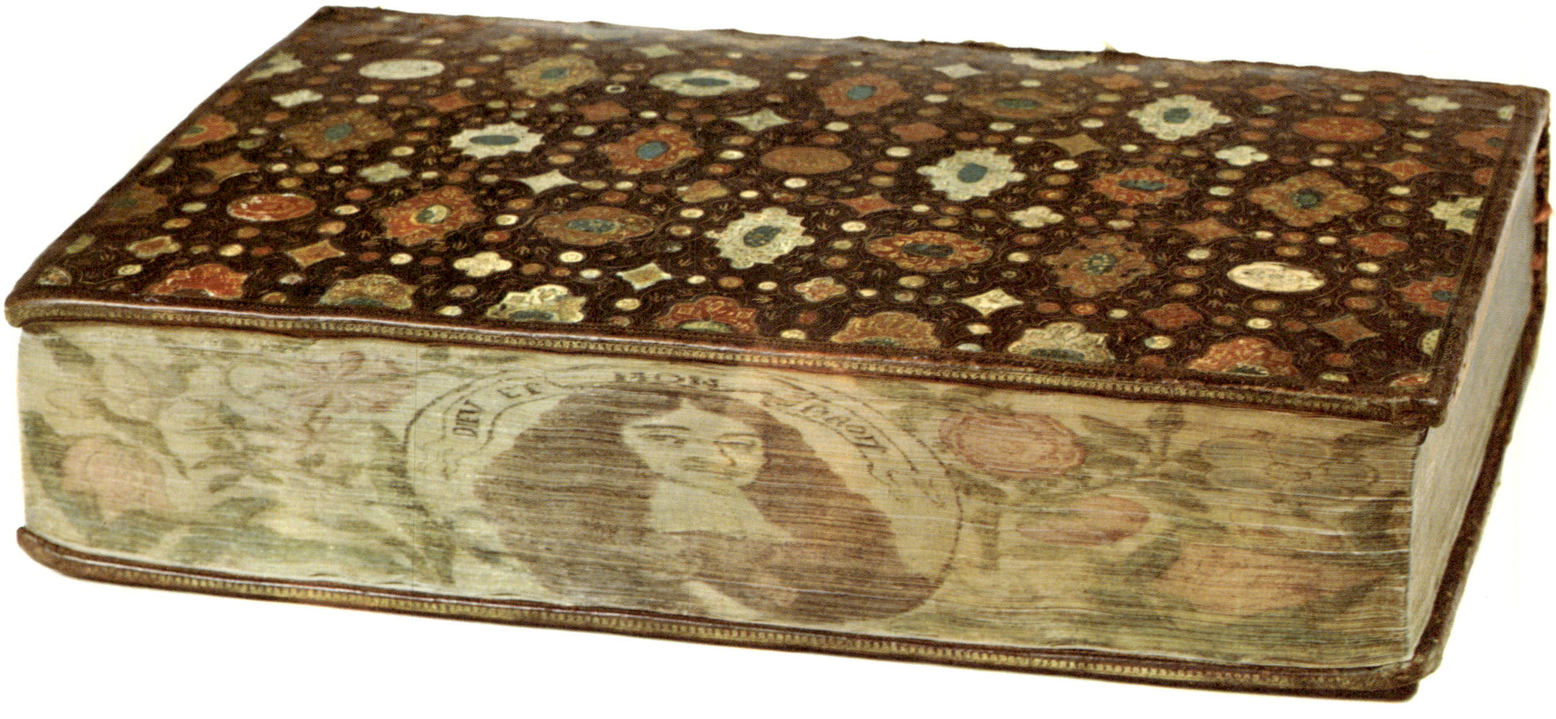

BINDING BY ROGER PAYNE ON BODONI'S EDITION
OF ANACREON, PARMA, 1791
Bequeathed in 1951 by William King Richardson, H 1880

BINDING FOR JEAN GROLIER ON
LARGE-PAPER ALDINE OVID, VENICE, 1533
Bequeathed in 1951 by William King Richardson, H 1880

The Richardson Library 43

POWDERED GOLD BINDING ON JACOBUS DE STRADA:
EPITOME DU THRESOR DES ANTIQUITEZ, LYONS, 1553
Bequeathed in 1951 by William King Richardson, H 1880

DEDICATION BINDING TO ARCHBISHOP WILLIAM LAUD ON
FRANCIS WHITE: *A TREATISE OF THE SABBATH-DAY*, LONDON, 1635
    Bequeathed in 1951 by William King Richardson, H 1880

The Richardson Library   45

THE TRVE COPIE OF AL THE BVRIALS AND CHRISTNINGS

aswell within the Citie of LONDON as the Liberties thereof, as in other Parishes in the skirts of the City, and out of the Freedome, according to the report made to the Kinges most excellent Maiesty, by the Company of Parish Clearkes of the said Cittie, From the 6. of October, 1603. to the 13. of the same. Whereunto is added the true Relation of the whole number of all that haue dyed of this Visitation, from the 17. of December, 1602 to the 13. of this present moneth of October. 1603. with the whole number of all that haue dyed in Westminster, in the Sauoy, in Stepney, Newington, and sundry other places, since the sicknesse beganne there.

London within the Walles.

Parish	Buried in all	Of the Plague
Albones in Woodstreet	14	13
Allhallowes Lombarstreet	5	5
Alhallowes the Great	13	11
Alhallowes the Lesse	14	14
Alhallowes Bredstreet	3	3
Alhallowes staynings	6	5
Alhallowes the wall	8	6
Alhallowes Hony-Lane	0	0
Alhallowes Barking	13	11
Alphage at Cripplegate	3	3
Androws by the Wardrope	7	7
Androwes vnder shaft	6	6
Androwes Eastcheape	5	5
Annes at Aldersgate	6	5
Annes Black Friers	7	7
Auntlins Parish	3	3
Austines Parish	7	7
Barthelmew at the Exch.	3	1
Bennets at Paules-wharfe	9	7
Bennets Grace-Church	2	2
Bennet Fincke	7	7
Bennets Sherhog	1	1
Buttols Billingsgate	4	2
Christ Church Parish	11	9
Christophers Parish	3	3
Clements by Eastcheape	7	6
Dennis Back-Church	8	2
Dunstones in the East	6	5
Edmunds in Lombardst.	2	2
Ethelborowes Parish	5	6
Faythes Parish	6	6
Fosters Parish	7	7
Gabriell Fan-Church	8	7
George in Buttolph Lane	4	4
Gregories by Paules	14	9
Hellens within Bishopsg.	4	3
Iames by Garlick-hithe	11	11
S. Iohn Euangelist	0	0
Iohn Zacharies	10	10
Iohns in the Walbrooke	8	7
Katherins Cree-Church	16	12
Katherine Coleman	9	8
Laurence in the Iury	10	8
Laurence Pountney	11	9
Leonardes Foster-Lane	14	8
Leonardes Eastcheape	4	3
Magnus Parish	9	6
Margrets New-fish street	4	3
Margrets Pattons	1	1
Margrets Moises	1	1
Margrets Lothbery	5	5
Martins in the Vintrie	12	11
Martins Ogars	2	2
Martins Outwich	2	2
Martins Iremonger-Lane	1	1
Martins at Ludgate	8	7
Mary le Booe	3	3
Mary Bothawe	4	4
Mary at the hill	4	2
Mary Abchurch	5	5
Mary Woolchurch	1	1
Mary Cole-Church	0	0
Mary Woolnoth	4	3
Mary Aldermary	2	2
Mary Aldermanbery	5	4
Mary staynings	2	1
Mary Mountawe	2	2
Mary Sommersets	10	10
Mathew Friday-street	1	1
Maudlins Milke-street	5	5
Maudlins by old-fishstreet	7	6
Mighels Bassie-shaw	5	3
Mighels in Corne-hill	8	6
Mighels in the Riall	4	3
Mighels in the Querne	3	2
Mighels Queane-hith	10	7
Mighels in Crooked-Lane	4	4
Mighels in Woodstreet	12	10
Mildreds in the Poultry	1	1
Mildreds in Bredstreet	3	3
Nicholas Acons	4	4
Nicholas Col-Abbay	16	16
Nicholas Olaues	6	4
Olaues in the Iury	6	4
Olaues in Hartstreet	9	9
Olaues in Siluerstreet	4	3
Pancras by Soper-Lane	0	0
Peters in Corne-hill	5	2
Peters in Cheape	2	2
Peters the poore	4	3
Peters at Pauleswharfe	4	3
Steuens in Colmanstreet	17	14
Steuens in the Walbroke	2	2
Swithins at London-stone	9	9
Thomas Apostles	13	11
Trinity Parish	4	4

The number buried with.in the wals of London is 576. Whereof, of the Plague 497.

London without the Wals, and within the Liberties.

Parish	Buried in all	Of the Plague
Androwes in Holborne	63	60
Barthelmew the great Smit.	6	6
Barthelmew the lesse Smithf.	4	4
Brides parish	43	36
Buttols Algate	25	20
Bridewell Precinct	9	9
Buttols Bishopsgate	23	20
Buttols without Aldersg.	35	32
Dunstones in the West	25	22
Georges in Southwarke	12	9
Giles without Criplegate	67	46
Olaues in Southwarke	51	48
Sauiours in Southwarke	91	84
Sepulchers parish	74	65
Thomas in Southwarke	3	2
Trinity in the Minories	2	2

The number buried without the wals, and within the liberties is 533. Whereof of the plague 465.

Out Parishes adioining to the Citie.

Parish	Buried in all	Of the Plague
Clements without Templeb.	41	38
Giles in the Fieldes	31	29
Iames at Clearkenwel	13	10
Katherines by the tower	19	16
Leonards in Shordich	20	14
Martins in the Fieldes	31	29
Mary Whitechappel	28	28
Magdalens in Barmondsey-street	16	16
At the Pest-house	4	4

Buried without 203. Whereof, Of the Plague 184.

From the first great plague in our memory after the losse of New-hauen, from the first of January, 1562. to December, 1563. there dyed of the Plague, twenty thousand, one hundred, thirty sixe

And in the last Visitation, from the 20. of December, 1592, to the 23 of the same moneth in the yeare 1593. dyed in all, 25886, of the Plague in and about London, 11003. And in the yeare before, 2000.

And now in this present Visitation which it pleaseth God to strike vs with, there hath dyed from the 17. of December, 1602. to the 14. of July, 1603. the whole number in London and the Liberties, 4314. Whereof, of the Plague, 3310. The rest are set down, as they haue followed weeckely.

	Buried	Plague
From the 14. of July, to the 21. of the same	867	—
Whereof of the plague	646	In the out Parishes 319, whereof, of the plague 271
Buried in all this weeke, 1186. Whereof, of the plague, 917		
From the 21. of July, to the 28. of the same	1312	In the out parishes 398, whereof of the Plague. 354
Whereof of the plague	1025	Out of the Pesthouse 18
Buried in all this weeke 1728. whereof of the plague 1396		
From the 28. of July, to the 4. of August	1700	In the out parishes 537, whereof of the plague 464
Whereof, of the plague	1439	Pesthouse 19
Buried in all this weeke, 2256. Whereof of the Plague 1922.		
From the 4. of August to the 11. of the same	1655	In the out parishes 410, whereof of the plague 361
whereof of the plague	1372	Pesthouse 12
Buried in all this weeke 2077. Whereof of the Plague 1745		
From the 11. of August, to the 18. of the same	2486	In the out Parishes 568, whereof of the plague 514
wherof of the plague	2199	In Bridewell 7. Pesthouse, 21
Buried in all this weeke, 3054. Whereof of the plague. 2713.		
From the 18. of August, to the 25. of the same	2343	In the out parishes 510, Whereof of the plague 448
whereof of the plague	2091	In Bridewell 8, Pesthouse, 12
Buried in all this weeke, 2853. Whereof of the plague, 2539.		
From the 25. of August, to the 1. of September	2798	In the out parishes 587, whereof of the plague 540
wherof of the plague	2495	In Bridewell, 5. pesthouse, 6
Buried in all this weeke, 3385. Whereof of the plague, 3035.		
From the 1. of September to the 8. of the same	2581	In the out parishe 495, whereof of the plague 441
whereof of the plague	2281	In Bridewell, 17 Pesthouse, 5
Buried in all this weeke, 3078. Whereof, of the plague, 2724.		
From the 8. of September to the 15. of the same	2676	In the out parishes, 453, whereof, of the plague, 407
whereof, of the plague,	2411	In Bridewell, 7. Pesthouse, 10
Buried in all this weeke, 3129. Whereof, of the plague, 2818.		
From the 15. of September to the 22. of the same	2080	In the out parishes, 376, whereof of the plague, 344
wherof, of the plague	1851	In Bridewell, 19. Pesthouse 10
Buried in all this weeke, 2456. whereof of the plague. 2195.		
From the 22. of September, to the 29 of the same,	1668	In the out parishes 295, whereof of the Plague 254
whereof of the plague,	1478	
Buried in all this weeke, 1961. Whereof, of the Plague, 1732.		
From the 29. of September, to the 6. of October	1525	In the out parishes 306, Whereof of the plague 274
Whereof of the plague,	1367	
Buried in all this weeke, 1831. Whereof of the plague, 1641.		
From the 6. of October, to the 13. of the same	1109	In the out parishes 203, whereof of the plague 184
whereof, of the plague,	962	
Buried in all this weeke 1312. Whereof, of the plague 1146		

Buried in all within London and the liberties and suburbes, since the sicknes beganne, 34620. Whereof of the plague, 28856.

The time when it began in the Citty of Westminster, and these places following.

Buried in Westminster, from the 14. of Iuly to the 13. of October, in the whole number, 794. whereof of the plague, 695.

Buried in the Sauoy, from the first of Iune to the 13. of October, in the whole number, 183. whereof, of the plague, 169.

Buried in the Parish of Stepney, from the 25. of March, to the 13 of October in all, 1882. whereof, of the plague, 1819.

Buried at Newington-buts from the 14. of Iune, to the 13. of October, in all, 614. whereof of the plague, 552.

Buried in Islington, 193. whereof of the plague, 162.
Buried in Lambeth, 363. whereof, of the plague, 352.
Buried in Hackney, 189. whereof, of the plague. 166.

Buried in all, within the 7. seuerall places last aforenamed, 4116. Whereof of the Plague, 3885.

The whole number that hath beene buried in all, both within London, and the liberties and the 7. other seuerall places last before mentioned is, 38614. whereof the number of the plague is, 31967.

Christnings 73. Parishes cleere of the Plague 5. Parishes infected 107.

Buried in all, within the places aforesaid 1312.
Whereof, of the Plague 1146.

Printed by Iohn Windet, Printer to the Honourable Citie of London.

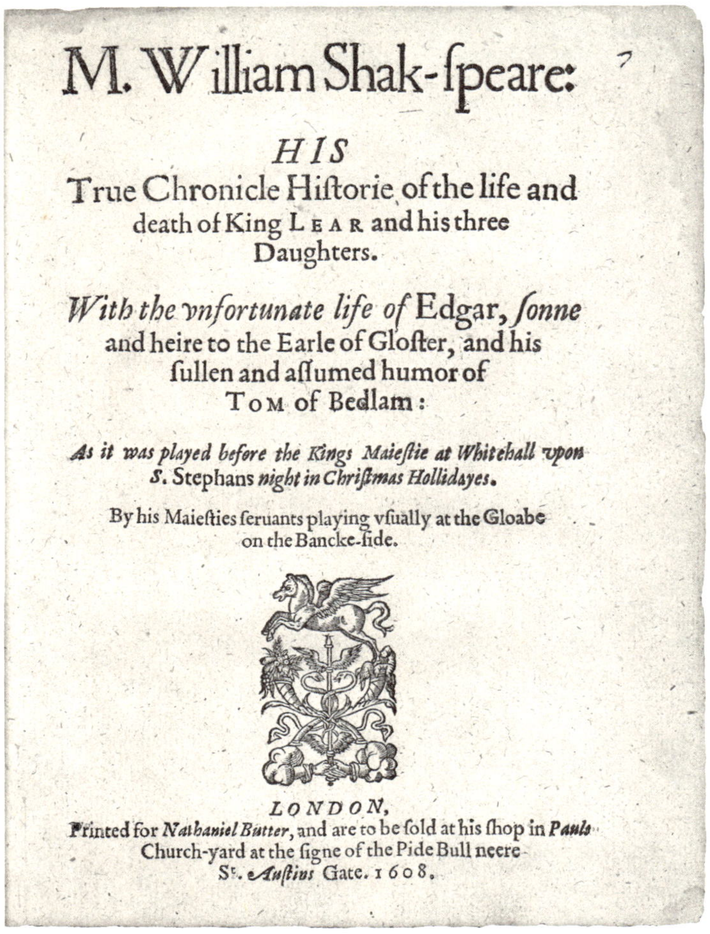

WILLIAM SHAKESPEARE: *KING LEAR*, 1608 (*STC* 22292)
7⅛ × 5¼ inches   Possibly the finest known copy of the first quarto
Given in 1929 by members of the family of William Augustus White, H 1863

THOMAS HARMAN: *A CAVEAT FOR COMMEN CUR-SETORS*, 1567 (*STC* 12787)   7 × 5 inches
One of three known copies of this edition
Given in 1941 by Harold T. White, H 1897, and Mrs. Hugh D. Marshall

S.T.C.

ENGLISH books of the period covered by Pollard and Redgrave's *Short-title Catalogue*—that is, printed from Caxton's day up to the year 1641—occupy a special place in the Harvard Library, headquarters for the revision of this bibliographical classic. The new *S.T.C.* was undertaken by Dr. F. S. Ferguson and the late Professor W. A. Jackson, and it continues in its office in the Houghton Library with completion expected about 1970.

Harvard's collection of *S.T.C.* books is one of the three most important in the United States, and in some fields (for example, law-books) it is unequalled anywhere. Recent collecting has been concentrated on publications of extreme rarity that are also significant in history and literature, such as the forty-four mortality bills of the plague years 1603–1604, of which seventeen are unique; or the five (out of six) controversial works of Giordano Bruno published in London with false imprints, the largest assemblage of them in America. The library also has a shelf of manuscript copies of works that circulated before their texts saw print.

A LONDON MORTALITY BILL OF 1603 (*STC* 16743.9)   15¾ × 10⅝ inches
The only copy in America
Acquired in 1960 with the Amy Lowell Fund

47

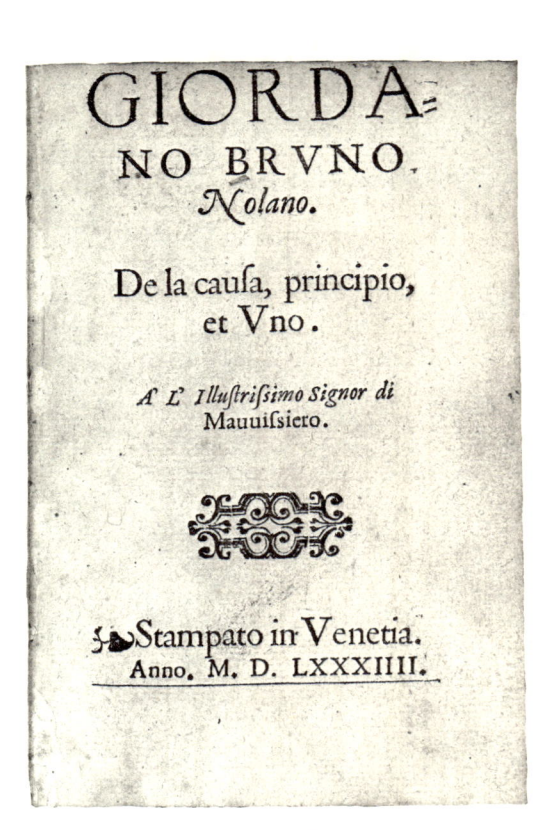

GIORDANO BRUNO: *DE LA CAUSA, PRINCIPIO, ET UNO* [LONDON] 1584 (*STC* 3936) 5⅜ × 3½ inches
Given in 1950 by Harrison D. Horblit, H 1933, in memory of his son, Mark M. Horblit II

GIORDANO BRUNO: *LA CENA DE LE CENERI* [LONDON] 1584 (*STC* 3935) 5⅜ × 3½ inches
Given in 1950 by Harrison D. Horblit, H 1933, in memory of his son, Mark M. Horblit II

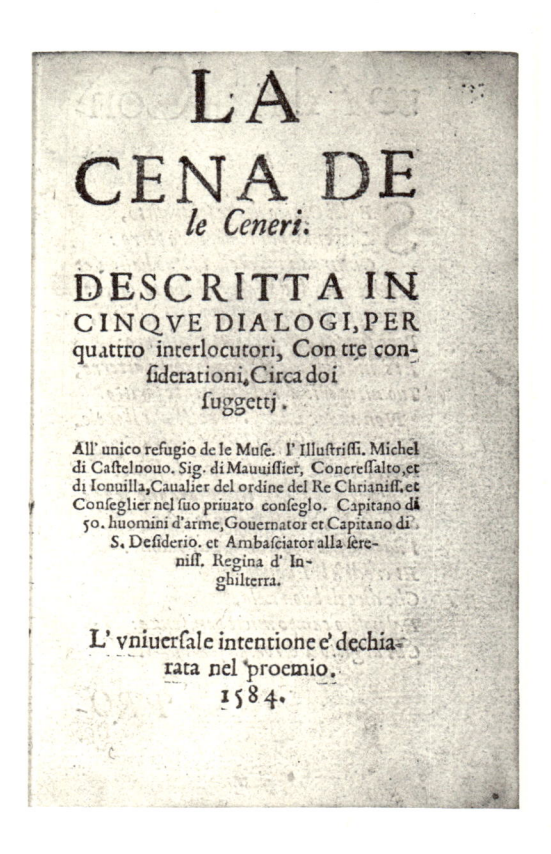

GIORDANO BRUNO: *DE GL'HEROICI FURORI* [LONDON] 1585 (*STC* 3937) 5½ × 3½ inches
Acquired in 1940 with the fund given in memory of Bennett Hubbard Nash, H 1856

GIORDANO BRUNO: *SPACCIO DE LA BESTIA TRIONFANTE* [LONDON] 1584 (*STC* 3940) 5¼ × 3½ inches
Acquired in 1954 with the Amy Lowell Fund

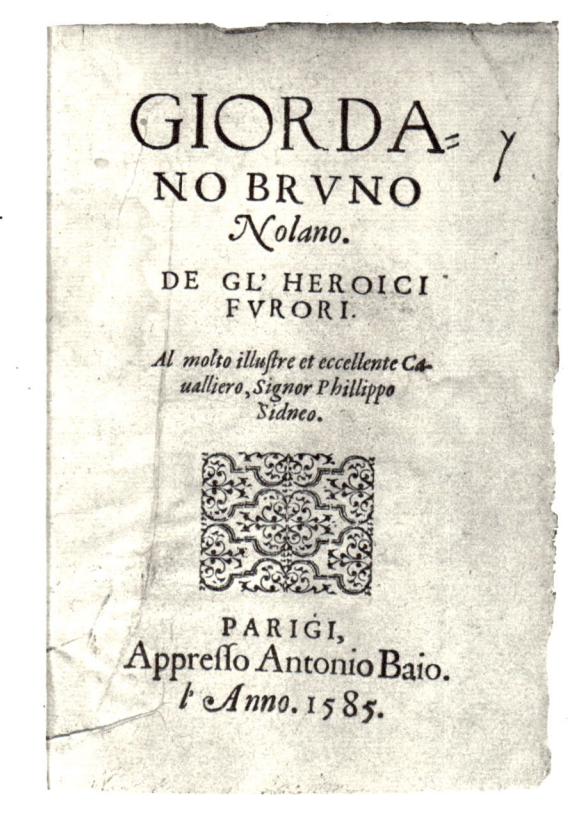

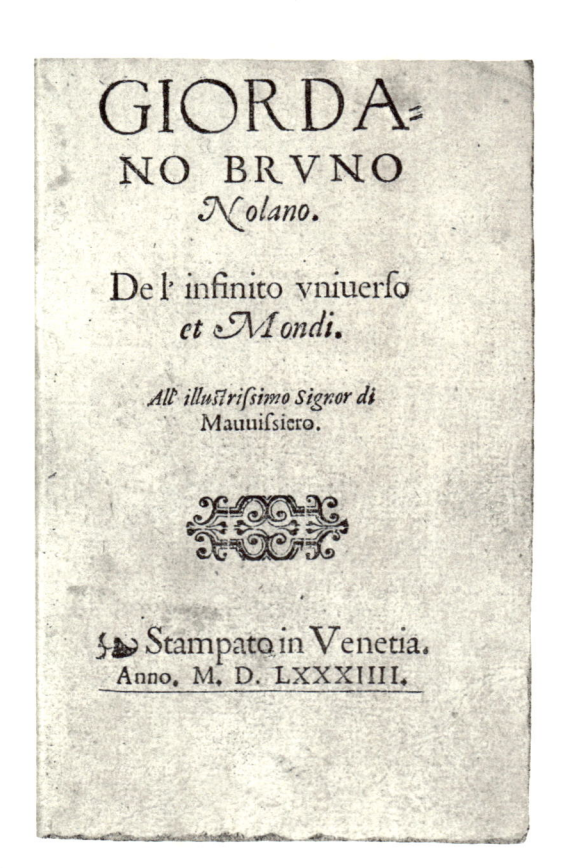

THE NEW TESTAMENT, 1637 (*STC* 2328.5) 5⅞ × 3¼ inches Forged title compartment, actually printed in the Netherlands
Given in 1964 by Robert S. Pirie, H 1956

GIORDANO BRUNO: *DE L'INFINITO UNIVERSO ET MONDI* [LONDON] 1584 (*STC* 3938) 5⅜ × 3½ inches
Given in 1950 by Henry S. Grew, H 1896

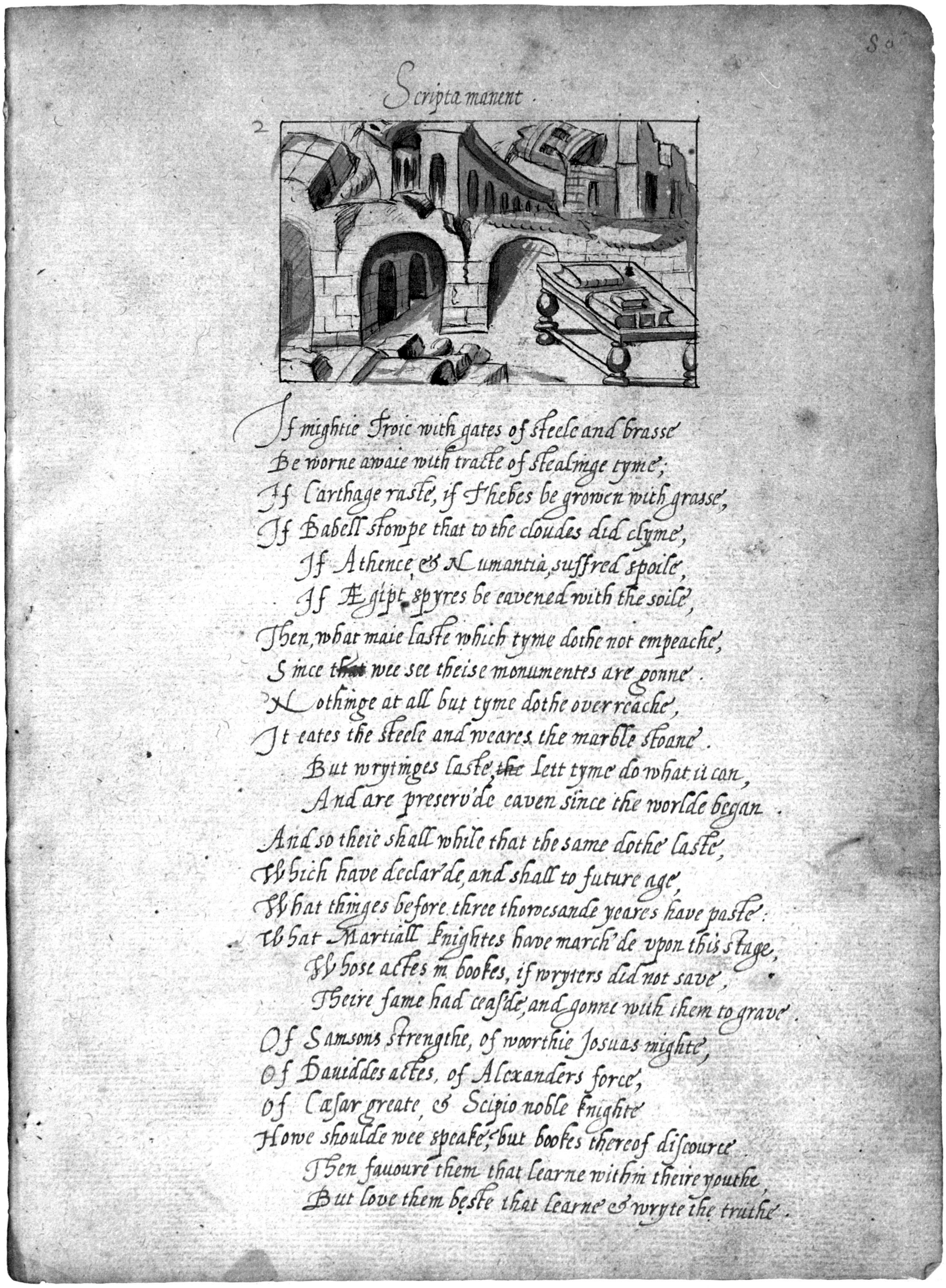

Scripta manent.

If mightie Troie with gates of steele and brasse
Be worne awaie with tracte of stealinge tyme;
If Carthage raste, if Thebes be growen with grasse,
If Babell stowpe that to the cloudes did clyme,
   If Athence, & Numantia, suffred spoile,
   If Ægipt spyres be eavened with the soile,
Then, what maie laste which tyme dothe not empeache,
Since that wee see theise monumentes are gonne.
Nothinge at all but tyme dothe overreache,
It eates the steele and weares the marble stoane.
   But wrytinges laste, lett tyme do what it can,
   And are preserv'de eaven since the worlde began.

And so theie shall while that the same dothe laste,
Which have declar'de, and shall to future age,
What thinges before three thowesande yeares have paste:
What Martiall knightes have march'de vpon this stage,
   Whose actes in bookes, if wryters did not save,
   Theire fame had ceasde, and gonne with them to grave.
Of Samsons strengthe, of woorthie Josuas mighte,
Of Dauiddes actes, of Alexanders force,
Of Cæsar greate, & Scipio noble knighte
Howe shoulde wee speake, but bookes thereof discource
   Then fauoure them that learne within theire youthe,
   But love them beste that learne & wryte the truthe.

GEOFFREY WHITNEY: *A CHOICE OF EMBLEMS* [1585]
Dedication manuscript given to the Earl of Leicester a year before publication
Given in 1941 by Harold T. White, H 1897, and Mrs. Hugh D. Marshall

                        use our time so well that
We'll ~~take it all before~~, and death shall find
No have drain'd life, & left a void behind. Exeunt
            Enter Lucifer

Luci: 'tis done.
Sure nature at that Instant, trembled round;
And mother earth, sigh'd, as she felt the wound.
Of how short durance was their new made state!
How far more mighty than Heav'n's Love, my hate!
His project ruin'd, and his King of Clay:
He form'd an Empire for his foe to Sway.
Heav'n let him Rule, which by his Arms he got;
I'm pleas'd to have obtain'd the second Lot.
This earth is mine; whose Lord I make my Thrall,
Annexing to my Crown, his Conquer'd ball.
Loos'd from the Lakes, my Legions I will Lead,
And, o're the darkned Ayr, Black banners spread:
Contagious damps, from hence, shall mount above,
And force him to his innmost Heav'ns remove.
      A Clap of Thunder is heard
He heares already, and I boast too soone;
I dread that Engine which serv'd his throne.
I'll dive below his wrath, into the deep,
And waste that Empire, which J canst keep. Descends
      Raphael & Gabriel descend

Rapha: As much of grief as happines admits
In Heaven, on each Celestial forehead sits:
Kindness for Man & pity for his ~~fall~~ fate,
May mixt with bliss, and yet not violate:)
their Heav'nly Harps a lower strain began,
And, in soft Musick, mourn'd the fall of Man.

JOHN DRYDEN: *THE FALL OF ANGELS* [1677]
Scribal manuscript with autograph corrections
Acquired in 1911 with funds given by the Saturday Club of Boston

English Literature

ENGLISH literature has always been one of the greatest strengths of the Harvard College Library. It could scarcely be otherwise, fostered by the devoted attention of such men as Francis James Child, George Lyman Kittredge, Fred Norris Robinson, Chester Noyes Greenough, Hyder Edward Rollins, and James Buell Munn, to name only a few of the faculty stalwarts who gave time, knowledge, books, and money to the library. Added to their benefactions are those of the men they educated and inspired with a love of English letters.

The collection is so eminent and so wide-ranging that it defies both brief description and comprehensive depiction. Perhaps this small selection of a few authors from a few periods, coupled with the separate notes on certain special collections, will provide a sufficient hint of its power and scope.

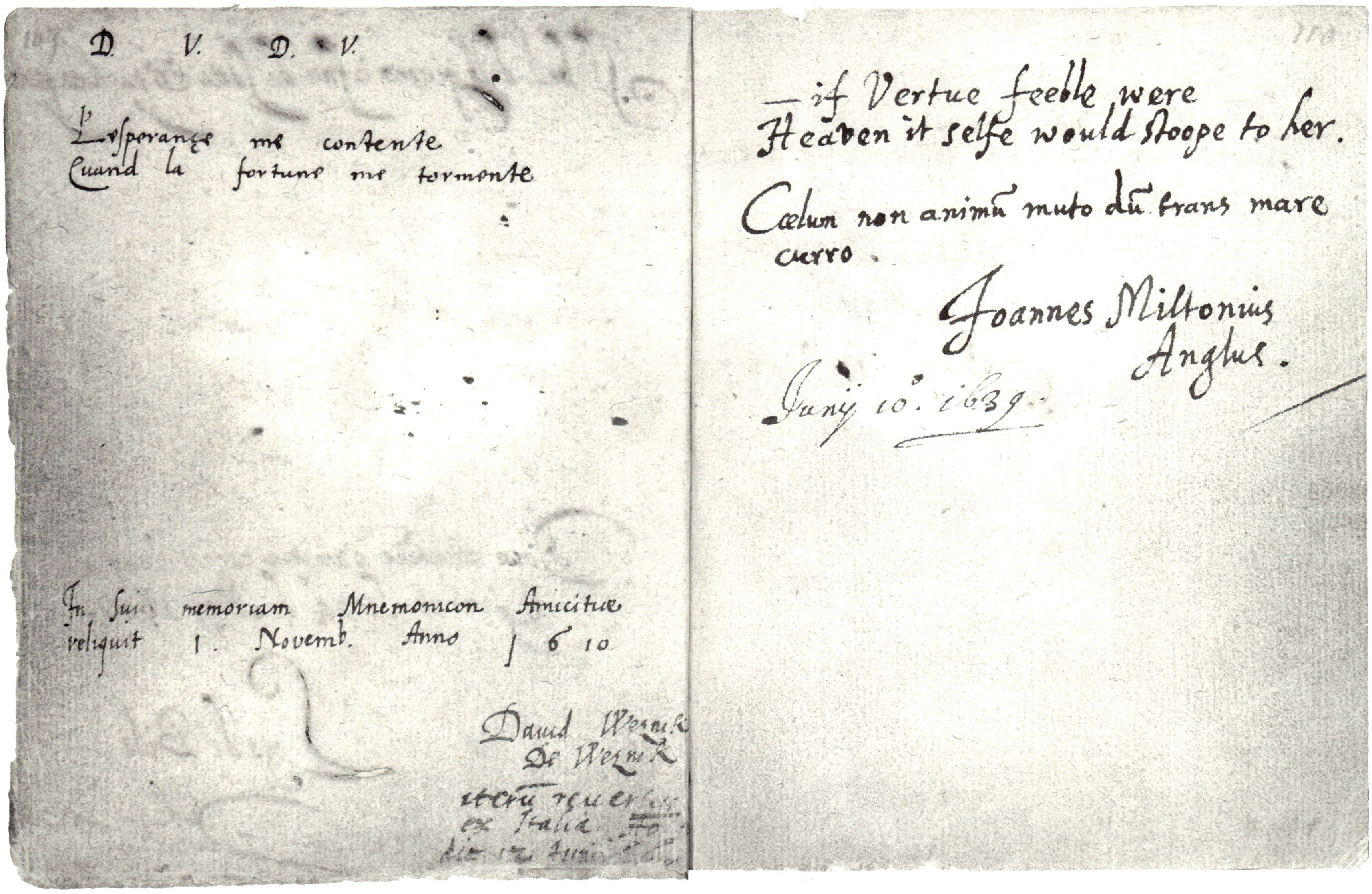

JOHN MILTON'S SIGNATURE IN THE *LIBER AMICORUM* OF CAMILLUS CARDOINUS
Bequeathed in 1874 by Charles Sumner, H 1830

DEATH-BED REPENTANCE OF JOHN WILMOT, 2ND EARL OF ROCHESTER ADDRESSED TO
BISHOP GILBERT BURNET   Acquired in 1944 with money from the sale of duplicates

GEORGE HERBERT: AUTOGRAPH LATIN VERSE
IN HIS COPY OF THE WORKS OF JAMES I, 162
Given in 1963 by the Hunt Foundatio

Peregrini Almam Matrem invisentibus Distichon ipsi
    libro inscriptum.
Quid Vaticanā Bodleiamq; objicis Hospes?
Unicus è nobis Bibliotheca Liber.

Carmina inscripta Pluteo cui opera Serenissi: Iacobi
    æternitati consecrauit.

Hic Iacobus inest, scilicet nunc Bajulus Atlas
    Ille sui Cælū sustinet ipse meum.
Inter Apollineas Norvex Regali columnas
    Cætera vexandi scripta labore levat.
Ni natura Animū clausisset corpore, nemo
    Crederet exiguo tanta latere specu.
Quem non trina capit Regio, non terminat Orbis
    Hunc ego claudo meo capsa beata sinu.

    In parte Exteriori
Nunquid miraris pluteū Peregrine? Recludas
    Interiori
Nunquid miraris tegmen inane? legas.
Cum notos Iacobi petas tua præmia cælos,
    Ne totus pereas cap͡sula ōra cavet.
                            G. Herbert.
                                Orator.

JOHN EVELYN: HOLOGRAPH OF *THE LIFE OF MRS. GODOLPHIN* [CA. 1678] IN EVELYN'S OWN BINDING 7⅝ × 5⅜ inches
Given in 1955 by Carleton R. Richmond, H 1909

JOHN DONNE'S COPY OF VIRGIL IN ITALIAN
6⅛ × 4 inches   Acquired in 1940 with the fund bequeathed by
Henry Saltonstall Howe, H 1869

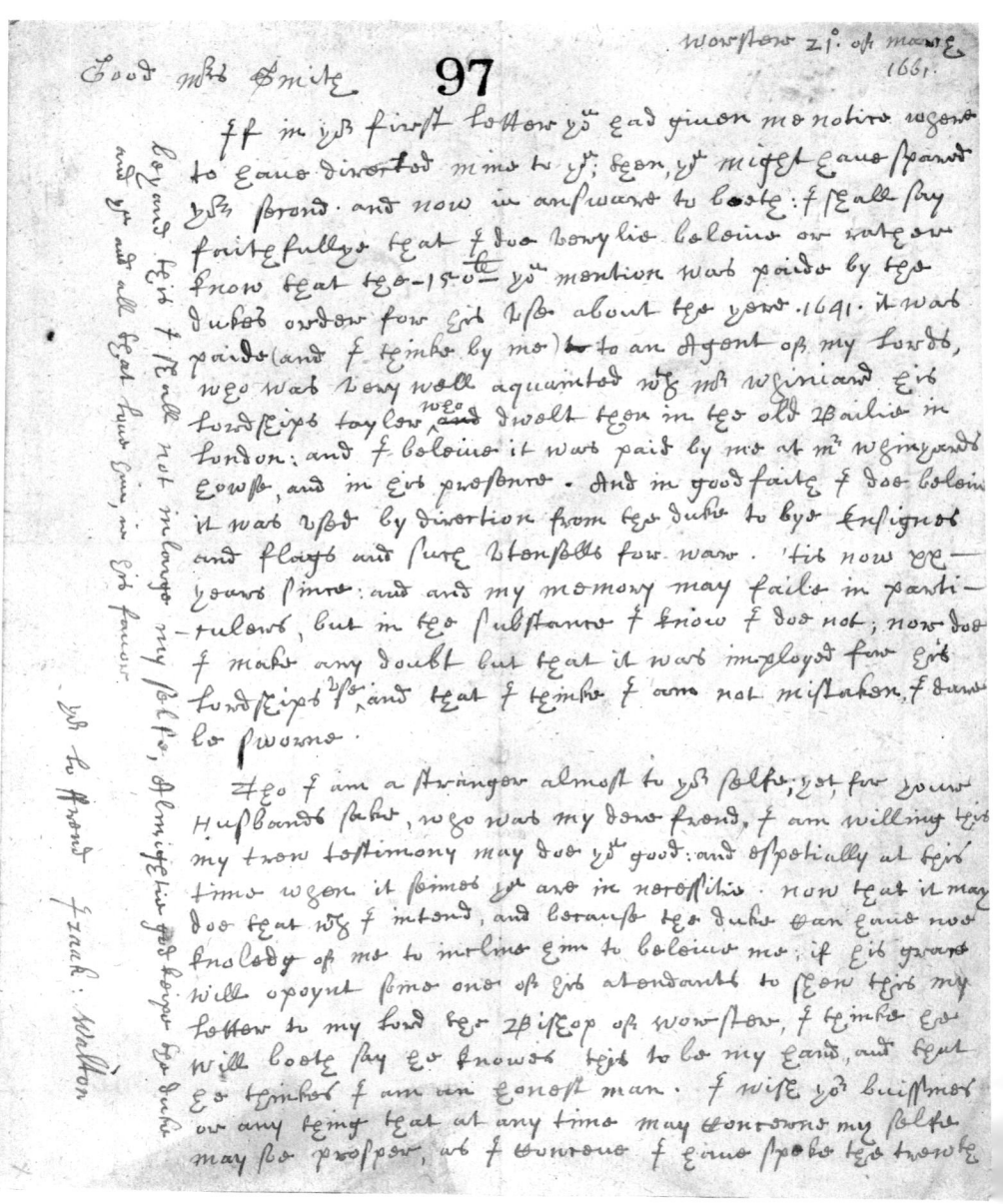

IZAAK WALTON: AUTOGRAPH LETTER TO DOROTHY SMITH 8 × 6½ inches
Bequeathed in 1947 by Gabriel Wells

JOHN LOCKE

GIOVANNI BATTISTA CIPRIANI: PORTRAIT OF JOHN LOCKE
Commissioned by Thomas Hollis of Lincoln's Inn

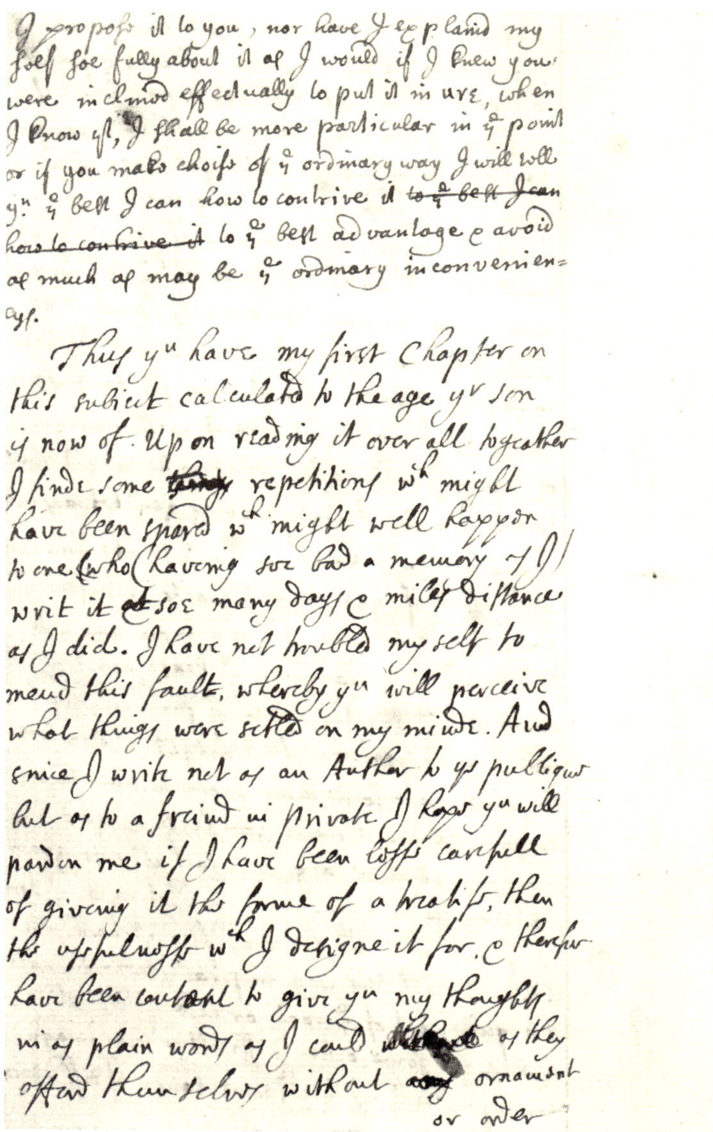

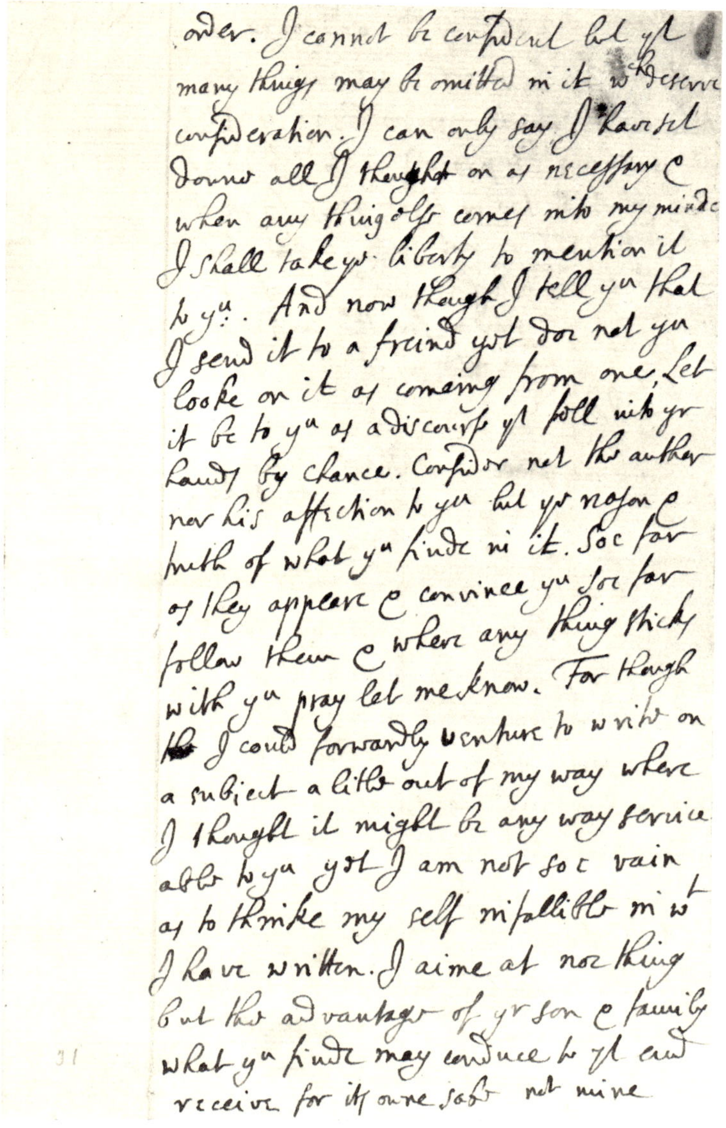

JOHN LOCKE: *OF EDUCATION* [1684]   Conclusion, in Locke's autograph
Given in 1946 by Mrs. Donald F. Hyde

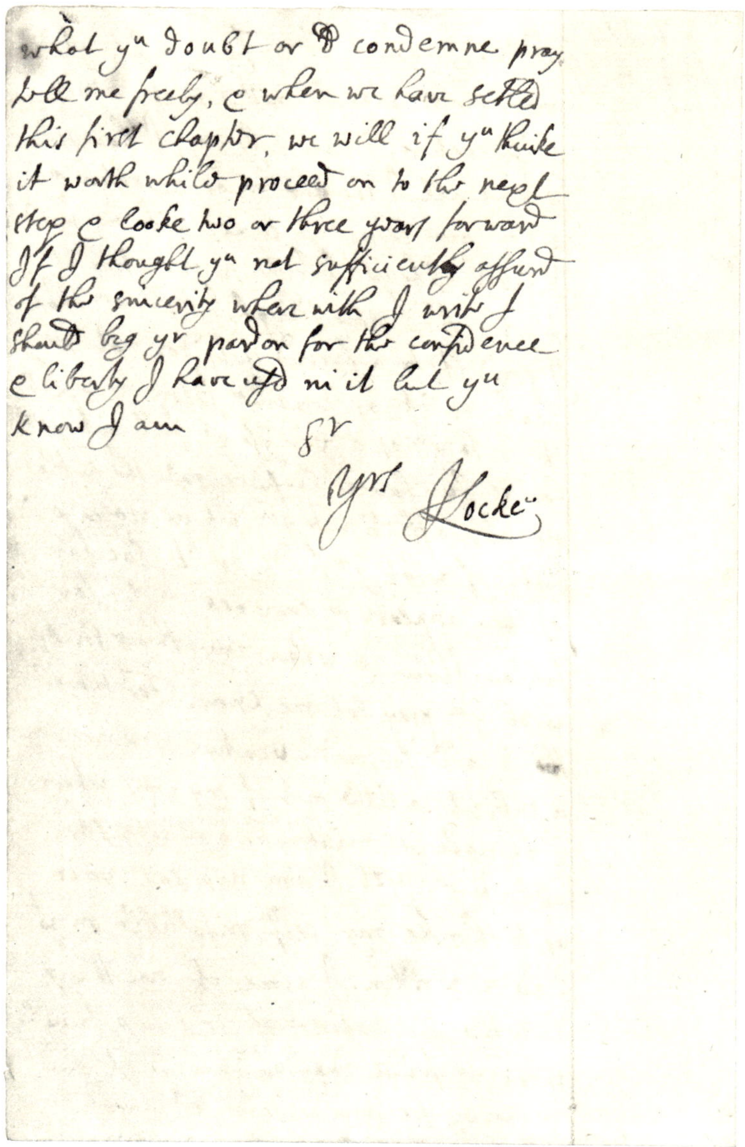

English Literature

JOSEPH ADDISON: AUTOGRAPH DRAFT OF *SPECTATOR* NO. 412   8½ × 10¼ inches
Given in 1949 by Stephen W. Phillips, H 1895

ALEXANDER POPE: HOLOGRAPH OF *AN ESSAY ON MAN*
Given in 1943 by Harold T. White, H 1897, William King Richardson,
H 1880, Carleton R. Richmond, H 1909, and others

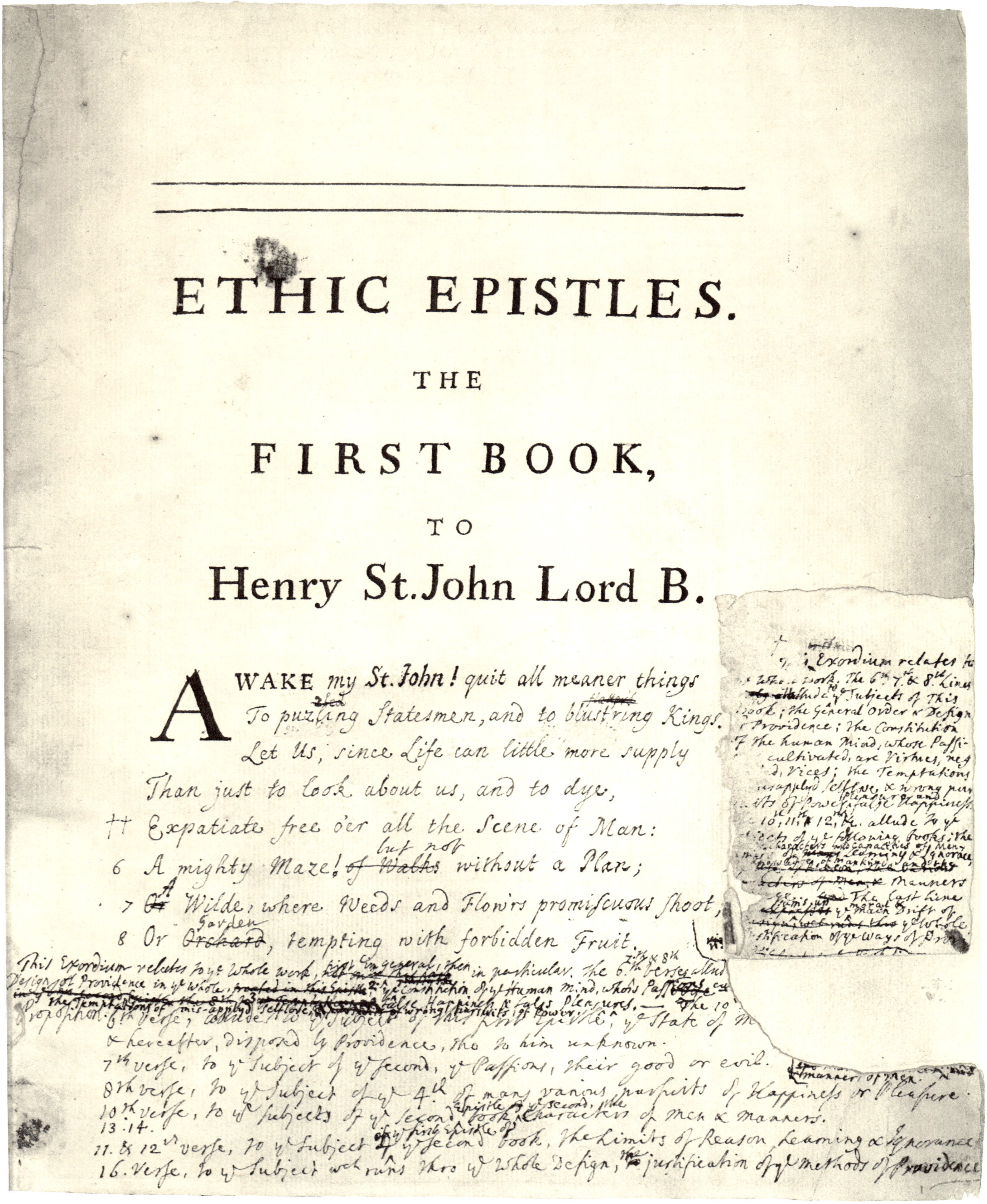

ETHIC EPISTLES.

THE

FIRST BOOK,

TO

Henry St. John Lord B.

AWAKE my St. John! quit all meaner things
To puzzling Statesmen, and to blust'ring Kings.
Let Us, since Life can little more supply
Than just to look about us, and to dye,
†† Expatiate free o'er all the Scene of Man:
6 A mighty Maze! but not without a Plan;
7 A Wilde, where Weeds and Flow'rs promiscuous shoot,
8 Or Garden, tempting with forbidden Fruit.

This Exordium relates to ye Whole work, first in general, then in particular. the 6th 7th & 8th verses allude to ye Design of Providence in ye Whole, ye Constitution of ye Human Mind, whose Passions, the Temptations of mis-applyd Selflove, wrong pursuits of Power, false Happiness & false Pleasures. — The 10
6th verse, alludes to ye Subject of this first Epistle, ye State of M
& hereafter, disposd by Providence, tho to him unknown.
7th verse, to ye Subject of ye second, ye Passions, their good or evil.
8th verse, to ye Subject of ye 4th of many various pursuits of Happiness or Pleasure.
10th verse, to ye subjects of ye second book, Characters of Men & Manners.
13. 14.
11. & 12th verse, to ye Subject of ye second book, the Limits of Reason Learning & Ignorance
16. Verse, to ye Subject wch runs thro ye Whole Design, the justification of ye methods of Providence

† ... Exordium relates to ... whole work. The 6th 7th & 8th Lines allude to ye Subjects of This book; the General Order & Design of Providence; the Constitution of the human Mind, whose Passions cultivated, are Virtues, neglected, Vices; the Temptations of misapplyd Selflove, & wrong pursuits of Power, pleasure and false Happiness. 10th, 11th & 12th, &c. allude to ye Subjects of ye following Books; the Characters and capacities of Men, ... Learning & Ignorance, knowledge of mankind, ... Manners ... The last Line sums up ye moral & main Drift of ye whole, ... Justification of ye ways of Providence.

SAMUEL JOHNSON:
IN THEATRO, 1771   4⅞ × 3⅛ inches
In the hand of Mrs. Thrale, annotated by Boswell
Given in 1946 by Kenneth B. Murdock, H 1916

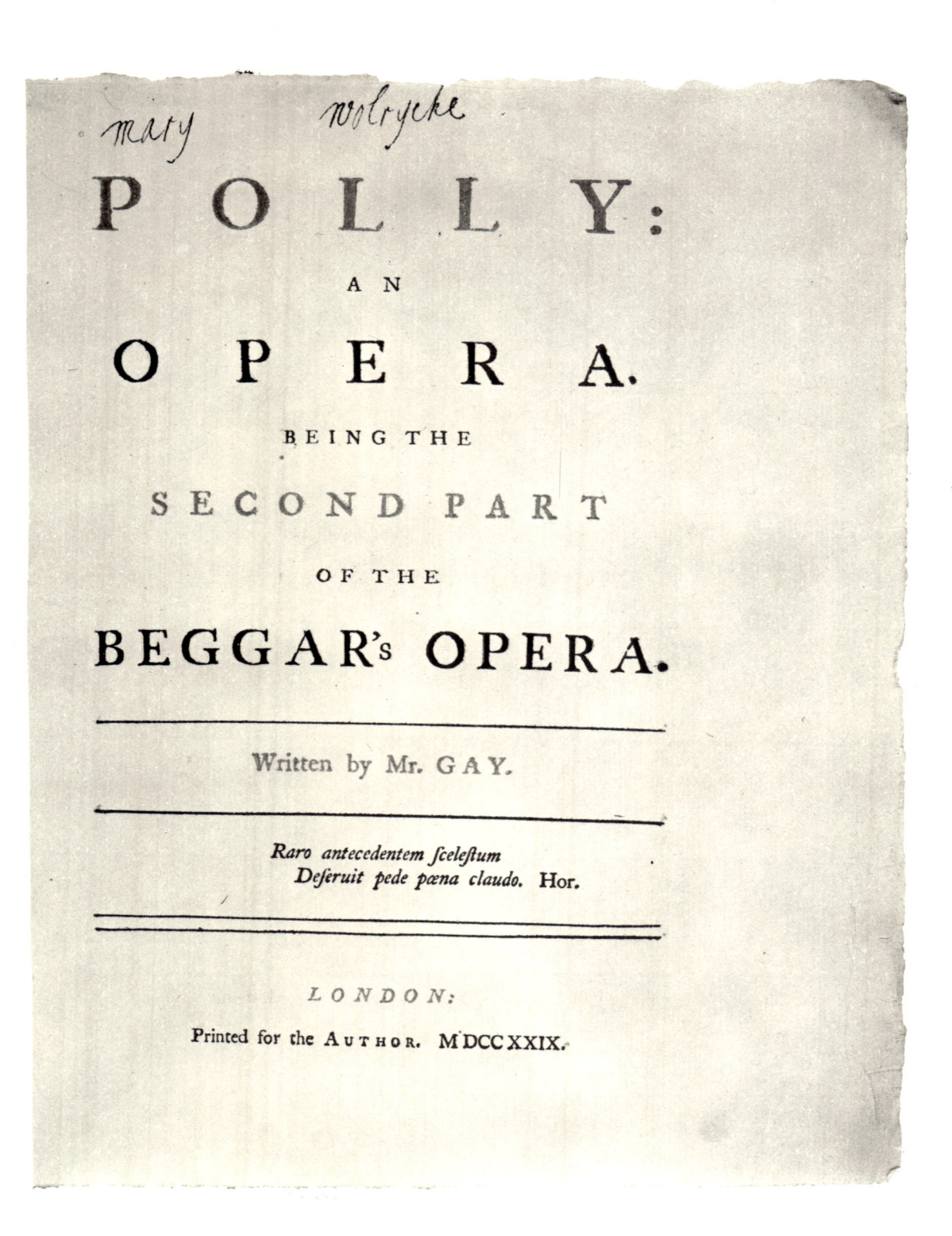

JOHN GAY: *POLLY*, 1729   9¾ × 7½ inches
Uncut and in original wrapper
From the collection of Ernest Lewis Gay, H 1897,
given in 1927 by George Henry Gay

HORACE WALPOLE:
POCKET NOTEBOOK
6⅛ × 3¾ inches
Given in 1934 by Elisabeth Merritt in
memory of Percival Merritt, H 1882

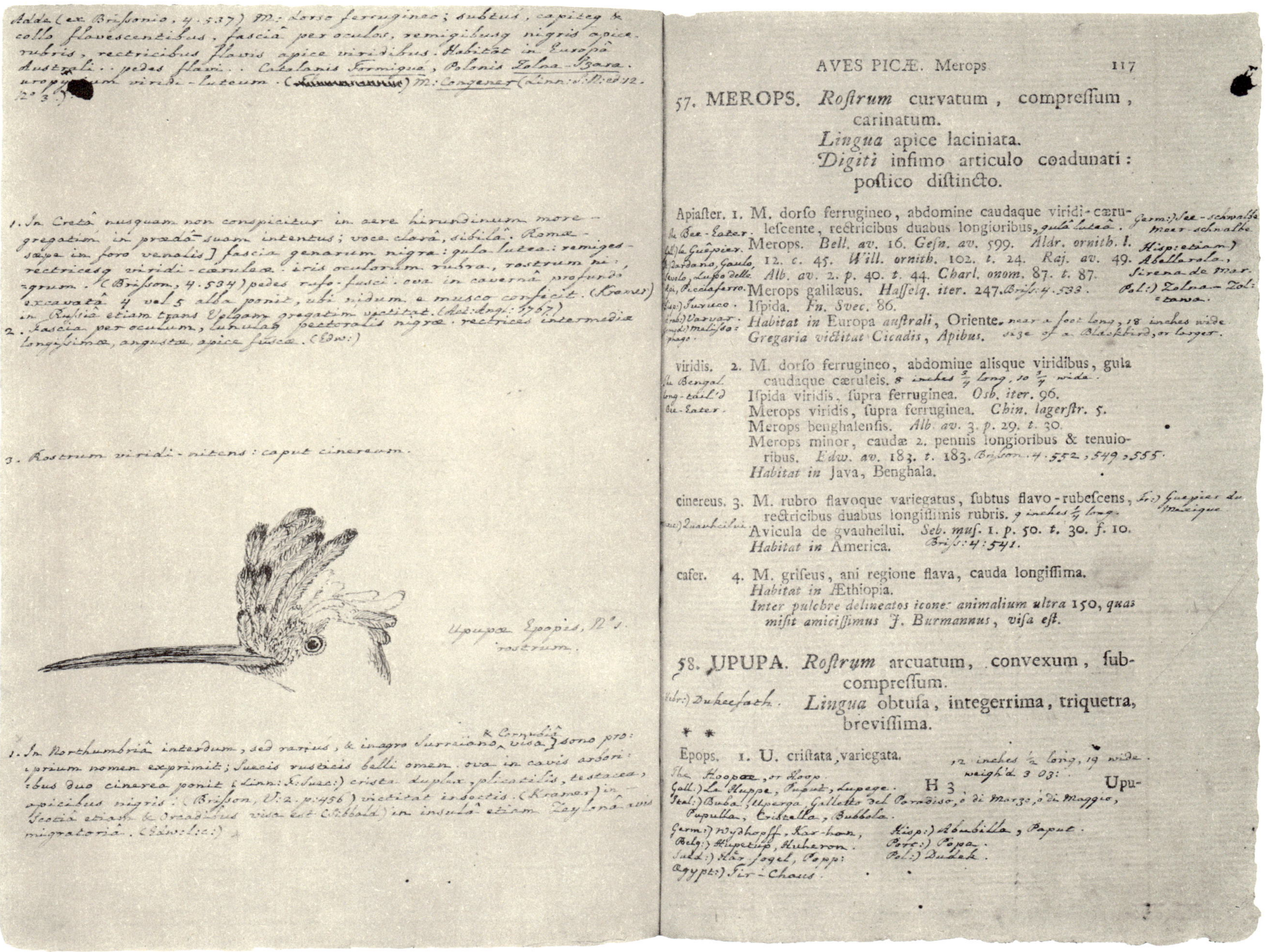

LINNAEUS: *SYSTEMA NATURAE*, 1758   8½ × 11 inches
Thomas Gray's annotated copy
    Acquired in 1908 from the library of Charles Eliot Norton, H 1846

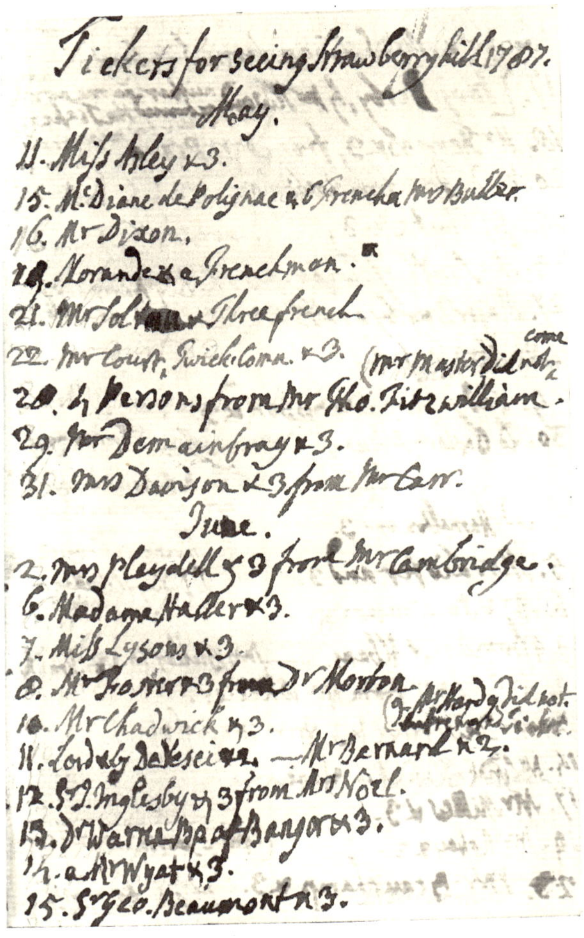

OLIVER GOLDSMITH:
*THE DESERTED VIL-
LAGE* [1772]   6½ × 4 inches
The edition produced by J. H. Merck
at the request of Goethe
Given in 1943 by
Augustin H. Parker, H 1897

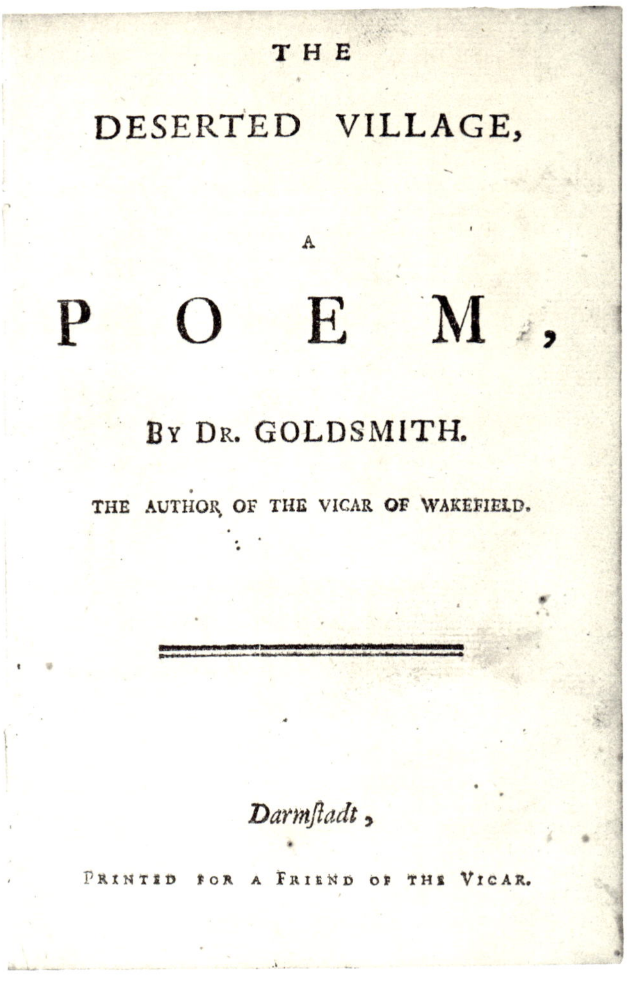

English Literature

3. Let Elizur rejoice with the Partridge, who is a prisoner of state and is proud of his keepers.
Let Shedeur rejoice with Pyrausta, who dwelleth in a medium of fire, which God hath adapted for him.
Let Shelumiel rejoice with Olor, who is of a goodly savour, and the very look of him harmonizes the mind.
Let Jael rejoice with the Plover, who whistles for his live, and foils the marksmen and their guns.
Let Raguel rejoice with the Cock of Portugal — God send good Angels to the allies of England.
Let Hobab rejoice with Necydalus, who is the Greek of a Grub.
Let Zurishaddai with the Polish Cock rejoice — The Lord restore peace to Europe.
Let Zuar rejoice with the Guinea Hen — The Lord add to his mercies in the WEST!
Let Chesed rejoice with Strepsiceros, whose weapons are the ornaments of his peace.
Let Hagar rejoice with Gnesion, who is the right sort of eagle, and towers the highest.
Let Libni rejoice with the Redshank, who migrates not but is translated to the upper regions.
Let Nahshon rejoice with the Seabreese, the Lord give the sailors of his Spirit.
Let Helon rejoice with the Woodpecker — the Lord encourage the propagation of trees!
Let Amos rejoice with the Coot — prepare to meet thy God, O Israel.
Let Ephah rejoice with Buprestis, the Lord endue us with temperance & humanity, till every cow have her mate!
Let Sarah rejoice with the Redwing, whose harvest is in the frost and snow.
Let Rebekah rejoice with Jynx, who holds his head on one side to deceive the adversary.
Let Shuah rejoice with Boa, which is the vocal serpent.
Let Ehud rejoice with Onocrotalus, whose braying is for the glory of God, because he makes the best musick in his power.
Let Shamgar rejoice with Otis, who looks about him for the glory of God, & sees the horizon complete at once.
Let Bohan rejoice with the Scythian Stag — he is beef and breeches against want & nakedness.
Let Achsah rejoice with the Pigeon who is an antidote to malignity and will carry a letter.
Let Tohu rejoice with the Grouse — the Lord further the cultivating of heaths & the peopling of deserts.
Let Hillel rejoice with Ammodytes, whose colour is deceitful and he plots against the pilgrim's feet.
Let Eli rejoice with Leucon — he is an honest fellow, which is a rarity.
Let Jemuel rejoice with Charadrius, who is from the HIGHT & the sight of him is good for the jaundice.
Let Pharaoh rejoice with Anataria, whom God permits to prey upon the ducks to check their increase.
Let Lotan rejoice with Sauterelle. Blessed be the name of the Lord from the Lote-tree to the Palm.
Let Dishon rejoice with the Landrail, God give his grace to the society for preserving the game.
Let Hushim rejoice with the King's Fisher, who is of royal beauty, tho' plebeian size.
Let Machir rejoice with Convolvulus from him to the ring of Saturn, which is the girdle of Job; to the sight of God from Job & his daughters BLESSED BE JESUS.
Let Atad bless with Eleos, the nightly Memorialist ελεησον κυριε.
Let Jamim rejoice with the Bittern blessed be the name of Jesus for Denver sluice, Ruston, & the draining of the fens.
Let Ohad rejoice with Byheros who eateth the vine and is a minister of temperance.
Let Zohar rejoice with Cychramus who cometh with the quails on a particular affair.
Let Serah, the daughter of Asher, rejoice with Ceyx, who maketh his cabin in the Halcyon's hold.
Let Magdiel rejoice with Ascarides, which is the life of the bowels — the worm hath a part in our frame.
Let Becher rejoice with Oscen who terrifies the wicked as trumpet and alarm the coward.
Let Shaul rejoice with Circos, who hath clumsy legs, but he can wheel it the better with his wings.
Let Hamul rejoice with the Crystal, who is pure and translucent.
Let Ziphion rejoice with the Tit-Lark who is a groundling, but he raises the spirits.
Let Mibzar rejoice with the Cadess, as is their number, so are their names, blessed be the Lord Jesus for them all.
Let Jubal rejoice with Cæcilia, the woman and the slow-worm praise the name of the Lord.
Let Arodi rejoice with the Royston Crow, there is a society of them at Trumpington & Cambridge.
Let Areli rejoice with the Criel, who is a dwarf that towereth above others.
Let Phuvah rejoice with Platycerotes, whose weapons of defence keep them innocent.
Let Shimron rejoice with the Kite, who is of more value than many sparrows.
Let Sered rejoice with the Wittal, a silly bird is wise unto his own preservation.
Let Elon rejoice with Attelabus, who is the Locust without wings.
Let Jahleel rejoice with the Woodcock, who liveth upon suction and is pure from his diet.
Let Shuni rejoice with the Gull, who is happy in not being good for food.
Let Ezbon rejoice with Musimon, who is from the ram and she-goat.
Let Barkos rejoice with the Black Eagle, which is the least of his species and the best-natured.
Let Bedan rejoice with Ossifrage — the bird of prey and the man of prayer.
Let Naomi rejoice with Pseudosphece, who is between a wasp and a hornet.
Let Ruth rejoice with the Tumbler — it is a pleasant thing to feed him and be thankful.
Let Ram rejoice with the Fieldfare, who is a good gift from God in the season of scarcity.
Let Manoah rejoice with Cerastes, who is a Dragon with horns.
Let Talmai rejoice with Alcedo, who makes a cradle for its young, which is rocked by the winds.
Let Bukki rejoice with the Buzzard, who is clever, with the reputation of a silly fellow.
Let Michal rejoice with Leucocruta who is a mixture of beauty and magnanimity.
Let Abiah rejoice with Morphnus who is a bird of passage to the Heavens.
Let Hur rejoice with the Water-wag-tail, who is a neighbour, and loves to be looked at.
Let Dodo rejoice with the purple Worm, who is cloathed sumptuously, tho' he fares meanly.
Let Ahio rejoice with the Merlin who is a cousin german of the hawk.
Let Joram rejoice with the Water Rail, who takes his delight in the river.
Let Chileab rejoice with Ophion who is clean made, less than an hart, and a Sardinian.
Let Shephatiah rejoice with the little Owl, which is the wingged cat.
Let Ithream rejoice with the great Owl, who understandeth that which he professes.
Let Abigail rejoice with Lethophagus God be gracious to the widows indeed.
Let.

CHRISTOPHER SMART: HOLOGRAPH OF *JUBILATE AGNO* [1756–1763]
Acquired in 1941 with gifts of Friends of the Library

3. For I am not without authority in my jeopardy, which I derive inevitably from the glory of the name of the Lord.
For I bless God whose name is Jealous — and there is a zeal to deliver us from everlasting burning.
For my extimation is good even amongst the slanderers and my memory shall arise for a sweet savour unto the Lord.
For I bless the PRINCE of PEACE and pray that all the guns may be naild up, save such as are for the rejoicing days.
For I have abstained from the blood of the grape and that even at the Lord's table.
For I have glorified God in GREEK and LATIN, the consecrated languages spoken by the Lord on earth.
For I meditate the peace of Europe amongst family bickerings and domestic jars.
For the HOST is in the WEST — the Lord make us thankful unto salvation.
For I preach the very GOSPEL of CHRIST without comment & with this weapon shall I slay envy.
For I bless God in the rising generation, which is on my side.
For I have translated in the charity, which makes things better & I shall be translated myself at the last.
For he that walked upon the sea, hath prepared the floods with the Gospel of peace.
For the merciful man is merciful to his beast, and to the trees that give them shelter.
For he hath turned the shadow of death into the morning, the Lord is his name.
For I am come home again, but there is nobody to kill the calf or to pay the musick.
For the hour of my felicity, like the womb of Sarah, shall come at the latter end.
For I should have availd myself of waggery, had not malice been multitudinous.
For there are still serpents that can speak — God bless my head, my heart & my heel.
For I bless God that I am of the same seed with Ehud, Mutius Scævola, and Colonel Draper.
For the word of God is a sword on my side — no matter what other weapon a stick or a straw.
For I have adventured myself in the name of the Lord, and he hath markd me for his own.
For I bless God for the Postmaster general & all conveyancers of letters under his care especially Allen & Shelvock.
For my grounds in New Canaan shall infinitely compensate for the flats & maynes of Staindrop Moor.
For the praise of God can give to a mute fish the notes of a nightingale.
For I have seen the white Raven & Thomas Hall of Willingham & am myself a greater curiosity than both.
For I look up to heaven which is my prospect to escape envy by surmounting it.
For if Pharaoh had known Joseph, he would have blessed God & me for the illumination of the people.
For I pray God to bless improvements in gardening till London be a city of palm-trees.
For I pray to give his grace to the poor of England, that Charity be not offended & that benevolence may increase.
For in my nature I quested for beauty, but God, God hath sent me to sea for pearls.
For there is a blessing from the STONE of JESUS which is founded upon hell to the precious jewell on the right hand of God.
For the nightly Visitor is at the window of the impenitent, while I sing a psalm of my own composing.
For there is a note added to the scale, which the Lord hath made fuller, stronger & more glorious.
For I offer my goat as he browses the vine, bless the Lord from chambering & drunkenness.
For there is a traveling for the glory of God without going to Italy or France.
For I bless the children of Asher for the evil I did them & the good I might have received at their hands.
For I rejoice like a worm in the rain in him that cherishes and from him that tramples.
For I am ready for the trumpet & alarm to fight, to die & to rise again.
For the banishd of the Lord shall come about again, for so he hath prepared for them.
For sincerity is a jewel which is pure & transparent, eternal & inestimable.
For my hands and my feet are perfect as the sublimity of Naphtali and the felicity of Asher.
For the names and number of animals are as the names and number of the stars.
For I pray the Lord Jesus to translate my MAGNIFICAT into verse and represent it.
For I bless the Lord Jesus from the bottom of Royston Cave to the top of King's Chapel.
For I am a little fellow, which is intitled to the great mess by the benevolence of God my father.
For I this day made over my inheritance to my mother in consideration of her infirmities.
For I this day made over my inheritance to my mother in consideration of her age.
For I this day made over my inheritance to my mother in consideration of her poverty.
For I bless the thirteenth of August, in which I had the grace to obey the voice of Christ in my conscience.
For I bless the thirteenth of August, in which I was willing to run all hazards for the sake of the name of the Lord.
For I lent my flocks and my herds and my lands at once unto the Lord.
For nature is more various than observation tho' observers be innumerable.
For ~~Agricola is Ingers~~
For I pray God to bless POLLY in the blessing of Naomi and assign her to the house of DAVID.
For I am in charity with the French who are my foes and Moabites because of the Moabitish woman.
For my Angel is always ready at a pinch to help me out and to keep me up.
For ~~   CHRISTOPHER~~ must slay the Dragon with a PHEON's head.
For they have seperated me and my bosom, whereas the right comes by setting us together.
For silly fellow! silly fellow! is against me and belongeth neither to me nor my family.
For he that scorneth the scorner hath condescended to my low estate.
For Abiah is the father of Joab and Joab of all Romans and English Men.
For they pass by me in their tour, and the good Samaritan is not yet come.
For I bless God in the behalf of TRINITY COLLEGE in CAMBRIDGE & the society of PURPLES in LONDON.
For I have a nephew CHRISTOPHER, to whom I implore the grace of God.
For I pray God bless the CAM — Mr HIGGS & Mr & Mrs WASHBOURNE at the drops of the dew.
For I pray God bless the king of Sardinia and make him an instrument of his peace.
For I am possessed of a cat, surpassing in beauty, from whom I take occasion to bless Almighty God.
For I pray God for the professors of the University of Cambridge to attend & to amend.
For the fatherless children and widows are never deserted of the Lord.
For.

English Literature 61

Peblis is the County Town of Tweedale. Etrick Forrest is not far distant, wch was a Royal Chase hence the Kgs of Scotland frequently resided there: Darnley was there the Winter before his Death

Maitland's MS. pag. 155.

Peblis to the Play

By K. James I of Scotland, vid. Majoris Hist. L. b. 6. c. 14. p. 309. Ed. 1740

1

At *Beltane, quhen ilk bodie bownis
    To Peblis to the Play,
To heir the singin and the soundis
    The solace, suth to say;
Be firth and forest furth thay found;
    Thay graythit thame full gay;
God wait, that wald thai do that stound,
    For it wes thair feist day,
        Thay said,
Of Peblis to the Play.

2

All the Wenchis of the west
    War up, or the Cok crew;
For reiling thair micht na man rest,
    For garray and for *glew:
Ane said my Curches ar nocht prest.
    Than answerit Meg full blew,
To get ane hude I hald it best;
    Be goddis saull, that is trew,
        Quod scho,
Of Peblis to the Play.

3

Scho tuik the tippet be the end,
    To lat it hing scho leit nocht.
Quod he, Thy bak sall beir ane bend.
    In fayth, quod scho, we meit nocht.
Scho wes so guckit and so gend
    That day ane byt scho eit nocht,
That spak hir fallowis that hir kend,
    Be still, my Joy, and greit nocht,
        Now
Of Peblis to the Play.

BISHOP THOMAS PERCY: ANNOTATED BALLAD TRANSCRIPT
Acquired in 1884 by Justin Winsor, H 1853, and Francis James Child, H 1846

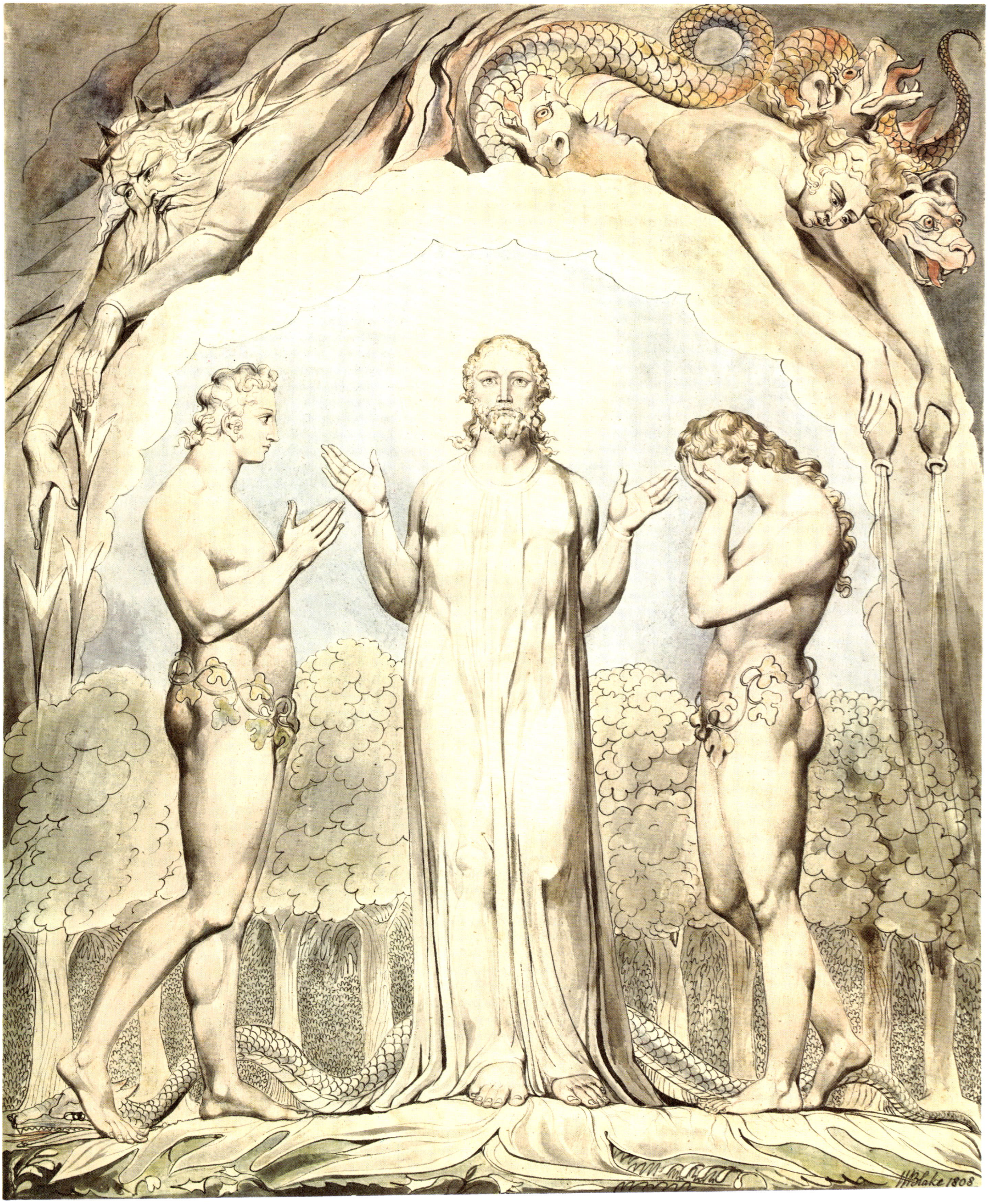
W Blake 1808

WILLIAM BLAKE: THE JUDGMENT OF ADAM AND EVE, 1808
One of the 'major series' of Blake's illustrations for *Paradise Lost*
Given in 1966 by John U. White, H 1934, and Harold T. White, H 1937

19½ × 15⅜ inches

Bannockburn —— Bruce to his troops ——
   Tune, Louis Gordon.

Scots, wha hae wi' Wallace bled;
Scots, whom Bruce has often led;
Welcome to your gory bed,
   Or to glorious victorie. ——

Now's the day, & now's the hour;
See the front of battle lour;
See approach proud Edward's power,
   Edward! Chains & Slaverie!

Wha will be a traitor knave?
Wha can fill a coward's grave?
Wha sae base as be a Slave?
   Traitor! Coward! turn & flee!

Wha for Scotland's king & law,
Freedom's sword will strongly draw,
Free-man stand, or Free-man fa',
   Caledonian, on wi' me.

By Oppression's woes & pains!
By your sons in servile chains!
We will drain our dearest veins,
   But they shall—they shall be free!

ROBERT BURNS: AUTOGRAPH MANUSCRIPT
Early version in a letter to the Earl of Buchan, 12 January 1794
Bequeathed in 1874 by Charles Sumner, H 1830

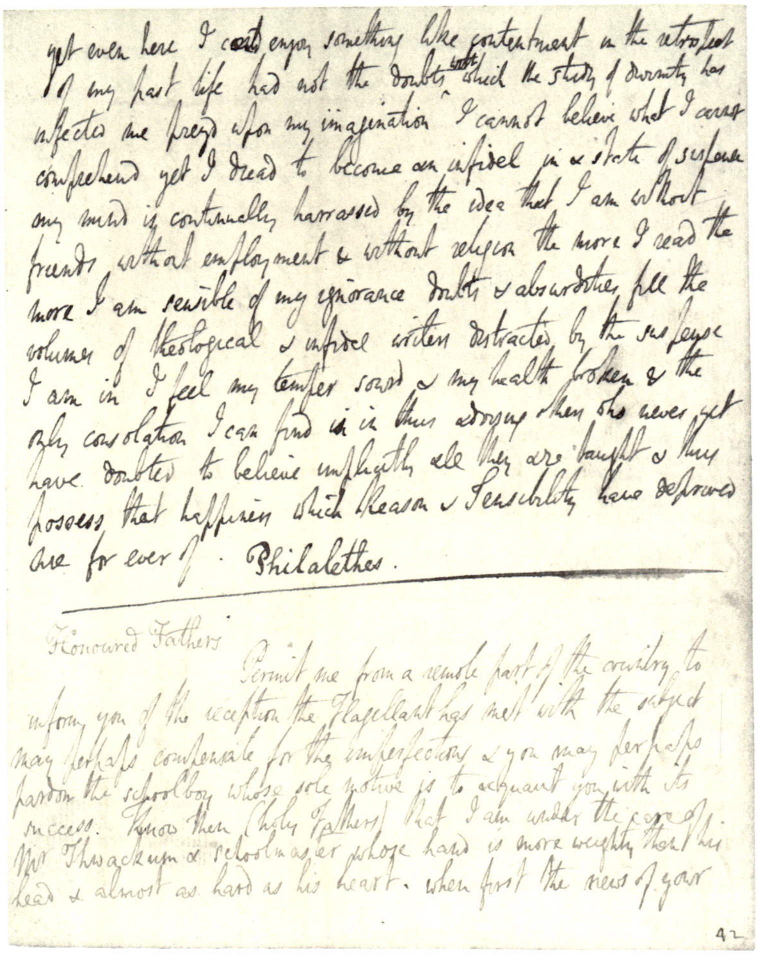

ROBERT SOUTHEY: HOLOGRAPH OF *THE FLAGELLANT*,
1792   7¾ × 6⅛ inches
Acquired in 1928 with the fund in memory of Norton Perkins, H 1898

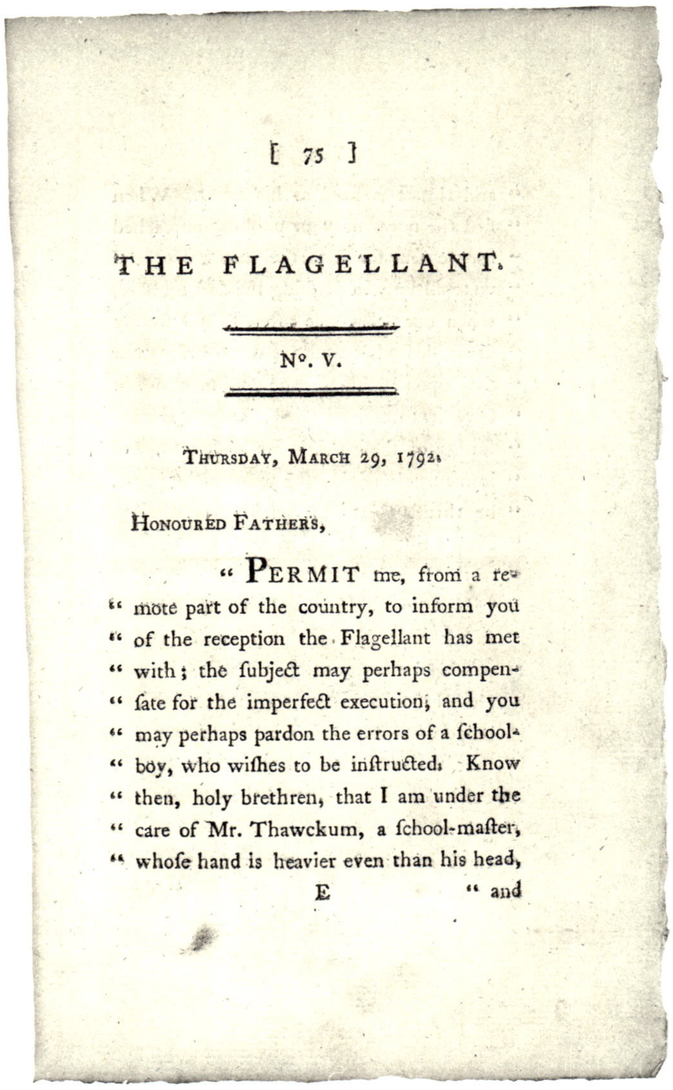

ROBERT SOUTHEY: *THE FLAGELLANT*, 1792
8⅞ × 5⅛ inches   Acquired in 1946 with the Bemis Fund

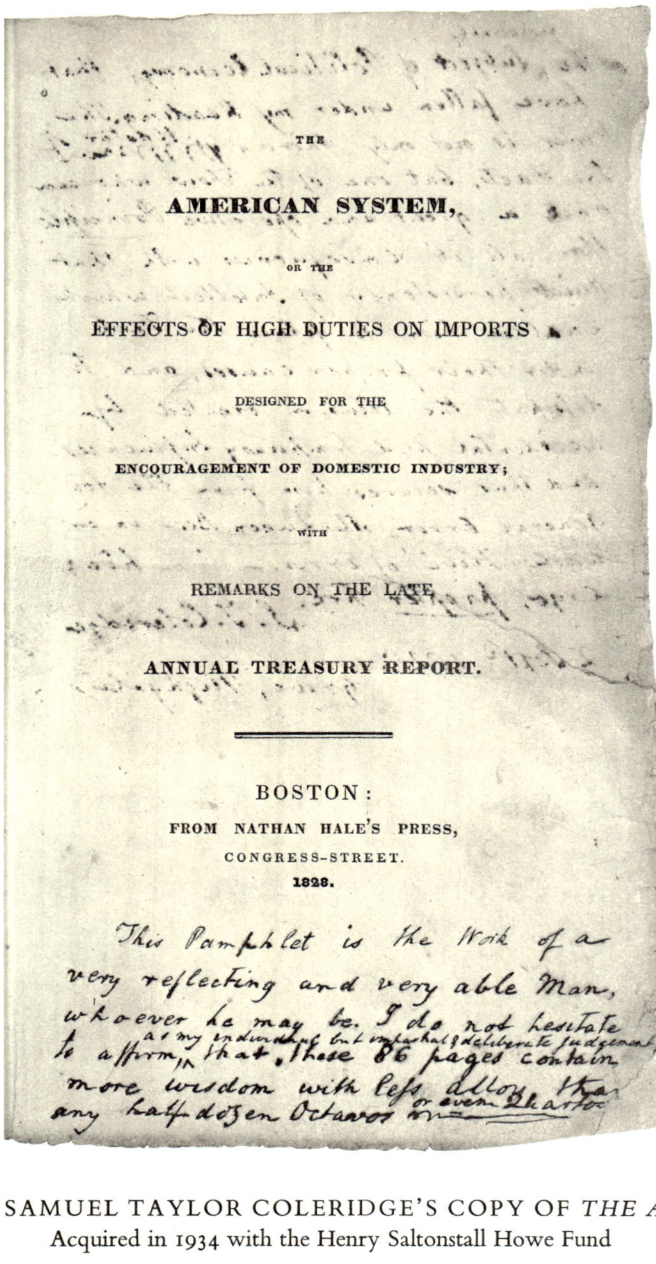

SAMUEL TAYLOR COLERIDGE'S COPY OF *THE AMERICAN SYSTEM*, 1828   9½ × 5⅜ inches
Acquired in 1934 with the Henry Saltonstall Howe Fund

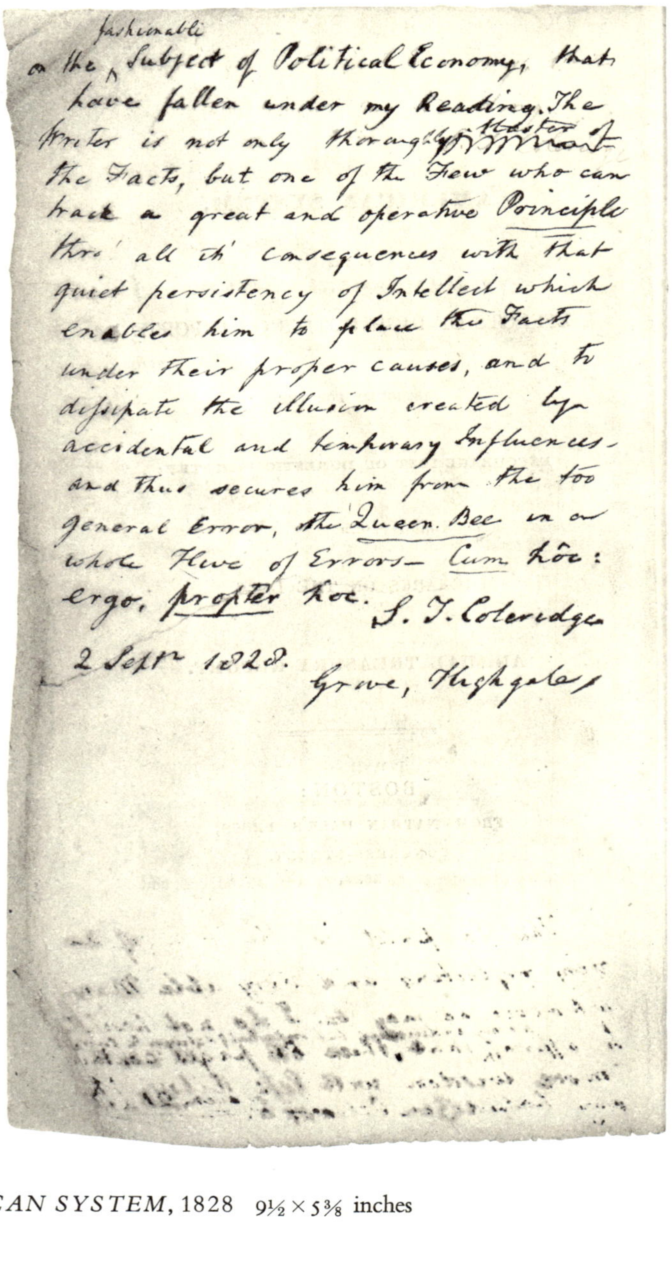

PERCY BYSSHE SHELLEY: HOLOGRAPH NOTEBOOK 7¾ × 6⅛ inches
Given in 1887 by Edward A. Silsbee

WILLIAM WORDSWORTH: *SONNETS*, 1838 6¾ × 7¾ inches Autograph revisions and additions for a new edition
Acquired in 1944 with the Henry Saltonstall Howe Fund

English Literature

JOHN LEECH: PRELIMINARY STUDY TO
ILLUSTRATE CHARLES DICKENS,
A CHRISTMAS CAROL, 1843   5½ × 3⅞ inches
Acquired in 1962 with funds from the sale of duplicates

WILLIAM MAKEPEACE THACKERAY:
DRAWING TO ILLUSTRATE *PENDENNIS*, 1848   7 × 4¾ inches
Given in 1947 by Herbert L. Carlebach, H 1909

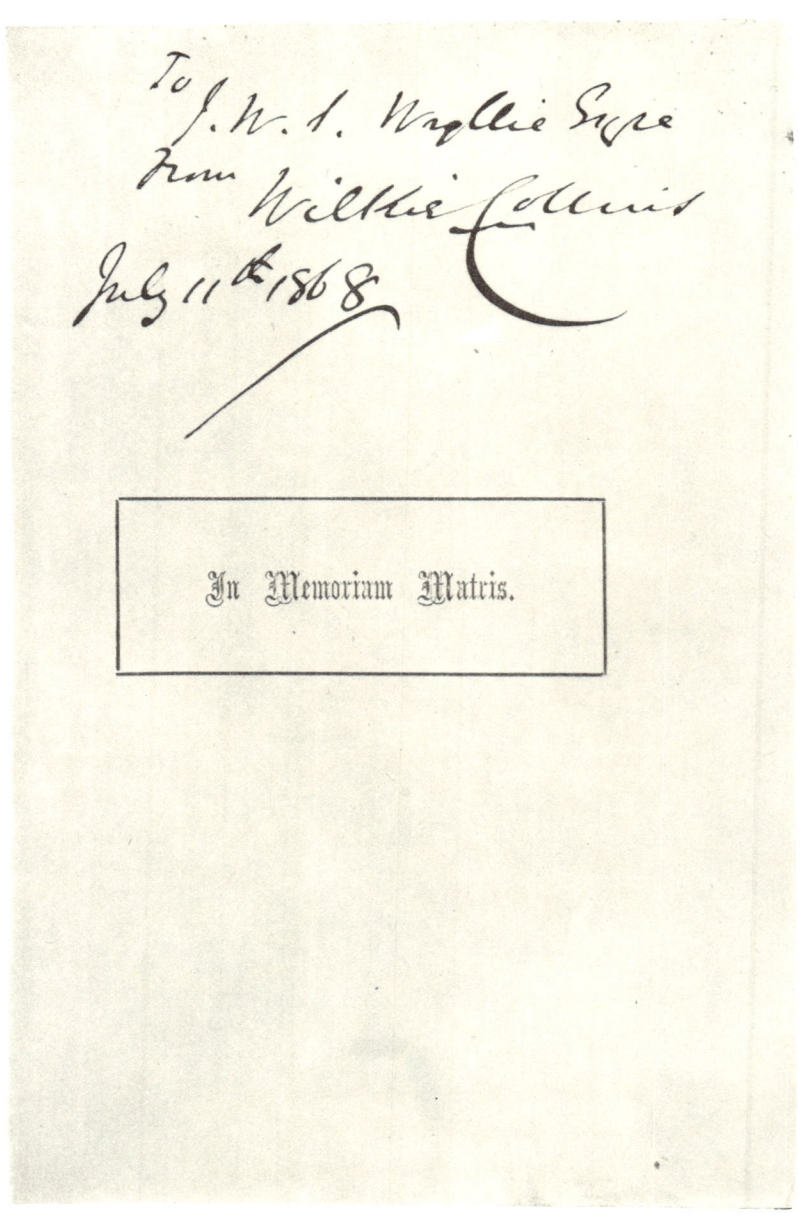

WILKIE COLLINS: *THE MOONSTONE*, 1868   7½ × 4⅞ inches
Presentation copy dated before publication day
Acquired in 1962 with the Amy Lowell Fund

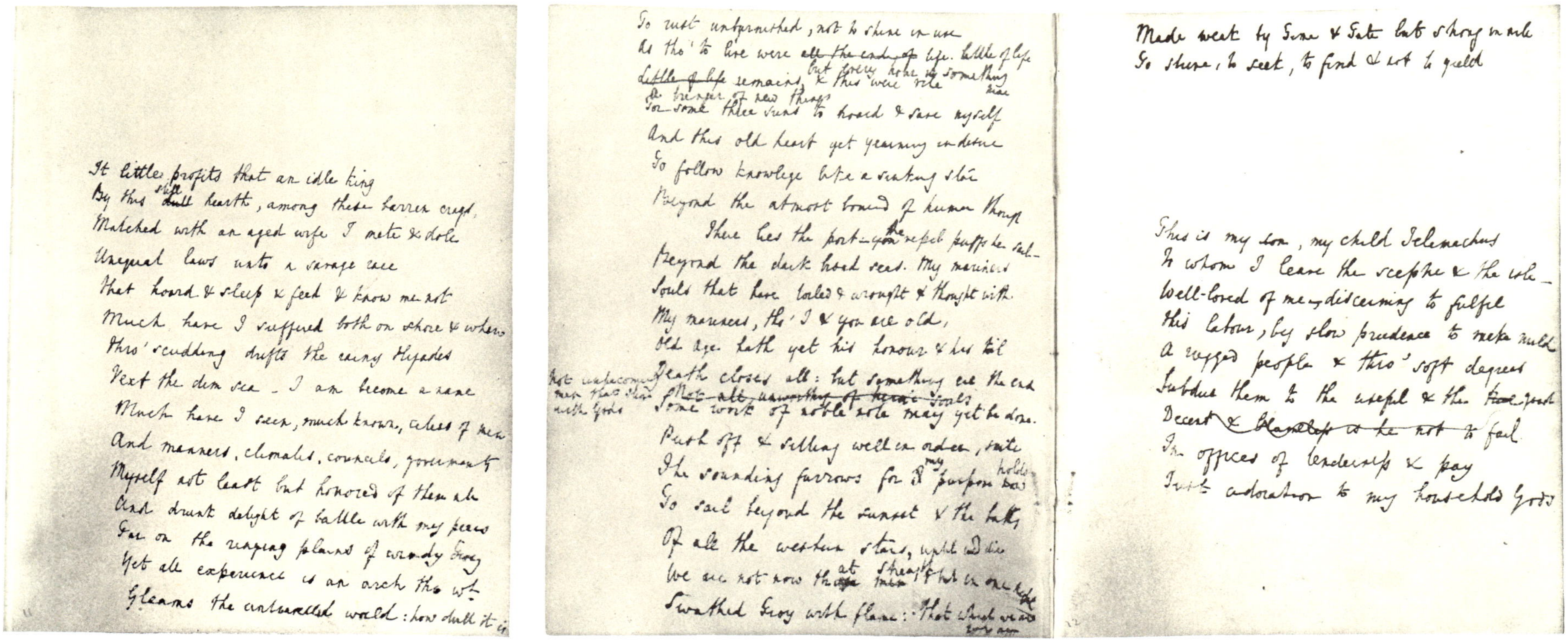

ALFRED, LORD TENNYSON: FIRST DRAFT OF *ULYSSES* 4⅝ × 7¼ inches
Acquired in 1954 with the Amy Lowell Fund

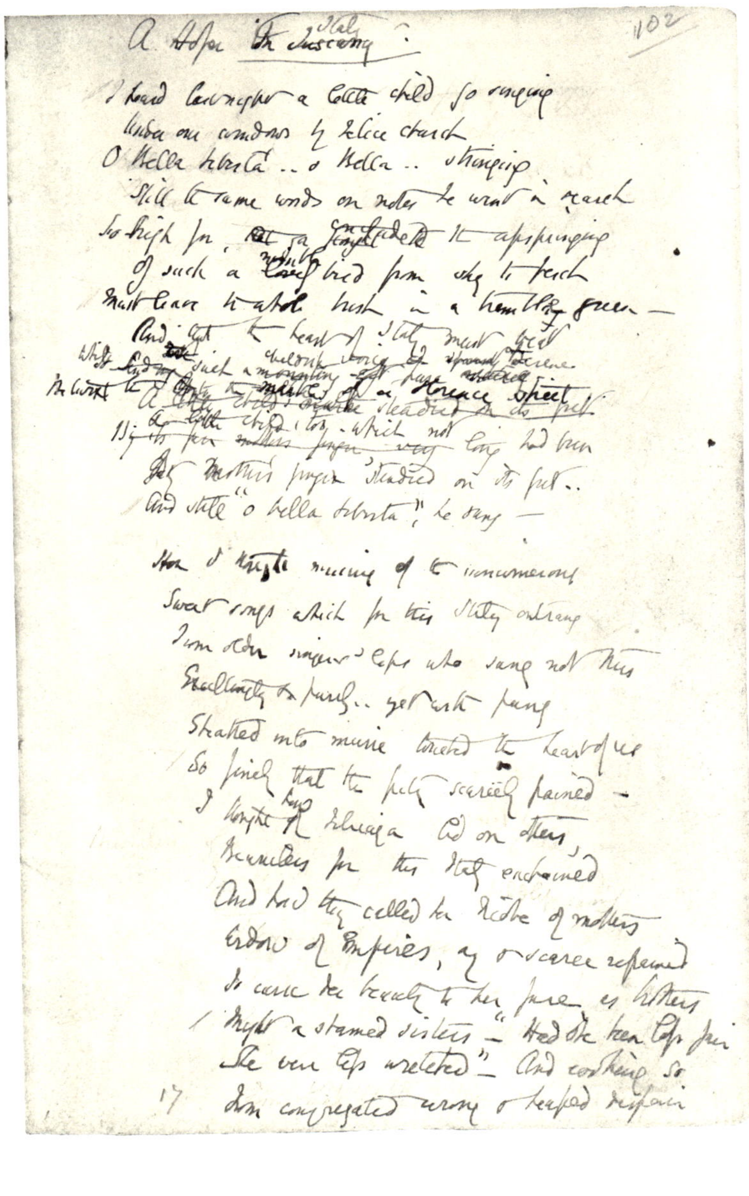

ELIZABETH BARRETT BROWNING: FIRST DRAFT OF
CASA GUIDI WINDOWS 7⅛ × 4½ inches
Bequeathed in 1947 by Gabriel Wells

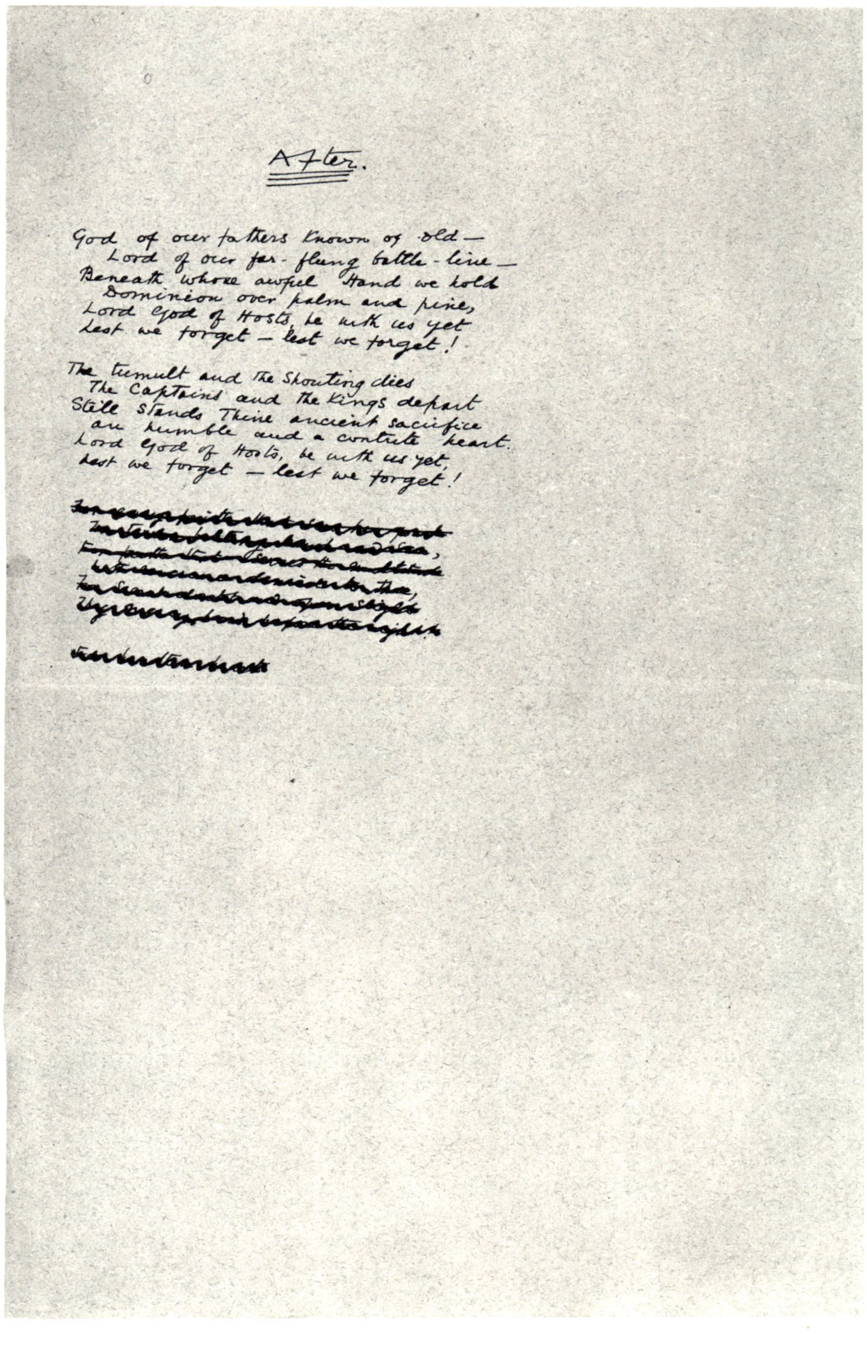

RUDYARD KIPLING: FIRST DRAFT OF *RECESSIONAL*
8¼ × 5¼ inches   Given in 1921 by William Norton Bullard, H 1875

English Literature   67

MRS WARREN'S PROFESSION.

Act I.

Summer afternoon. Garden of ~~a small~~ an old cottage near Haslemere, in Surrey, with a thatched roof and porch. Right hand corner occupied by the cottage, ~~a new one in the Bedford Park style.~~ One large latticed window in the front with the ~~door~~ porch beside it, on its left ~~the window R. and the door L.~~ Further back a little wing is built out, making a right angle with the left side wall. From the end of this wing a paling curves ~~round to down L.~~ across and forward, completely shutting in the garden ~~scene~~, except for a gate ~~opposite L.2 E.~~ on the left. The common rises in a high hill beyond the paling to the sky line. ~~Two~~ Three folded canvas garden chairs are ~~leaning against the cottage front beside the door.~~ leaning against the side bench in the cottage porch. A lady's bicycle is propped against the wall, under the window. A little to the left of the porch A hammock is slung from two posts ~~along the paling L.C.~~ A big canvas umbrella is stuck in the ground to keep the sun off, the hammock, in which a young lady lies. ~~Vivie is lying in the hammock~~ reading and making notes, her head ~~to the R.~~ towards the cottage & her feet towards the gate. In front of the hammock, & within reach of her hand, a ~~cheap~~ common kitchen chair, with a pile of serious looking books upon it and a supply of MS paper.

Enter Praed, L.U.E, behind the paling. ~~He seems not~~ A gentleman coming into sight from behind the ~~...~~ He is hardly certain of his way. He looks over the paling; takes stock of the place; and sees Vivie.

~~PRAED~~ The Gentleman

(taking off his hat) I beg your pardon. Can you direct me to Hindhead View? ~~Mrs Warren's.~~ Alison's.

VIVIE

GEORGE BERNARD SHAW: DRAFT OF *MRS. WARREN'S PROFESSION*
Given in 1953 by L. Richard Bamberger, H 1926

WILLIAM BUTLER YEATS: DRAFT OF *THE COUNTESS CATHLEEN*
Acquired in 1934 with the Morris Gray Fund

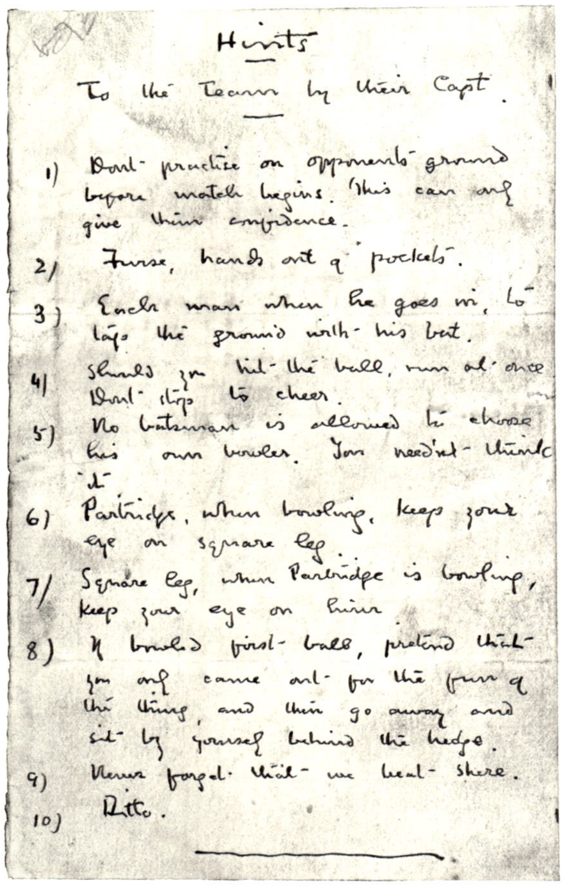

J. M. BARRIE: HOLOGRAPH OF *ALLAHAKBARRIES C. C.*, 1893
5⅞ × 3½ inches
Acquired in 1948 with the Henry Saltonstall Howe Fund

MAX BEERBOHM: DRAWING IN *THE BOOK OF THE RHYMERS' CLUB*, 1892   6¼ × 4¾ inches
Given in 1948 by Albert E. Gallatin

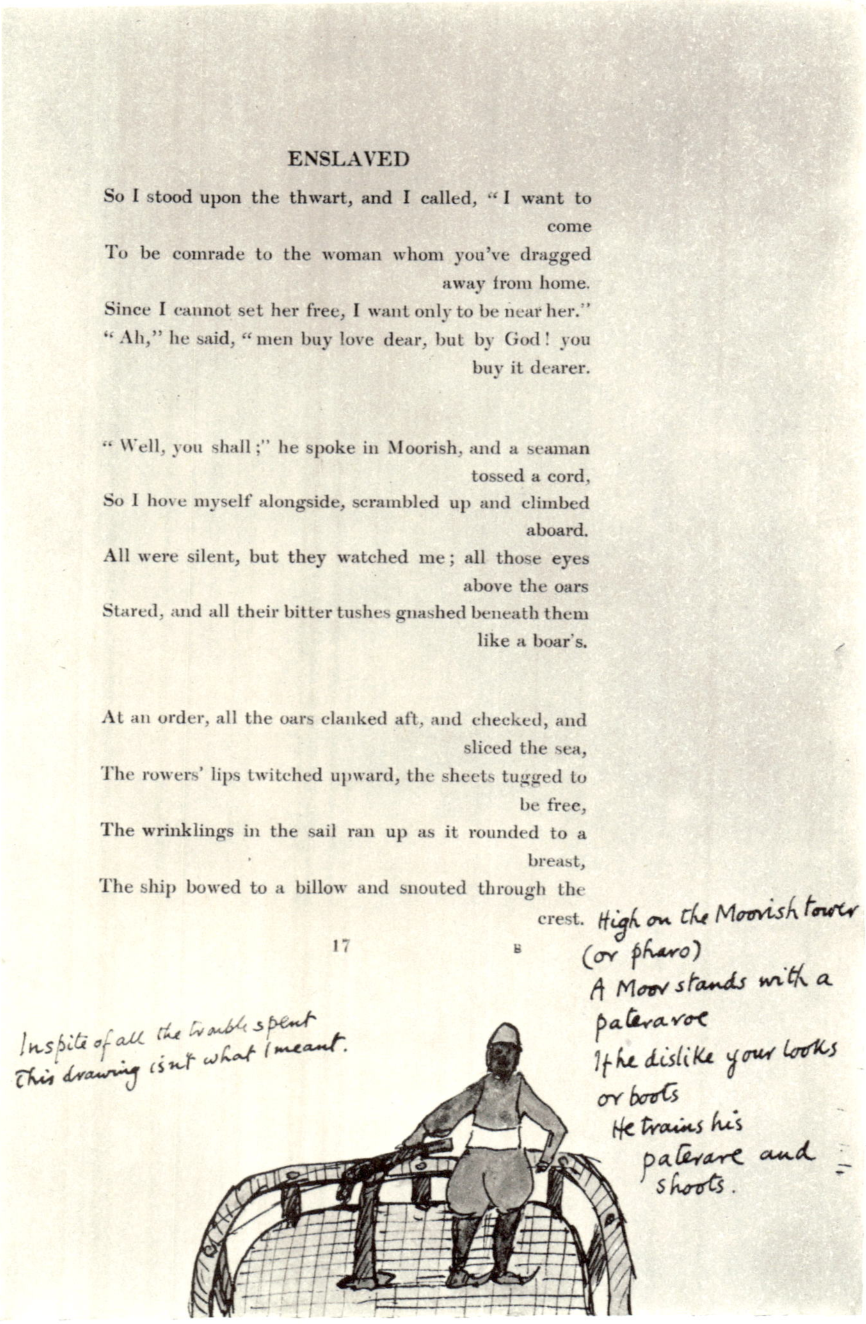

JOHN MASEFIELD: *ENSLAVED*, 1920   9 × 5¾ inches
Illuminated by the author for Thomas W. Lamont
Given in 1942 by Thomas W. Lamont, H 1892

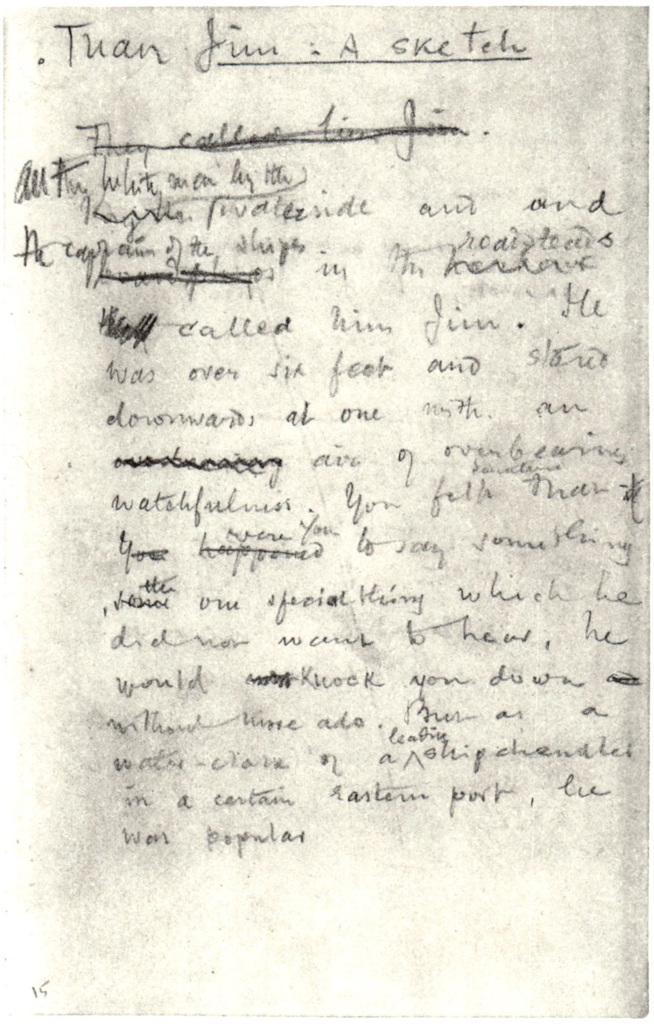

> POEMS 3
>
> I
>
> (a)
>
> The sprinkler on the lawn
> Weaves a cool vertigo, and stumps are drawn;
> The last boy vanishes,
> A blazer half-on, through the rigid trees.
>
> (b)
>
> Bones wrenched, weak whimper, lids wrinkled, first
>   dazzle known,
> World-wonder hardened as bigness, years, brought
>   knowledge, you,
> Presence a rich mould augured for roots urged, but
>   gone,
> The soul is tetanous: gun-barrel burnishing

About 45 copies.
No 19

W. H. AUDEN: *POEMS*, 1928   4⅞ × 7½ inches
Given in 1963 by H. Bradley Martin

JOSEPH CONRAD:
FIRST DRAFT OF *LORD JIM*
6¾ × 4¼ inches
Given in 1925 in memory of
Lionel de Jersey Harvard, H 1915

JAMES JOYCE: HOLOGRAPH OF
STEPHEN HERO 8⅜ × 6½ inches
Acquired in 1938 with gifts of
Friends of the Library

English Literature 71

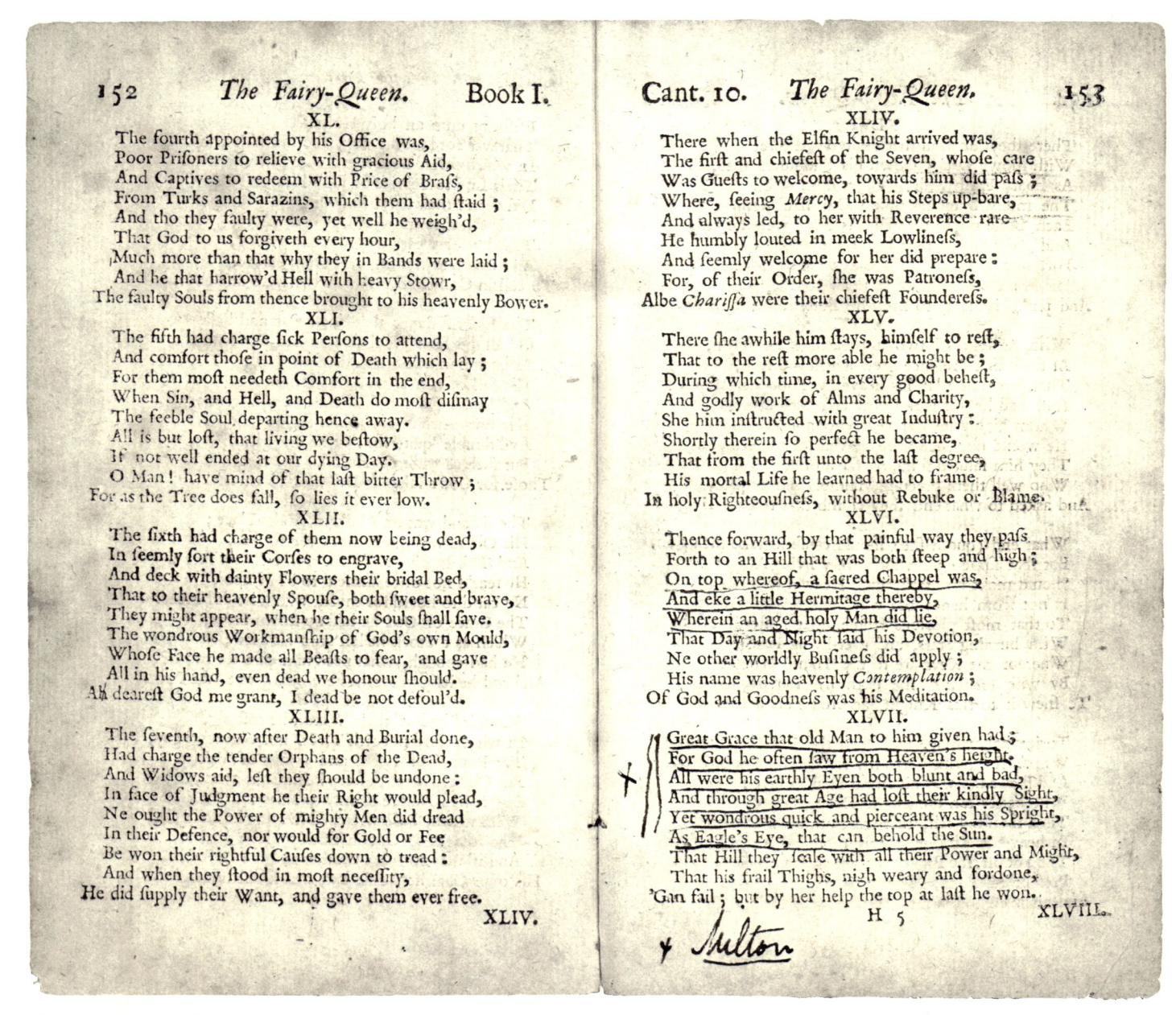

GEORGE KEATS'S SPENSER, MARKED BY JOHN KEATS
Bequeathed in 1925 by Amy Lowell

AUTOGRAPH MS.
'ON FIRST LOOKING INTO
CHAPMAN'S HOMER'
Bequeathed in 1925 by Amy Lowell

John Keats

THE Keats Room on the second floor of the Houghton Library, panelled in walnut and presided over by the calm and confident life mask of the poet, contains the source for more than two thirds of the known letters of Keats, along with numerous autograph manuscripts, first and other editions, association books, material on the Keats circle, and Keatsiana of all kinds. The foundation of the collection came with Amy Lowell's bequest in 1925, since augmented by John Gregory's run of 19th and 20th century editions, Louis A. Holman's iconographic collection, and most of all by the collection of Arthur A. Houghton, Jr., H 1929. This, together with Mr. Houghton's subsequent additions, more than doubled Miss Lowell's collection in both numbers and importance.

The Room has become a world center for Keats studies, and one can scarcely imagine an important work of scholarship in the field that would not draw heavily upon its resources.

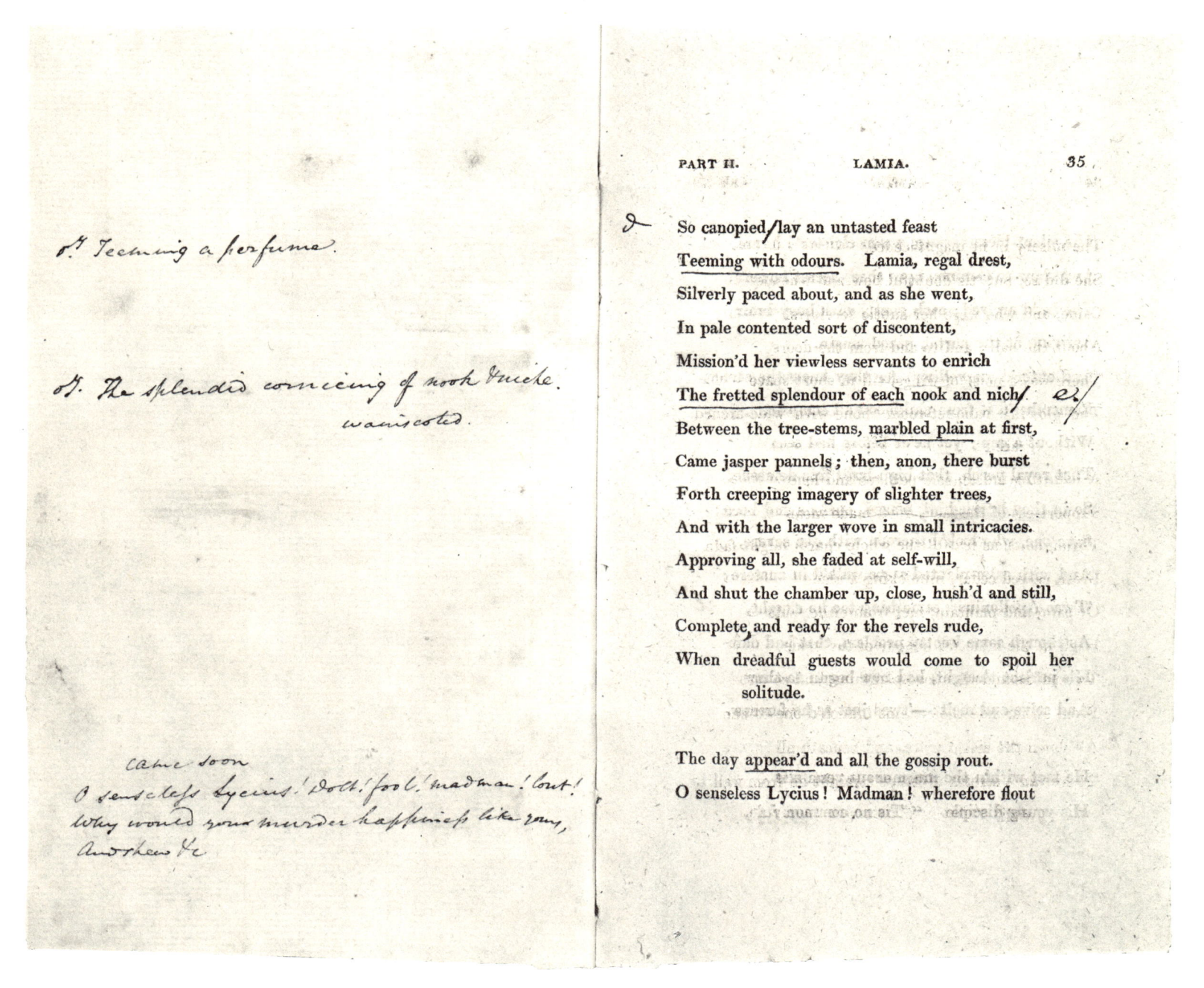

PROOFSHEETS OF *LAMIA*, 1820
CORRECTED BY KEATS, ANNOTATED BY RICHARD WOODHOUSE
Given by Arthur A. Houghton, Jr., H 1929

EARLY DRAFT
OF *LAMIA*
Given by
Arthur A. Houghton, Jr.,
H 1929

5 A haunting Music sole perhaps and love
Supportress of the fairy roof — made moan
Through out as fearful the whole charm might fade.
Fresh Carved Cedar — a mimicking a glade
Of Palm and Plantain met from either side
In the high midst in honor of the Bride —
Two Palms, and then two Plantains and so on
From either side their stems branch'd one to one
All down the aisled place — and beneath all
There ran a stream of Lamps straight from wall to wall
So canopied lay an untasted feast
Teeming a perfume. Lamia regal dresst
Silently pac'd about and as she went
Mission'd her viewless servants to enrich
The splendid furniture of each nook and niche
Between the tree-stems wainscoated at first
Came gasper pannels — then anon there burst
Forth creeping imagery of lighter trees
And with the larger more smaller trees embranch'd
And so till she was sated; then came down
Soft lighting on her head a brilliant crown
Wreath'd turban-wise of tender wannish fire
And sprinkled over with stars like Ariadne's tear
Approving all — she faded at self will
And shut the Chamber up close, hush'd and still,
Complete, and ready for the revel roses
When dreadful Guests would come to spoil her solitude
The day came soon and all the gossip rout
O senseless Lycius Dolt! Fool! Madman! Lout!

Silently pac'd about, and as she went,
In pale contented sort of discontent,
Mission'd her viewless servants to enrich
The fretted splendor of each nook and niche.
Between the tree-stems, marbled plain at first,
Came jasper pannels; then, anon, there burst
Forth creeping imagery of slighter trees
And with the larger wove in small intricacies.
Approving all, she faded at self-will,
And shut the chamber up, close, hush'd and still,
Complete and ready for the revels rude
When dreadful guests would come to spoil her solitude.

The day appear'd, and all the gossip rout.
O senseless Lycius! Madman! wherefore flout
The silent-blessing Fate, warm cloister'd hours,
And shew to common eyes these secret bowers?
The Herd arriv'd, each guest, with busy brain,
Arriving at the Portal, gaz'd amain,
And enter'd marveling: for they knew the Street,
Remember'd it from childhood all complete
Without a gap; yet ne'er before had seen
That royal Porch, that high-built fair demesne;
So in they hurried all, maz'd, curious and keen:
Save one, who look'd thereon with eye severe,
And with calm-planted steps walk'd in austere;
'Twas Apollonius: something too he laugh'd,
As though some knotty Problem that had daft
His patient thought, had now begun to thaw,
And solve and melt:— 'twas just as he foresaw.

THE ONLY RECORDED COPY OF THE 1865 *ALICE* STILL IN A PRESENTATION BINDING 7¾ × 11 inches
Given in 1925 by Mrs. Harcourt Amory

Lewis Carroll

HARCOURT AMORY, H 1876, was responsible for Harvard's great strength in the works of Charles Lutwidge Dodgson, or Lewis Carroll, as the world knows him. Mr. Amory began where many Carrollians end, or try to end: with a copy of the fabulous 1865 *Alice*, which he bought in order to secure the illustrations as models for toy theatre figures he proposed to carve. He later wrote, 'The play [based on the figures] never came off . . .; and my energies were transferred to searching for bibliographical rarities strictly limited to one subject.'

After his death in 1925, Mrs. Amory and her children gave the collection to Harvard. By that time it included *two* copies of the 1865 *Alice*, first and other editions of all Carroll's major and many of his minor works, translations, manuscripts, letters, original drawings by Tenniel and others, and all manner of Carrolliana. Subsequent donors have continued to enrich the collection.

LEWIS CARROLL: STUDIES FOR *THROUGH THE LOOKING-GLASS*
   Given in 1927 by Mrs. Harcourt Amory

SIR JOHN TENNIEL: PENCIL DRAWINGS FOR *THROUGH THE LOOKING-GLASS*
   Given in 1925 by Mrs. Harcourt Amory

"Vanished that dim and ghostly bed,
(The hangings, tape; the tape was red:)
'Tis o'er, and Doe and Roe are dead!

Oh yet my spirit inly crawls,
What time it shudderingly recalls
That horrid dream of marble halls!

Oxford. 1855.

STANZA OF ANGLO-SAXON POETRY.

> TWAS BRYLLYG, AND YE SLYTHY TOVES
> DID GYRE AND GYMBLE IN YE WABE:
> ALL MIMSY WERE YE BOROGOVES;
> AND YE MOME RATHS OUTGRABE.

This curious fragment reads thus in modern characters:

TWAS BRYLLYG, AND THE SLYTHY TOVES
DID GYRE AND GYMBLE IN THE WABE:
ALL MIMSY WERE THE BOROGOVES;
AND THE MOME RATHS OUTGRABE.

The meanings of the words are as follows:

BRYLLYG. (derived from the verb to BRYL or BROIL). "the time of broiling dinner, i.e. the close of the afternoon."

SLYTHY. (compounded of SLIMY and LITHE)."smooth and active"

TOVE. a species of Badger. They had smooth white hair, long

LEWIS CARROLL: AUTOGRAPH MS. OF *MISCHMASCH*
THE FIRST STANZA OF *JABBERWOCKY*
   Given in 1925 by Mrs. Harcourt Amory

hind legs, and short horns like a stag: lived chiefly on cheese.

GYRE. verb. (derived from GYAOUR or GIAOUR, "a dog".) - "to scratch like a dog."

GYMBLE. (whence GIMBLET). "to screw out holes in anything."

WABE. (derived from the verb to SWAB or SOAK). "the side of a hill." (from it's being soaked by the rain.)

MIMSY. (whence MIMSERABLE and MISERABLE). "unhappy."

BOROGOVE. An extinct kind of Parrot. The had no wings, beaks turned up, and made their nests under sun-dials: lived on veal.

MOME. (hence SOLEMOME, SOLEMONE, and SOLEMN). "grave."

RATH. A species of land turtle. Head erect: mouth like a shark: the ~~front~~ fore legs curved out so that the animal walked on it's knees: smooth green body. lived on swallows and oysters.

OUTGRABE. past tense of the verb to OUTGRIBE. (it is connected with the old verb to GRIKE or SHRIKE, from which are derived "shriek" and "creak".) "squeaked."

Hence the literal English of the passage is: "It was evening, and the smooth active badgers were scratching and boring holes in the hill-side: all unhappy were the parrots; and the grave turtles squeaked out."

There were probably sun-dials on the top of the hill, and the "borogoves" were afraid that their nests would be undermined. The hill was probably full of the nests of "raths", which ran out, squeaking with fear, on hearing the "toves" scratching outside. This is an obscure, but yet deeply-affecting, relic of ancient Poetry.

Croft - 1855.   Ed:

CHAPTER

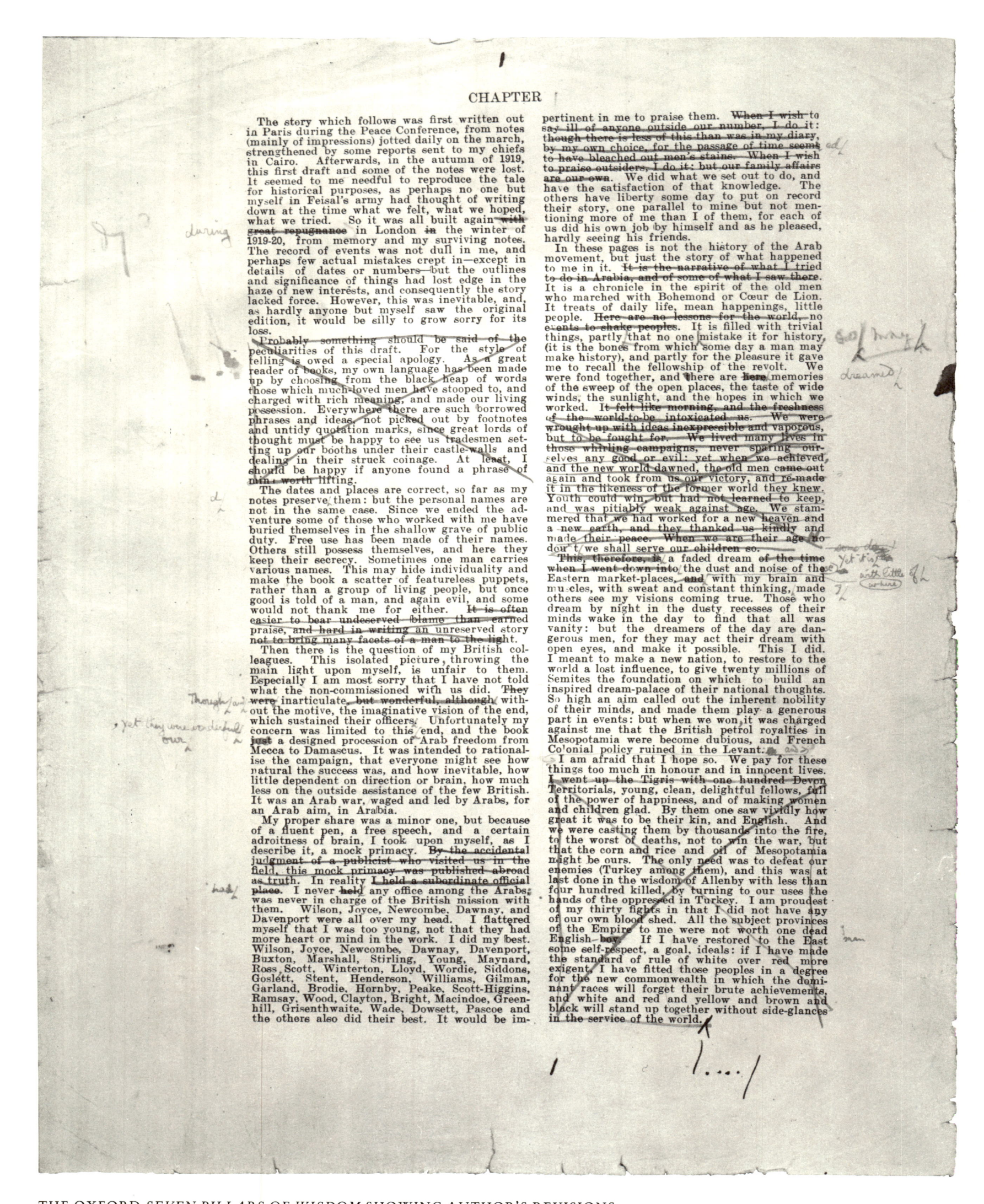

The story which follows was first written out in Paris during the Peace Conference, from notes (mainly of impressions) jotted daily on the march, strengthened by some reports sent to my chiefs in Cairo. Afterwards, in the autumn of 1919, this first draft and some of the notes were lost. It seemed to me needful to reproduce the tale for historical purposes, as perhaps no one but myself in Feisal's army had thought of writing down at the time what we felt, what we hoped, what we tried. So it was all built again with great repugnance in London in the winter of 1919-20, from memory and my surviving notes. The record of events was not dull in me, and perhaps few actual mistakes crept in—except in details of dates or numbers—but the outlines and significance of things had lost edge in the haze of new interests, and consequently the story lacked force. However, this was inevitable, and, as hardly anyone but myself saw the original edition, it would be silly to grow sorry for its loss.

Probably something should be said of the peculiarities of this draft. For the style of telling is owed a special apology. As a great reader of books, my own language has been made up by choosing from the black heap of words those which much-loved men have stooped to, and charged with rich meaning, and made our living possession. Everywhere there are such borrowed phrases and ideas, not picked out by footnotes and untidy quotation marks, since great lords of thought must be happy to see us tradesmen setting up our booths under their castle-walls and dealing in their struck coinage. At least, I should be happy if anyone found a phrase of mine worth lifting.

The dates and places are correct, so far as my notes preserve them: but the personal names are not in the same case. Since we ended the adventure some of those who worked with me have buried themselves in the shallow grave of public duty. Free use has been made of their names. Others still possess themselves, and here they keep their secrecy. Sometimes one man carries various names. This may hide individuality and make the book a scatter of featureless puppets, rather than a group of living people, but once good is told of a man, and again evil, and some would not thank me for either. It is often easier to bear undeserved blame than earned praise, and hard in writing an unreserved story not to bring many facets of a man to the light.

Then there is the question of my British colleagues. This isolated picture, throwing the main light upon myself, is unfair to them. Especially I am most sorry that I have not told what the non-commissioned with us did. They were inarticulate, but wonderful, although without the motive, the imaginative vision of the end, which sustained their officers. Unfortunately my concern was limited to this end, and the book just a designed procession of Arab freedom from Mecca to Damascus. It was intended to rationalise the campaign, that everyone might see how natural the success was, and how inevitable, how little dependent on direction or brain, how much less on the outside assistance of the few British. It was an Arab war, waged and led by Arabs, for an Arab aim, in Arabia.

My proper share was a minor one, but because of a fluent pen, a free speech, and a certain adroitness of brain, I took upon myself, as I describe it, a mock primacy. By the accidental judgment of a publicist who visited us in the field, this mock primacy was published abroad as truth. In reality I held a subordinate official place. I never held any office among the Arabs; was never in charge of the British mission with them. Wilson, Joyce, Newcombe, Dawnay, and Davenport were all over my head. I flattered myself that I was too young, not that they had more heart or mind in the work. I did my best. Wilson, Joyce, Newcombe, Dawnay, Davenport, Buxton, Marshall, Stirling, Young, Maynard, Ross, Scott, Winterton, Lloyd, Wordie, Siddons, Goslett, Stent, Henderson, Williams, Gilman, Garland, Brodie, Hornby, Peake, Scott-Higgins, Ramsay, Wood, Clayton, Bright, Macindoe, Greenhill, Grisenthwaite, Wade, Dowsett, Pascoe and the others also did their best. It would be impertinent in me to praise them. When I wish to say ill of anyone outside our number, I do it: though there is less of this than was in my diary, by my own choice, for the passage of time seems to have bleached out men's stains. When I wish to praise outsiders, I do it: but our family affairs are our own. We did what we set out to do, and have the satisfaction of that knowledge. The others have liberty some day to put on record their story, one parallel to mine but not mentioning more of me than I of them, for each of us did his own job by himself and as he pleased, hardly seeing his friends.

In these pages is not the history of the Arab movement, but just the story of what happened to me in it. It is the narrative of what I tried to do in Arabia, and of some of what I saw there. It is a chronicle in the spirit of the old men who marched with Bohemond or Cœur de Lion. It treats of daily life, mean happenings, little people. Here are no lessons for the world, no events to shake peoples. It is filled with trivial things, partly that no one mistake it for history, (it is the bones from which some day a man may make history), and partly for the pleasure it gave me to recall the fellowship of the revolt. We were fond together, and there are here memories of the sweep of the open places, the taste of wide winds, the sunlight, and the hopes in which we worked. It felt like morning, and the freshness of the world-to-be intoxicated us. We were wrought up with ideas inexpressible and vaporous, but to be fought for. We lived many lives in those whirling campaigns, never sparing ourselves any good or evil: yet when we achieved, and the new world dawned, the old men came out again and took from us our victory, and re-made it in the likeness of the former world they knew. Youth could win, but had not learned to keep, and was pitiably weak against age. We stammered that we had worked for a new heaven and a new earth, and they thanked us kindly and made their peace. When we are their age no doubt we shall serve our children so.

This, therefore, is a faded dream of the time when I went down into the dust and noise of the Eastern market-places, and with my brain and muscles, with sweat and constant thinking, made others see my visions coming true. Those who dream by night in the dusty recesses of their minds wake in the day to find that all was vanity: but the dreamers of the day are dangerous men, for they may act their dream with open eyes, and make it possible. This I did. I meant to make a new nation, to restore to the world a lost influence, to give twenty millions of Semites the foundation on which to build an inspired dream-palace of their national thoughts. So high an aim called out the inherent nobility of their minds, and made them play a generous part in events: but when we won, it was charged against me that the British petrol royalties in Mesopotamia were become dubious, and French Colonial policy ruined in the Levant.

I am afraid that I hope so. We pay for these things too much in honour and in innocent lives. I went up the Tigris with one hundred Devon Territorials, young, clean, delightful fellows, full of the power of happiness, and of making women and children glad. By them one saw vividly how great it was to be their kin, and English. And we were casting them by thousands into the fire, to the worst of deaths, not to win the war, but that the corn and rice and oil of Mesopotamia might be ours. The only need was to defeat our enemies (Turkey among them), and this was at last done in the wisdom of Allenby with less than four hundred killed, by turning to our uses the hands of the oppressed in Turkey. I am proudest of my thirty fights in that I did not have any of our own blood shed. All the subject provinces of the Empire to me were not worth one dead English boy. If I have restored to the East some self-respect, a goal, ideals: if I have made the standard of rule of white over red more exigent, I have fitted those peoples in a degree for the new commonwealth in which the dominant races will forget their brute achievements, and white and red and yellow and brown and black will stand up together without side-glances in the service of the world.

THE OXFORD *SEVEN PILLARS OF WISDOM* SHOWING AUTHOR'S REVISIONS
Given in 1961 by Bayard L. Kilgour, Jr., H 1927

T. E. Lawrence

One of the most comprehensive collections of Lawrence of Arabia ever formed was given to Harvard by Bayard L. Kilgour, Jr., H 1927, who built it up over a period of years. It contains letters, manuscripts, memorabilia and iconographic material of all kinds, together with a comprehensive run of editions of books by and about Lawrence, including translations of his works into many foreign languages. More than two hundred letters include long and important series to Robert Graves and to Bruce Rogers. A shelf of books once owned by Lawrence includes the Greek edition of Aristophanes that he carried with him during the entire desert campaign.

The rarest important printed book in the canon is the Oxford newsprint edition of *Seven Pillars of Wisdom*; the Kilgour Collection contains the copy extensively revised by Lawrence and Edward Garnett in preparation for the 1926 edition, together with the revised proofsheets of the latter including the suppressed Chapter I. Outstanding among the manuscripts is the holograph of *The Mint*, presented to Garnett, accompanied by the privately printed first edition (New York, 1936).

HOLOGRAPH MS. OF *THE MINT* 7 × 5 inches
Given in 1960 by Bayard L. Kilgour, Jr., H 1927

The Amy Lowell Collection

THE bequest of Amy Lowell's library, received in 1925, and the residuary bequest of income from the trust she established, beginning in 1952, constitute between them one of the greatest resources now available to the Houghton Library. Miss Lowell was a discriminating and knowledgeable collector. Her library consisted mainly of English literature from the 18th to the 20th century, with some American and some Continental authors as well, and it was rich in manuscripts and association books.

Her collecting was usually directed by her intellectual interests. When she undertook a biography of John Keats, she acquired primary materials, including first editions, letters, and manuscripts. Her books are shelved in a room next to the Keats Room, as they are in fact inseparably associated with the Keats Collection.

For fifteen years the Harvard Library has received a substantial portion of the income from the trust she established for the purpose of increasing the collections along the lines that she laid down. Many of the most important recent acquisitions, from the papers of Tennyson to those of E. E. Cummings, would have been impossible without the Lowell Fund.

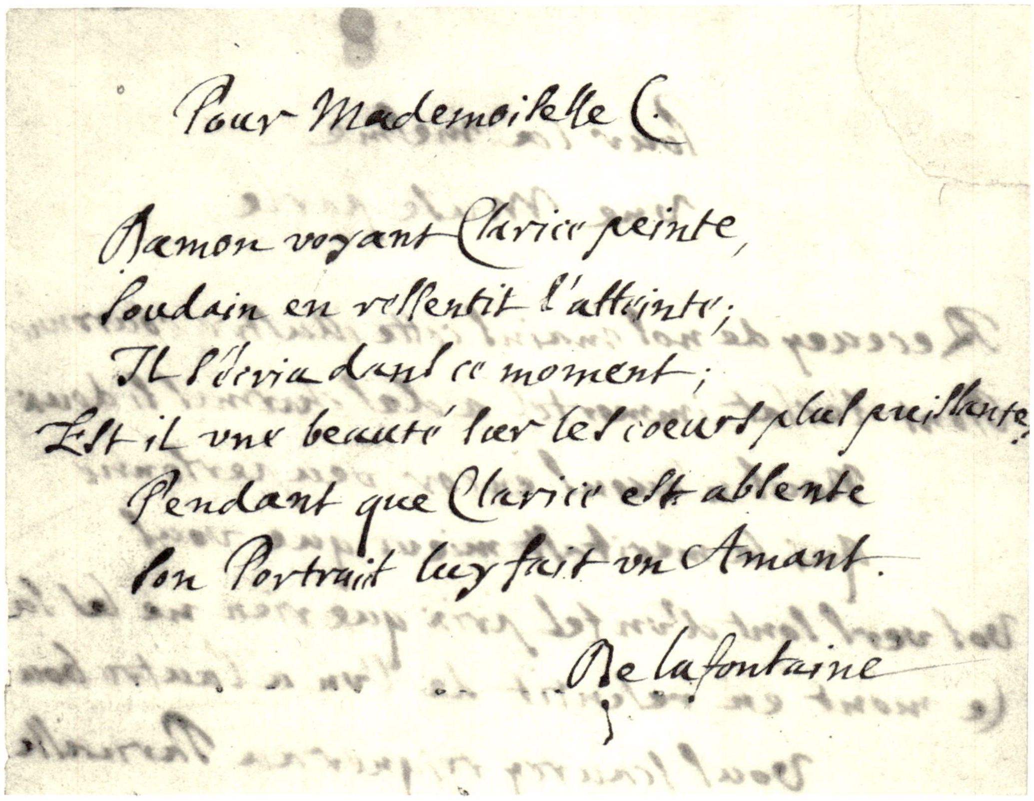

JEAN DE LA FONTAINE: AUTOGRAPH POEM
Bequeathed in 1925 by Amy Lowell

BEN JONSON: AUTOGRAPH LETTER TO GEORGE GARRARD,
WITH EPITAPH ON CECILIA BULSTRODE
   Bequeathed in 1925 by Amy Lowell

JAMES BOSWELL:
THE LIFE OF SAMUEL JOHNSON, 8TH ED., 1816
MRS. PIOZZI'S COPY, WITH HER MARGINALIA
Bequeathed in 1925 by Amy Lowell

474   THE LIFE OF

1765.
Ætat. 56.

married to a nobleman. It was not fit that a peer should continue the business. On the old man's death, therefore, the brewery was to be sold. To find a purchaser for so large a property was a difficult matter; and, after some time, it was suggested, that it would be adviseable to treat with Thrale, a sensible, active, honest man, who had been employed in the house, and to transfer the whole to him for thirty thousand pounds, security being taken upon the property. This was accordingly settled. In eleven years Thrale paid the purchase-money. He acquired a large fortune, and lived to be a member of Parliament for Southwark.[5] But what was most remarkable was the liberality with which he used his riches. He gave his son and daughters the best education. The esteem which his good conduct procured him from the nobleman who had married his master's daughter, made him be treated with much attention; and his son, both at school and at the University of Oxford, associated with young men of the first rank. His allowance from his father, after he left college, was splendid; not less than a thousand a year. This, in a man who had risen as old Thrale did, was a very extraordinary instance of generosity. He used to say, 'If this young dog does not find so much after I am gone as he expects, let him remember that he has had a great deal in my own time.'"

The son, though in affluent circumstances, had good sense enough to carry on his father's trade,

paling, ermine, on a chief indented vert, three wolves (or gryphons') heads, or, couped at the neck:—Crest on a ducal coronet, a tree, vert. BLAKEWAY.]

[5] [In 1733 he served the office of High Sheriff for Surrey; and died April 9, 1758. A. CHALMERS.]

SAMUEL JOHNSON: *RASSELAS*, 3D ED., 1760
THE AUTHOR'S COPY
Bequeathed in 1925 by Amy Lowell

CHARLES LAMB: AUTOGRAPH MS. OF
GRACE BEFORE MEAT 14½ × 9½ inches
Bequeathed in 1925 by Amy Lowell

84

Grace before Meat.

The custom of saying Grace at meals had probably its origin in the early times of the world, and the hunter-state of man, when dinners were precarious things, and a full meal was something more than a common blessing; when a belly-full was a windfall, and looked like a special providence. In the shouts and triumphal songs, with which after a season of sharp abstinence a lucky booty of deer's or goat's flesh would naturally be ushered home, existed perhaps the germ of the modern Grace. It is not otherwise easy to be understood why the blessing of food — the act of eating — should have had a particular expression of thanksgiving annexed to it, distinct from that implied and silent gratitude with which we are expected to enter upon the enjoyment of the many other various gifts and good things of existence.

I own that I am disposed to say Grace upon twenty other occasions in the course of the day besides my dinner. I want a form for setting out upon a pleasant walk, for a moonlight ramble, for a friendly meeting, or a solved problem. Why have we none for books, those spiritual repasts — a Grace before Milton — a Grace before Shakspeare — a Devotional Exercise proper to be said before reading the Fairy Queen? — but, the received ritual having prescribed these forms to the solitary ceremony of manducation, I shall confine my observations to the experience which I have had of the Grace, properly so called; commending my new scheme for extension to a niche in the grand philosophical, poetical, and perchance in part heretical, Liturgy, now compiling by my friend Homo Humanus, for the use of a certain snug congregation of Utopian Rabelæsian Christians, no matter where assembled.

The form then of the benediction before eating has its beauty, at a poor man's table, or at the simple and unprovocative repasts of children. It is here that the Grace becomes exceedingly graceful. The indigent man, who hardly knows whether he shall have a meal the next day or not, sits down to his fare with a present sense of the blessing, which can be but feebly acted by the rich, into whose minds the conception of ever wanting a dinner could never but by some extreme theory have entered. The proper end of food — the animal sustenance — is barely contemplated by them. The poor man's bread is his daily bread, literally his bread for the day. Their courses are perennial.

Again, the plainest diet seems the fittest to be preceded by the Grace. That which is least stimulative to appetite, leaves the mind most free for foreign considerations. A man may feel thankful, heartily thankful, over a dish of plain mutton with turnips, and have leisure to reflect upon the ordinance

MINIATURE MSS. OF CHARLOTTE AND PATRICK BRANWELL BRONTË
Bequeathed in 1925 by Amy Lowell

GEORGE ELIOT: MS. 'QUARRY' FOR *MIDDLEMARCH* 6⅛ × 8 inches
Bequeathed in 1925 by Amy Lowell

ROBERT BROWNING: *PAULINE,* 1833, REVISED BY THE AUTHOR IN 1867 FOR
A SECOND EDITION THAT WAS NEVER PUBLISHED 8 × 10 inches
Bequeathed in 1925 by Amy Lowell

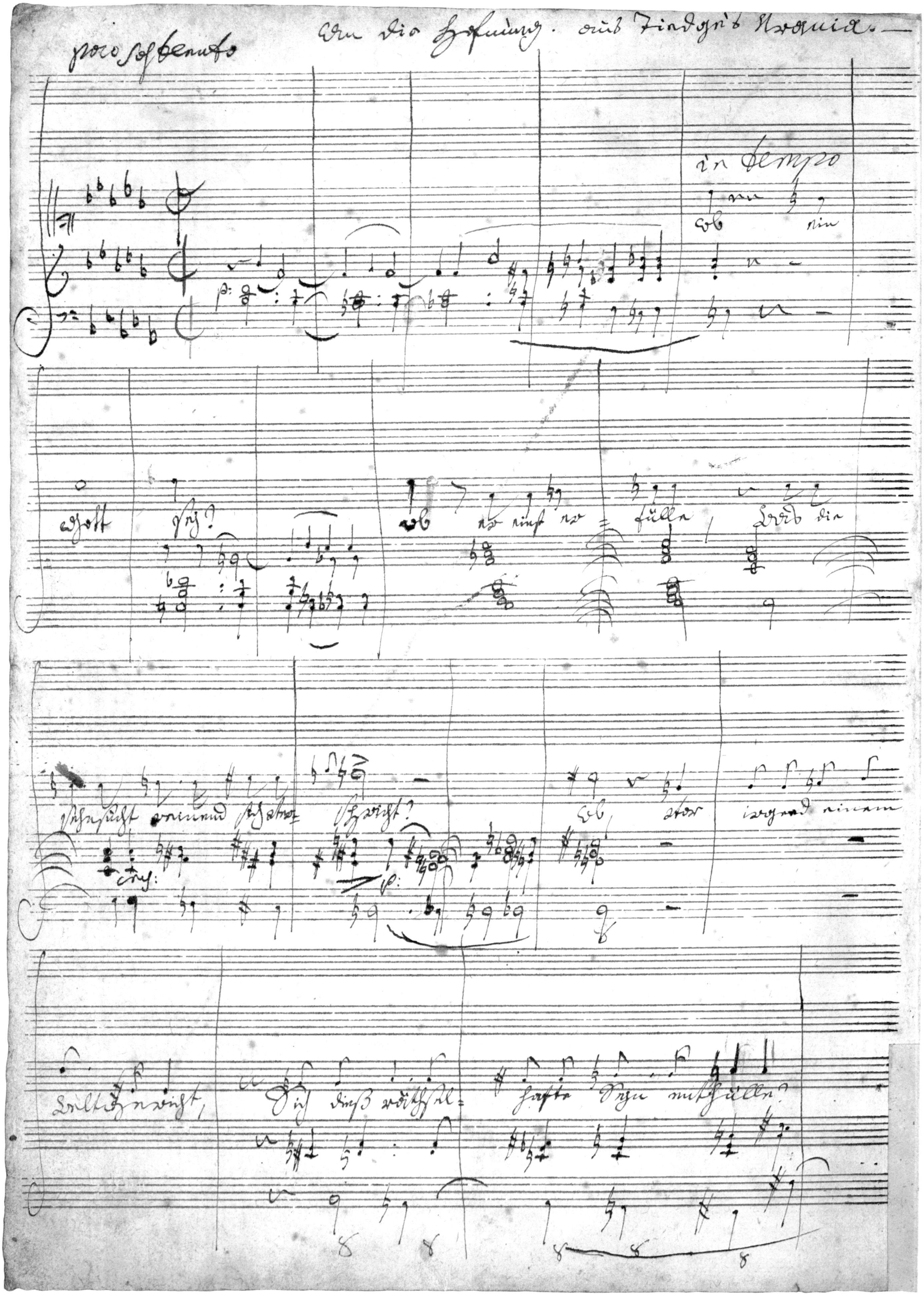
poco sostenuto
An die Hoffnung. aus Tiedges Urania.
in tempo

(As a projectile, form'd, impell'd, passing a certain line, still keeps on,
So the present, utterly form'd, impell'd by the past.)

Passage to India! clue and rapport
But ~~Passage first~~ to the ~~primal~~ myths and the fables!

Not you alone, O truths of the world!
Not you ~~alone~~, ye facts of modern science!
But fables — ~~the splendid fables~~! the far-back fables, Asia's Africa's fables!

> The far darting beams of the spirit!—the unloos'd dreams!
> The deep diving ~~fables—the mythical~~ bibles and legends;
> The daring plots of the poets — the elder ~~and newer~~ religions; *myths*
> —O you temples fairer than lilies, pour'd over by the rising sun!
> O you fables, spurning the known, eluding the hold of the known, mounting to heaven!
> You lofty and dazzling towers, pinnacled, red as roses, burnish'd with gold!
> Towers of fables immortal, fashion'd from mortal dreams!
> You too I welcome, and fully, the same as the rest;
> You too with joy I sing.

With such, the past, the accepted present
And thee and I, O soul, chanting our chant ~~singing~~ the ~~song~~ of pleasant exploration.

WALT WHITMAN: AUTOGRAPH MS. OF *PASSAGE TO INDIA*
Bequeathed in 1925 by Amy Lowell

BEETHOVEN: AUTOGRAPH MS.
OF *AN DIE HOFFNUNG*   13 7/8 × 9 3/4 inches
Bequeathed in 1925 by Amy Lowell

JOHN ELIOT: *NEW ENGLANDS FIRST FRUITS*, 1643   7⅛ × 10½ inches
Bequeathed in 1883 by Joseph J. Cooke

American History

HARVARD has always been properly assiduous in the gathering and study of material bearing upon the history of the United States. Moreover, in a real sense the University Archives and the records of the library constitute an important source for historical studies, since they are the papers of the oldest continuing corporate body, the senior institution of higher learning, and the largest university library in the country.

During most of the library's growth, this effort was directed towards printed books, pamphlets, maps, and newspapers. Certain special collections added to the library's strength in Americana. For example, the association books bequeathed in 1931 by Henry Saltonstall Howe included a complete run of books owned by Presidents of the United States, a run that has been kept up to date ever since. Another collection in this field consists of works by members of the Mather family, and it has long since overflowed the large case devoted to it in the entrance lobby.

For many years the library made no special effort to collect historical manuscripts, but manuscripts nevertheless came to the library from time to time in the natural course of events. They ranged from those in the collection of Christoph Daniel Ebeling (acquired in 1818) to the political and military Americana of Frederick M. Dearborn (bequeathed in 1961). These have been joined by the personal papers of historians, statesmen, and diplomats (Jared Sparks, Charles Sumner, and Joseph C. Grew, to name only one in each category), and the collections continue to grow in response to increasing demands by scholarly users.

FATHER SEBASTIAN RÂLE: DICTIONARY
OF THE ABENAKI LANGUAGE
CAPTURED AT NORRIDGEWOCK CA. 1724
9⅛ × 6⅝ inches
Given in 1764 by Middlecott Cooke, H 1723

AGREEMENT TO SUPPORT THE
ROXBURY LATIN SCHOOL, 1646
SIGNED BY JOHN ELIOT AND OTHERS 7⅝ × 11¼ inches
Deposited in 1957 by the Trustees of the Roxbury Latin School
and reproduced with their consent

Lexington April 23. 1775.

We Nathan Barret. Captain. Jonathan Farrar, Joseph Butler & Francis Wheeler. Lieutenants, John Barret. Ensign. John Brown, Silas Walker, Ephraim Melvin, Nathan Buttrick, Stephen Hosmer Jr Samˡ Barret, Thomas Jones, Joseph Chandler, Peter Wheeler, Nathan Peirce and Edward Richardson all of Concord in the County of Middlesex in the Province of the Massachusetts Bay of lawfull age testify & declare that on wednesday the nineteenth instant about an hour after sunrise, we assembled on a hill near the meeting house in Concord aforsᵈ in consequence of an information that a number of regular troops had killed six of our countrymen at Lexington & were on their march to said Concord, and about an hour afterwards we saw them approaching to the number, as we imagine, of about twelve hundred, on which we retreated to a hill about eighty rods back, and the aforsaid troops then took posession of a hill where we were first posted. — Presently after this, we saw them moving towards the north bridge about one mile from said meeting house. We then immediately went before them, and passed the bridge just before a party of them to the number of about two hundred arrived — They there left about one half of these two hundred at the bridge and proceeded with the rest towards Colˡ Barrets, about two miles from the said bridge.

We then seeing several fires in the Town thought our houses were in danger, and immediately marched back towards said bridge, and the troops, who were stationed there, observing our approach marched back over the bridge and then took up some of the planks. — We then hastned our steps towards the bridge, and when we had got near the bridge they fired on our men, first three guns one after the other, and then a considerable number more upon which, and not before (having orders from our commanding officer not to fire till we were fired upon) we fired upon the regulars, and they retreated. — At Concord & on their retreat thro Lexington they plundered many houses, burnt three at Lexington togeather with a shop and a barn — and committed damage more or less to almost every house from Concord to Charlestown —

Peter Wheeler
Nathan Peirce
Edward Richardson

Nathan Barrett
Jonathan Farrar
Joseph Butler
Francis Wheeler
John Barrett
John Brown
Silas Walker
Ephraim Melvin
Nathan Buttrick
Stephen Hosmer Jur
Samuel Barrett
Thomas Jones
Joseph Chandler

DEPOSITION SIGNED BY MINUTE MEN, 23 APRIL 1775
From the Arthur Lee Papers, given in 1827 by Richard Henry Lee

JAMES MONROE: *A VIEW OF THE CONDUCT OF THE EXECUTIVE*, 1797
ANNOTATED BY GEORGE WASHINGTON   9 × 10½ inches
Bequeathed in 1847 by Justice Joseph Story, H 1798

[322]

state of things, are palpable. They almost deprive the republic of the advantage it ought to derive from this article of the treaty.

2. The admission of English vessels of war into the ports of the United States, against the express stipulation of the 17th article of the treaty; that is to say, when they have made prizes upon the republic, or its citizens. The weakness with which the federal government yielded this point in the beginning, tended to increase the pretensions of Great Britain ; so that, at present, the ports of the United States have become a station for the squadron of Admiral Murray; which, for two years past, has stationed there, to make excursions thence upon the American commerce, and destroy our property. This division carries its audacity even farther, by conducting its prizes into those ports. (1)

3. The consular convention, which makes a part of our treaties, is equally unexecuted in two of its most important clauses: The first, which grants to our consuls the right of judging exclusively all controversies which take place between French citizens, has become illusory, from a defect in the law which gives to our consuls the means of executing their judgments. (2) The consequences of this defect tend to annihilate the prerogatives of our consuls, and by means thereof, to injure essentially our merchants. The second gives to our consuls the right of arresting our marine deserters. The inexecution of this part of the convention affects beyond all expression our maritime service, whilst our vessels are stationed in the American ports. The judges charged, by the law, to deliver mandats of arrest, have lately required the presentation of the original register of the equipage, in despite of the 5th article of the treaty, which admits to the tribunals of the two powers copies certified by the consuls. (3) Particular local considerations oppose, in a thousand circumstances, the presentation of the original register, and, under these circumstances, the sailors always make their escape.

4. The arrestation in the port of Philadelphia, in the month of August, 1795, of the Captain of the Corvette Cassius, for an act committed by him on the high seas. This measure is contrary to the 19th article of the treaty of commerce, which stipulates : " that the commandants of public and private vessels shall not be detained in any manner." It violates moreover the right of nations, the most common ; which puts the officers of public vessels under the safeguard of their flag. (4) The United States had sufficient proof of the respect, which the republic entertained for them, to have counted upon its

[323]

justice, upon this occasion. The Captain has been imprisoned, though the consul of the republic supported the action; and, with difficulty, has he been released. The Corvette, though regularly armed at the Cape by the General Lavaud, has been arrested (as it appears she still is) under the pretext, that eight months before she sailed from Philadelphia, she was suspected of having been armed in that port.

Second COMPLAINT. The impunity of the outrage made to the republic, in the person of its minister, the citizen Fauchet, by the English vessel, the Africa, in concert with the vice-consul of that nation.

The arrestation, in the waters of the United States, of the packet boat in which the minister sailed : The search made in his trunks, with the avowed object of seizing his person and his papers, committed on the first of August 1795, and after which this insult was vessel (the Africa) blocked up the rest of that month, at Newport, the frigate Medusa of the republic ; nor was that vessel ordered to depart 'till after this frigate had sailed, and which order was given for a new outrage committed against the United States, by a menacing letter ; and, for a participation in which last insult, the exequatur of the English consul was withdrawn.

Third COMPLAINT. The treaty concluded in November, 1794, between the United States, and Great Britain. It would be easy to prove, that the United States, in that treaty, have sacrificed, *knowingly* and *evidently*, their connection with the republic ; and the rights, the most essential and least contested, of neutrality. (2)

1. The United States, have not only departed from the principles that were consecrated by the armed neutrality, during the war of their independence ; but they have also given to England, to the injury of their first allies, a mark the most striking of a *condescension*, without limits, in abandoning the rule, which the rights of nations, their treaties with all other powers and even the treaties of England with most of the maritime powers, have given to contraband. To sacrifice, exclusively to this power, the objects which are necessary for the equipment and construction of vessels,—is not this to depart evidently from the principles of neutrality ? (3)

2. But they have even gone further. They have consented to extend the denomination of contraband, even to provi-

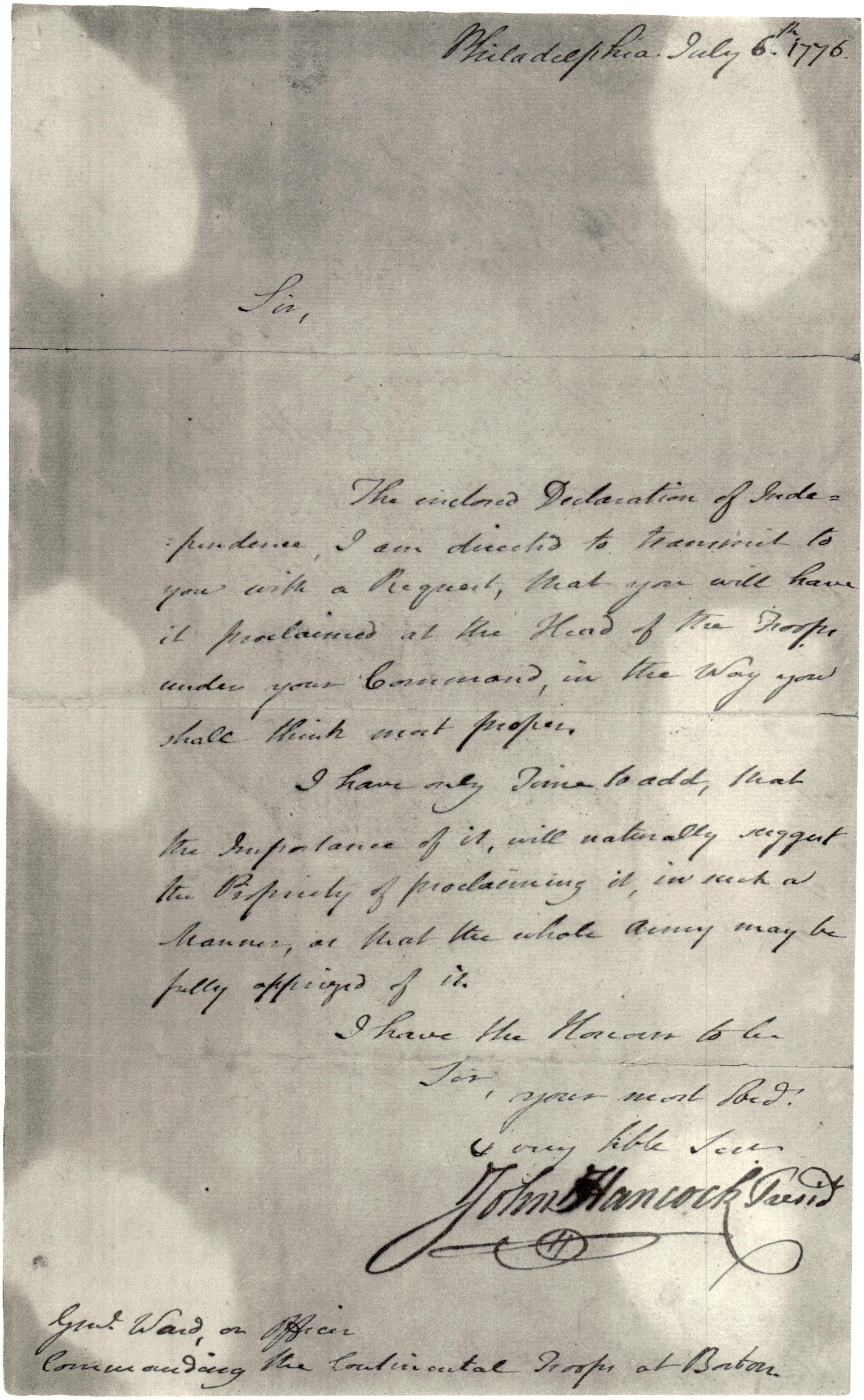

Philadelphia July 6th 1776.

Sir,

The enclosed Declaration of Independence, I am directed to transmit to you with a Request, that you will have it proclaimed at the Head of the Troops under your Command, in the Way you shall think most proper.

I have only Time to add, that the Importance of it, will naturally suggest the Propriety of proclaiming it, in such a Manner, as that the whole Army may be fully apprized of it.

I have the Honour to be
Sir, your most Obed.
& very hble Serv.
John Hancock Presid.

Genl Ward, or Officer
Commanding the Continental Troops at Boston.

LETTER FROM JOHN HANCOCK TO ARTEMAS WARD, 6 JULY 1776
From the set of Signers given in 1945 by Helen Fahnestock Hubbard in memory of her husband, John Hubbard, H 1892

IN CONGRESS, JULY 4, 1776.

A DECLARATION

BY THE REPRESENTATIVES OF THE

UNITED STATES OF AMERICA,

IN GENERAL CONGRESS ASSEMBLED.

WHEN in the Courſe of human Events, it becomes neceſſary for one People to diſſolve the Political Bands which have connected them with another, and to aſſume among the Powers of the Earth, the ſeparate and equal Station to which the Laws of Nature and of Nature's God entitle them, a decent Reſpect to the Opinions of Mankind requires that they ſhould declare the cauſes which impel them to the Separation.

We hold theſe Truths to be ſelf-evident, that all Men are created equal, that they are endowed by their Creator with certain unalienable Rights, that among theſe are Life, Liberty, and the Purſuit of Happineſs--That to ſecure theſe Rights, Governments are inſtituted among Men, deriving their juſt Powers from the Conſent of the Governed, that whenever any Form of Government becomes deſtructive of theſe Ends, it is the Right of the People to alter or to aboliſh it, and to inſtitute new Government, laying its Foundation on ſuch Principles, and organizing its Powers in ſuch Form, as to them ſhall ſeem moſt likely to effect their Safety and Happineſs. Prudence, indeed, will dictate that Governments long eſtabliſhed ſhould not be changed for light and tranſient Cauſes; and accordingly all Experience hath ſhewn, that Mankind are more diſpoſed to ſuffer, while Evils are ſufferable, than to right themſelves by aboliſhing the Forms to which they are accuſtomed. But when a long Train of Abuſes and Uſurpations, purſuing invariably the ſame Object, evinces a Deſign to reduce them under abſolute Deſpotiſm, it is their Right, it is their Duty, to throw off ſuch Government, and to provide new Guards for their future Security. Such has been the patient Sufferance of theſe Colonies; and ſuch is now the Neceſſity which conſtrains them to alter their former Syſtems of Government. The Hiſtory of the preſent King of Great-Britain is a Hiſtory of repeated Injuries and Uſurpations, all having in direct Object the Eſtabliſhment of an abſolute Tyranny over theſe States. To prove this, let Facts be ſubmitted to a candid World.

He has refuſed his Aſſent to Laws, the moſt wholeſome and neceſſary for the public Good.

He has forbidden his Governors to paſs Laws of immediate and preſſing Importance, unleſs ſuſpended in their Operation till his Aſſent ſhould be obtained; and when ſo ſuſpended, he has utterly neglected to attend to them.

He has refuſed to paſs other Laws for the Accommodation of large Diſtricts of People, unleſs thoſe People would relinquiſh the Right of Repreſentation in the Legiſlature, a Right ineſtimable to them, and formidable to Tyrants only.

He has called together Legiſlative Bodies at Places unuſual, uncomfortable, and diſtant from the Depoſitory of their public Records, for the ſole Purpoſe of fatiguing them into Compliance with his Meaſures.

He has diſſolved Repreſentative Houſes repeatedly, for oppoſing with manly Firmneſs his Invaſions on the Rights of the People.

He has refuſed for a long Time, after ſuch Diſſolutions, to cauſe others to be elected; whereby the Legiſlative Powers, incapable of Annihilation, have returned to the People at large for their exerciſe; the State remaining in the mean time expoſed to all the Dangers of Invaſion from without, and Convulſions within.

He has endeavoured to prevent the Population of theſe States; for that Purpoſe obſtructing the Laws for Naturalization of Foreigners; refuſing to paſs others to encourage their Migrations hither, and raiſing the Conditions of new Appropriations of Lands.

He has obſtructed the Adminiſtration of Juſtice, by refuſing his Aſſent to Laws for eſtabliſhing Judiciary Powers.

He has made Judges dependent on his Will alone, for the Tenure of their Offices, and the Amount and Payment of their Salaries.

He has erected a Multitude of new Offices, and ſent hither Swarms of Officers to harraſs our People, and eat out their Subſtance.

He has kept among us, in Times of Peace, Standing Armies, without the conſent of our Legiſlatures.

He has affected to render the Military independent of and ſuperior to the Civil Power.

He has combined with others to ſubject us to a Juriſdiction foreign to our Conſtitution, and unacknowledged by our Laws; giving his Aſſent to their Acts of pretended Legiſlation:

For quartering large Bodies of Armed Troops among us:

For protecting them, by a mock Trial, from Puniſhment for any Murders which they ſhould commit on the Inhabitants of theſe States:

For cutting off our Trade with all Parts of the World:

For impoſing Taxes on us without our Conſent:

For depriving us, in many Caſes, of the Benefits of Trial by Jury:

For tranſporting us beyond Seas to be tried for pretended Offences:

For aboliſhing the free Syſtem of Engliſh Laws in a neighbouring Province, eſtabliſhing therein an arbitrary Government, and enlarging its Boundaries, ſo as to render it at once an Example and fit Inſtrument for introducing the ſame abſolute Rule into theſe Colonies:

For taking away our Charters, aboliſhing our moſt valuable Laws, and altering fundamentally the Forms of our Governments:

For ſuſpending our own Legiſlatures, and declaring themſelves inveſted with Power to legiſlate for us in all Caſes whatſoever.

He has abdicated Government here, by declaring us out of his Protection and waging War againſt us.

He has plundered our Seas, ravaged our Coaſts, burnt our Towns, and deſtroyed the Lives of our People.

He is, at this Time, tranſporting large Armies of foreign Mercenaries to compleat the Works of Death, Deſolation, and Tyranny, already begun with circumſtances of Cruelty and Perfidy, ſcarcely paralleled in the moſt barbarous Ages, and totally unworthy the Head of a civilized Nation.

He has conſtrained our fellow Citizens taken Captive on the high Seas to bear Arms againſt their Country, to become the Executioners of their Friends and Brethren, or to fall themſelves by their Hands.

He has excited domeſtic Inſurrections amongſt us, and has endeavoured to bring on the Inhabitants of our Frontiers, the mercileſs Indian Savages, whoſe known Rule of Warfare, is an undiſtinguiſhed Deſtruction, of all Ages, Sexes and Conditions.

In every ſtage of theſe Oppreſſions we have Petitioned for Redreſs in the moſt humble Terms: Our repeated Petitions have been anſwered only by repeated Injury. A Prince, whoſe Character is thus marked by every act which may define a Tyrant, is unfit to be the Ruler of a free People.

Nor have we been wanting in Attentions to our Britiſh Brethren. We have warned them from Time to Time of Attempts by their Legiſlature to extend an unwarrantable Juriſdiction over us. We have reminded them of the Circumſtances of our Emigration and Settlement here. We have appealed to their native Juſtice and Magnanimity, and we have conjured them by the Ties of our common Kindred to diſavow theſe Uſurpations, which, would inevitably interrupt our Connections and Correſpondence. They too have been deaf to the Voice of Juſtice and of Conſanguinity. We muſt, therefore, acquieſce in the Neceſſity, which denounces our Separation, and hold them, as we hold the reſt of Mankind, Enemies in War, in Peace, Friends.

We, therefore, the Repreſentatives of the UNITED STATES OF AMERICA, in GENERAL CONGRESS, Aſſembled, appealing to the Supreme Judge of the World for the Rectitude of our Intentions, do, in the Name, and by Authority of the good People of theſe Colonies, ſolemnly Publiſh and Declare, That theſe United Colonies are, and of Right ought to be, FREE AND INDEPENDENT STATES; that they are abſolved from all Allegiance to the Britiſh Crown, and that all political Connection between them and the State of Great-Britain, is and ought to be totally diſſolved; and that as FREE AND INDEPENDENT STATES, they have full Power to levy War, conclude Peace, contract Alliances, eſtabliſh Commerce, and to do all other Acts and Things which INDEPENDENT STATES may of right do. And for the ſupport of this Declaration, with a firm Reliance on the Protection of divine Providence, we mutually pledge to each other our Lives, our Fortunes, and our ſacred Honor.

Signed by ORDER *and in* BEHALF *of the* CONGRESS,

JOHN HANCOCK, PRESIDENT.

ATTEST.
CHARLES THOMSON, SECRETARY.

PHILADELPHIA: PRINTED BY JOHN DUNLAP.

FIRST EDITION OF THE DECLARATION OF INDEPENDENCE 17¾ × 15⅛ inches
Given in 1947 by Carleton R. Richmond, H 1909

PEYTON RANDOLPH: AUTOGRAPH LETTER
TO GEORGE WASHINGTON,
3 MAY 1756   7½ × 6⅛ inches
From the Sparks Papers, collected
by Jared Sparks, H 1815

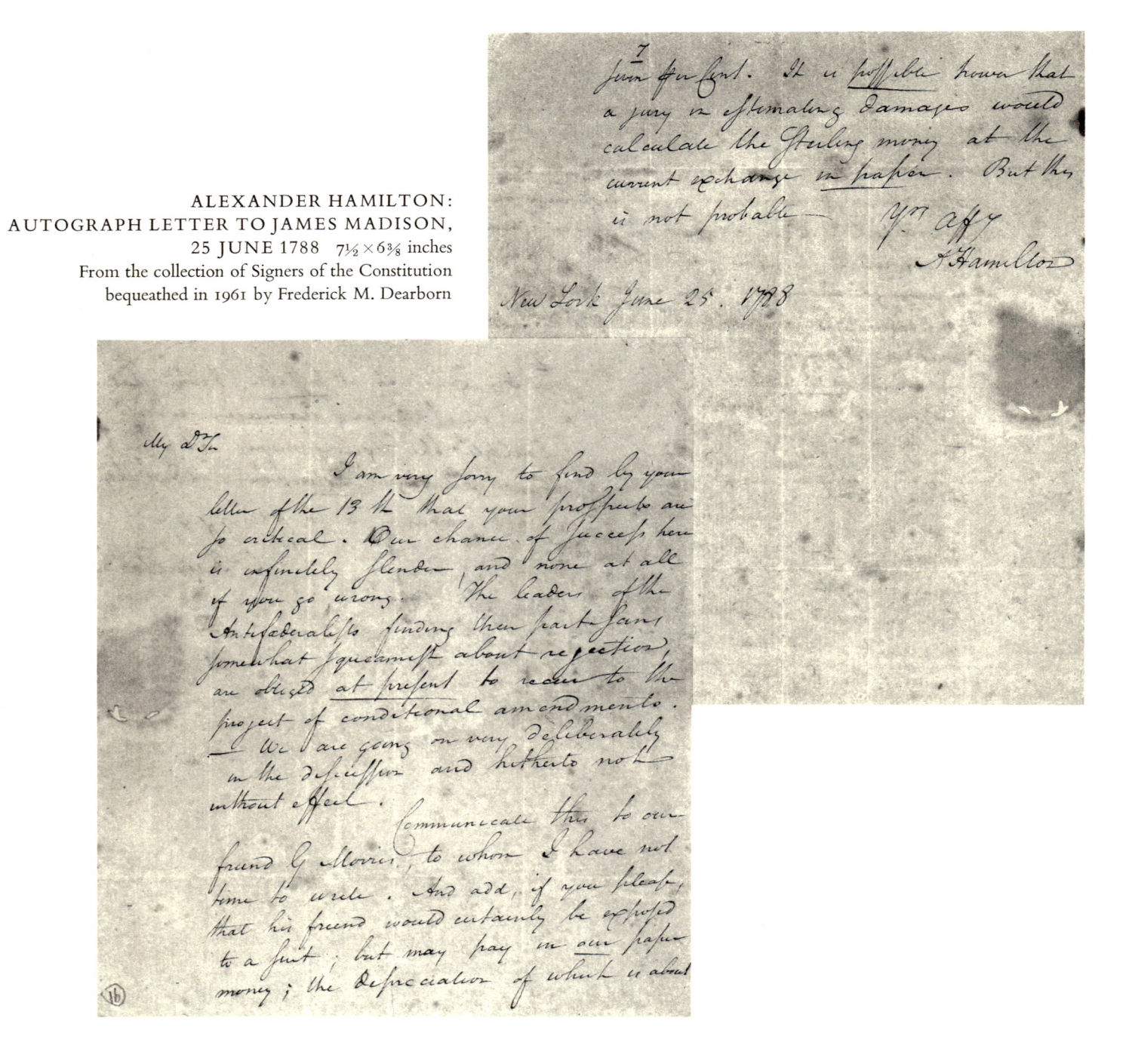

ALEXANDER HAMILTON:
AUTOGRAPH LETTER TO JAMES MADISON,
25 JUNE 1788   7½ × 6⅜ inches
From the collection of Signers of the Constitution
bequeathed in 1961 by Frederick M. Dearborn

JOHN JAMES AUDUBON: ORIGINAL DRAWING 15¾ × 9¾ inches
Bequeathed in 1930 by Joseph Y. Jeanes through his son, Joseph Y. Jeanes 2nd, H 1924

"Tell ye your CHILDREN of it, and let your CHILDREN tell their CHILDREN, and their CHILDREN another generation."

CELEBRATION
OF
AMERICAN INDEPENDENCE,
BY THE
BOSTON SABBATH SCHOOL UNION,
AT PARK STREET CHURCH, JULY 4, 1831.

ORDER OF EXERCISES.

1. SINGING.
[By the Juvenile Choir.]

This is the youthful choir that comes,
  All dressed so neat and gay;
As bright as birds that soar and sing,
  And warble all the day.

This is the youthful choir that loves
  The teacher to obey;
That meets to sing, and pray, and learn,
  On every Sabbath day.

This is the youthful choir that goes
  Through wind and storm away,
From peaceful home to Sabbath school,
  To learn salvation's way.

This is the youthful choir that sings,
  When all the town is gay;
That praises God with gratitude
  On Independent day.

2. READING THE SCRIPTURES.

3. SINGING.
[By the Choir.]

With joy we meet,
With smiles we greet
  Our schoolmates bright and gay:
Be dry each tear
Of sorrow here—
  'Tis Independent day.

'Tis freedom's sound
That rings around,
  And brightens every ray,
On banner floats,
And trumpet-notes:
  On Independent day.

O who from home
Would fail to come
  And join the children's lay—
When praise we bring
To God our king,
  On Independent day.

For liberty,
Great God, to thee
  Our grateful thanks we pay;
For thanks, we know,
To thee, we owe,
  On Independent day.

While thunder breaks,
And music wakes
  Its patriotic lay,
At temple-gate
Our feet shall wait,
  On Independent day.

O Saviour, shine,
With beams divine,
  And take our sins away;
And give us grace
To seek thy face,
  On Independent day.

4. PRAYER.

5. SINGING.
[By the Choir.]

My country! 'tis of thee,
Sweet land of liberty—
  Of thee I sing:
Land, where my fathers died;
Land of the pilgrim's pride;
From every mountain-side,
  Let freedom ring.

My native country! thee—
Land of the noble free—
  Thy name I love:
I love thy rocks and rills,
Thy woods and templed hills;
My heart with rapture thrills,
  Like that above.

No more shall tyrants here
With haughty steps appear,
  And soldier-bands;
No more shall tyrants tread
Above the patriot dead—
No more our blood be shed
  By alien hands.

Let music swell the breeze,
And ring from all the trees
  Sweet freedom's song:
Let mortal tongues awake—
Let all that breathes partake—
Let rocks their silence break—
  The sound prolong.

Our fathers' God! to thee,
Author of liberty!
  To thee we sing;
Long may our land be bright
With freedom's holy light—
Protect us by thy might,
  Great God, our King!

6. ADDRESS TO THE CHILDREN.
By Rev. Dr. WISNER.

7. SINGING.
[By the Choir.]
Hosanna, Hosanna, Hosanna in the highest.
[By the Congregation.]
    Tune—DUKE STREET.
What are those soul reviving strains
That echo thus from Salem's plains?
What anthems loud, and louder still,
So sweetly sound from Zion's hill?
[By the Choir.]
Hosanna, Hosanna, Hosanna in the highest.
[By the Congregation.]
Behold a youthful chorus sings
Hosanna to the King of kings,
The Saviour comes—and they proclaim
Salvation sent in Jesus' name.
[By the Choir.]
Blessed is he who cometh in the name of the Lord.
[By the Congregation.]
Proclaim hosannas loud and clear,
See David's Son and Lord appear,
All praise on earth to him be given,
And glory shout through highest heaven.
[By the Choir.]
Hosanna, Hosanna, Hosanna in the highest.

8. CONCLUDING PRAYER AND BENEDICTION.

THE FIRST PRINTING OF *AMERICA*   11¾ × 6¾ inches
Acquired in 1948 with the F. B. Bemis Fund

SAMUEL FRANCIS SMITH:
ORIGINAL DRAFT OF *AMERICA*
6½ × 3 inches
Given in 1914 by the
Reverend D. A. W. Smith, H 1859

By the frame of the government under which we live, this same people have wisely given their public servants but little power for mischief; and have, with equal wisdom, provided for the return of that little to their own hands at very short intervals.

While the people ~~retain their virtue and vigilance~~ retain their virtue and vigilance, no administration ~~by any extreme of wickedness or folly~~, can very seriously injure the government in the short space of four years.

~~My~~ My countrymen, one and all, think calmly and well, upon this whole subject. Nothing valuable can be lost by taking time. ~~~~ If there be an object to *hurry* any of you, in hot haste, to a step which you would never take *deliberately*, that object will be frustrated by taking time; but no good object can be frustrated by it. Such of you as are now dissatisfied, still have the old Constitution unimpaired, and, on the sensitive point, the laws of your own framing under it; while the new administration will have no immediate power, if it would, to change either. If it were admitted that you who are dissatisfied, hold the right side in the dispute, there still is no single good reason for precipitate action. Intelligence, patriotism, Christianity, and a firm reliance on Him, who has never yet forsaken this favored land, are still competent to adjust, in the best way, all our present difficulty.

In *your* hands, my dissatisfied fellow countrymen, and not in *mine*, is the momentous issue of civil war. The government will not assail *you*. You can have no conflict, without being yourselves the aggressors. *You* have no oath registered in Heaven to destroy the government, while *I* shall have the most solemn one to "preserve, protect and defend" it.

I am loth to close. We are not enemies, but friends. We must not be enemies. Though passion may have strained, it must not break our bonds of affection. The mystic chords of memory, stretching from every battle field and patriot grave to every living heart and hearth-stone all over this broad land, will yet swell the chorus of the Union, when again touched, as surely they will be, by the better angels of our nature.

END

CLOSE OF LINCOLN'S FIRST INAUGURAL ADDRESS
PROOFS REVISED BY JOHN G. NICOLAY   12 × 8¾ inches
Received in 1914 with the autograph collection of Charles Eliot Norton, H 1846

RICHARD MATHER, BY JOHN FOSTER
The first American woodcut portrait, 1670

COTTON MATHER, BY PETER PELHAM 13⅝ × 9⅞ inches
The first American mezzotint portrait, 1727

Cottonus Matherus
*S. Theologiæ Doctor Regiæ Societatis Londinensis Socius
et Ecclesiæ apud Bostonum Nov-Anglorum nuper Præpositus.*
Ætatis Suæ LXV, MDCCXXVII.   P. Pelham ad vivum pinxit ab origin Fecit et ex

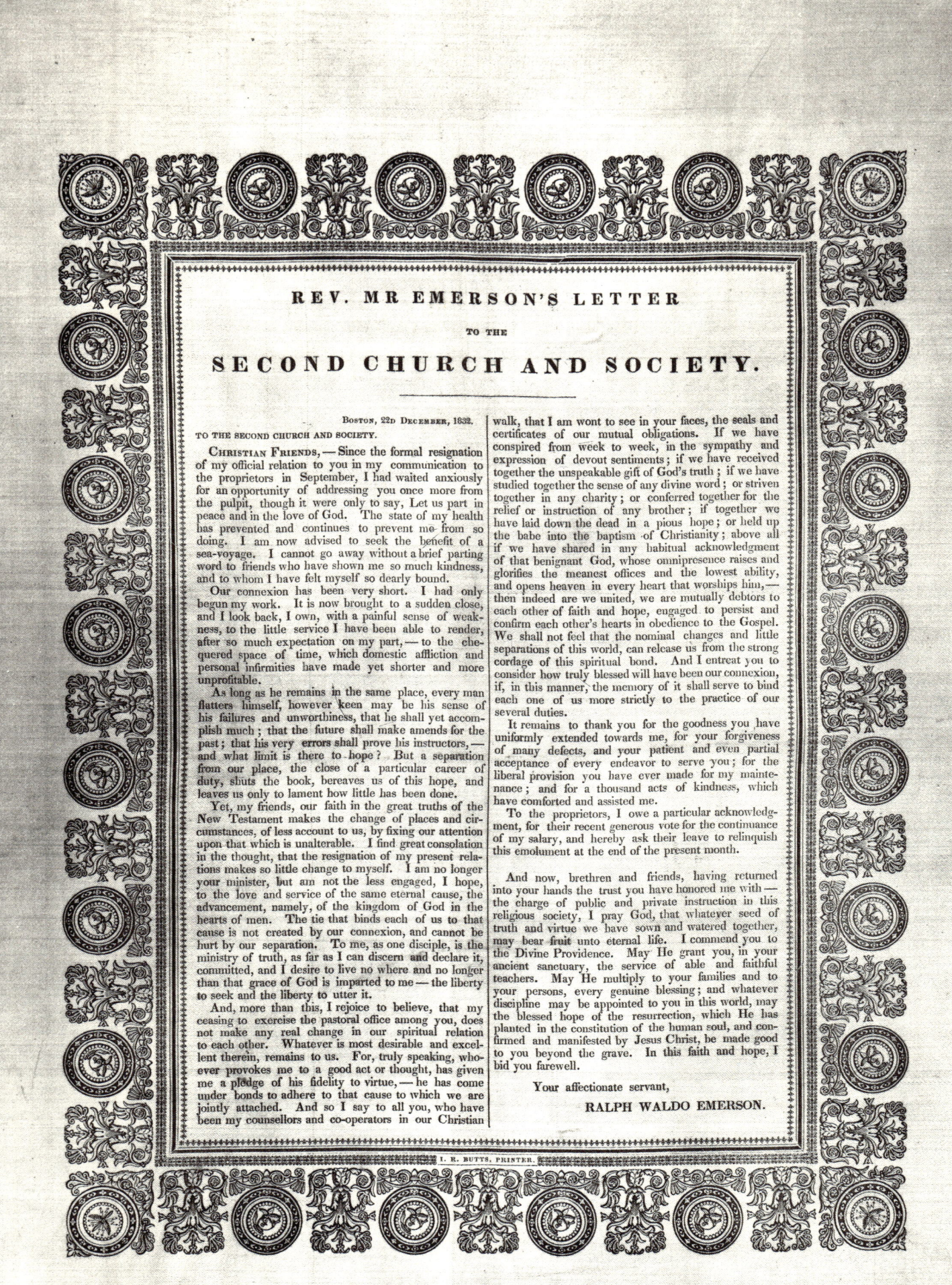

REV. MR EMERSON'S LETTER
TO THE
SECOND CHURCH AND SOCIETY.

BOSTON, 22D DECEMBER, 1832.

TO THE SECOND CHURCH AND SOCIETY.

CHRISTIAN FRIENDS,—Since the formal resignation of my official relation to you in my communication to the proprietors in September, I had waited anxiously for an opportunity of addressing you once more from the pulpit, though it were only to say, Let us part in peace and in the love of God. The state of my health has prevented and continues to prevent me from so doing. I am now advised to seek the benefit of a sea-voyage. I cannot go away without a brief parting word to friends who have shown me so much kindness, and to whom I have felt myself so dearly bound.

Our connexion has been very short. I had only begun my work. It is now brought to a sudden close, and I look back, I own, with a painful sense of weakness, to the little service I have been able to render, after so much expectation on my part,—to the chequered space of time, which domestic affliction and personal infirmities have made yet shorter and more unprofitable.

As long as he remains in the same place, every man flatters himself, however keen may be his sense of his failures and unworthiness, that he shall yet accomplish much; that the future shall make amends for the past; that his very errors shall prove his instructors,—and what limit is there to hope? But a separation from our place, the close of a particular career of duty, shuts the book, bereaves us of this hope, and leaves us only to lament how little has been done.

Yet, my friends, our faith in the great truths of the New Testament makes the change of places and circumstances, of less account to us, by fixing our attention upon that which is unalterable. I find great consolation in the thought, that the resignation of my present relations makes so little change to myself. I am no longer your minister, but am not the less engaged, I hope, to the love and service of the same eternal cause, the advancement, namely, of the kingdom of God in the hearts of men. The tie that binds each of us to that cause is not created by our connexion, and cannot be hurt by our separation. To me, as one disciple, is the ministry of truth, as far as I can discern and declare it, committed, and I desire to live no where and no longer than that grace of God is imparted to me — the liberty to seek and the liberty to utter it.

And, more than this, I rejoice to believe, that my ceasing to exercise the pastoral office among you, does not make any real change in our spiritual relation to each other. Whatever is most desirable and excellent therein, remains to us. For, truly speaking, whoever provokes me to a good act or thought, has given me a pledge of his fidelity to virtue,—he has come under bonds to adhere to that cause to which we are jointly attached. And so I say to all you, who have been my counsellors and co-operators in our Christian walk, that I am wont to see in your faces, the seals and certificates of our mutual obligations. If we have conspired from week to week, in the sympathy and expression of devout sentiments; if we have received together the unspeakable gift of God's truth; if we have studied together the sense of any divine word; or striven together in any charity; or conferred together for the relief or instruction of any brother; if together we have laid down the dead in a pious hope; or held up the babe into the baptism of Christianity; above all if we have shared in any habitual acknowledgment of that benignant God, whose omnipresence raises and glorifies the meanest offices and the lowest ability, and opens heaven in every heart that worships him,—then indeed are we united, we are mutually debtors to each other of faith and hope, engaged to persist and confirm each other's hearts in obedience to the Gospel. We shall not feel that the nominal changes and little separations of this world, can release us from the strong cordage of this spiritual bond. And I entreat you to consider how truly blessed will have been our connexion, if, in this manner, the memory of it shall serve to bind each one of us more strictly to the practice of our several duties.

It remains to thank you for the goodness you have uniformly extended towards me, for your forgiveness of many defects, and your patient and even partial acceptance of every endeavor to serve you; for the liberal provision you have ever made for my maintenance; and for a thousand acts of kindness, which have comforted and assisted me.

To the proprietors, I owe a particular acknowledgment, for their recent generous vote for the continuance of my salary, and hereby ask their leave to relinquish this emolument at the end of the present month.

And now, brethren and friends, having returned into your hands the trust you have honored me with — the charge of public and private instruction in this religious society, I pray God, that whatever seed of truth and virtue we have sown and watered together, may bear fruit unto eternal life. I commend you to the Divine Providence. May He grant you, in your ancient sanctuary, the service of able and faithful teachers. May He multiply to your families and to your persons, every genuine blessing; and whatever discipline may be appointed to you in this world, may the blessed hope of the resurrection, which He has planted in the constitution of the human soul, and confirmed and manifested by Jesus Christ, be made good to you beyond the grave. In this faith and hope, I bid you farewell.

Your affectionate servant,
RALPH WALDO EMERSON.

I. R. BUTTS, PRINTER.

CHRISTOPHER PEARSE CRANCH: CARICATURE TO ILLUSTRATE EMERSON
Given in 1925 by Miss Elizabeth Gaskell Norton

American Literature

THE collections in American literature range far beyond the regional boundaries of New England, but we have chosen mainly to display in these pages a selection of local writers in order to suggest the depth of Harvard's resources. New England authors and those with Harvard connections have received the special attention of the university library for at least as long as American literature has been regarded as an academic subject in its own right.

Largely within the last twenty-five years the Houghton Library has acquired the most extensive holdings anywhere of the literary papers and correspondence of the New England school. These were added to already strong runs of first and early editions, and with them have come whole libraries of association copies, all the more interesting because they reveal the intricate interrelation of these men. The collection still strives to keep pace with the constantly increasing interest in our national literature.

RALPH WALDO EMERSON: *LETTER TO THE SECOND CHURCH AND SOCIETY*, 1832   18⅛ × 12⅛ inches
Special edition printed on satin
Deposited in 1943 by the Ralph Waldo Emerson Memorial Association

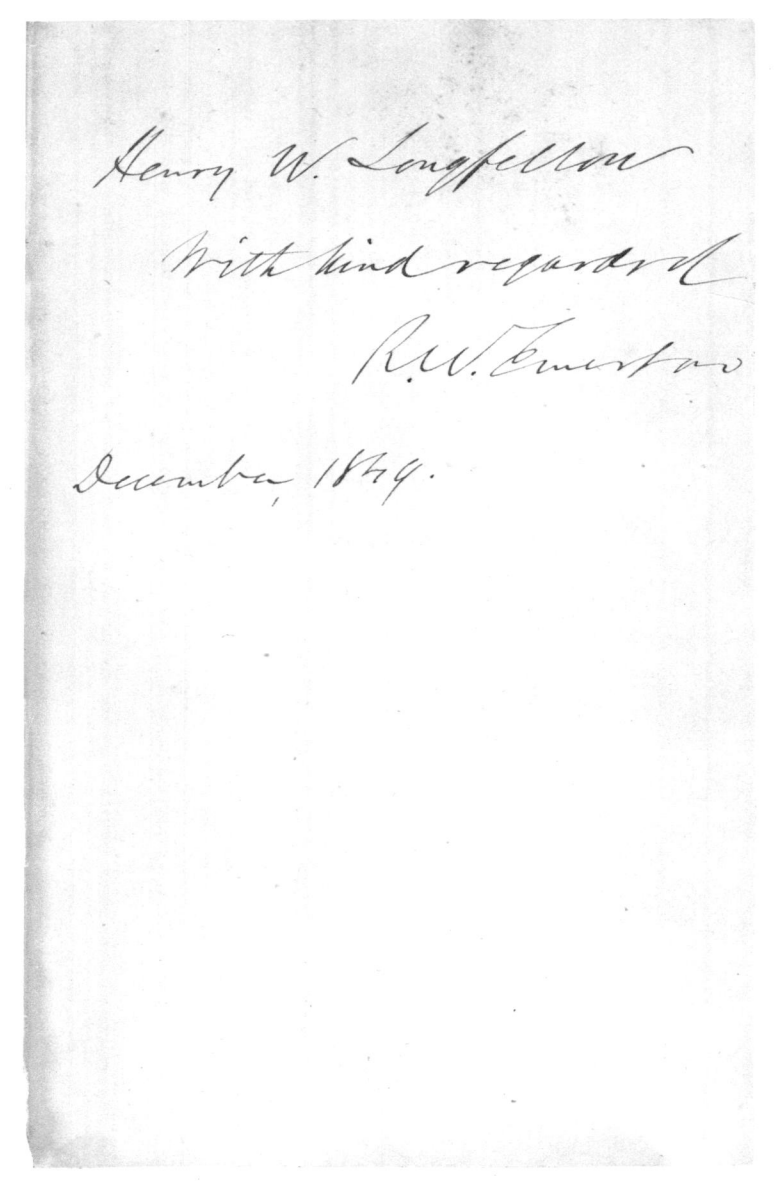

RALPH WALDO EMERSON: *REPRESENTATIVE MEN*,
1850   7¼ × 4½ inches
Deposited in 1954 by the Trustees of the Longfellow House Trust

LOUISA MAY ALCOTT: *FLOWER FABLES*, 1855
6⅞ × 3⅞ inches   The dedication copy
Deposited in 1944 by the Ralph Waldo Emerson Memorial Association

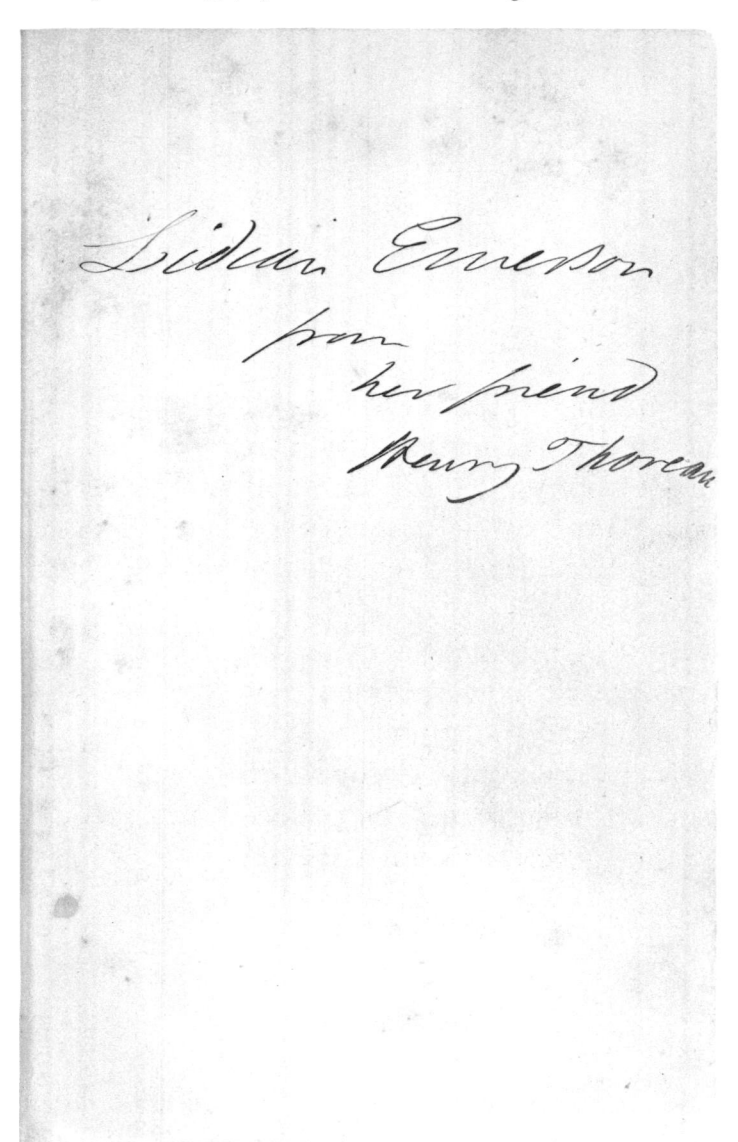

HENRY DAVID THOREAU: *WALDEN*, 1854
7 × 4¼ inches   Deposited in 1944 by the Ralph Waldo Emerson Memorial Association

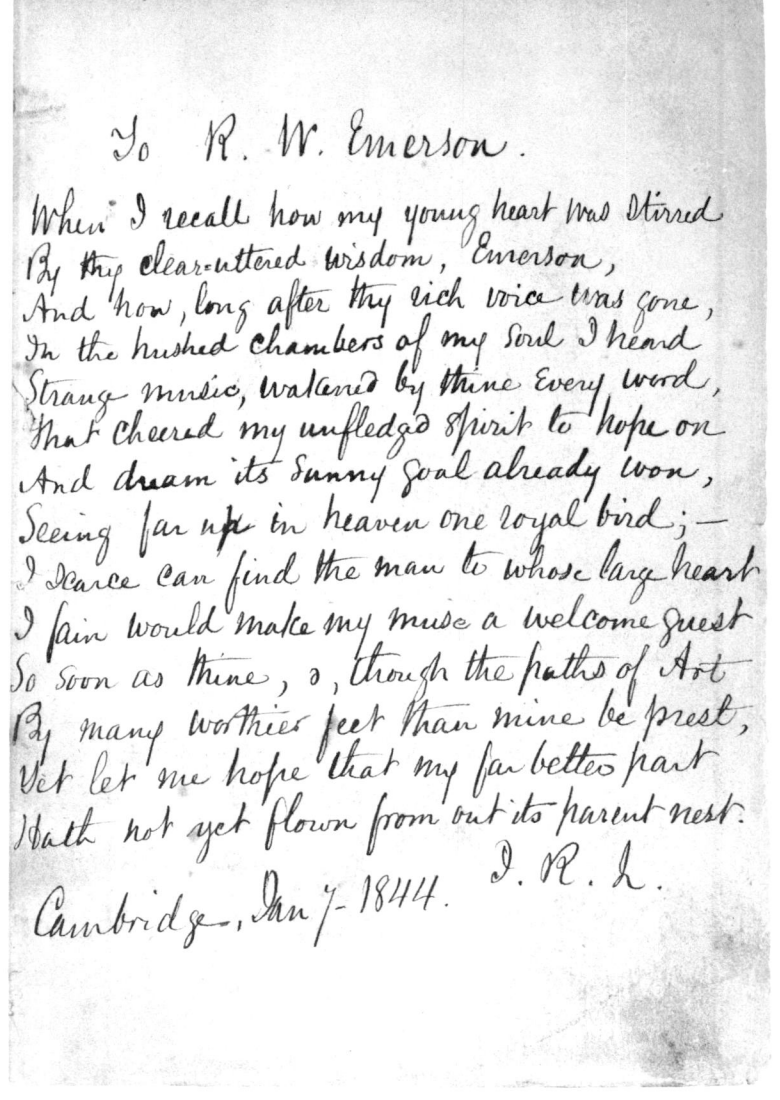

JAMES RUSSELL LOWELL: *POEMS*, 1844   7 × 4¾ inches
Deposited in 1944 by the Ralph Waldo Emerson Memorial Association

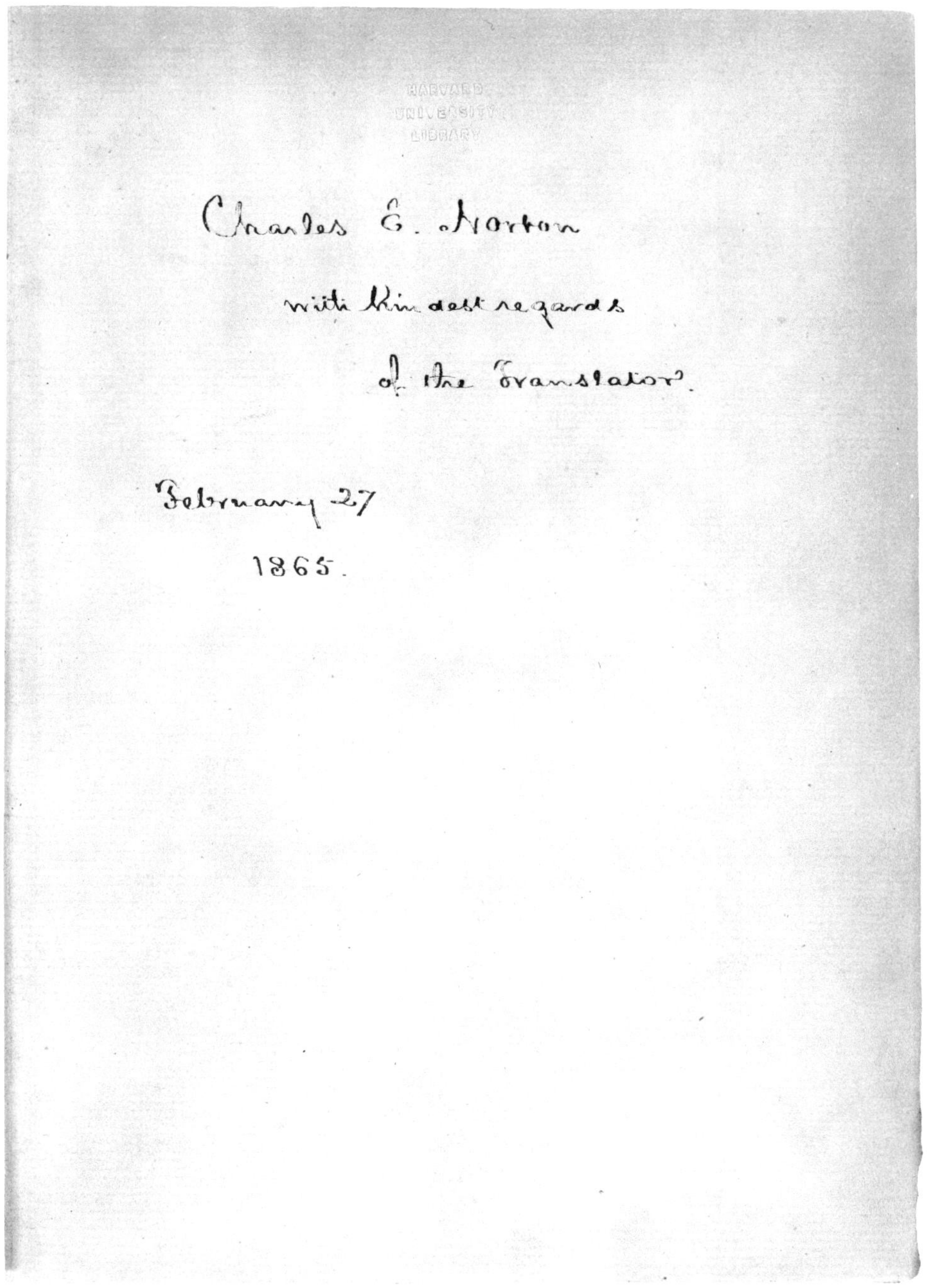

HENRY WADSWORTH LONGFELLOW: PRIVATE EDITION OF
THE DIVINE COMEDY, 1865   10 × 7 inches
    Acquired in 1905 from the library of Charles Eliot Norton, H 1846

OLIVER WENDELL HOLMES:
ELSIE VENNER, 1861   7¼ × 4½ inches
    Deposited in 1954 by the Trustees of the
    Longfellow House Trust

WILLIAM DEAN HOWELLS:
THE RISE OF SILAS LAPHAM,
1885   7⅜ × 4½ inches
    Bequeathed in 1963 by
    Mrs. A. Kingsley Porter

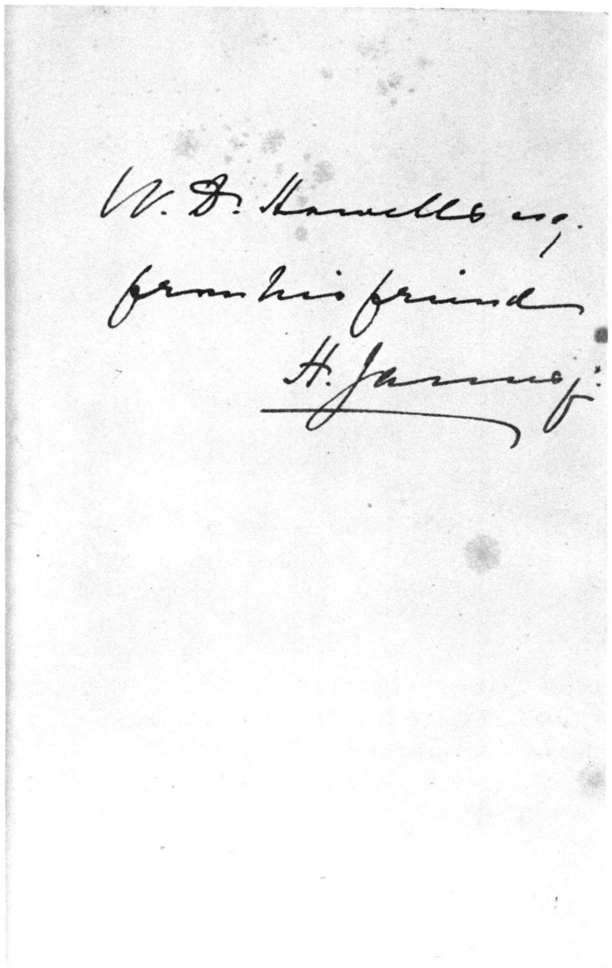

A GALAXY OF
PRESENTATION
COPIES

HENRY JAMES: *A PASSIONATE PILGRIM*,
1875   7⅜ × 4½ inches
    Given in 1953 by Miss Mildred Howells

American Literature   105

HERMAN MELVILLE: HOLOGRAPH OF *BILLY BUDD* 7 × 5½ inches
Given in 1938 by Eleanor Melville Metcalf

OWEN CHASE: *SHIPWRECK OF THE WHALE-SHIP ESSEX*, 1821 6½ × 7⅜ inches
Annotated and completed by Herman Melville
Given in 1960 by Alfred C. Berol, H 1913

Preface.

When a writer calls his work a Romance, it need hardly be observed that he wishes to claim a certain latitude, both as to its fashion and material, which he would not have felt himself entitled to assume, had he professed to be writing a novel. The latter form of composition is presumed to aim at a very minute fidelity, not merely to the possible, but to the probable and ordinary course of man's experience. The former — while, as a work of art, it must rigidly subject itself to laws, and while it sins unpardonably, so far as it may swerve aside from the truth of the human heart — has fairly a right to present that truth under circumstances, to a great extent, of the writer's own choosing or creation. If he think fit, also, he may so manage his atmospherical medium as to bring out or mellow the lights and deepen and enrich the shadows of the picture. He will be wise, no doubt, to make a very moderate use of the privileges here stated, and, especially, to mingle the Marvellous rather as a slight, delicate, and evanescent flavor, than as any portion of the actual substance of the dish offered to the Public. He can hardly be said, however, to commit a literary crime, even if he disregard this caution.

In the present work, the Author has proposed to himself (but with what success, fortunately, it is not for him to judge) to keep undeviatingly within his immunities. The point of view in which this Tale comes under the Romantic definition, lies in the attempt to connect a bygone time with the very Present that is flitting away from us. It is a Legend, prolonging itself, from an epoch now gray in the distance, down into our own broad daylight,

NATHANIEL HAWTHORNE: HOLOGRAPH OF *THE HOUSE OF THE SEVEN GABLES*, 1851
Bequeathed in 1915 by Mrs. James T. Fields

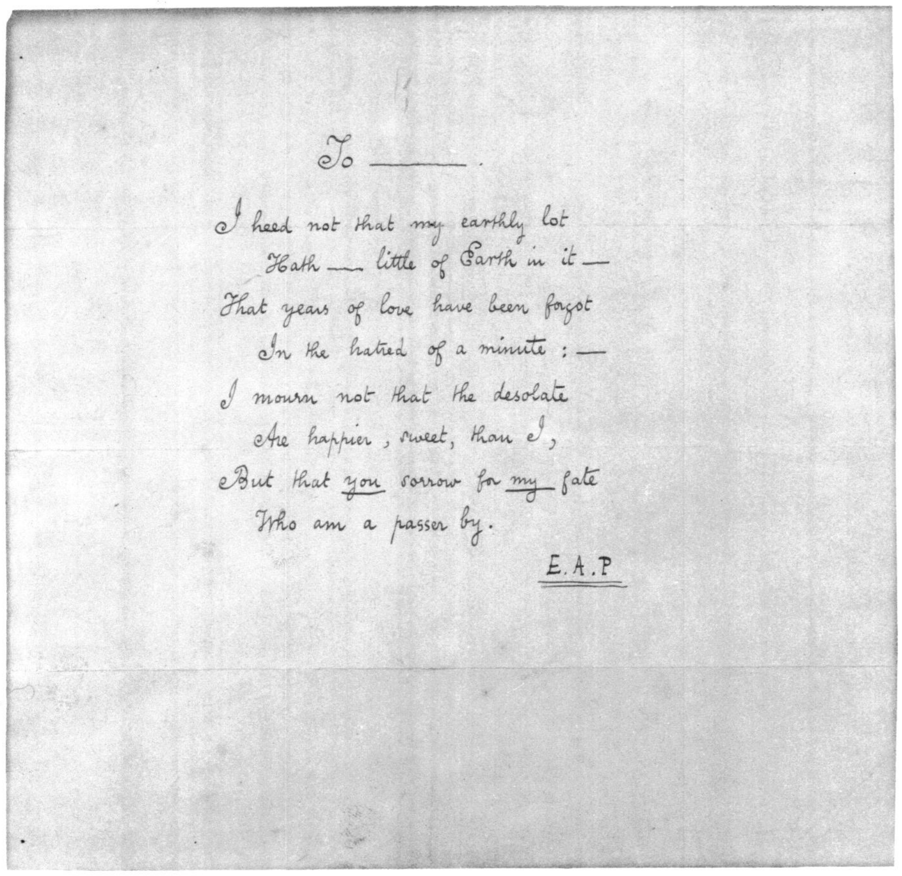

EDGAR ALLAN POE: HOLOGRAPH OF *TO – – –*   7¾ × 7¾ inches
Given in 1960 by Merrill Griswold, H 1907

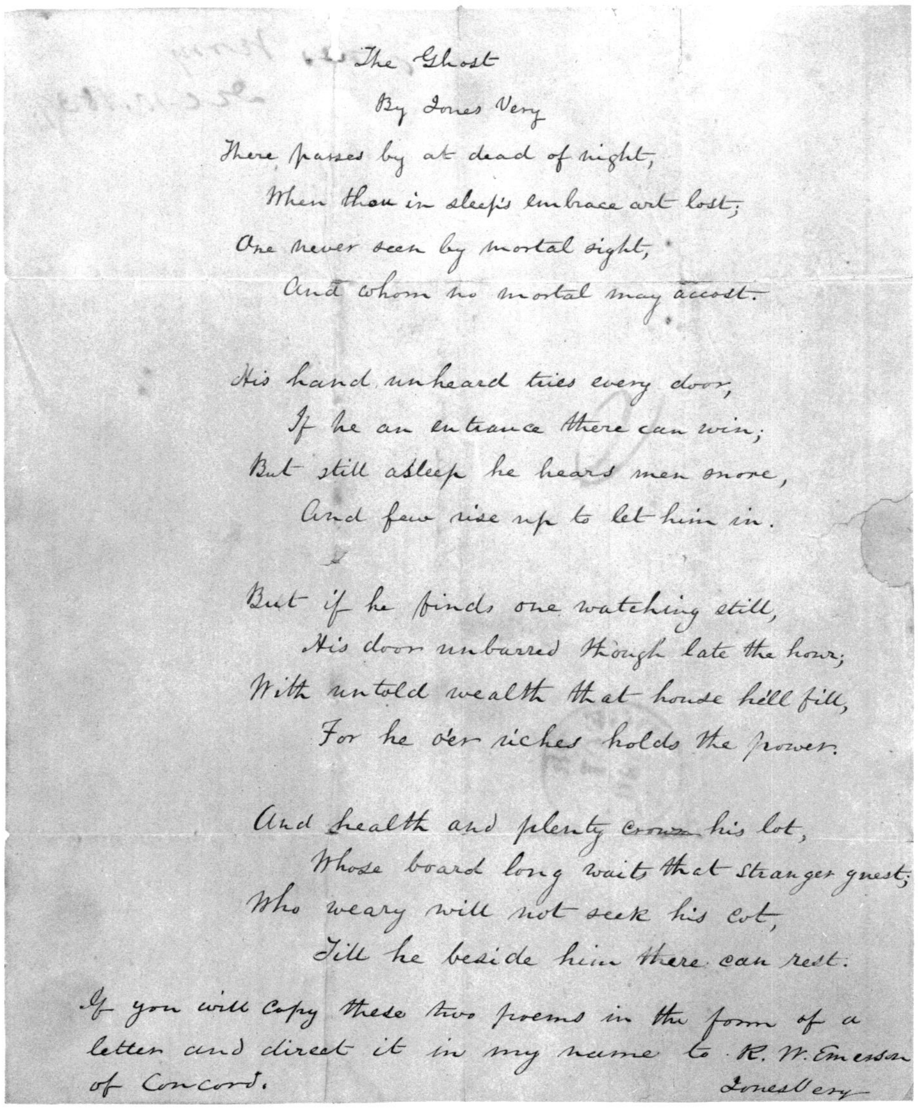

JONES VERY: AUTOGRAPH LETTER TO C. B. FARNSWORTH,
10 DECEMBER 1839   9¾ × 7¾ inches
Given in 1961 by W. B. Farnsworth

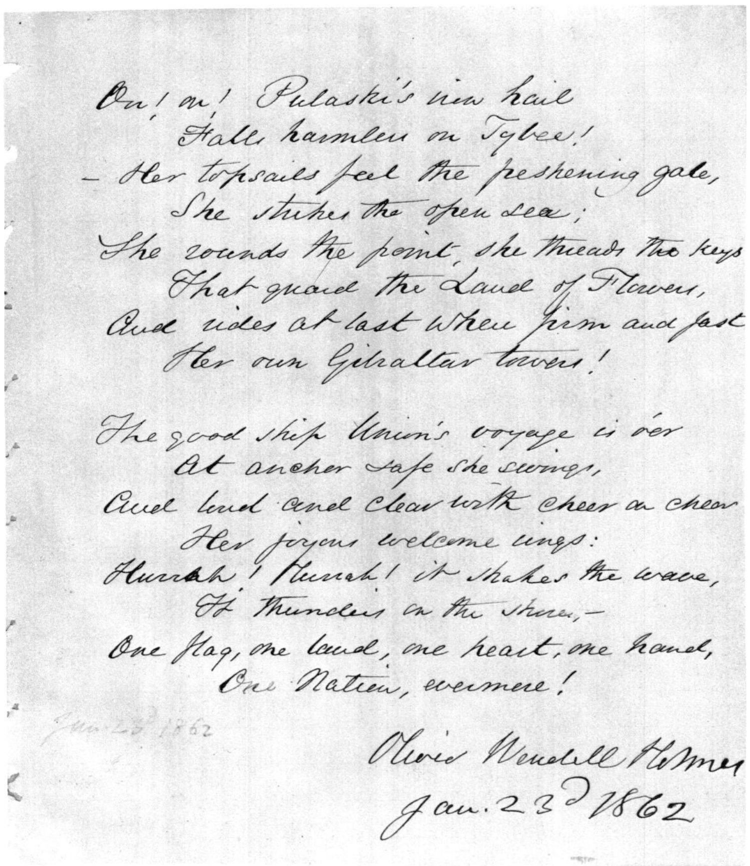

JAMES RUSSELL LOWELL: *COMMEMORATION ODE*, 1865
9⅝ × 6¾ inches   Copy inscribed to Oliver Wendell Holmes
Given in 1951 by Mr. and Mrs. Edward Jackson Holmes, H 1895

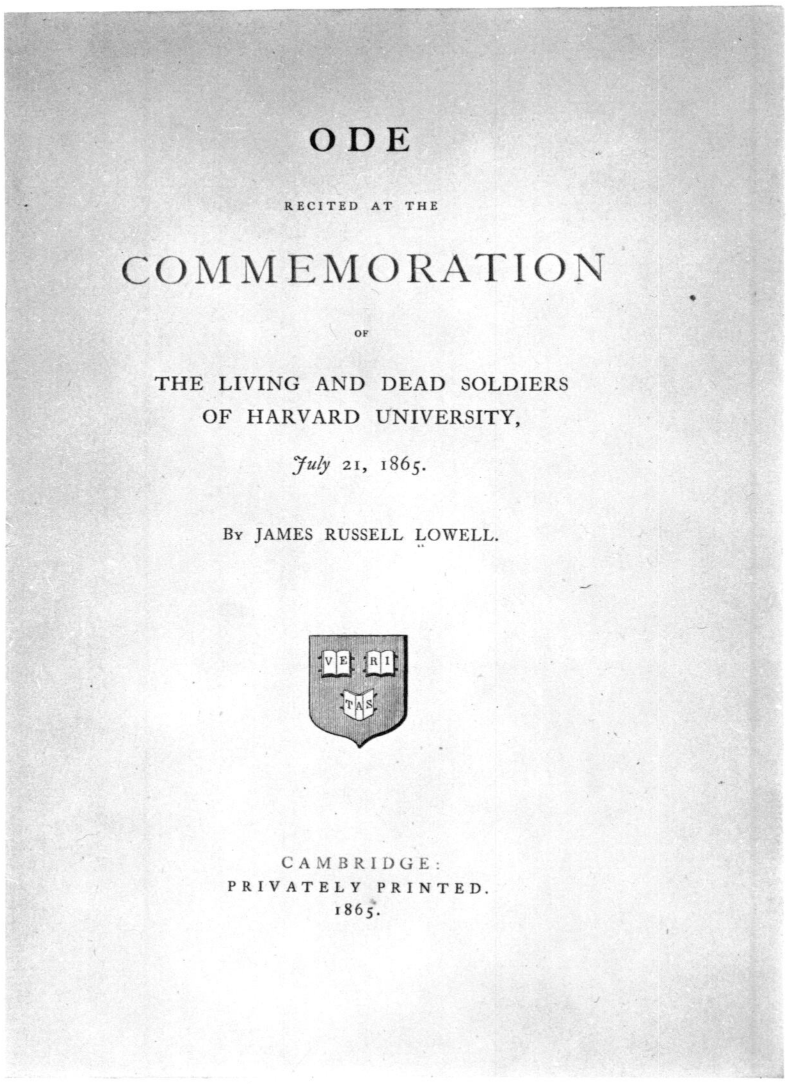

OLIVER WENDELL HOLMES: HOLOGRAPH OF
THE VOYAGE OF THE GOOD SHIP UNION, 1865
7¾ × 6⅜ inches
Given in 1871 by James T. Fields, A.M. (Hon.) 1858

HENRY WADSWORTH LONGFELLOW: FIRST DRAFT OF
HIAWATHA, 1854   10 × 6⅜ inches
Deposited in 1954 by the Trustees of the Longfellow House Trust

HENRY DAVID THOREAU: HOLOGRAPH TRANSLATION OF
AESCHYLUS   9¾ × 7¾ inches
Acquired in 1965 with the Amy Lowell Fund

JOHN GREENLEAF WHITTIER: HOLOGRAPH OF *MEMORIES*
10 × 7¼ inches   Bequeathed in 1915 by Mrs. James T. Fields

HENRY ADAMS: HOLOGRAPH OF TWO LETTERS ON
A PRUSSIAN GYMNASIUM, 1859   8¼ × 6¾ inches
Given in 1941 in memory of Henry Adams, H 1858, by his niece,
Louisa Hooper Thoron

American Literature   109

Lecture XIX

Other Characteristics.

We have wormed our way back, after our excursion through mysticism and philosophy, to where we were before: — the uses of religion (its uses) to the individual who has it, and the uses of the individual himself to the world, are the best arguments that truth is in it. We return to the empirical philosophy: The true is what works well, even though the qualification "on the

WILLIAM JAMES: HOLOGRAPH OF *THE VARIETIES OF RELIGIOUS EXPERIENCE*
Presented in 1928 by the James Family

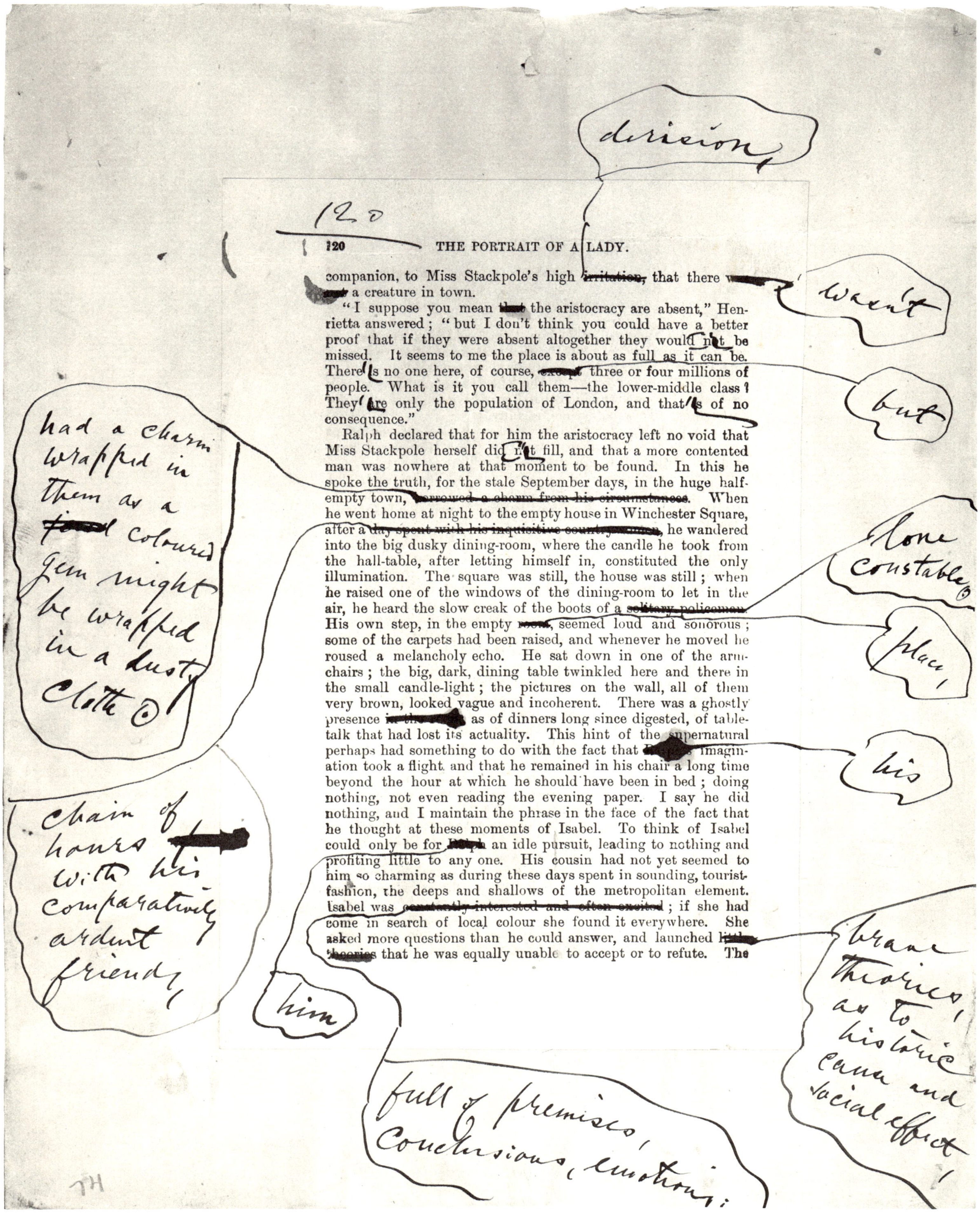

120 THE PORTRAIT OF A LADY.

companion, to Miss Stackpole's high ~~irritation~~ *derision*, that there ~~was~~ *wasn't* ~~a~~ creature in town.

"I suppose you mean ~~that~~ the aristocracy are absent," Henrietta answered; "*but* I don't think you could have a better proof that if they were absent altogether they would *n't* be missed. It seems to me the place is about as full as it can be. There *'s* no one here, of course, ~~except~~ *but* three or four millions of people. What is it you call them—the lower-middle class? They *'re* only the population of London, and that *'s* of no consequence."

Ralph declared that for him the aristocracy left no void that Miss Stackpole herself did *n't* fill, and that a more contented man was nowhere at that moment to be found. In this he spoke the truth, for the stale September days, in the huge half-empty town, ~~borrowed a charm from his circumstances~~ *had a charm wrapped in them as a ~~faded~~ coloured gem might be wrapped in a dusty cloth.* When he went home at night to the empty house in Winchester Square, ~~after a day spent with his inquisitive countrywoman~~, he wandered into the big dusky dining-room, where the candle he took from the hall-table, after letting himself in, constituted the only illumination. The square was still, the house was still; when he raised one of the windows of the dining-room to let in the air, he heard the slow creak of the boots of a ~~solitary policeman~~ *lone constable*. His own step, in the empty ~~room~~ *place*, seemed loud and sonorous; some of the carpets had been raised, and whenever he moved he roused a melancholy echo. He sat down in one of the armchairs; the big, dark, dining table twinkled here and there in the small candle-light; the pictures on the wall, all of them very brown, looked vague and incoherent. There was a ghostly presence ~~in the~~ as of dinners long since digested, of table-talk that had lost its actuality. This hint of the supernatural perhaps had something to do with the fact that ~~his~~ imagination took a flight, and that he remained in his chair a long time beyond the hour at which he should have been in bed; doing nothing, not even reading the evening paper. I say he did nothing, and I maintain the phrase in the face of the fact that he thought at these moments of Isabel. To think of Isabel could only be for ~~Ralph~~ *him* an idle pursuit, leading to nothing and profiting little to any one. His cousin had not yet seemed to him so charming as during these days *chain of hours with his comparatively ardent friend* spent in sounding, tourist-fashion, the deeps and shallows of the metropolitan element. Isabel was ~~constantly interested and often excited~~ *full of premises, conclusions, emotions*; if she had come in search of local colour she found it everywhere. She asked more questions than he could answer, and launched ~~him~~ ~~theories~~ *brave theories as to historic cause and social effect* that he was equally unable to accept or to refute. The

---

HENRY JAMES: *THE PORTRAIT OF A LADY*
 Revised for the New York Edition
 Acquired in 1943 with the Norton Perkins Fund

American Literature

EDWIN ARLINGTON ROBINSON: *THE TORRENT AND THE NIGHT BEFORE*, 1896
 6¾ × 4 inches
 Given in 1919 by Talbot Aldrich, H 1892

EDWIN ARLINGTON ROBINSON: HOLOGRAPH NOTEBOOK 7¾ × 5¼ inches
 Given in 1939 by Louis V. Ledoux

ROBERT FROST: LAWRENCE HIGH SCHOOL *CLASS HYMN*, 1892
 7¾ × 10 inches
 The first printing, in the program of graduation exercises Given in 1963 by Parkman D. Howe, H 1911

112

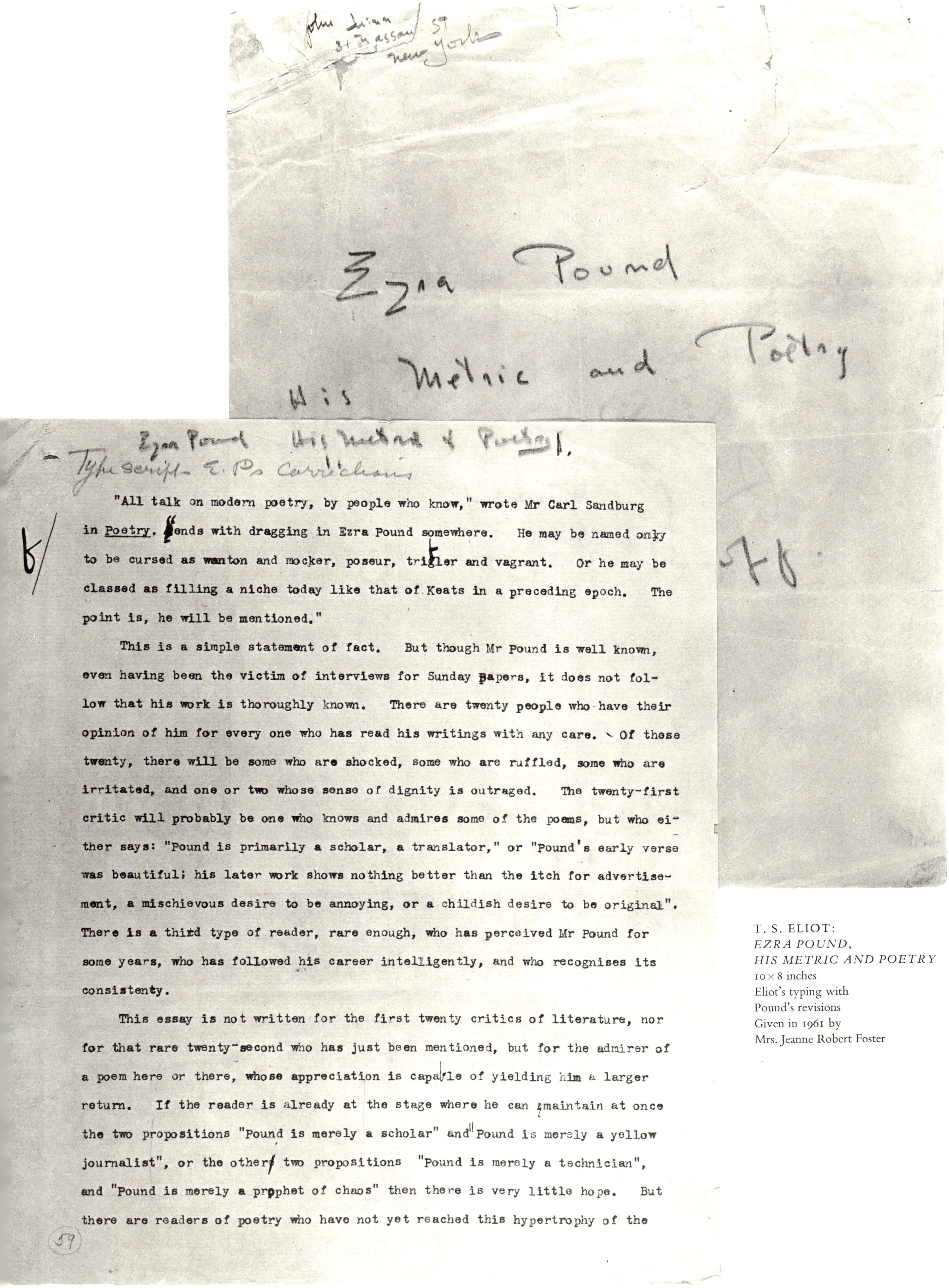

Ezra Pound

His Metric and Poetry

"All talk on modern poetry, by people who know," wrote Mr Carl Sandburg in *Poetry*, "ends with dragging in Ezra Pound somewhere. He may be named only to be cursed as wanton and mocker, poseur, trifler and vagrant. Or he may be classed as filling a niche today like that of Keats in a preceding epoch. The point is, he will be mentioned."

This is a simple statement of fact. But though Mr Pound is well known, even having been the victim of interviews for Sunday papers, it does not follow that his work is thoroughly known. There are twenty people who have their opinion of him for every one who has read his writings with any care. Of these twenty, there will be some who are shocked, some who are ruffled, some who are irritated, and one or two whose sense of dignity is outraged. The twenty-first critic will probably be one who knows and admires some of the poems, but who either says: "Pound is primarily a scholar, a translator," or "Pound's early verse was beautiful; his later work shows nothing better than the itch for advertisement, a mischievous desire to be annoying, or a childish desire to be original". There is a third type of reader, rare enough, who has perceived Mr Pound for some years, who has followed his career intelligently, and who recognises its consistency.

This essay is not written for the first twenty critics of literature, nor for that rare twenty-second who has just been mentioned, but for the admirer of a poem here or there, whose appreciation is capable of yielding him a larger return. If the reader is already at the stage where he can maintain at once the two propositions "Pound is merely a scholar" and "Pound is merely a yellow journalist", or the other two propositions "Pound is merely a technician", and "Pound is merely a prophet of chaos" then there is very little hope. But there are readers of poetry who have not yet reached this hypertrophy of the

T. S. ELIOT:
*EZRA POUND,
HIS METRIC AND POETRY*
10 × 8 inches
Eliot's typing with
Pound's revisions
Given in 1961 by
Mrs. Jeanne Robert Foster

CONRAD AIKEN: HOLOGRAPH NOTEBOOK 9 × 6¾ inches
Given in 1936 by Alfred Claghorn Potter, H 1889

lady it is your frailness which overthrows me
who being clumsy am without defence:
your least smile easily will unclose me
though i have closed myself as fingers,

lady it is your frailness which overthrows me

out of your slightest look is a flower born
having a fragrance more subtle than any fear;
in your most faint gesture are things which enclose me,
or which i cannot touch because they are too near

    VII
i do not know what it is about you that closes
and opens:only something in me understands
the voice of your eyes is deeper than all roses;
nobody,not even the rain,has such small hands

    IV
somewhere i have never travelled,a little beyond
any experience,your eyes have their silence;
in your most frail gesture are things which enclose me,
or which i cannot touch because they are too near

    II
your slightest look easily will unclose me
though i have closed myself as fingers,
you open always petal by petal myself as Spring opens
(touching skilfully,mysteriously)her first rose

    III
or if your wish be to close me,i and
my life will shut very beautifully,suddenly,
as when the heart of this flower imagines
it feels the snow carefully everywhere descending;

    V
nothing which we are to perceive in this world equals
the power of your intense fragility:whose texture
compels me with the colours of its countries
rendering death and forever with each breathing

i

E. E. CUMMINGS:
WORKING DRAFTS
Acquired in 1965 with
the Amy Lowell Fund

---

your slightest look easily will unclose me
though i have closed myself as fingers,   ) 2
you open always petal by petal myself as Spring opens
(touching skilfully,mysteriously)her first rose

or if your wish be to close me,i and
my life will shut very beautifully,suddenly,) 3
as when the heart of this flower imagines
it feels the snow carefully everywhere descending;

somewhere i have never travelled,a little beyond
any experience,your eyes have their silence:) 1
in your most frail gesture are things which enclose me,
or which i cannot touch because they are too near

nothing which we are to perceive in this world equals
the power of your intense fragility:whose texture   ) 4 X
compels me with the colour of its countries
rendering death and forever with each breathing

i am unable

i do not know what it is about you that closes
and opens:only something in me understands   ) 5
the voice of your eyes is deeper than all roses;
nobody,not even the rain,has such small hands

American Literature 115

THE DICKINSON CHILDREN, BY OTIS A. BULLARD 28×24 inches
Given in 1950 by Gilbert H. Montague, H 1901

Emily Dickinson

IN May, 1950, Gilbert H. Montague, H 1901, presented to Harvard the principal collection of Emily Dickinson papers, formerly in the possession of Martha Dickinson Bianchi and A. L. Hampson. It includes holograph poems, letters, ancillary papers, and the family library, and appropriate material continues to be added whenever possible. The collection is housed on the second floor of the Houghton Library in a special room containing furniture and pictures from the Dickinson home in Amherst, Massachusetts.

Many of Emily's manuscript poems were stitched in a series of forty 'packets' whose identity has been carefully preserved. About two-thirds of them are fair copies prepared by the poet, who usually threw away the earlier drafts, but from time to time a manuscript shows a text in the process of development, or a choice of readings.

The portrait of the three Dickinson children, Emily, Austin, and Lavinia, hangs in the room between portraits of the poet's father and mother. They are the work of an itinerant painter, Otis Allen Bullard (1816–1853), who visited Amherst in 1840.

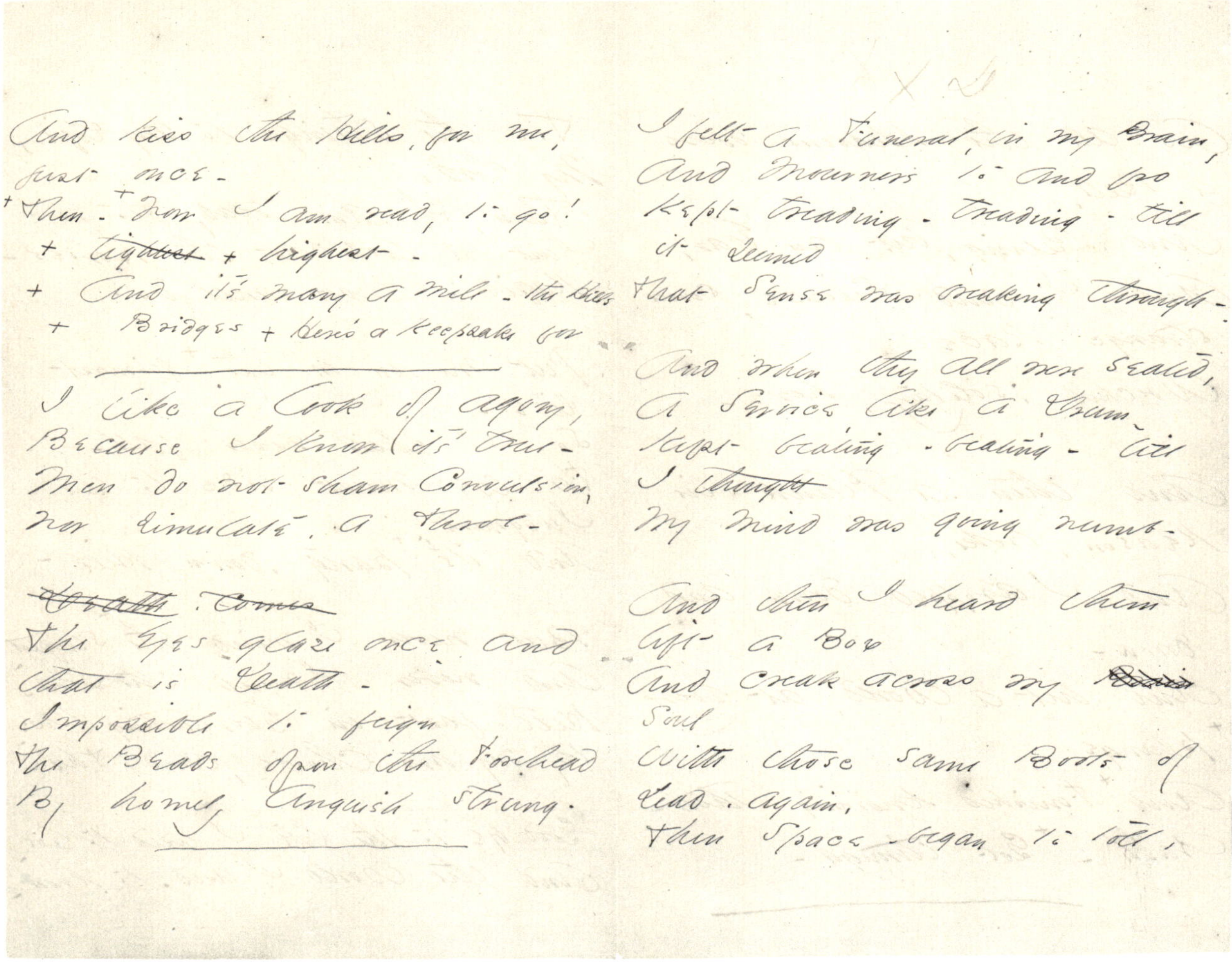

'I FELT A FUNERAL IN MY BRAIN' FROM PACKET XXXIII 8⅛ × 9⅞ inches
Given in 1950 by Gilbert H. Montague, H 1901

A LEAF FROM ONE OF WOLFE'S NOTEBOOKS
Given in 1947 by William B. Wisdom

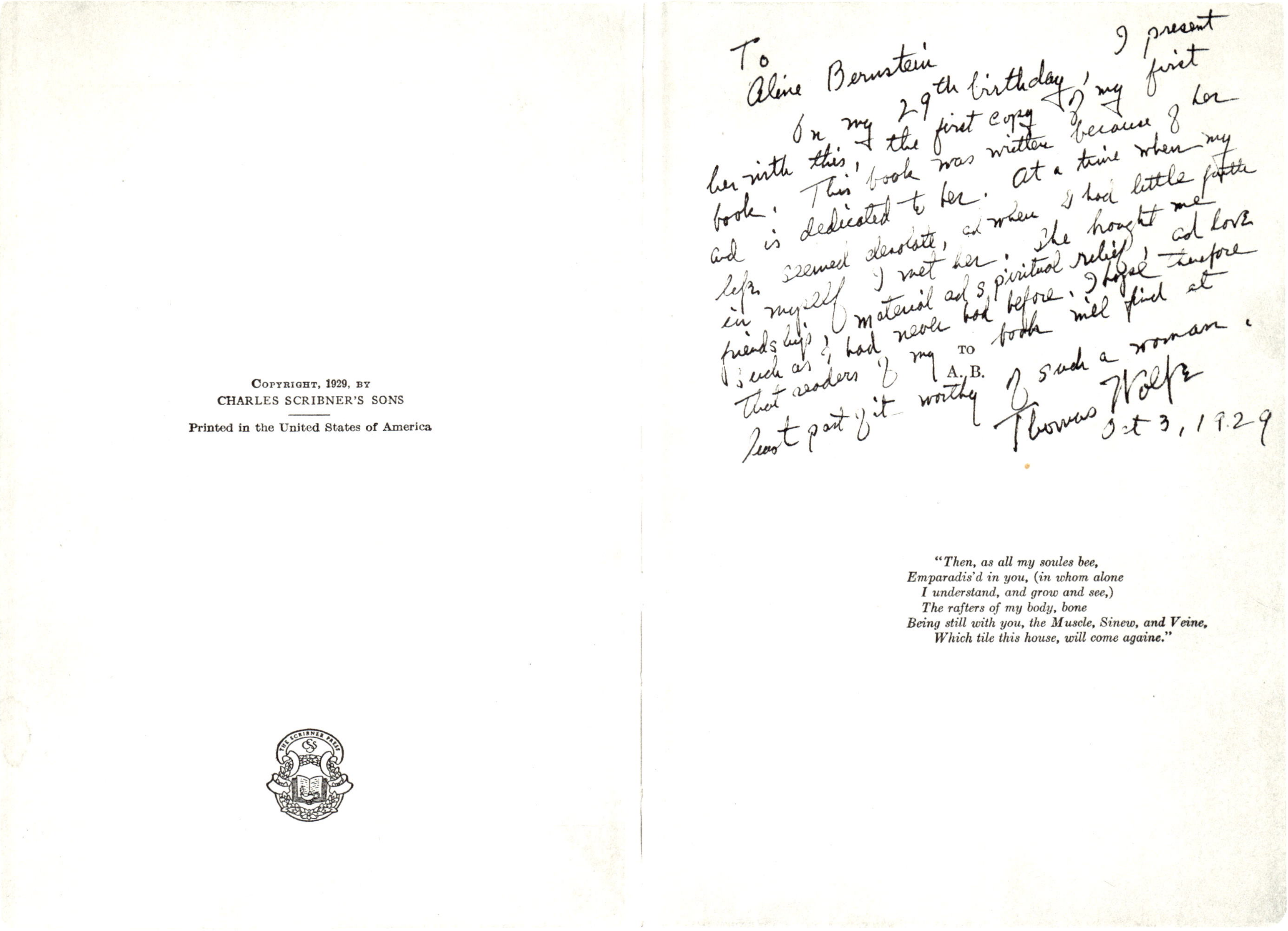

THE DEDICATION COPY OF *LOOK HOMEWARD, ANGEL*, 1929
7⅝ × 10¼ inches   Given in 1945 by Aline Bernstein

Thomas Wolfe

WHEN the Thomas Wolfe Collection of William B. Wisdom came to the Library in 1947, first as the deposit and later as the gift of Mr. Wisdom, the most convenient way to describe it was as a ton and a half of material. It contained all Wolfe's working papers and correspondence in his possession at the time of his death, together with his own library and a comprehensive collection of first and other editions of his works. The seventeen folio ledger books in which he wrote the first draft of *Look Homeward, Angel* were already in the Houghton Library, the gift in 1939 of Gabriel Wells. Books and manuscripts from many sources have been added to the basic collection.

The first page of one of Wolfe's exercises in total recall typifies the documents in the Wisdom Collection as a source that must be taken into account by every serious student of Wolfe. He crossed these notes out when he made use of them as raw material for the great saga of the Gant family, starting with his first novel, *Look Homeward, Angel*.

Canadiana

CANADIAN history has been intensively collected by the Harvard College Library since at least 1845, when the bequest of the Honorable William Prescott, H 1783, made it possible to secure a nearly complete run of Jesuit relations. Important additions were later made by the bequest of Francis Parkman, H 1844, and by many other donors.

But the great source of strength in recent years has been first the gifts and later the generous bequest of Dr. William Inglis Morse, a Canadian by birth and until his death in 1952 the Honorary Curator of Canadiana in the Harvard College Library. His benefactions capped an already remarkable collection, and the fund he established enables the library to maintain and enlarge its resources in a subject to which historians are devoting increasing attention.

VIEW OF QUEBEC, BY THOMAS JOHNSTON, CA. 1759   8 × 9¾ inches

END OF ARTICLES OF
AGREEMENT, COMPAGNIE
DES CENT ASSOCIÉS, 1627
6½ × 8½ inches
Acquired in 1956 with the Morse Fund

LAST PAGE OF LESCARBOT:
A DIEU AUX FRANCOIS [1606]
TITLE-PAGE OF BIENCOURT:
FACTUM DU PROCEZ, 1633
8⅛ × 11¼ inches
Given in 1948 by
Dr. William Inglis Morse

A MONSIEVR DE POV-
TRINCOVRT LIEVTENANT DE MONSIEVR
De Monts en la nouuelle France.
SONNET.

SCIPION ennuyé de la trompeuse vie
D'vn siecle corrompu, passa de ses vieux ans
Le chagrin au deduit des jardins & des champs,
Dedaignant les douceurs d'vne ingrate patrie.
Ton ame, POVTRINCOVRT, d'iniustice enne-
mie,
En nos mœurs corrompus ne prend nul passe temps,
Et comme Scipion tu cherches dés long temps
Vn seiour d'innocence eloigné de l'enuie.
Mais en ce poinct icy tu passes Scipion,
C'est que fuiant si loin des hommes la malice
Non seulement tu sers à la religion,
Mais tu t'acquiers encor vn renom glorieux:
Et l'autre s'escartant loin de ses enuieux
Se contenta d'auoir aux pieds foulé le vice.

Par MARC LESCARBOT Veruinois.

Escrit au Port Royal de l'Equille
le 24. d'Aoust 1606.

FACTVM
DV PROCEZ

Entre Messire Iean de Biencourt
Cheualier sieur de Poutrin-
court, Baron de S. Iust,
appellant d'vne part,

Et Pierre Biard, Euemond Massé & consorts,
soy disans Prestres de la Societé de
Iesus, intimez.

*Cœlum, non animum, mutant qui
trans mare currunt.*

M. DC. XIIII.

121

Dear Sir

Since our arrival in this Country, the news of my Father's death has reached me; I left him in so weak a condition, that it was not probable, we shou'd ever meet again; the general tenour of his conduct thro' life, has been extreamly upright, & benevolent; from whence one may hope, that little failings, & imperfections, were overbalanced by his many good Qualities. I am exceeding sorry, it so fell out, that I had it not in my power to assist him in his illness, and to leave my Mother in her distress, and the more, as her relations are not affectionate, and you are too far off to give her help. I have writ to Mr Fisher, to continue the Pensions, which my Father had assign'd to his Kindred, my easy circumstances enabling me to fulfill all his intentions.

We are order'd to attack Quebeck, a very nice operation. The fleet consists of 22 sail of the Line & many Frigates; the Army of 9000 men (in England it is called 12). We have 10 Battalions 3 Companies of Grenadiers, some Marines (if the Admiral can spare them), and 6 new rais'd Companies of North American Rangers, not compleat, & the worst Soldiers in the Universe; a great train of Artillery – Plenty of Provisions, Tools, & implements of all sorts. Three Brigadiers under me, all men of great Spirit; some Colonels of reputation; Carleton, for a Quarter Master General; and upon whom I chiefly rely for the Engineering part. Engineers very indifferent, and of little experience, but we have none better. The Regular Troops in Canada consists of 8 Battalions of old Foot, about 400 a Battalion & 40 Companies of Marines (or Colony Troops) 40 men a Company. They can gather together 8 or 10 thousand Canadians, and perhaps a thousand Indians. As they are attack'd on the side of Mont-real, by an Army of 12 thousand fighting men, they must necessarily divide their Force — but, as the loss of the Capital implys the loss of the Colony, their chief attention will naturally be there

BEGINNING OF AUTOGRAPH LETTER FROM JAMES WOLFE TO MAJOR WALTER WOLFE, LOUISBOURG, 19 MAY 1759 Given in 1945 by Dr. William Inglis Morse

and therefore, I reckon we may find at Quebeck, 6 Battalions, some Companies of Marines, 4 or 5 thousand Canadians, and some Indians, altogether not much inferior in Number to their Enemy. Rear Admiral Durelle with ten Sail, is gone up the River; he has orders to take such a station, as will effectually cut off all Succour; but as he sail'd late from Halifax (Le M'mey) there is reason to think, that some store Ships have already got up. If so, our difficulties are like to increase. I have sent a detachment with M.r Durelle, to assist his first operations; and to seize the Islands in those parts of the River, where the Navigation is most dangerous. This Admiral had positive instructions to watch the first opening of the River S.t Lawrence, & to push with his Squadron, as high as the Isle de Bic; and from thence to detach some small Ships to the Bason of Quebeck, that all might be taken & shown behind. The Admiral Commander in Chief, of the Fleet, is a zealous, brave Officer, I don't exactly know, what disposition he intends to make in the River after the junction of the two Squadrons, but I conclude he will send four, or five of his smallest Ships of the Line, to assist us at Quebeck, and remain with the rest at an anchor below the Isle aux Coudres, ready to fight whatever Fleet the Enemy may send to disturb us. The Town of Quebeck is poorly fortified, but the ground round about it, is rocky. To invest the Place, & cut off all communication with the Colony, it will be necessary to encamp with our Right to the River S.t Lawrence, and our left to the River S.t Charles; from the River S.t Charles to Beauport, the communication must be kept open, by strong entrenched Posts, & Redoubts; (the Enemy can pass that River at Low Water), and it will be proper to establish ourselves, with small entrenched Posts, from the Point of Levy, to la Chaudiere. It is the business of our naval Force, to be Masters of the River, both above, & below the Town.

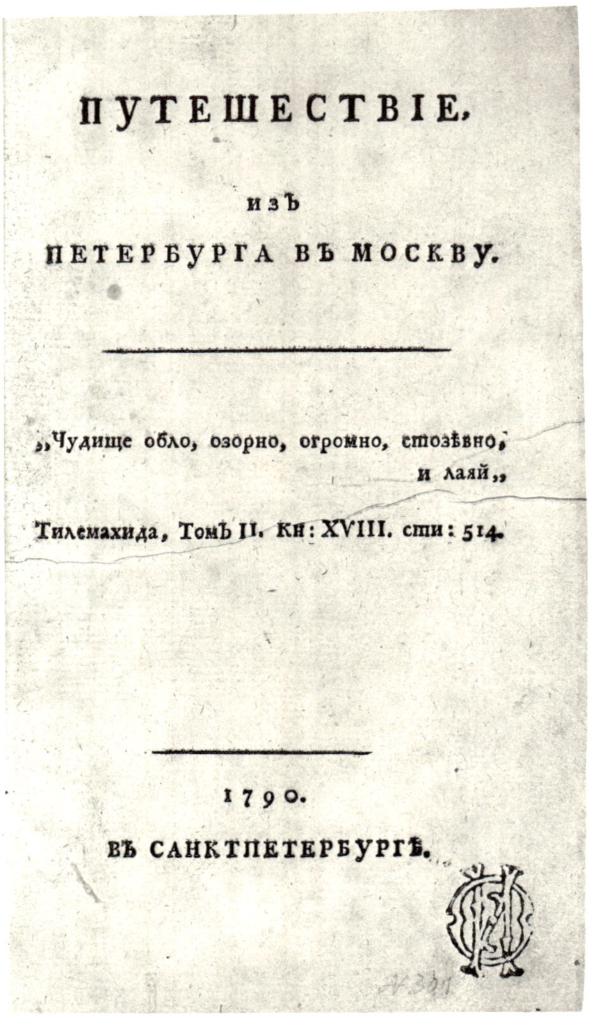

A. N. RADISHCHEV: *JOURNEY FROM PETERSBURG TO MOSCOW*, 1790 7¾ × 4⅜ inches
Suppressed first edition of an attack on the institution of serfdom, given in 1953 by Bayard L. Kilgour, Jr., H 1927

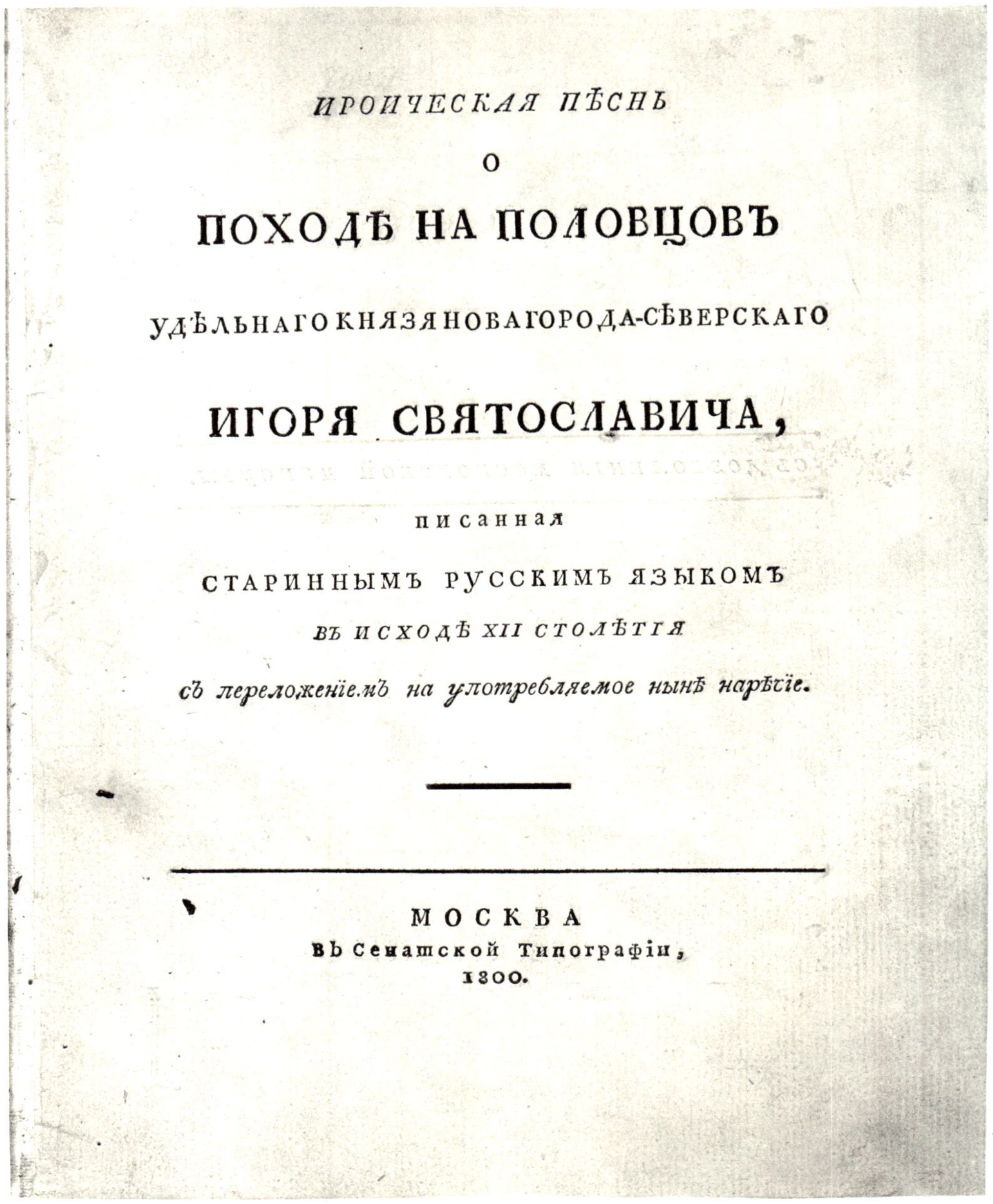

THE IGOR' TALE, 1800 9½ × 7½ inches
First edition, first issue, given in 1953 by Bayard L. Kilgour, Jr., H 1927

ALEKSANDR PUSHKIN: *EUGENE ONEGIN*, 1825 6½ × 3⅞ inches
The first edition of the first part, given in 1953 by Bayard L. Kilgour, Jr., H 1927

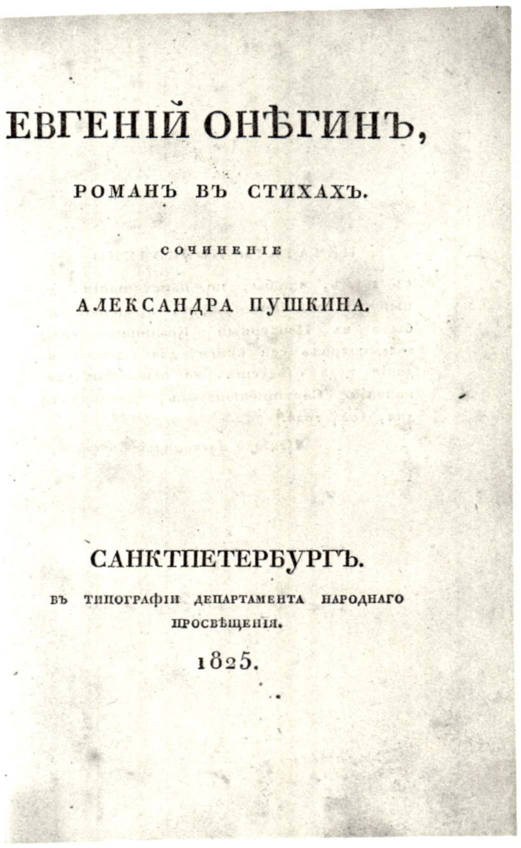

Russian Literature and History

RUSSIAN studies have long been a Harvard interest. As usual, this is reflected in the library's collections, just as recent acceleration in the field has its counterpart in increased library activity. The file of *Pravda* began to accumulate virtually as soon as publication commenced, and many similar sources have been acquired on a current basis.

But the great impulse towards retrospective acquisition was supplied by Bayard L. Kilgour, Jr., H 1927, who presented his magnificent library of Russian belles lettres and revolutionary ephemera together with funds to continue acquisition. While still an undergraduate, Mr. Kilgour was inspired by the scholar-librarians Archibald Cary Coolidge and Robert Pierpont Blake to visit Russia and to make Russian letters his sphere of collecting.

The Kilgour *Catalogue* with its more than 1,300 entries, published by the Harvard College Library in 1959, shows the range and depth of the literary resources now available.

THE FEDEROV *PRIMER*, LVOV, 1574
Unique copy of the first Russian grammar, given in 1953 by Bayard L. Kilgour, Jr., H 1927

Морю

Прощай, свободная стихія!
Въ послѣдній разъ передо мной
Ты катишь волны голубыя
И блещешь гордою красой.

Какъ друга ропотъ заунывный,
Какъ зовъ его въ прощальный часъ,
Твой грустный шумъ, твой шумъ призывный
Услышалъ я въ послѣдній разъ.

Моей души предѣлъ желанный!
Какъ часто по брегамъ твоимъ
Бродилъ я тихій и туманный,
Завѣтнымъ умысломъ томимъ!

Какъ я любилъ твои отзывы,
Глухіе звуки, бездны гласъ,
И тишину въ вечерній часъ,
И своенравные порывы!

Смиренный парусъ рыбарей,
Твоею прихотью хранимый,
Скользитъ отважно средь зыбей:
Но ты взыгралъ, неодолимый —
И стая тонетъ кораблей.

Не удалось навѣкъ оставить
Мнѣ скучный, неподвижный брегъ,
Тебя восторгами поздравить
И по хребтамъ твоимъ направить
Мой поэтическій побѣгъ!

Ты ждалъ, ты звалъ... я былъ окованъ;
Вотще рвалась душа моя;

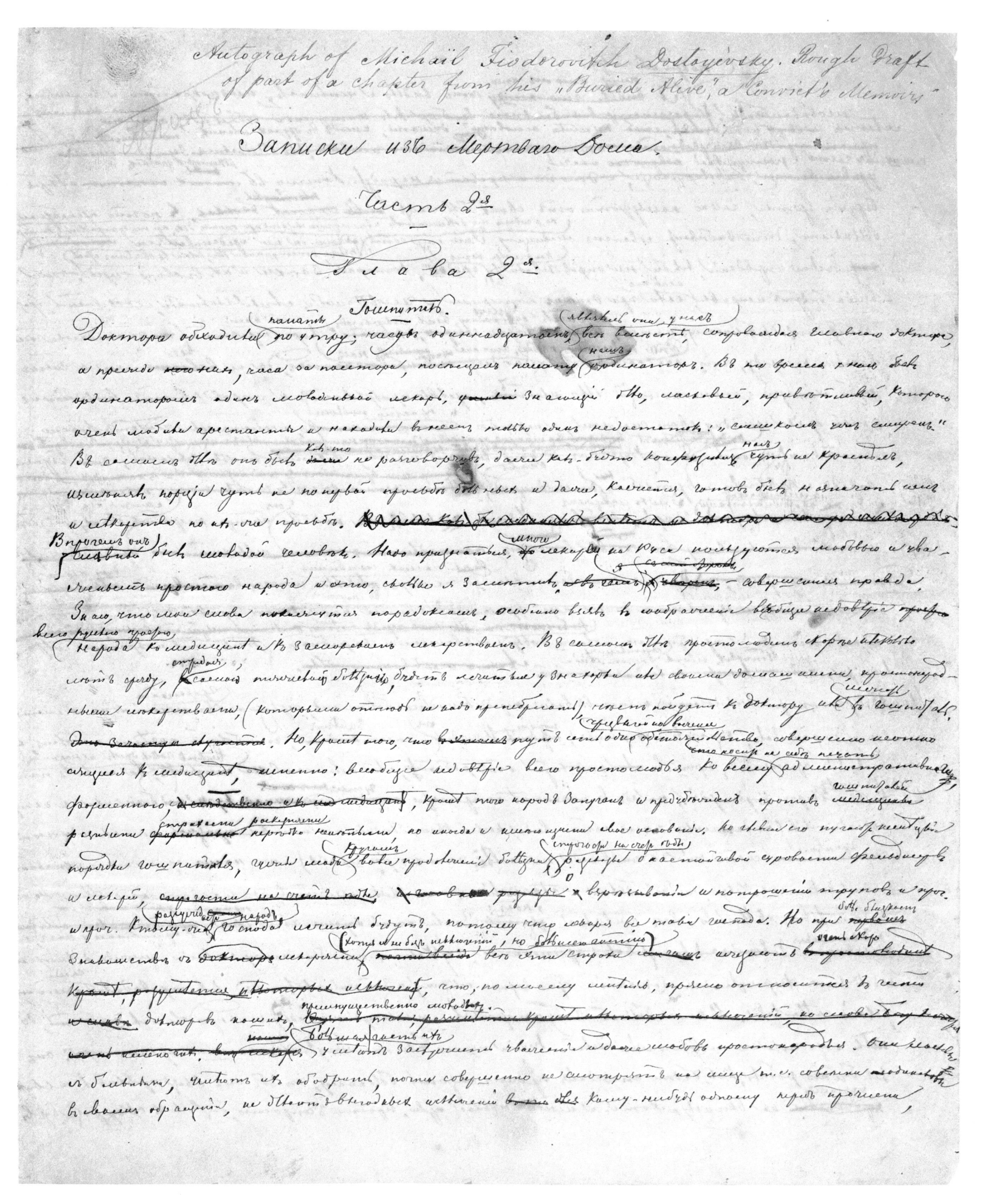

FEDOR DOSTOEVSKII: AUTOGRAPH MS., *THE HOUSE OF THE DEAD*
Bequeathed in 1919 by Theodore Whittemore

ALEKSANDR PUSHKIN:
AUTOGRAPH MS., *TO THE SEA*
Given in 1953 by Bayard L. Kilgour, Jr., H 1927

MARX AND ENGELS: THE COMMUNIST MANIFESTO, 1848   8⅜ × 9⅞ inches
First edition, first issue, given in 1953 by Bayard L. Kilgour, Jr., H 1927

PROCLAMATION OF THE PROVISIONAL COMMITTEE OF THE DUMA, 27 FEBRUARY 1917   5 × 8½ inches
Given in 1961 by Bayard L. Kilgour, Jr., H 1927

LEON TROTSKY: AUTOGRAPH DIARY, 1935
Acquired from the author in 1940

JOHANN WOLFGANG VON GOETHE: *NEUE LIEDER*, 1770   8 × 10⅛ inches
Given in 1954 by Carl M. Loeb

THE Harvard collections of German literature (the term is here restricted to the period beginning with such classical figures as Gottsched, Gellert, and Klopstock) date back well into the late eighteenth and early nineteenth centuries. They were notably enriched by the purchase, in 1945, of the library of Paul Hirsch of Frankfurt, while special attention more recently has resulted in further significant additions. Exceptionally strong collections of such authors as Heine and Rilke are given separate treatment elsewhere in this volume; the Hofmannsthal *Nachlass*, given by the author's family, is well known in the scholarly world; here it will be sufficient to remark that though other American institutional libraries may surpass Harvard in certain individual authors or limited periods, on overall balance the Harvard German collections are probably better than any other in this country, both in depth and quality. In so large a field, the books and manuscripts shown on the following pages must serve to represent far greater resources than their small number might seem to indicate.

German Literature

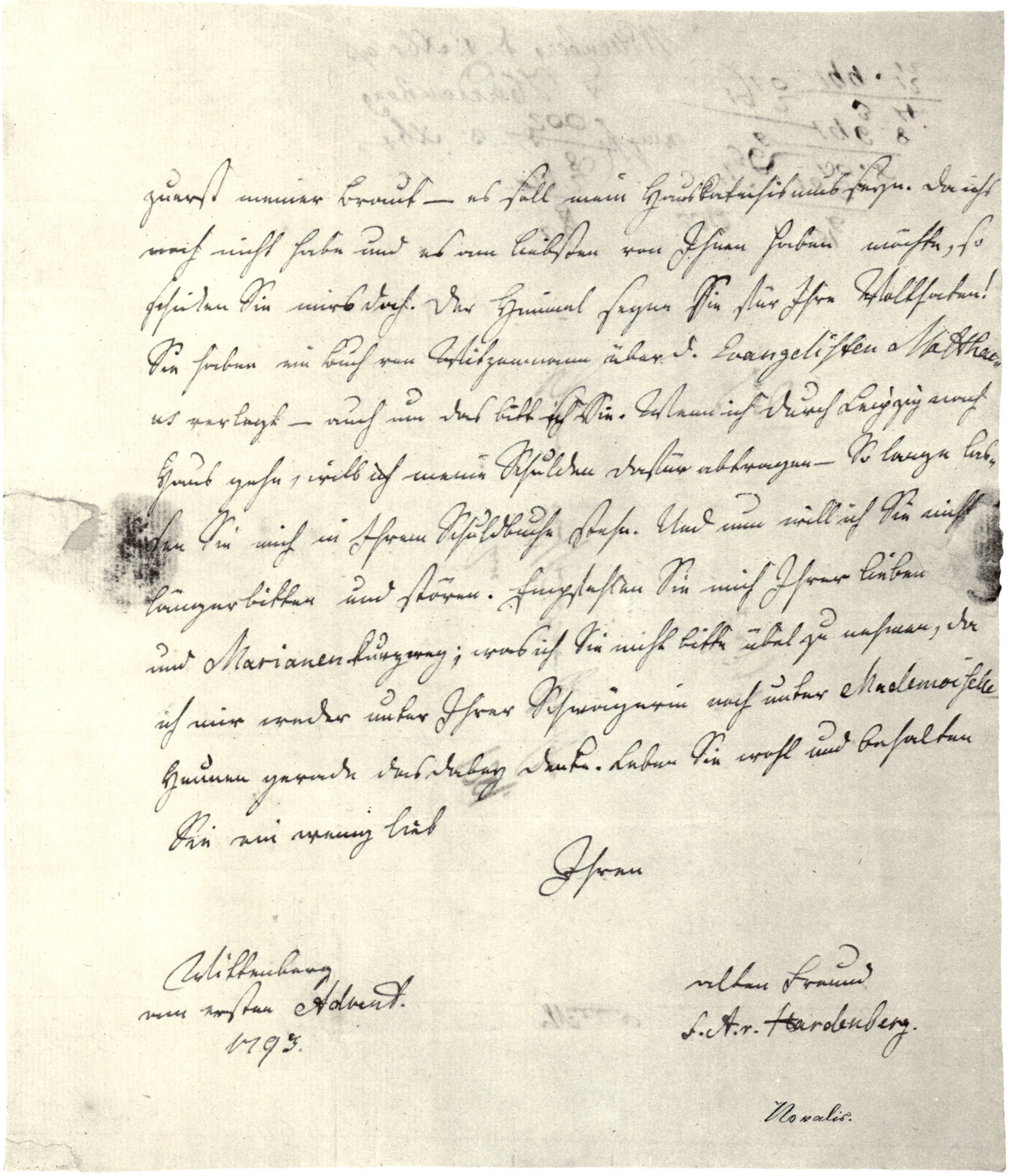

FRIEDRICH VON HARDENBERG (NOVALIS): AUTOGRAPH LETTER TO GEORG JOACHIM GÖSCHEN, 1 DECEMBER 1793
Given in 1965 by John L. Loeb, H 1924

JOHANN CHRISTOPH GOTTSCHED:
STERBENDER CATO, 1732 6 × 3¾ inches
  Acquired in 1966 with the fund bequeathed by
  George L. Lincoln, H 1895

CHRISTOPH MARTIN WIELAND:
LOBGESANG AUF DIE LIEBE, 1751 6½ × 3⅞ inches
  Acquired in 1965 with the fund bequeathed
  by George L. Lincoln, H 1895

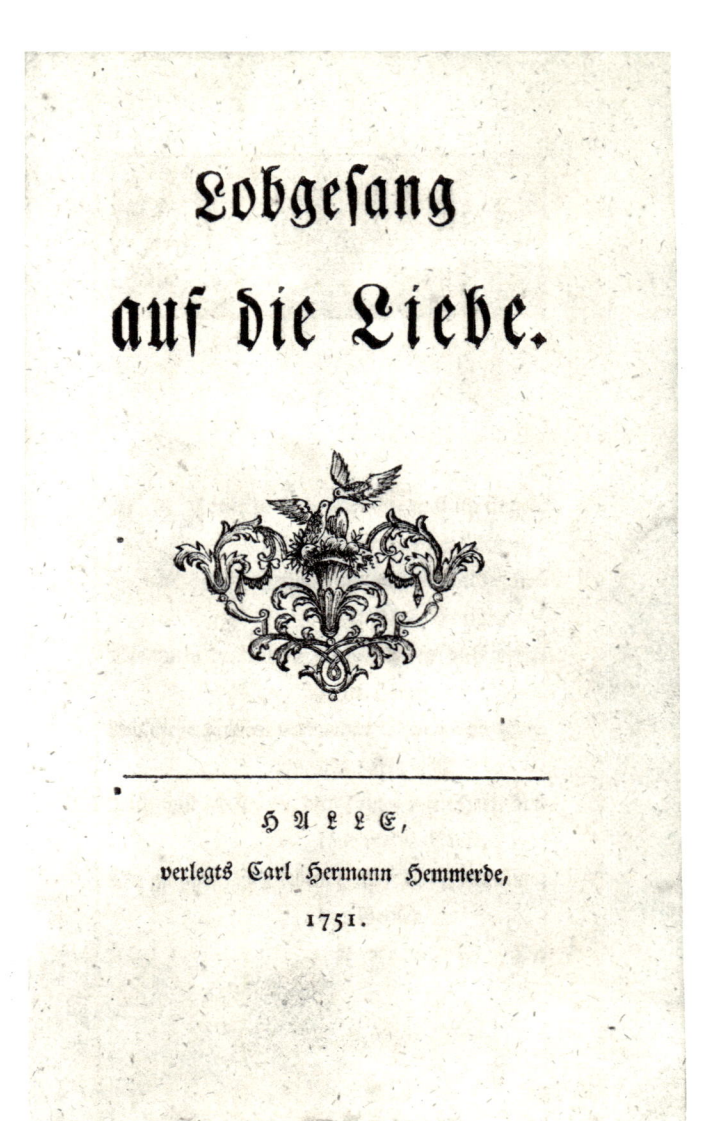

JOHANN GEORG HAMANN: *SOKRATISCHE
DENKWÜRDIGKEITEN*, 1759 6⅛ × 3¼ inches
  Acquired in 1966 with the fund bequeathed
  by George L. Lincoln, H 1895

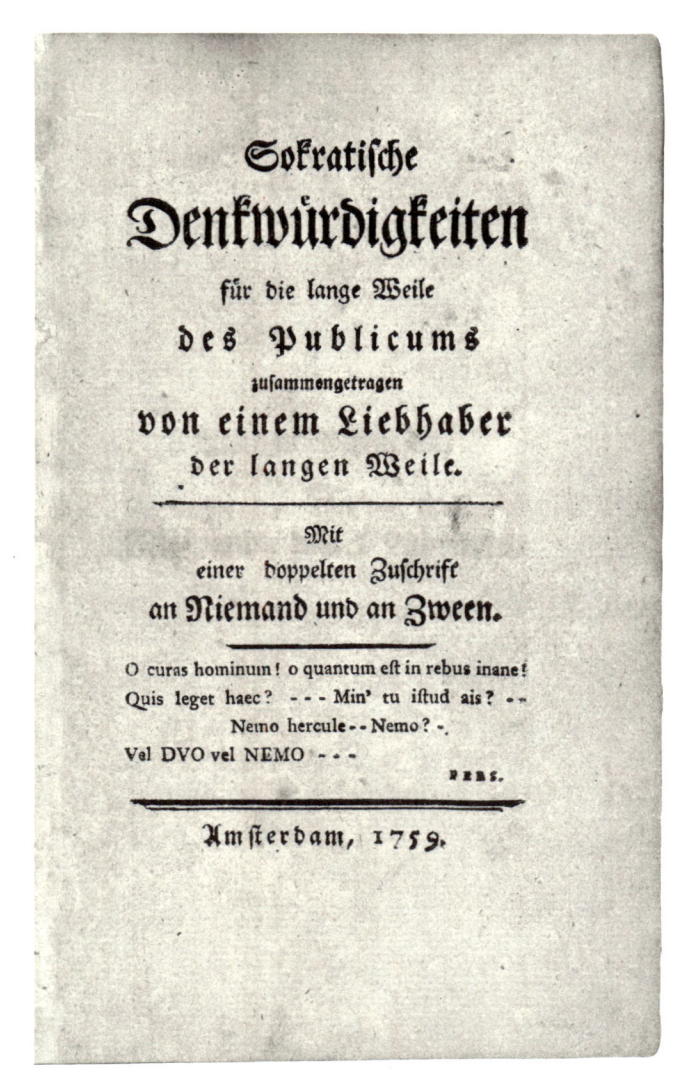

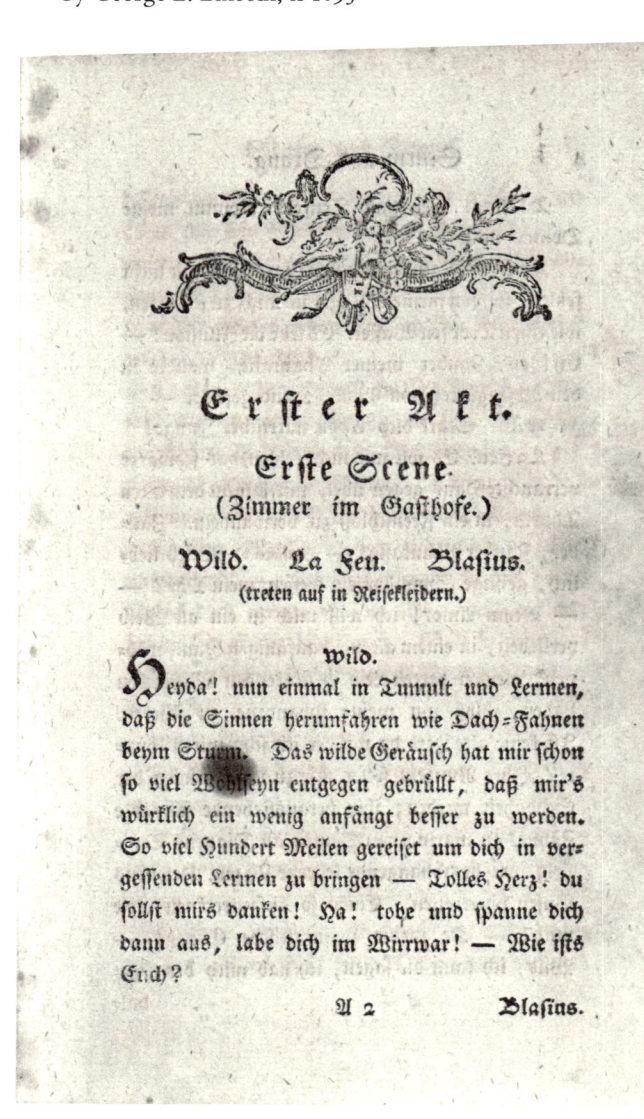

FRIEDRICH MAXIMILIAN VON KLINGER:
STURM UND DRANG, 1776 6⅜ × 3¾ inches
  Acquired in 1944 with the Grant Walker Fund

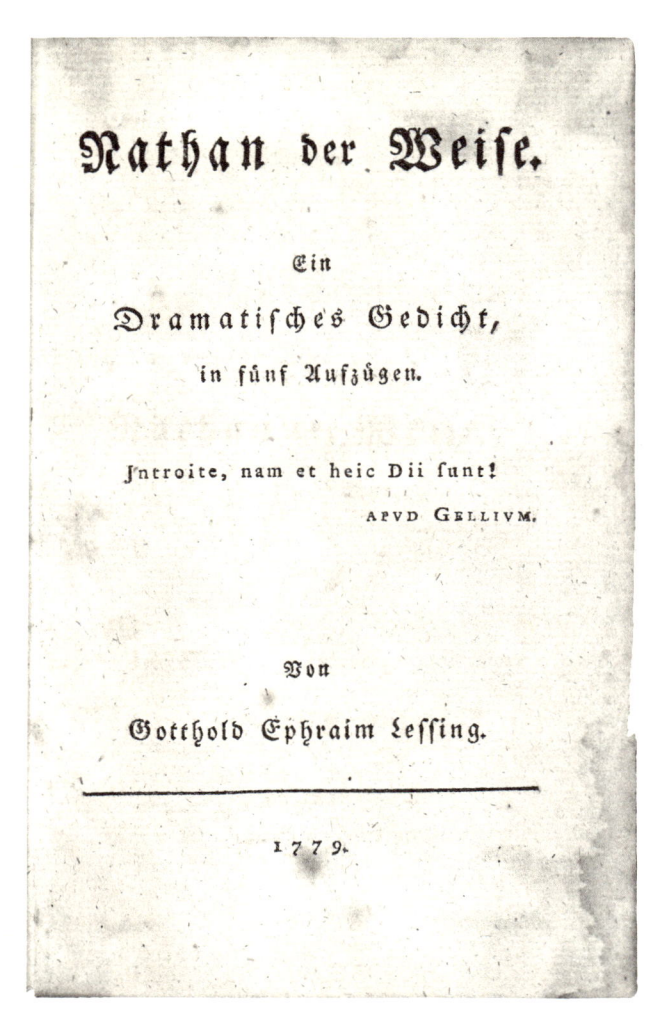

GOTTHOLD EPHRAIM LESSING:
NATHAN DER WEISE, 1779   5¾ × 3½ inches
Given in 1927 by Mrs. J. Montgomery Sears

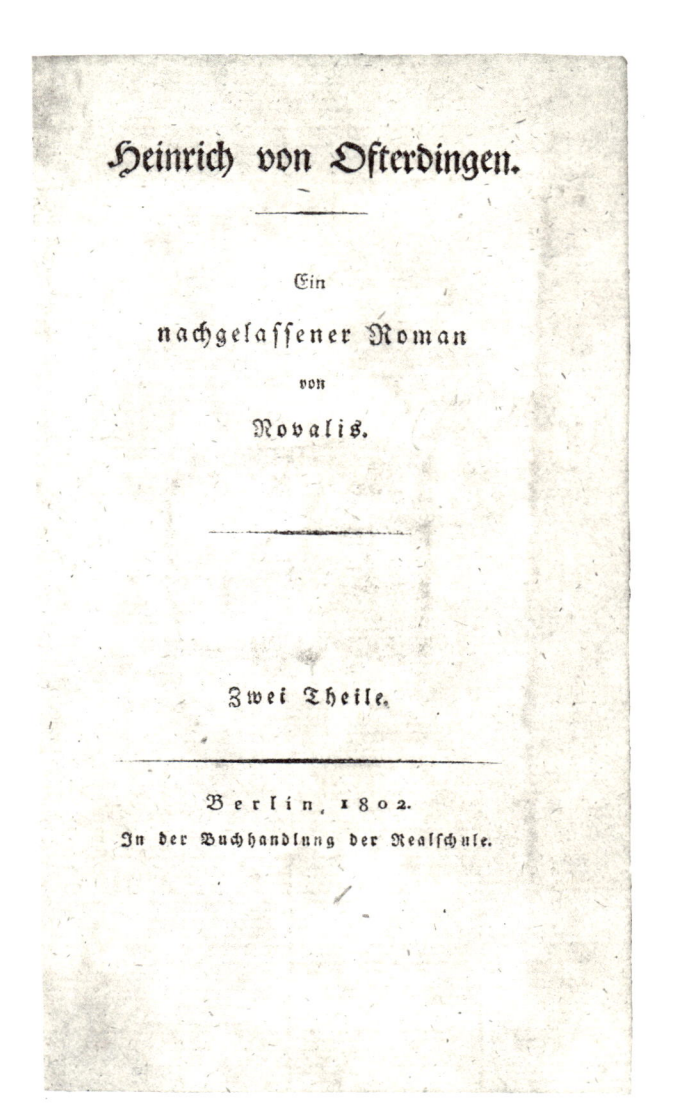

FRIEDRICH VON HARDENBERG (NOVALIS):
HEINRICH VON OFTERDINGEN, 1802   6¼ × 3½ inches
Acquired in 1966 with the fund bequeathed by
George L. Lincoln, H 1895

LUDWIG TIECK: *DER STURM*, 1796   7½ × 4½ inches
Acquired in 1966 with the fund bequeathed by George L. Lincoln, H 1895

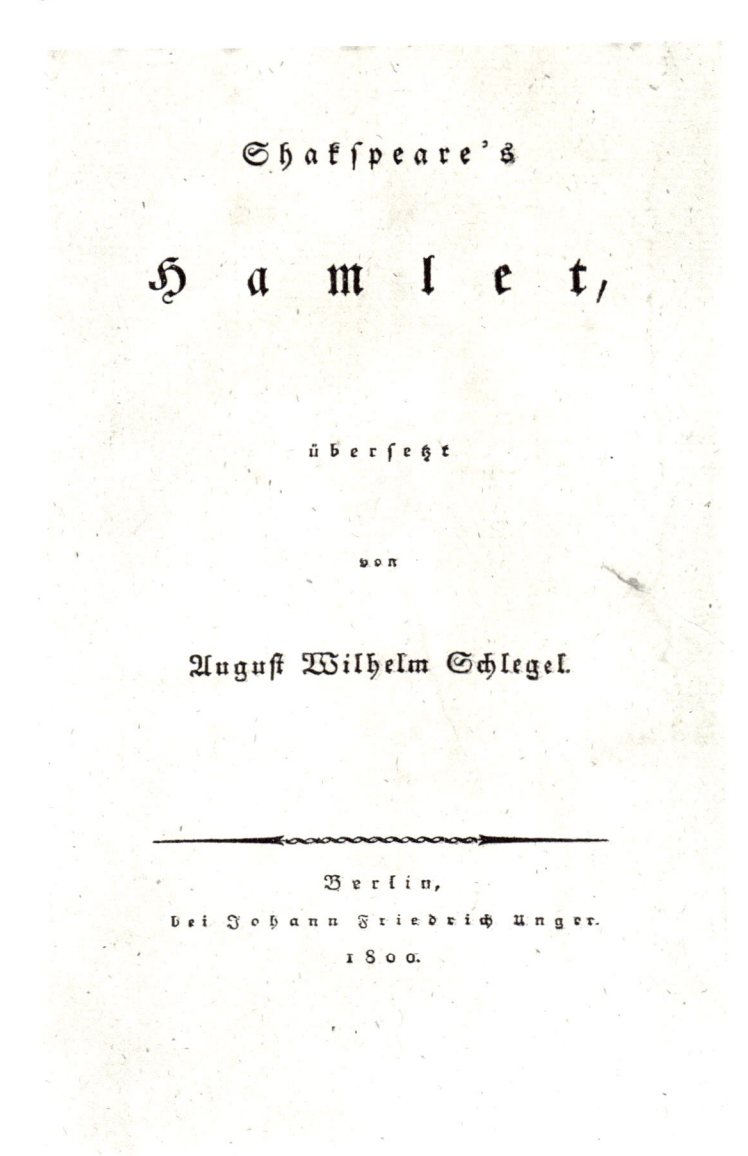

AUGUST WILHELM SCHLEGEL: *HAMLET*, 1800   6¾ × 4 inches
Acquired in 1966 with the fund bequeathed by George L. Lincoln, H 1895

German Literature   133

Gräfin.

Es ist zu spät.
In wenig Augenblicken ist mein Schicksal
Erfüllt. (Sie geht ab.)

Gordon.

O Haus des Mordes und Entsetzens!
(Ein Officier kommt und bringt einen Brief
mit großem Siegel.)

Gordon. (tritt ihm entgegen.)

Was giebts? Das ist das Kaiserliche Siegel.
(Er hat die Aufschrift gelesen, und über-
giebt den Brief dem Octavio mit einem
Blick des Vorwurfs, und einen Nach-
druck auf den Ton legend.)
Dem Fürsten Piccolomini.

Octavio.

(schrickt zusamen und blickt schmerzvoll
zum Himel.)

Der Vorhang fällt.

"Dieses Schauspiel ist nach meiner
eigenen Handschrift copiert und von
mir selbst durchgesehen, welcher
ich hiemit attestiere.
Jena 30 September 1799." Fridrich Schiller

FRIEDRICH SCHILLER: *WALLENSTEIN*, 1799 13½ × 7¾ inches
The manuscript sent to Samuel Taylor Coleridge for translation
Given in 1930 by Friends of the Library

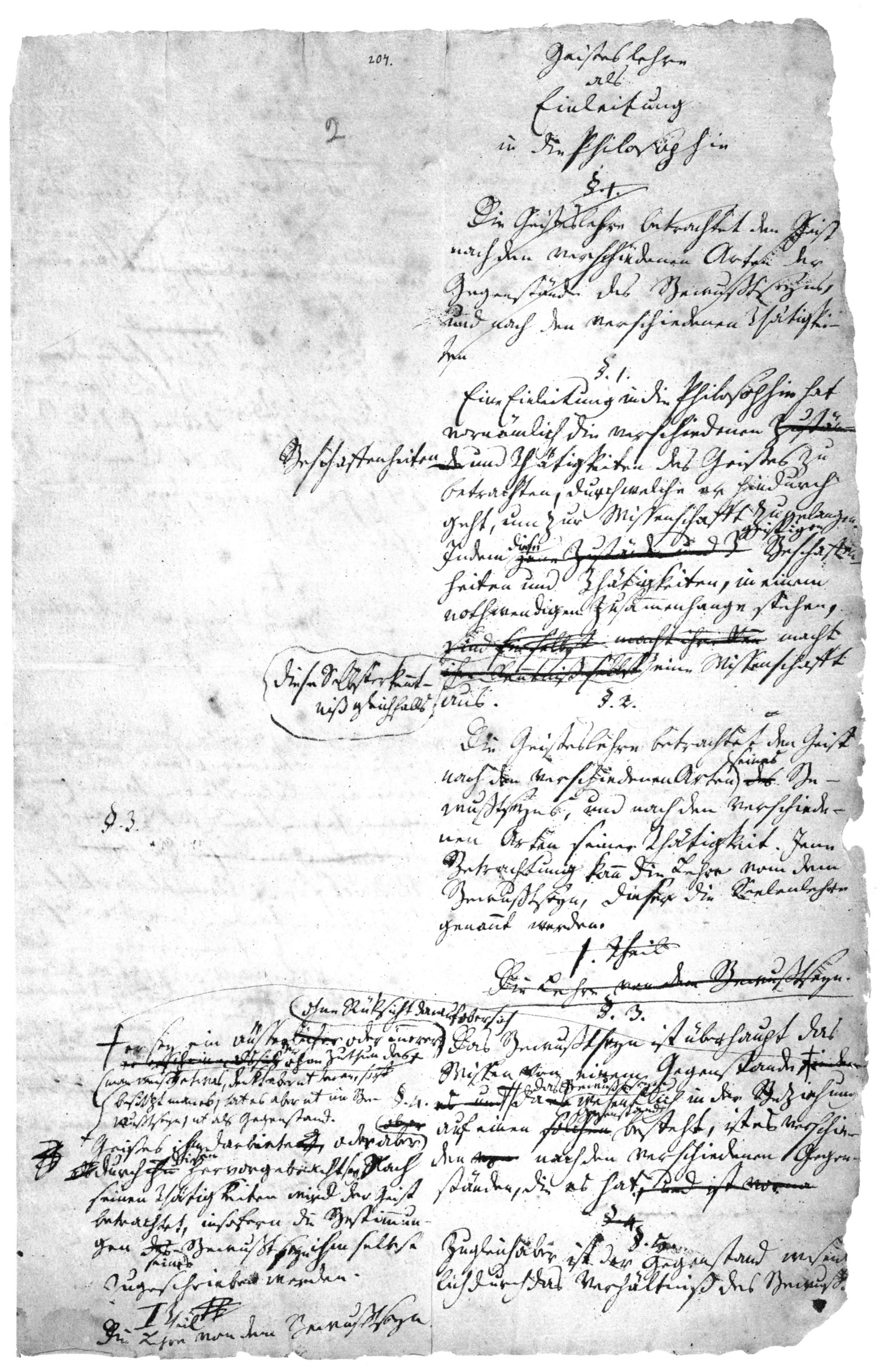

GEORG WILHELM FRIEDRICH HEGEL: HOLOGRAPH OF *GEISTESLEHREN ALS EINLEITUNG IN DIE PHILOSOPHIE* 13⅜ × 8¼ inches
Given in 1910 by George Herbert Palmer, H 1864

FRIEDRICH HÖLDERLIN: *GEDICHTE*, 1826   6½ × 3⅞ inches
Acquired in 1944 with the Holland Fund

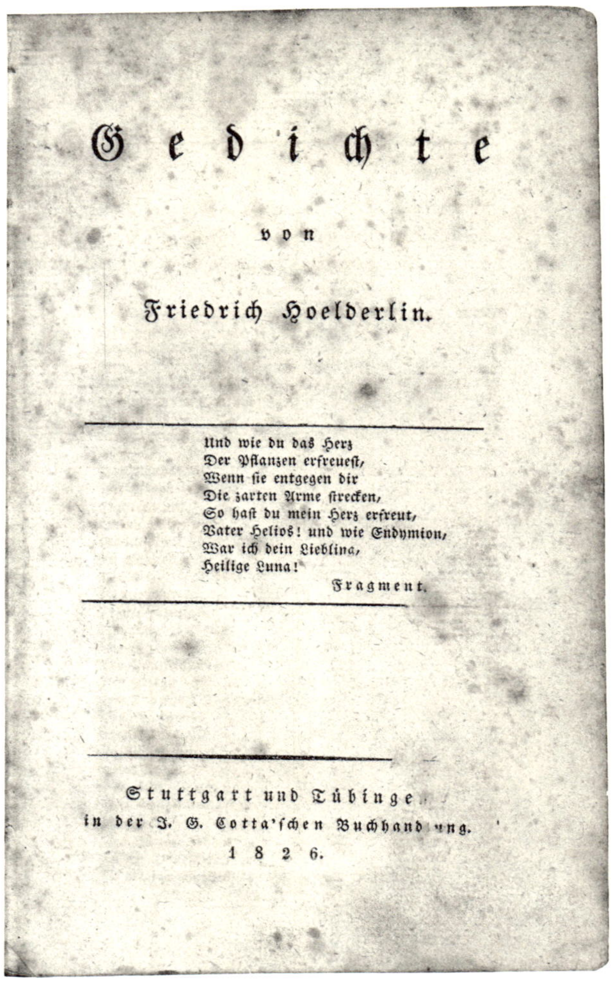

ACHIM VON ARNIM AND CLEMENS BRENTANO:
DES KNABEN WUNDERHORN, 1806   8 × 4⅝ inches
Given in 1938 by Philip Hofer, H 1921

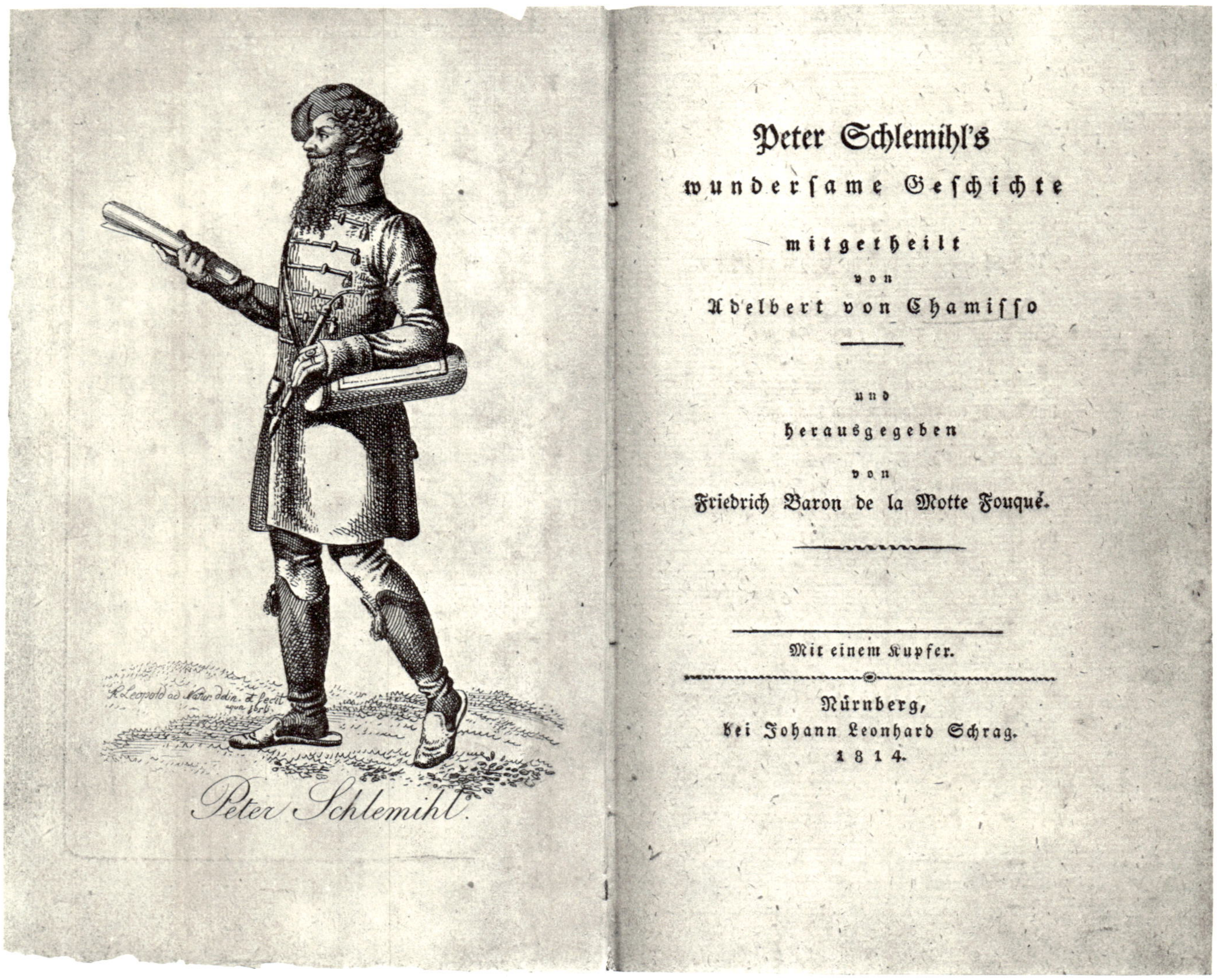

ADELBERT VON CHAMISSO: *PETER SCHLEMIHL'S WUNDERSAME GESCHICHTE*, 1814   7¼ × 8½ inches
Acquired in 1944 with the Peabody Fund

GEORG BÜCHNER: *DANTON'S TOD*, 1835   6½ × 4⅜ inches
Acquired in 1944 with the Dexter Fund

ADALBERT STIFTER: *WITIKO*, 1865   7¼ × 4⅞ inches
Acquired in 1964 with the Amy Lowell Fund

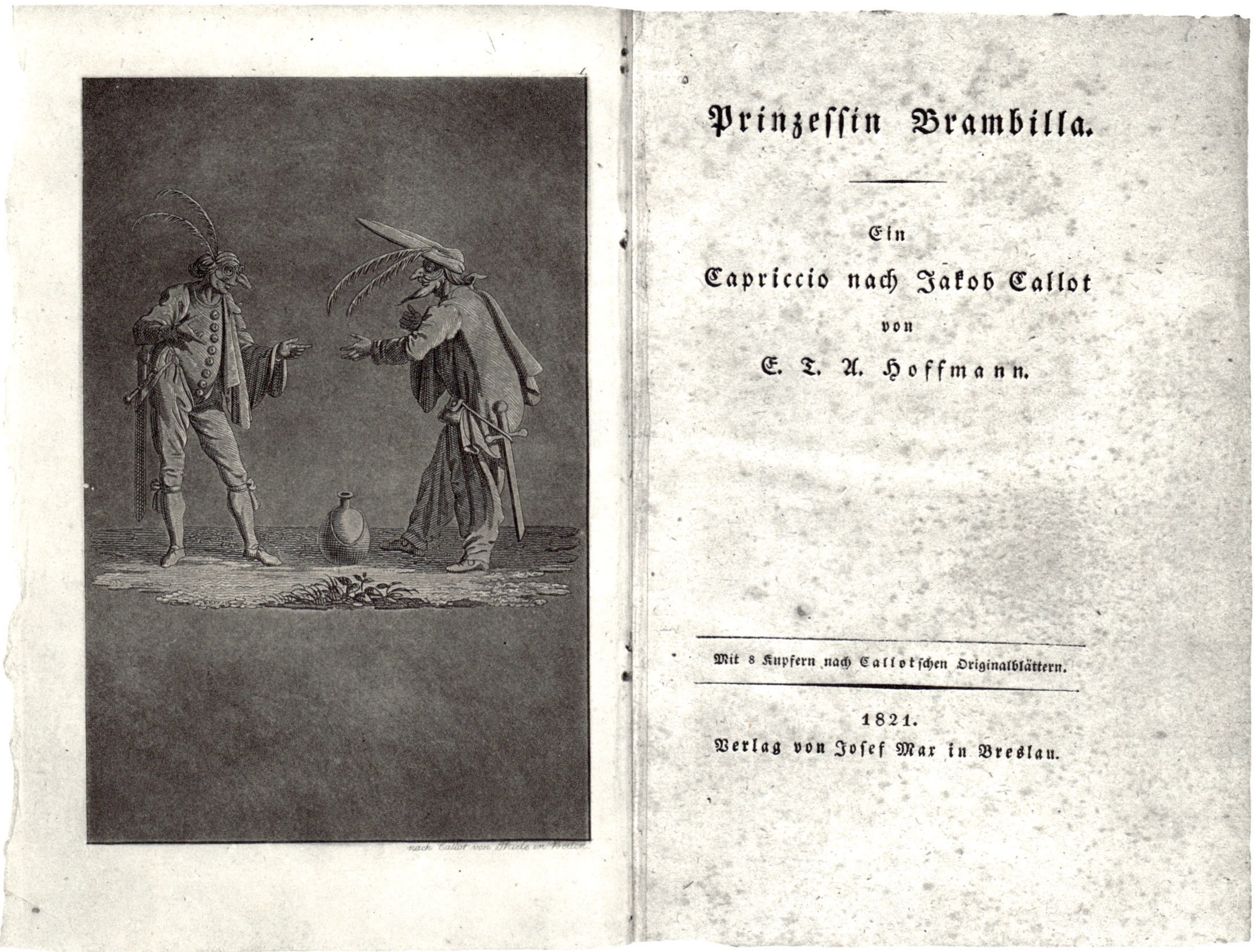

E. T. A. HOFFMANN: *PRINZESSIN BRAMBILLA*, 1821   6¾ × 8½ inches
With engravings after Jacques Callot
Given in 1941 by Philip Hofer, H 1921

German Literature · 137

DIE WALKÜRE. 45

das zaglos ich halte!
Wälfe verhiefs mir,
in höchfter Noth
follt' ich es finden:
ich fafs' es nun!
Heiligfter Liebe
höchfte Noth
brennt mir hell in der Bruft:
fchmachvoller Bande
fchmählichfte Noth
hält in Fefseln uns feft: —
Nothung! Nothung! —
fo nenn' ich dich Schwert —
Nothung! Nothung!
neidlicher Stahl!
Zeig' deiner Schärfe
fchneidenden Zahn:
heraus aus der Scheide zu mir!

Er zieht mit einem gewaltigen Zuck das Schwert aus dem Stamme, und zeigt es der von Staunen und Entzücken erfafsten Sieglinde.

Siegmund den Wälfung
fiehft du, Weib!
Als Brautgabe
bringt er diefs Schwert:
fo freit er fich

die feligfte Frau;
dem Feindeshaus
entführt er dich fo.
Fern von hier
folge ihm nun,
fort in des Lenzes
lachendes Haus:
dort fchützt dich Nothung das Schwert,
wenn Siegmund dir liebend erlag!

Er umfafst fie, um fie mit fich fortzuziehen.

SIEGLINDE,
in höchfter Trunkenheit.
Bift du Siegmund,
den ich hier fehe —
Sieglinde bin ich,
die dich erfehnt:
die eig'ne Schwefter
gewann'ft du zueins mit dem Schwert!

SIEGMUND.
Braut und Schwefter
bift du dem Bruder —
fo blühe denn Wälfungen-Blut!

Er zieht fie mit wüthender Gluth an fich: fie finkt mit einem Schrei an feine Bruft. — Der Vorhang fällt fchnell.

ZWEITER AUFZUG.

Wildes Felfengebirg.

Im Hintergrunde zieht fich von unten her eine Schlucht herauf, die auf ein erhöhtes Felsjoch mündet; von diefem fenkt fich der Boden dem Vordergrunde zu wieder abwärts.

WODAN, kriegerifch gewaffnet, und mit dem Speer: vor ihm BRÜNNHILDE, als Walküre, ebenfalls in voller Waffenrüftung.

WODAN.
Nun zäume dein Rofs,
reifsige Maid!
Bald entbrennt
brünftiger Streit:
Brünnhilde ftürme zum Kampf,
dem Wälfung kiefe fie Sieg!
Hunding wähle fich
wem er gehört:
nach Walhall taugt er mir nicht.

RICHARD WAGNER: *DER RING DES NIBELUNGEN*, LIBRETTO, 1853
The copy presented to Schopenhauer,
with his critical comments throughout
Given in 1957 by Mrs. Frederick W. Hilles
in memory of her parents,
Dr. and Mrs. William Inglis Morse

HUGO VON HOFMANNSTHAL: HOLOGRAPH OF *ÖDIPUS*
Given in 1948 by Gilbert H. Montague, H 1901

German Literature

ROBERT MUSIL: *DIE VERWIRRUNGEN DES ZÖGLINGS TÖRLESS*, 1906   7 × 4⅞ inches
Acquired in 1956 with the Amy Lowell Fund

STEFAN GEORGE: *DER SIEBENTE RING*, 1907   8⅞ × 7⅛ inches
Given in 1951 by Gilbert H. Montague, H 1901

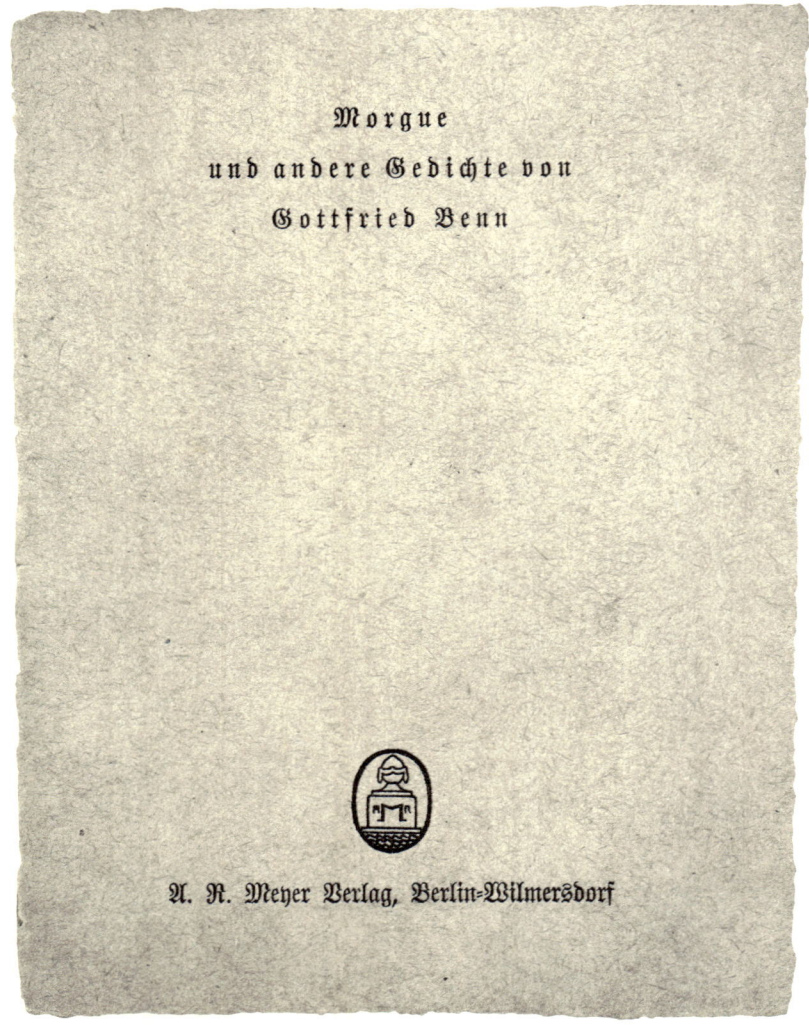

GOTTFRIED BENN:
MORGUE UND ANDERE GEDICHTE, 1912   7¼ × 5½ inches
Acquired in 1951 with the library of Karl Viëtor

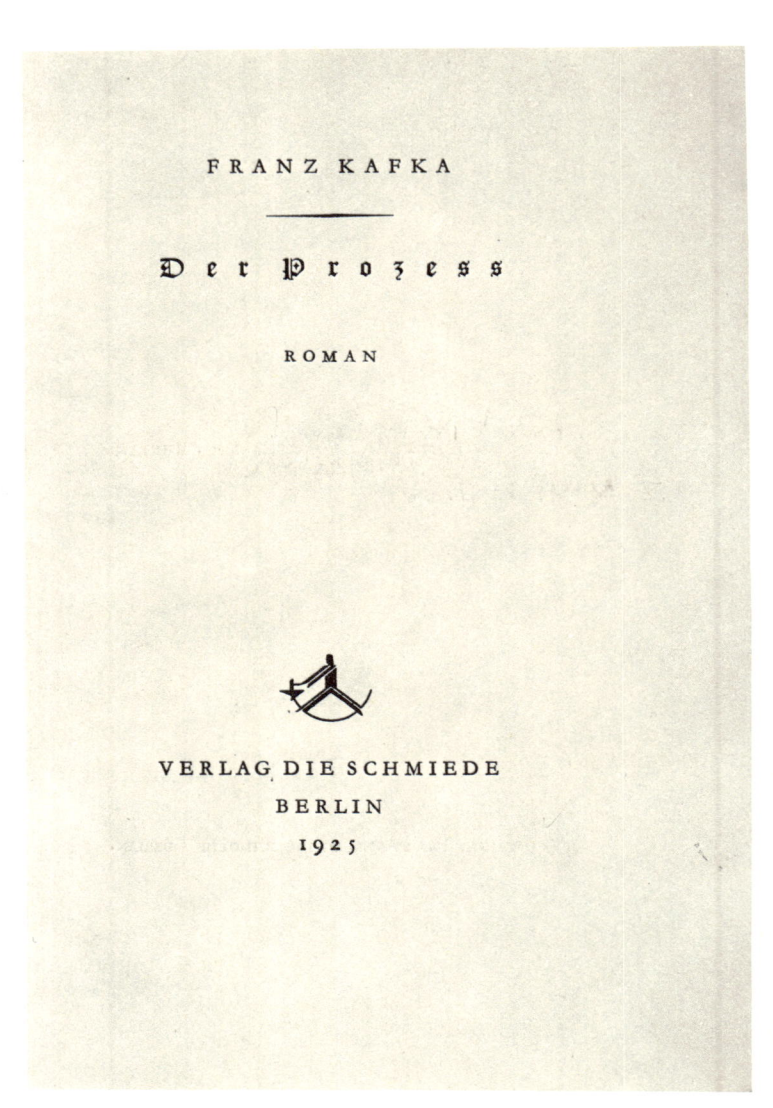

FRANZ KAFKA: *DER PROZESS*, 1925   7¾ × 5⅛ inches
Given in 1963 by Curt H. Reisinger, H 1912

THOMAS MANN: HOLOGRAPH OF *MEERFAHRT MIT DON QUIJOTE*
Given in 1935 by the author

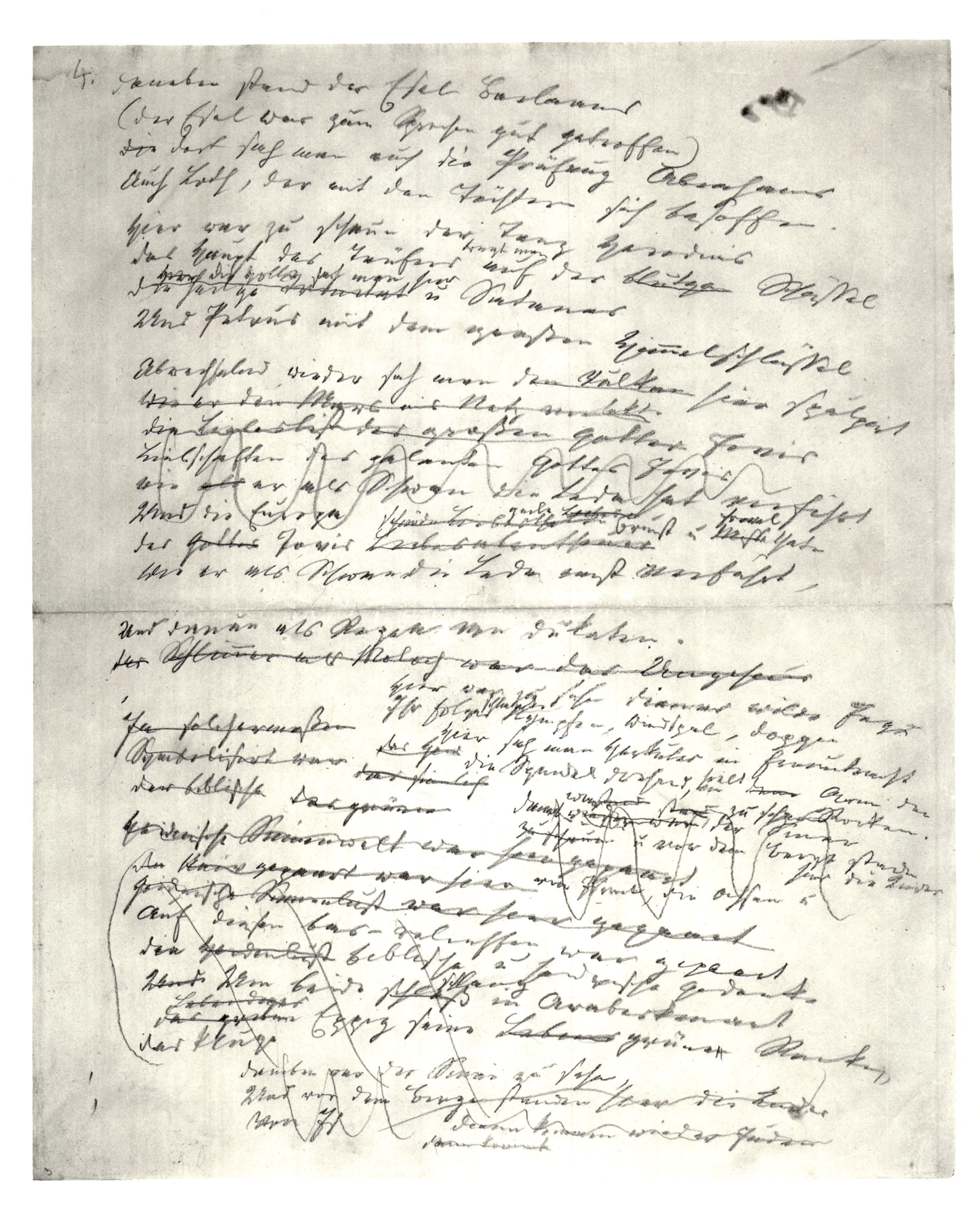

HEINRICH HEINE: *FÜR DIE MOUCHE* [1856?] 15½ × 12⅛ inches
Autograph manuscript of his last poem
  Given in 1950 by Carl M. Loeb

Heinrich Heine

IN 1935 the late Carl M. Loeb gave the Salli Kirschstein Collection to Harvard and in so doing he raised to the first rank the library's holdings of the works of Heinrich Heine. Kirschstein, an eminent collector in Berlin, had died earlier that year. His library was rich in first and other editions of the poet, often with interesting associations, and in manuscripts as well as secondary sources.

A single glass case in the Houghton Library now houses all twelve editions of the *Buch der Lieder* published in Heine's lifetime, along with one or more copies of each of his other first editions. More books and manuscripts are shelved in the stacks below. The collection is not static; Mr. Loeb continued to add to it after his initial gift, and since his death members of his family have contributed further significant documents.

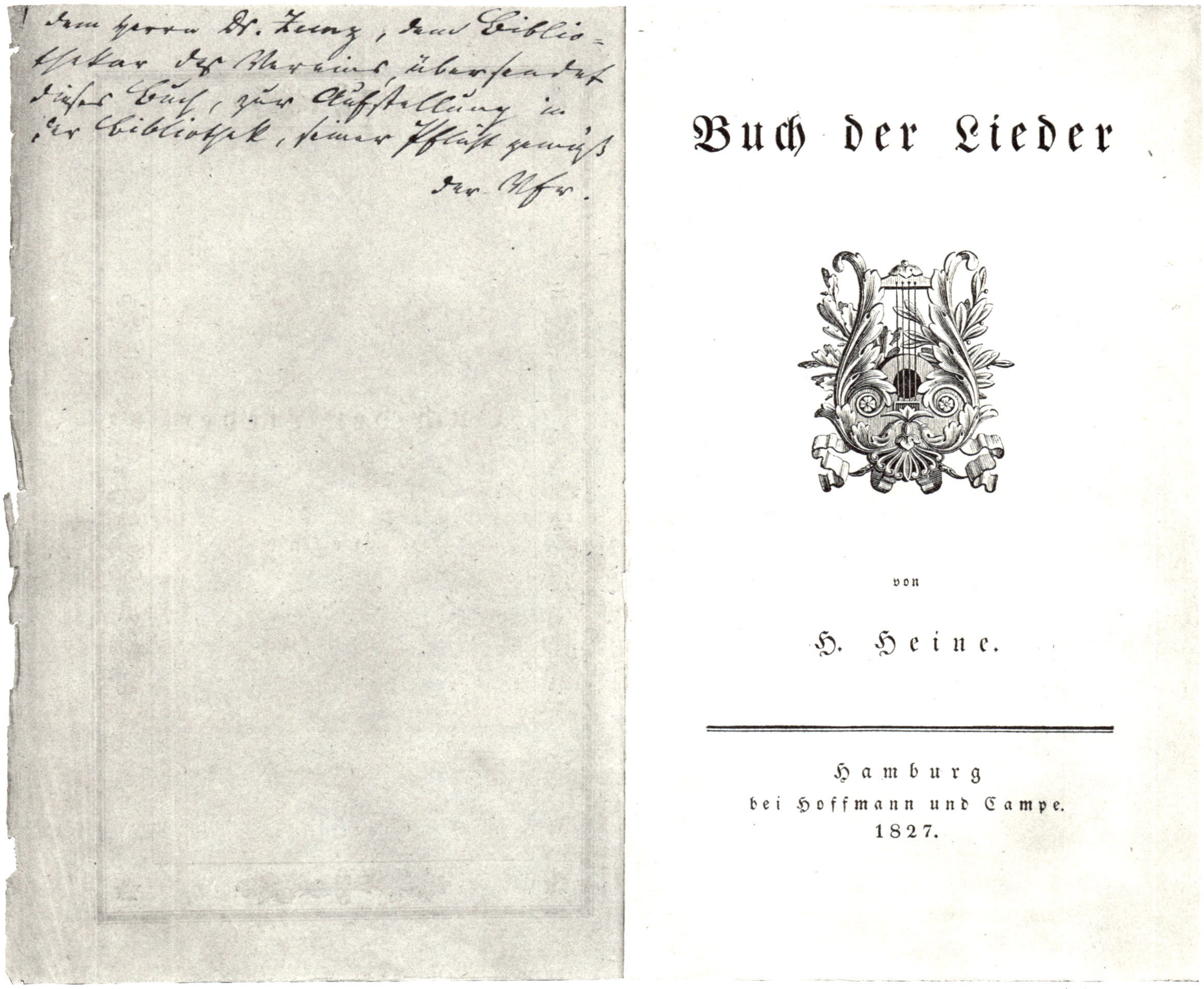

HEINRICH HEINE: *BUCH DER LIEDER*, 1827
Inscribed to Leopold Zunz
Given in 1935 by Carl M. Loeb

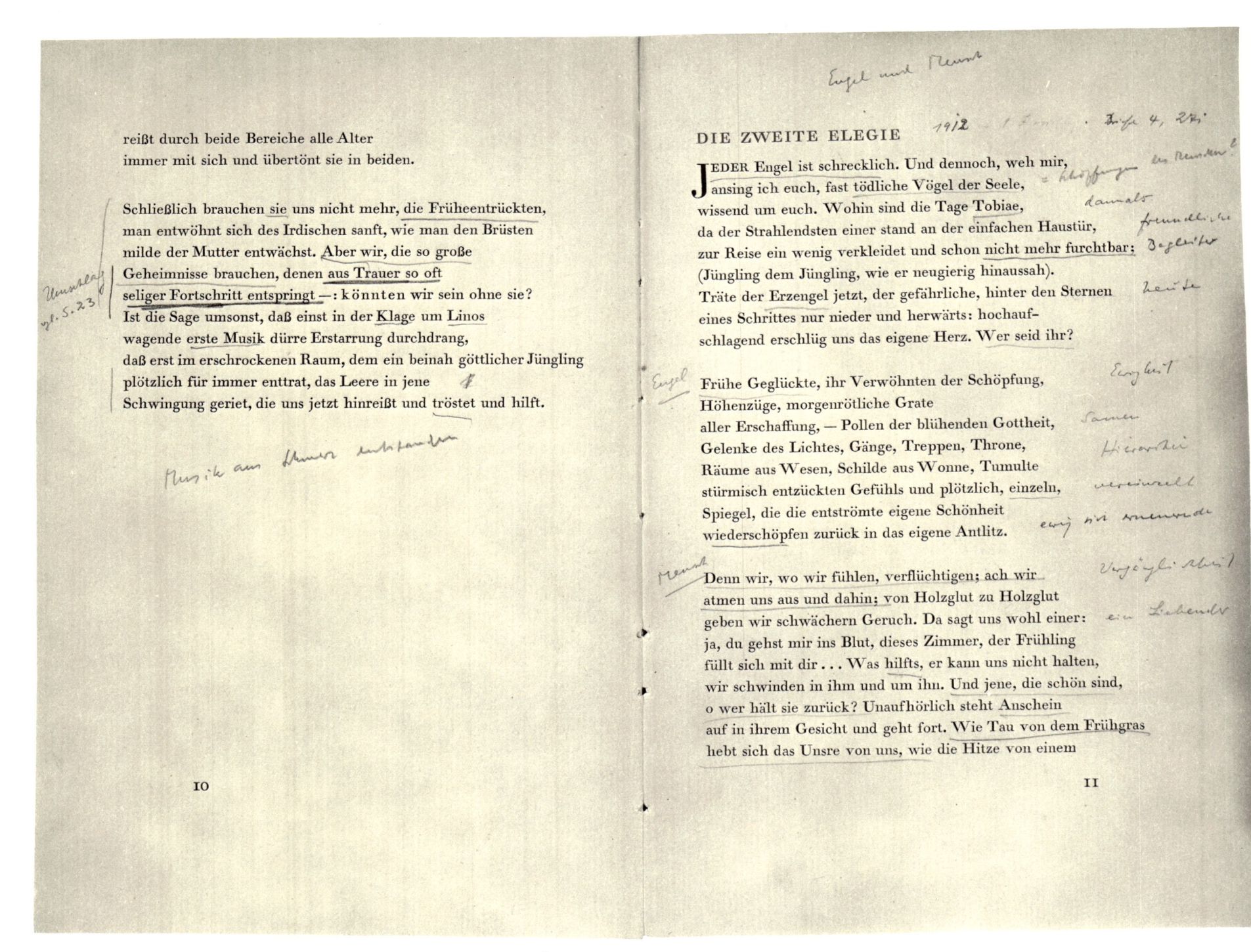

reißt durch beide Bereiche alle Alter
immer mit sich und übertönt sie in beiden.

Schließlich brauchen sie uns nicht mehr, die Früheentrückten,
man entwöhnt sich des Irdischen sanft, wie man den Brüsten
milde der Mutter entwächst. Aber wir, die so große
Geheimnisse brauchen, denen aus Trauer so oft
seliger Fortschritt entspringt —: könnten wir sein ohne sie?
Ist die Sage umsonst, daß einst in der Klage um Linos
wagende erste Musik dürre Erstarrung durchdrang,
daß erst im erschrockenen Raum, dem ein beinah göttlicher Jüngling
plötzlich für immer enttrat, das Leere in jene
Schwingung geriet, die uns jetzt hinreißt und tröstet und hilft.

DIE ZWEITE ELEGIE

JEDER Engel ist schrecklich. Und dennoch, weh mir,
ansing ich euch, fast tödliche Vögel der Seele,
wissend um euch. Wohin sind die Tage Tobiae,
da der Strahlendsten einer stand an der einfachen Haustür,
zur Reise ein wenig verkleidet und schon nicht mehr furchtbar;
(Jüngling dem Jüngling, wie er neugierig hinaussah).
Träte der Erzengel jetzt, der gefährliche, hinter den Sternen
eines Schrittes nur nieder und herwärts: hochauf-
schlagend erschlüg uns das eigene Herz. Wer seid ihr?

Frühe Geglückte, ihr Verwöhnten der Schöpfung,
Höhenzüge, morgenrötliche Grate
aller Erschaffung, — Pollen der blühenden Gottheit,
Gelenke des Lichtes, Gänge, Treppen, Throne,
Räume aus Wesen, Schilde aus Wonne, Tumulte
stürmisch entzückten Gefühls und plötzlich, einzeln,
Spiegel, die die entströmte eigene Schönheit
wiederschöpfen zurück in das eigene Antlitz.

Denn wir, wo wir fühlen, verflüchtigen; ach wir
atmen uns aus und dahin; von Holzglut zu Holzglut
geben wir schwächern Geruch. Da sagt uns wohl einer:
ja, du gehst mir ins Blut, dieses Zimmer, der Frühling
füllt sich mit dir... Was hilfts, er kann uns nicht halten,
wir schwinden in ihm und um ihn. Und jene, die schön sind,
o wer hält sie zurück? Unaufhörlich steht Anschein
auf in ihrem Gesicht und geht fort. Wie Tau von dem Frühgras
hebt sich das Unsre von uns, wie die Hitze von einem

KARL VIËTOR'S COPY OF THE FIRST EDITION 8¾ × 11¾ inches
Acquired in 1951 with Professor Viëtor's library

RAINER MARIA RILKE is one of the great seminal poets of the 20th century: his work has had an impact and an influence that have overleapt the boundaries of nationality and language to make him a universal, rather than a German—or even a European—poet. Harvard is fortunate in having been able to acquire in 1953, by means of the Amy Lowell Fund, the Richard von Mises collection of Rilke, which contains printed and manuscript material unsurpassed on this side of the Atlantic and approached by only one or two repositories in Europe. Its riches are listed in detail in a *Katalog* by Paul Obermüller, Herbert Steiner, and Ernst Zinn, published in 1966 by the Insel-Verlag.

Among Rilke's best-known and most powerful productions are his *Duineser Elegien*, begun at Duino in 1912, laid aside during the weary and unproductive years of World War I, and finally finished in an unparalleled burst of poetic inspiration in February of 1922. Shown here is the beginning of the second Elegy, written at Duino in 1912, in the autograph manuscript and in a copy of the first edition (Leipzig, 1923) owned and annotated by the late Karl Viëtor, Kuno Francke Professor of German Art and Culture at Harvard.

Rainer Maria Rilke

AUTOGRAPH MS., SECOND DUINO ELEGY 8¼ × 5¼ inches
Acquired in 1958 with the Amy Lowell Fund

French Literature

ALTHOUGH two early manuscripts of the *Roman de la rose* were acquired by Harvard in 1878, no doubt because of their Chaucerian interest, the library's collection of original editions and manuscripts in French literature is largely a creation of the present century. In 1903 James Hazen Hyde, H 1898, gave important runs of Montaigne, Molière, and Bossuet; in 1908 a gift in memory of Arthur Sturgis Dixey, H 1908, purchased early editions of Desportes, Pascal, and Ronsard; and in 1924 John B. Stetson, Jr., H 1906, enabled the library to make large acquisitions at the Moura sale.

In recent years the bequest of Amy Lowell has made it possible to strengthen immeasurably the holdings in this field, particularly in the nineteenth and twentieth centuries, adding manuscripts and correspondence as well as original editions.

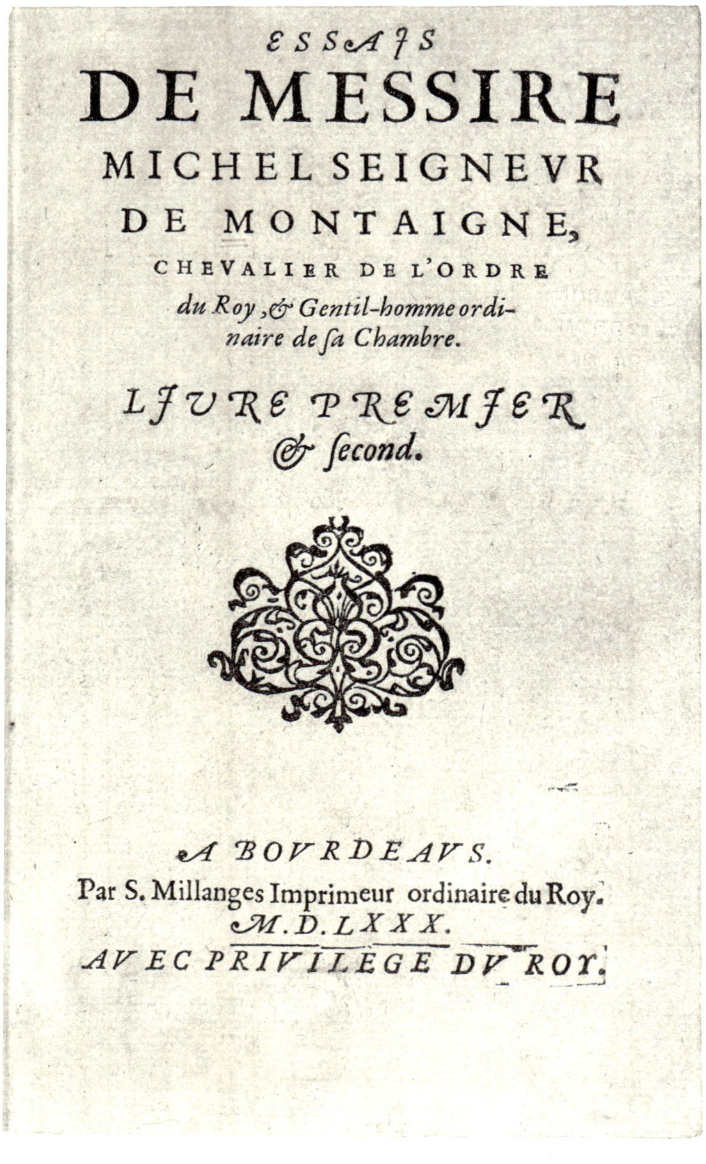

MICHEL DE MONTAIGNE: *ESSAIS*, 1580
Bequeathed in 1906 by Mrs. Martin Brimmer,
from the library of her husband, H 1849

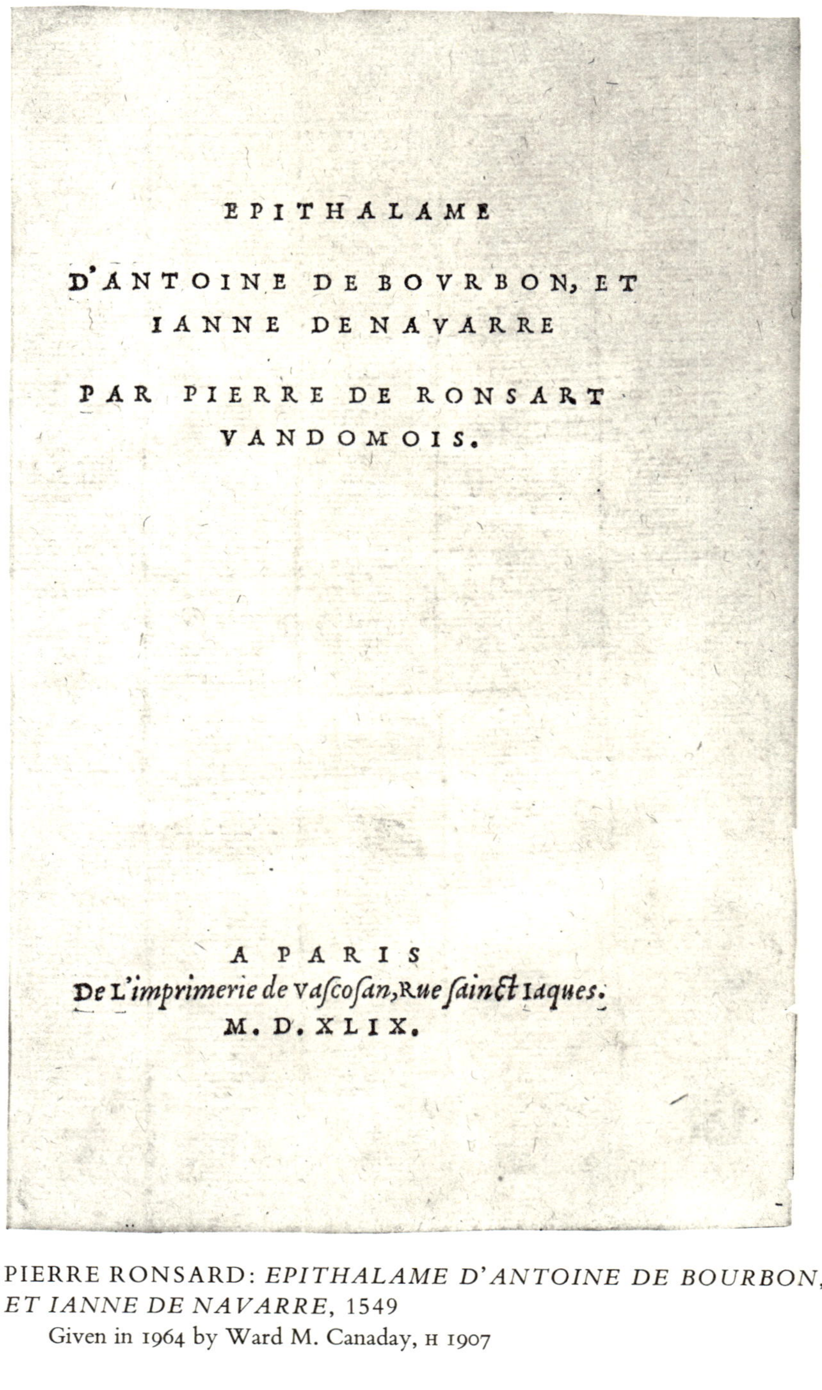

PIERRE RONSARD: *EPITHALAME D'ANTOINE DE BOURBON, ET IANNE DE NAVARRE*, 1549
Given in 1964 by Ward M. Canaday, H 1907

PIERRE CORNEILLE: *CINNA*, 1643 8½ × 6¼ inches
Copy bound for Louis II de Bourbon, Prince de Condé
Acquired in 1952 with the Amy Lowell Fund

MOLIÈRE: *LE DIVERTISSEMENT ROYAL*, 1670 8¼ × 6 inches
Given in 1960 by the estate of Templeton Crocker

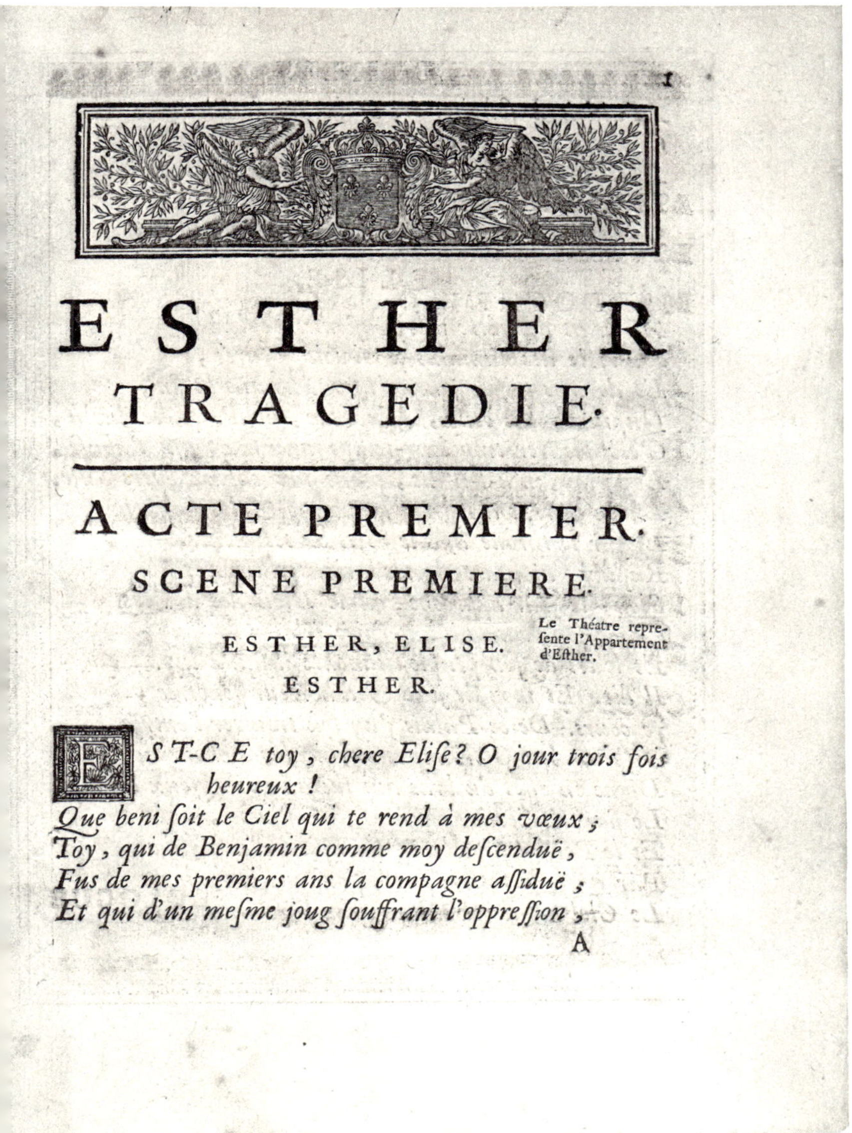

AN RACINE: *ESTHER*, 1689 9½ × 7 inches
Acquired in 1943 with the Dexter Fund

J. B. MOREAU: *CHOEURS DE LA TRAGÉDIE D'ESTHER*, 1689
10⅛ × 7¼ inches   Given in 1960 by George L. Lincoln, H 1895

VOLTAIRE: HOLOGRAPH OF *LA PUCELLE*,
CHANT XI 8¾ × 6½ inches
Acquired in 1950 with the H. S. Howe
and F. C. Lowell Funds

JEAN-JACQUES ROUSSEAU:
HOLOGRAPH OF *IDÉE DE LA METHODE
DANS LA COMPOSITION D'UN LIVRE* 8⅝ × 6½ inches
Acquired in 1958 with the Amy Lowell Fund

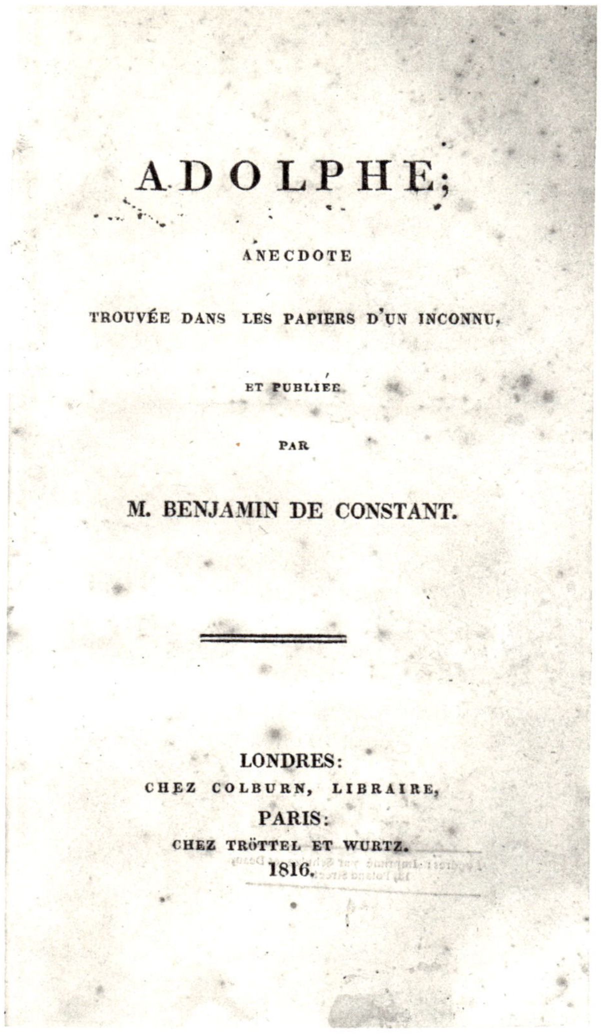

BENJAMIN CONSTANT
DE REBECQUE: *ADOLPHE*,
1816   7¼ × 4⅜ inches
Acquired in 1943 with gifts
of Friends of the Library

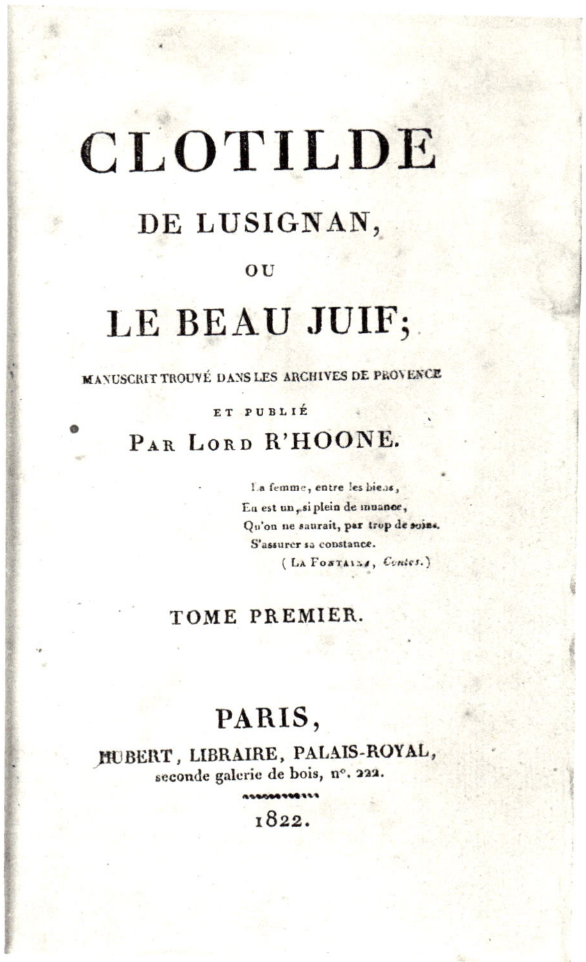

HONORÉ DE BALZAC:
CLOTILDE DE LUSIGNAN,
1822   6⅜ × 3¾ inches
Bequeathed in 1946 by
Gabriel Wells

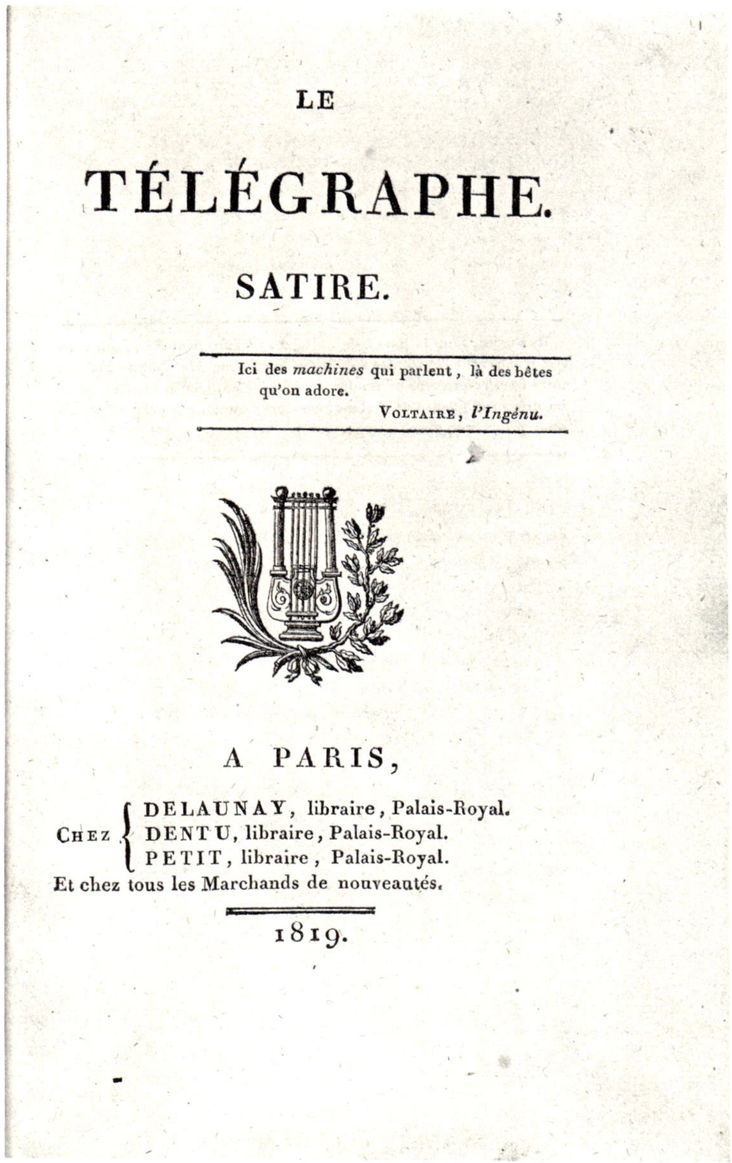

VICTOR HUGO: *LE TÉLÉGRAPHE*, 1819   7¾ × 4⅝ inches
Acquired in 1965 with the Amy Lowell Fund

MARCELINE DESBORDES-VALMORE: *POÉSIES*, 1820
7¾ × 4¾ inches   Acquired in 1965 with the Amy Lowell Fund

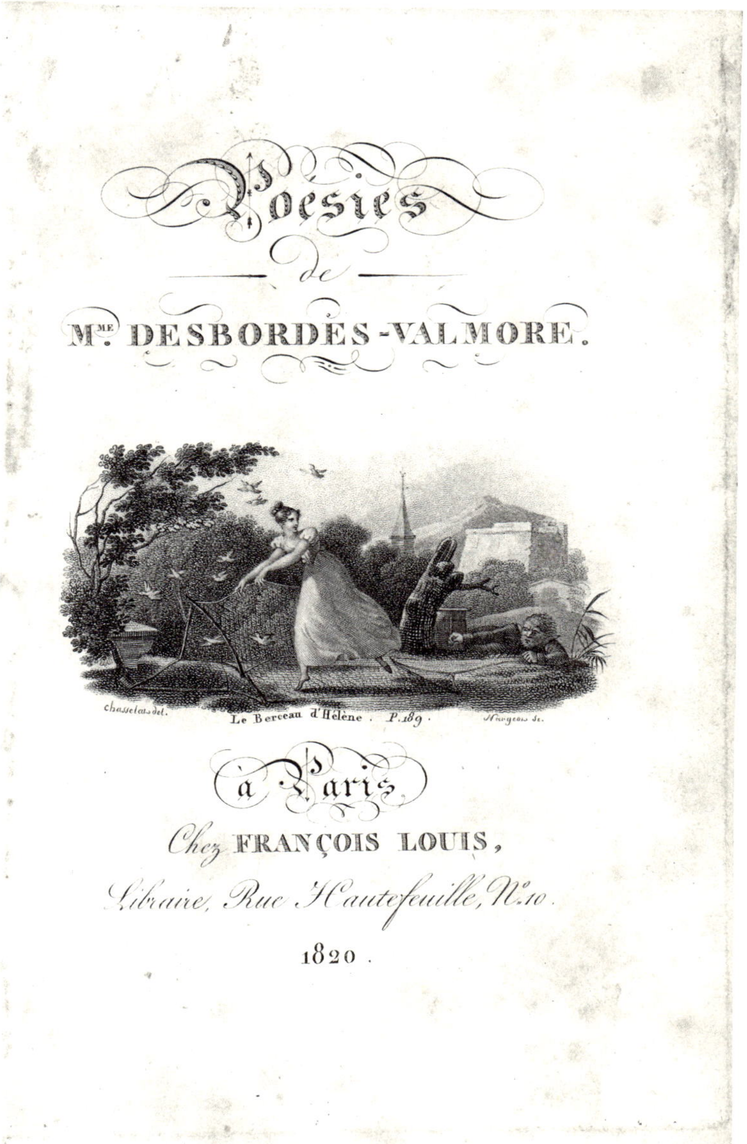

French Literature   149

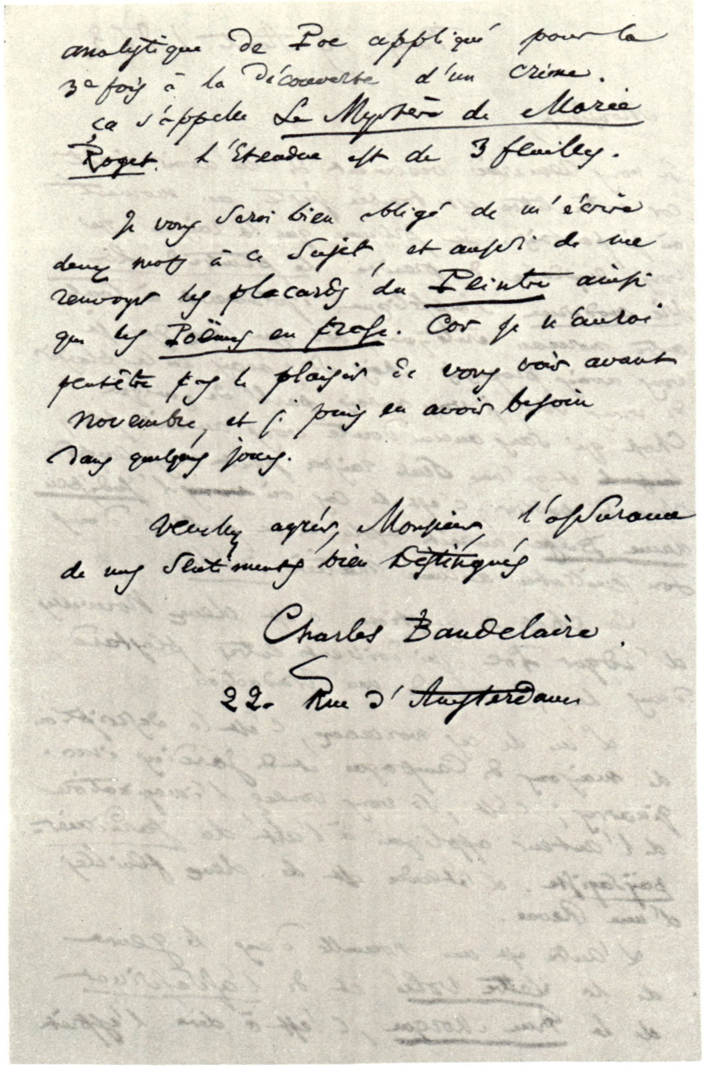

CHARLES BAUDELAIRE: AUTOGRAPH LETTER
TO M. BERARDI, 19 AUGUST 1863   8⅛ × 5⅛ inches
Given in 1963 by Lucien Wulsin, H 1910

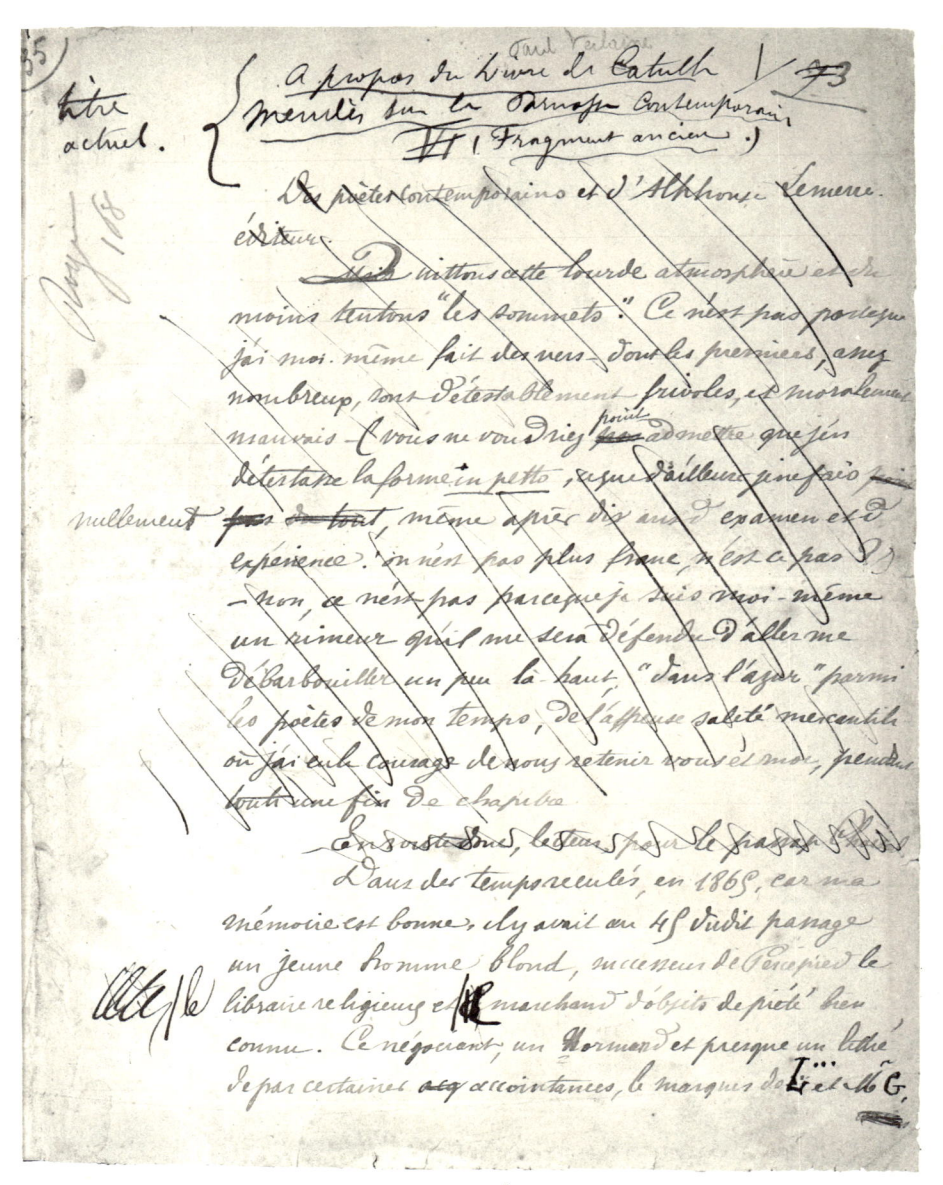

PAUL VERLAINE: HOLOGRAPH OF À PROPOS DU LIVRE DE
CATULLE MENDÈS SUR LE PARNASSE CONTEMPORAIN
8¾ × 6⅜ inches   Acquired in 1955 with the Amy Lowell Fund

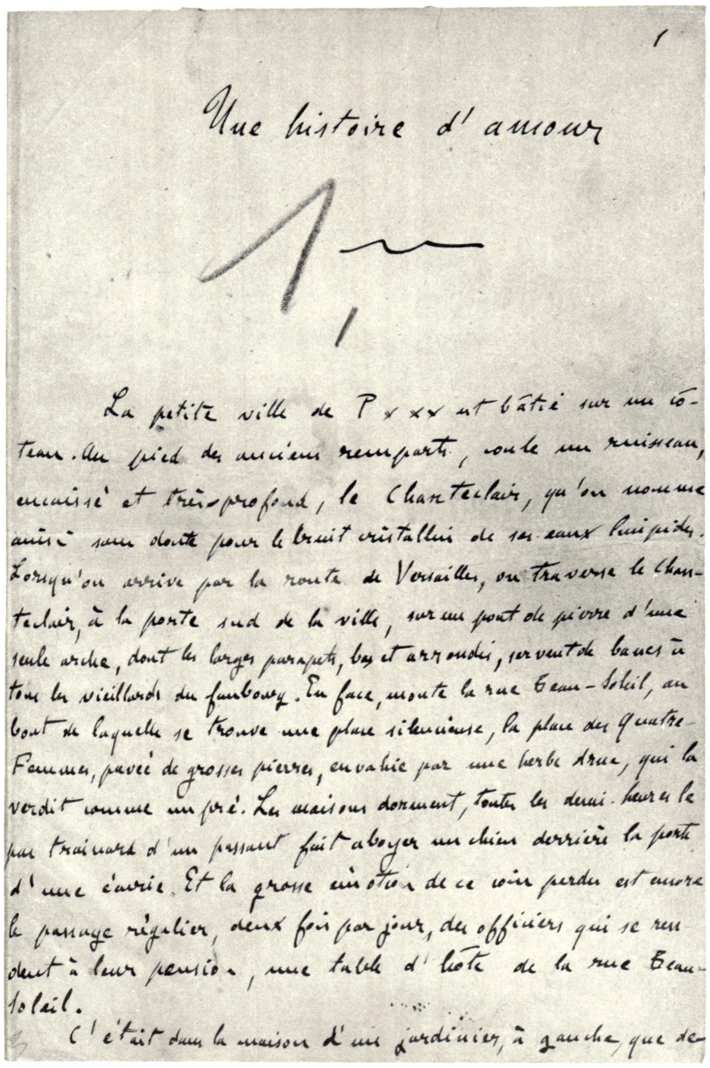

ÉMILE ZOLA: HOLOGRAPH OF POUR UNE NUIT
D'AMOUR, 1882   8⅛ × 5¼ inches
Given in 1944 by W. B. Osgood Field

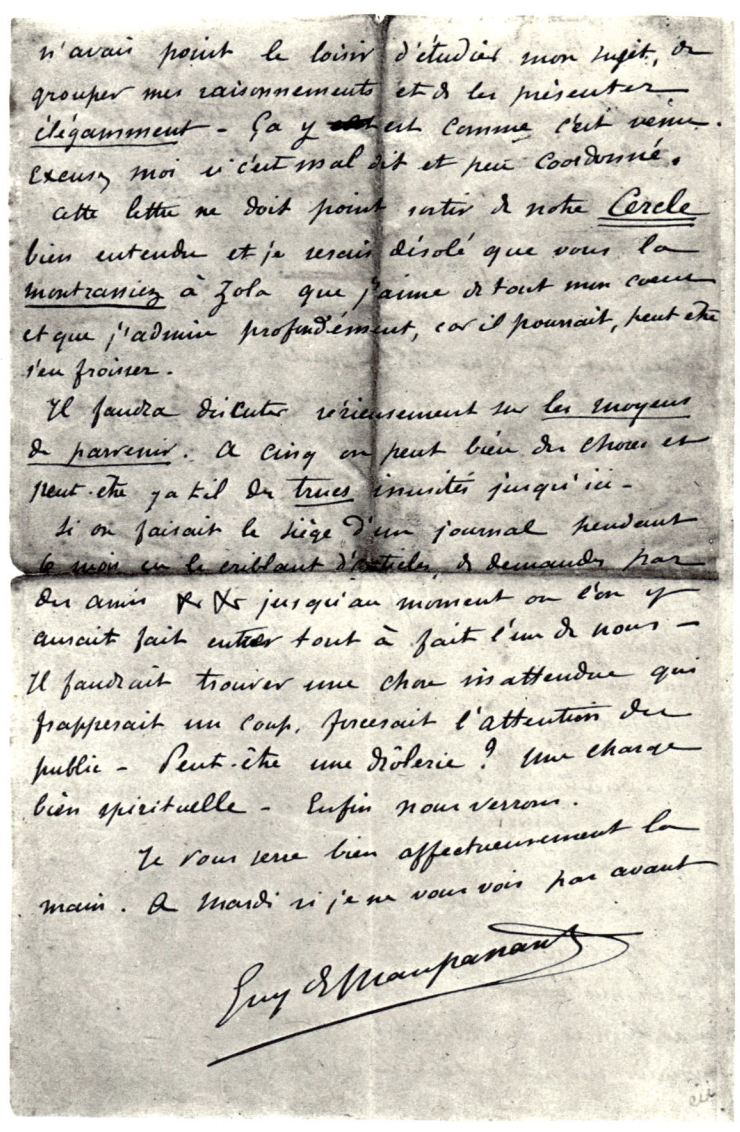

GUY DE MAUPASSANT: AUTOGRAPH LETTER TO
J. K. HUYSMANS, 17 JANUARY 1877   8½ × 5⅜ inches
Acquired in 1957 with the Amy Lowell Fund

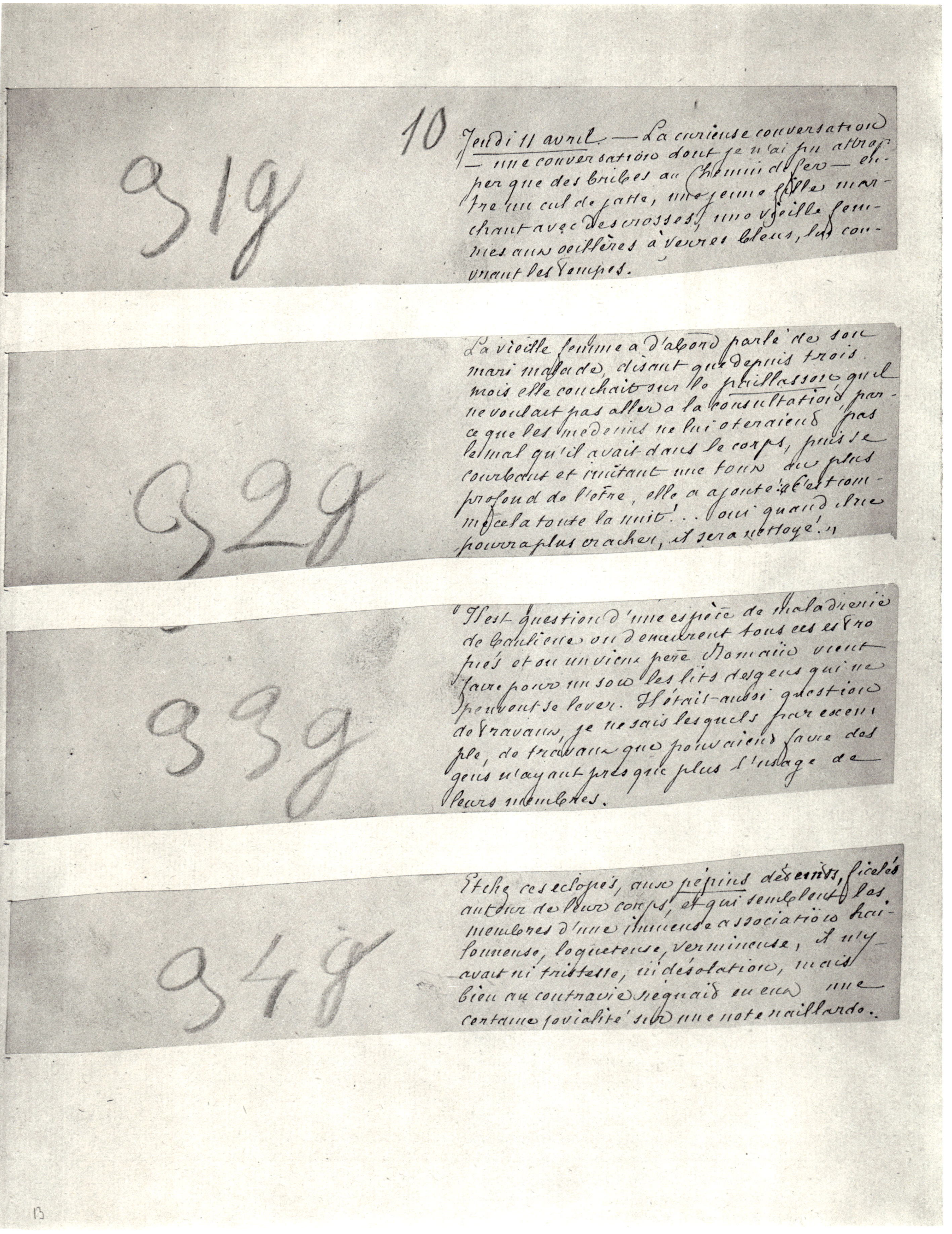

EDMOND DE GONCOURT: HOLOGRAPH JOURNAL, 1878
Acquired in 1957 with the Amy Lowell Fund

French Literature

GUSTAVE FLAUBERT: HOLOGRAPH OF *UNE NUIT DE DON JUAN*
Acquired in 1962 with the Amy Lowell Fund

ALBERT CAMUS: HOLOGRAPH OF *L'HOMME RÉVOLTÉ*

Italian Literature

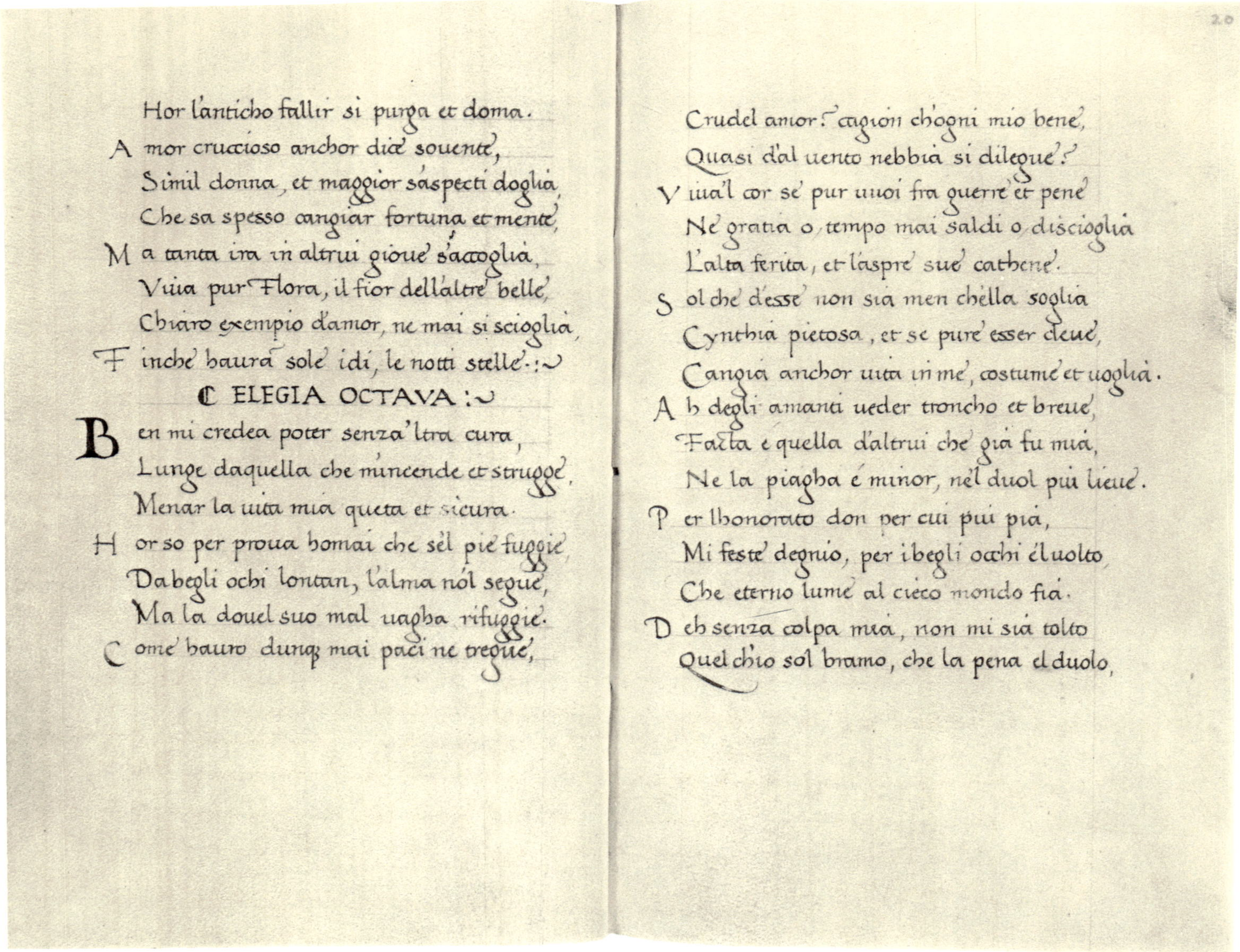

Hor l'anticho fallir si purga et doma.
Amor cruccioso anchor dicia souente,
  Simil donna, et maggior s'aspecti doglia
  Che sa spesso cangiar fortuna et mente,
Ma tanta ira in altrui gioue s'accoglia,
Viua pur Flora, il fior dell'altre belle,
Chiaro exempio d'amor, ne mai si scioglia
Finche haura sole idi, le notti stelle.

ELEGIA OCTAVA

Ben mi credea poter senza l'tra cura,
  Lunge daquella che m'incende et strugge,
  Menar la uita mia queta et sicura.
Hor so per proua homai che sel pie fugge,
  Da begli ochi lontan, l'alma nol segue,
  Ma la douel suo mal uagha rifugge.
Come hauro dunq mai paci ne tregue,
Crudel amor? cagion ch'ogni mio bene,
  Quasi dal uento nebbia si dilegue?
Viua'l cor se pur uuoi fra guerre et pene
  Ne gratia o tempo mai saldi o discioglia
  L'alta ferita, et l'aspre sue cathene.
Sol che d'esse non sia men ch'ella soglia
  Cynthia pietosa, et se pure esser deue,
  Cangia anchor uita in me, costume et uoglia.
Ah degli amanti ueder troncho et breue,
  Fatta e quella d'altrui che gia fu mia,
  Ne la piagha e minor, nel duol piu lieue.
Per lhonorato don per cui piu pia,
  Mi feste degnio, per i begli ochi el uolto,
  Che eterno lume al cieco mondo fia.
Deh senza colpa mia, non mi sia tolto
Quel ch'io sol bramo, che la pena el duolo,

LUIGI ALAMANNI: *OPERE TOSCANE*, MANUSCRIPT [CA. 1530]
Acquired in 1964 with the fund bequeathed by George L. Lincoln, H 1895

HARVARD'S Dante collection is based on the gift over a period of years by Charles Eliot Norton, H 1846, of most of his Dante library (see p. 15), to which that of George Ticknor, LL.D. (Hon.) 1850, was added in 1896. The acquisition of the Riant Library in 1899 brought a strong collection of Tasso, and from various sources came the foundation collections of Petrarch, Aretino, Ariosto, Boccaccio, Machiavelli, and other Italian classics.

The bequest in 1925 of the fund in memory of Bennett Hubbard Nash, H 1856, made possible extensive additions, particularly in later Italian literature, and the collection has been further augmented since receipt of the Amy Lowell bequest. In Italian history, the collection on the Risorgimento period formed by H. Nelson Gay, A.M. 1896, is virtually without a rival on either side of the Atlantic.

L obliuion gliaspecti obscuri & adri
   piu che mai bei tornando lasceranno
   a morte impetuosa igiorni ladri
N el eta piu fiorita et uerde aranno
   chon immortal bellezza eterna fama
   ma innanzi a tutti cha rifar si uanno
E t quella che piangendo il mondo chiama
   chon la mia lingua et chon la stanca penna
   mal ciel pur diuederla interra brama
A rriua un fiume che nasce in gebenna
   amor mi die per lui si lunga guerra
   che la memoria ancora el core accenna
F elice saxo chel bel uiso serra
   che poi chaura ripreso il suo bel uelo
   se fu beato chi la uide in terra
O r che fia dunque a riuederla in cielo?

:FINIS. M.CCCCLXX.

Quę fuerāt multis quōdam confusa tenebris
   Petrarcę laurę metra sacrata suę
Christophori et feruens pariter cyllenia cura
   Transcripsit nitido lucidiora die.
Vtq; superueniens nequeat corrumpere tēpus
   En Vindelinus ęnea plura dedit.

PETRARCH: *CANZONIERE E TRIONFI*
[VENICE] VINDELINUS DE SPIRA, 1470
The editio princeps
   Given in 1964 by Ward M. Canaday, H 1907

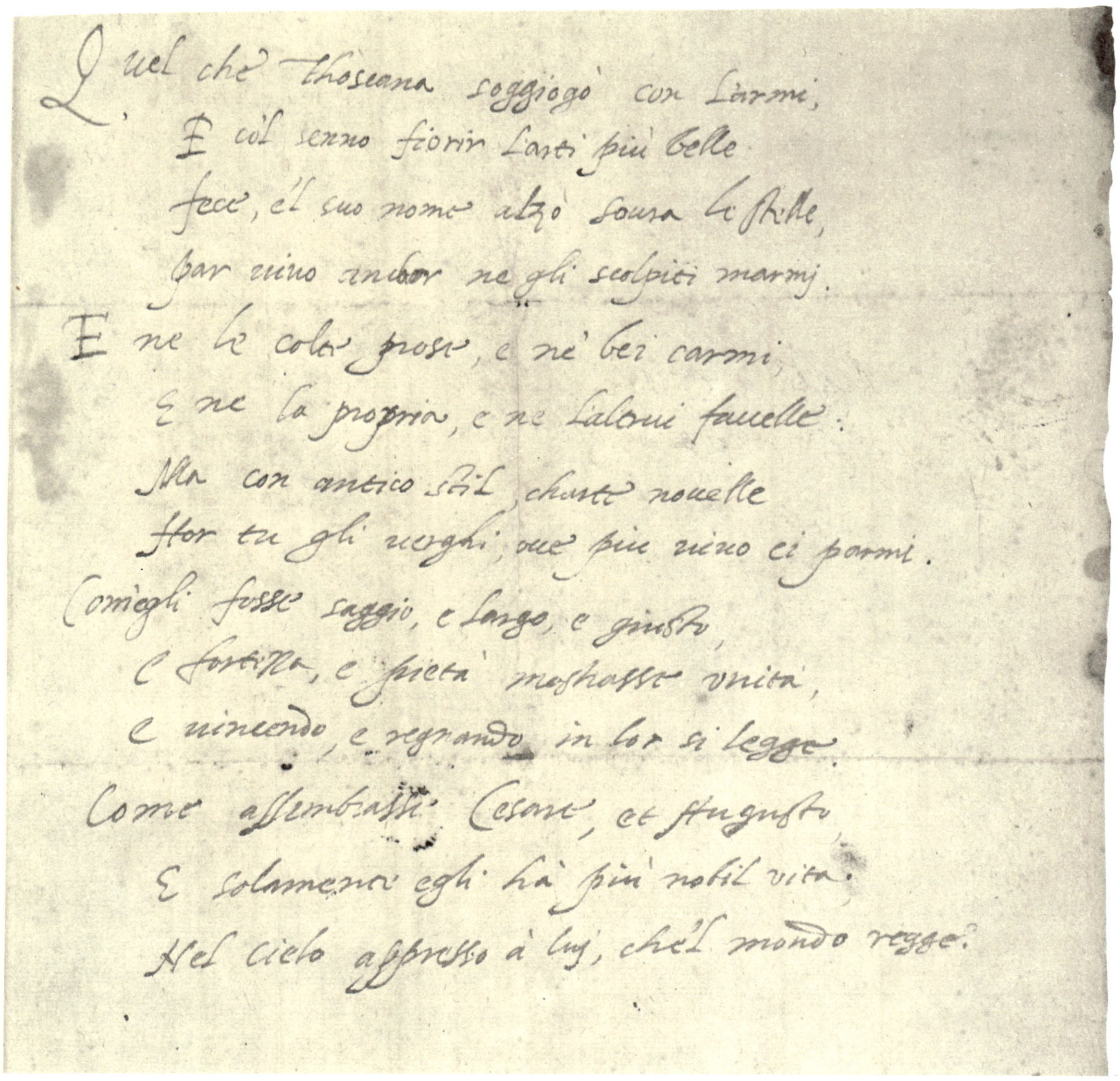

Quel che Thoscana soggiogò con l'armi,
E col senno fiorir l'arti più belle
fece, e'l suo nome alzò sovra le stelle,
par vivo ancor ne gli scolpiti marmj.

E ne le colte prose, e ne' bei carmi
E ne la propria, e ne l'altrui favelle.
Ma con antico stil, chiare novelle
Fior tu gli vergli, ove più vivo ci parmi.

Com'egli fosse saggio, e largo, e giusto,
E fortezza, e pietà mostrasse unita,
e vincendo, e regnando, in lor si legge.

Come assembrasti Cesare, et Augusto,
E solamente egli hà più nobil vita,
Nel cielo appresso à luj, che'l mondo regge.

TORQUATO TASSO:
HOLOGRAPH SONNET, 1582 8 × 7⅝ inches
Acquired in 1940 with the Nash Fund

LUDOVICO ARIOSTO: *ORLANDO FURIOSO*, 1516 8 × 11⅛ inches
Acquired in 1944 through gifts of Friends of the Library

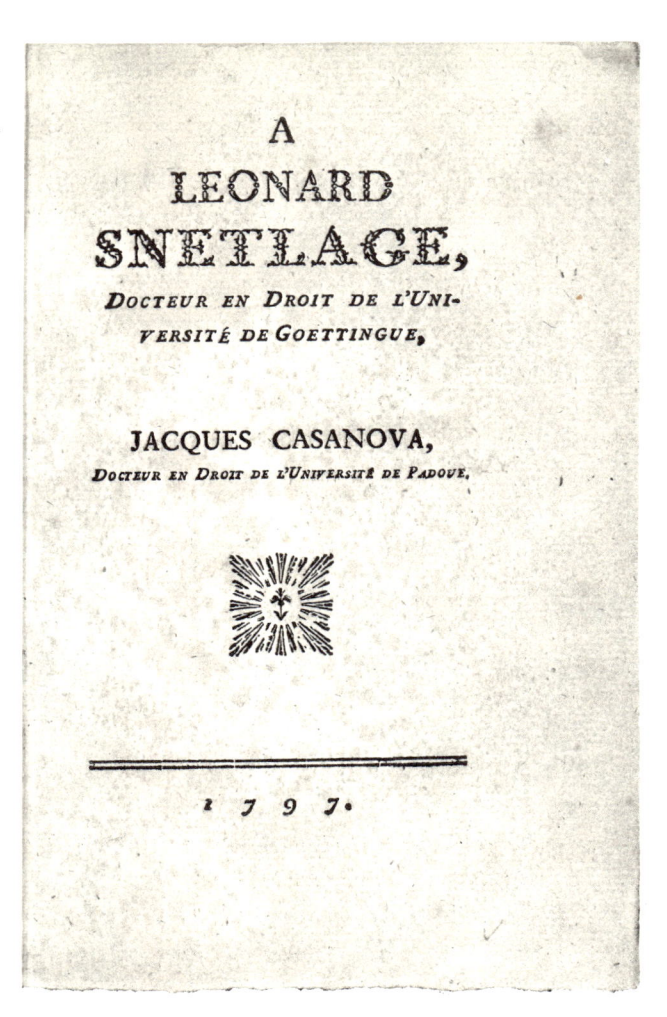

JACQUES CASANOVA: À LEONARD SNETLAGE, 1797   6¾ × 4¼ inches
Acquired in 1949 with the Norton Fund

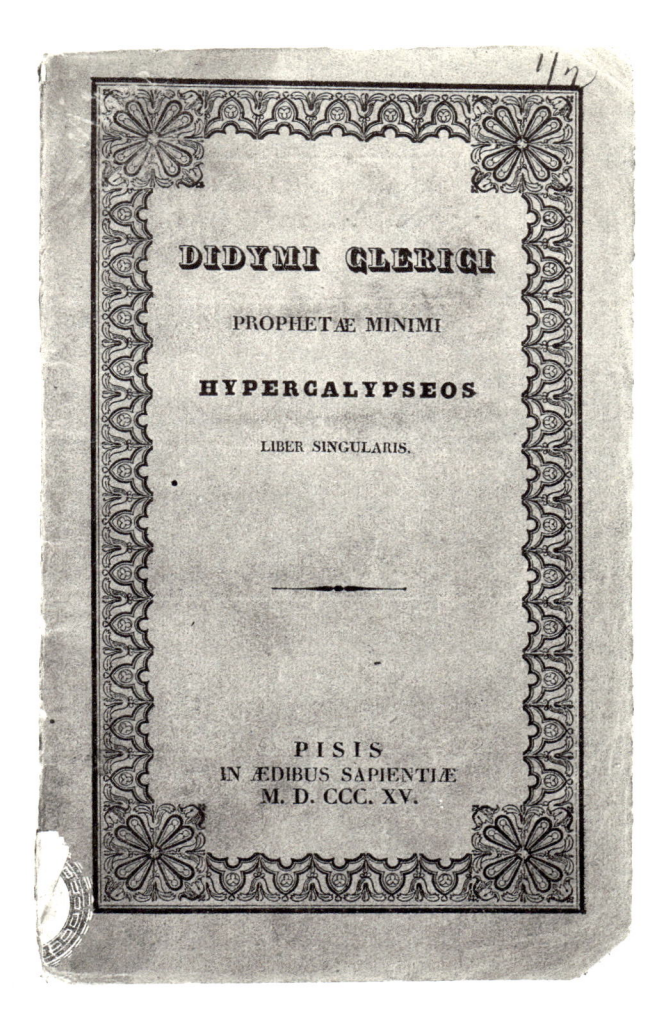

UGO FOSCOLO: HYPERCALYPSEOS LIBER SINGULARIS [ZURICH] 1815
6¾ × 4⅛ inches
Acquired in 1960 with the Amy Lowell Fund

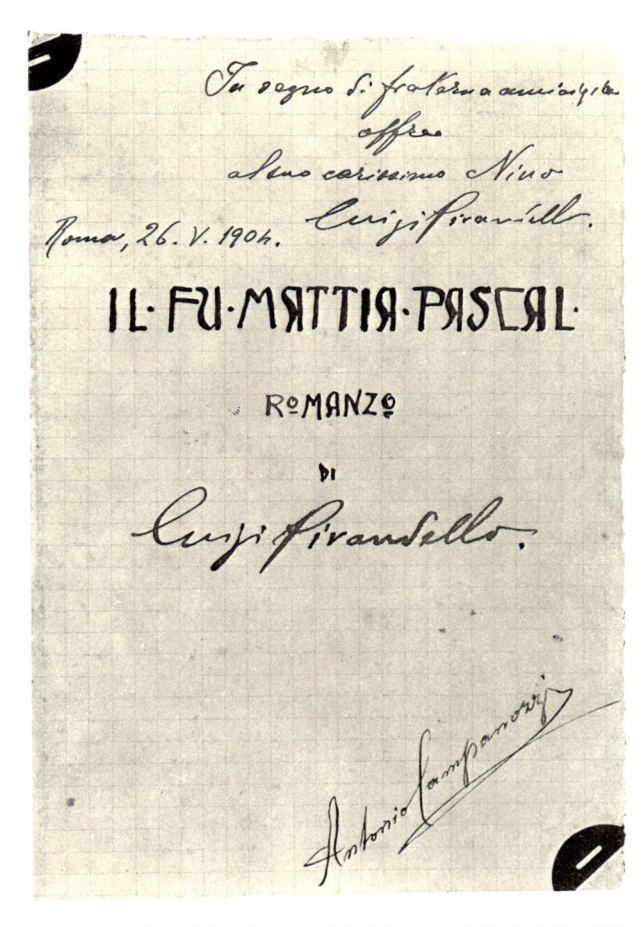

LUIGI PIRANDELLO: HOLOGRAPH OF IL FU MATTIA PASCAL, 1904   6⅛ × 4⅛ inches
Acquired in 1959 with the Amy Lowell Fund

GIACOMO LEOPARDI: SAGGIO CHE DEGLI STUDII DA LORO FATTI NEL DECORSO ANNO 1809,
1810   9⅝ × 7½ inches
Acquired in 1960 with the Amy Lowell Fund

Italian Literature   157

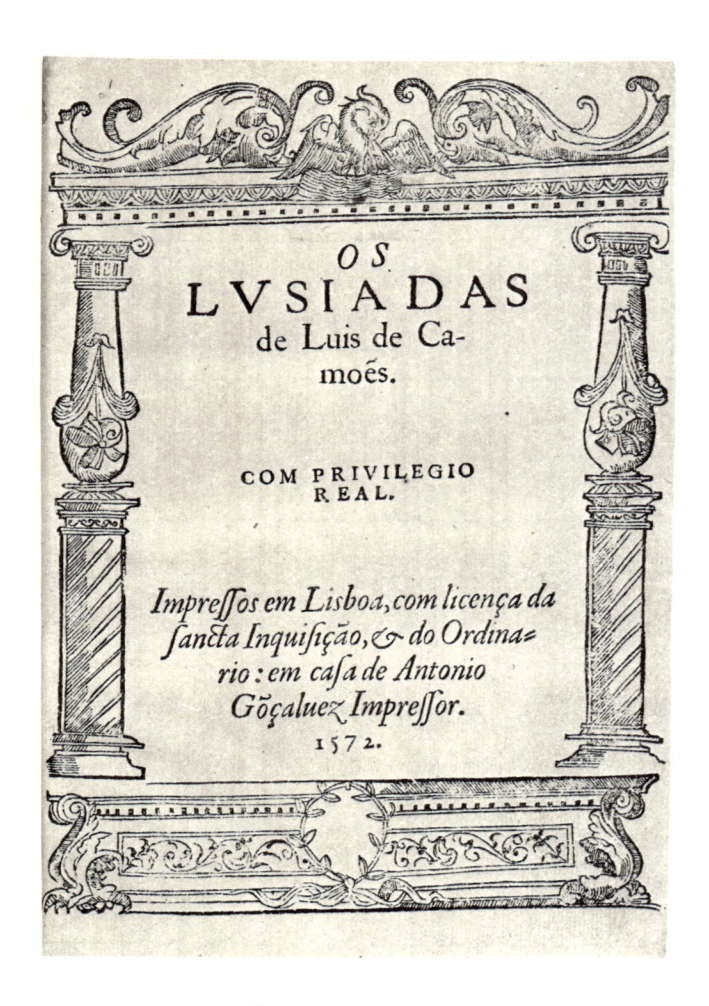

LUIS DE CAMOÊS: *OS LUSIADAS*, 1572   7 × 4¾ inches
The 'E' edition
Given in 1928 by John B. Stetson, Jr., H 1906

LUIS DE CAMOÊS: *OS LUSIADAS*, 1572   7¼ × 4¾ inches
The 'E e' edition
Given in 1928 by John B. Stetson, Jr., H 1906

Camoẽs and Cervantes

HARVARD'S collection of Portuguese belles lettres stems chiefly from the gift in 1928 by John B. Stetson, Jr., H 1906, of the great Palha Collection. Central to this collection is a long run of the national epic, the *Lusiadas* of Luis de Camoẽs, beginning with multiple copies of the first edition and its contemporary imitation.

At the foundation of Harvard's collection of Miguel de Cervantes Saavedra are the gifts over a long period of years of the late Carl T. Keller, H 1894. The Houghton Library now possesses first editions of all of Cervantes' works; translations into forty-seven languages, including a long and nearly complete run of 17th century versions and every English translation before 1800; together with association copies, illustrated editions, otherwise unrecorded early issues in parts, and Cervantica of every description.

Mr. Keller insured the continuity of the collection by bequeathing a fund for acquisitions in the field of Cervantes and Iberian letters generally, making it possible to fill the few remaining gaps as opportunities arise.

CERVANTES: *PRIMERA PARTE DE LA GALATEA*,
1585   5⅜ × 3⅝ inches   The author's first book
Given in 1928 by John B. Stetson, Jr., H 1906

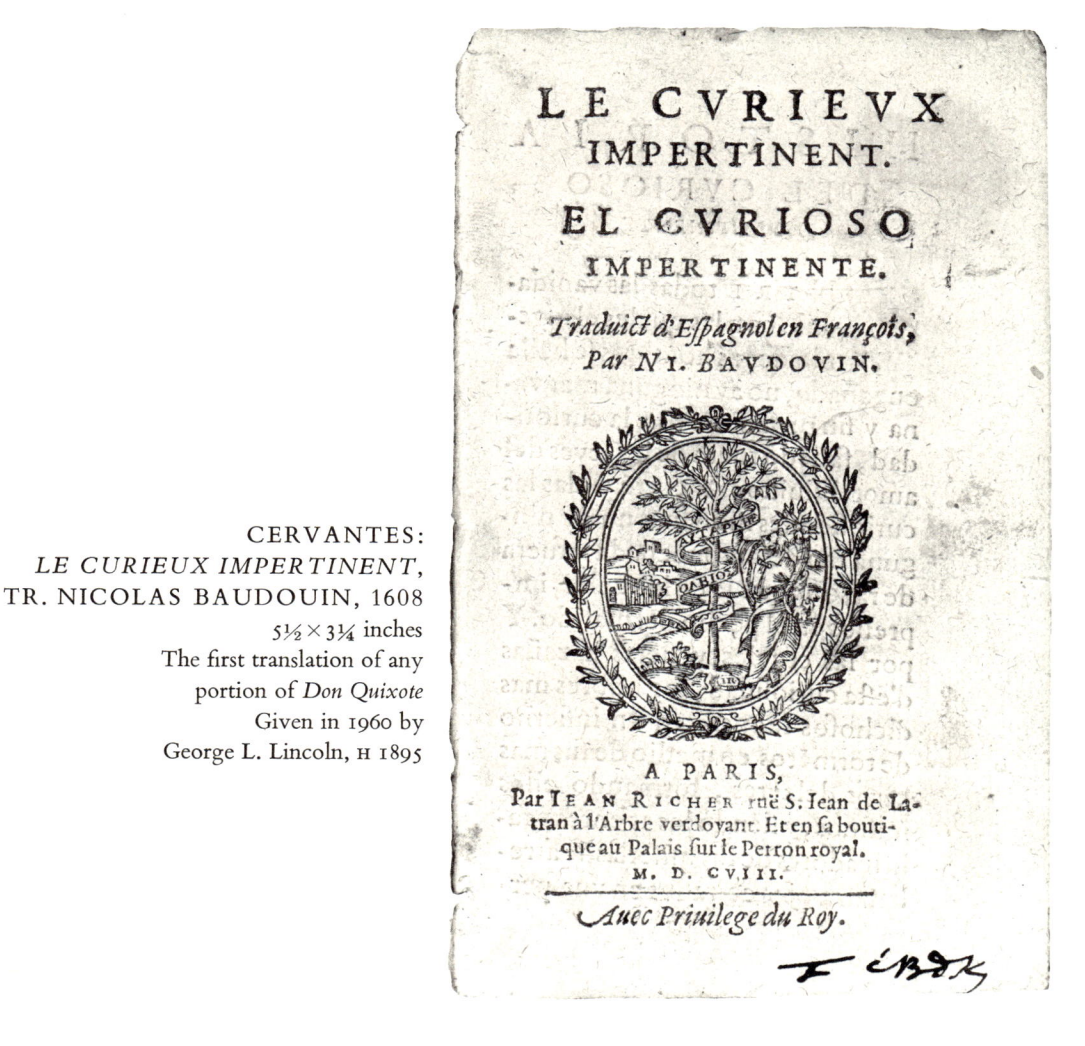

CERVANTES:
LE CURIEUX IMPERTINENT,
TR. NICOLAS BAUDOUIN, 1608
5½ × 3¼ inches
The first translation of any
portion of *Don Quixote*
Given in 1960 by
George L. Lincoln, H 1895

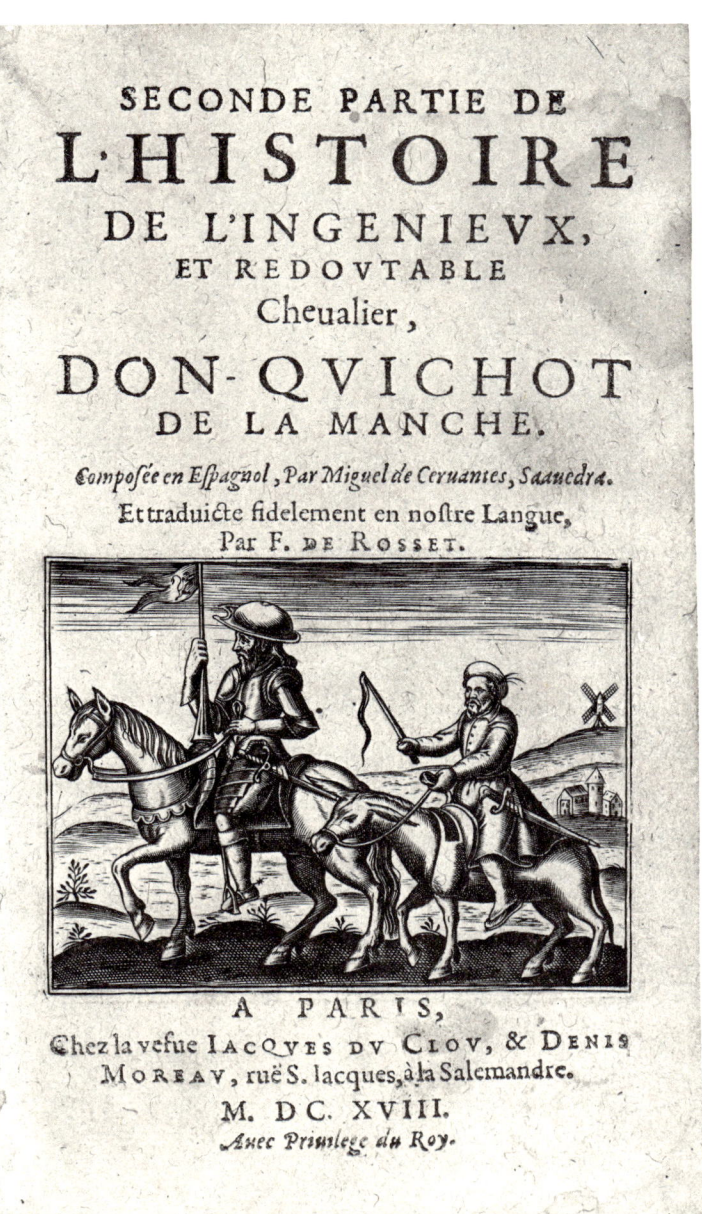

CERVANTES: *DON-QUICHOT*, PART II,
TR. FRANÇOIS DE ROSSET, 1618   6¾ × 4 inches
Acquired in 1965 with the Keller Fund

CERVANTES: *NOVELAS EXEMPLARES*, 1613   8⅛ × 5¼ inches
Acquired in 1947 through gifts of Friends of the Library

159

TYCHO BRAHE: *ASTRONOMIAE INSTAURATAE MECHANICA*, 1598   13⅜ × 9⅜ inches
Acquired in 1945 with the Hofer Fund

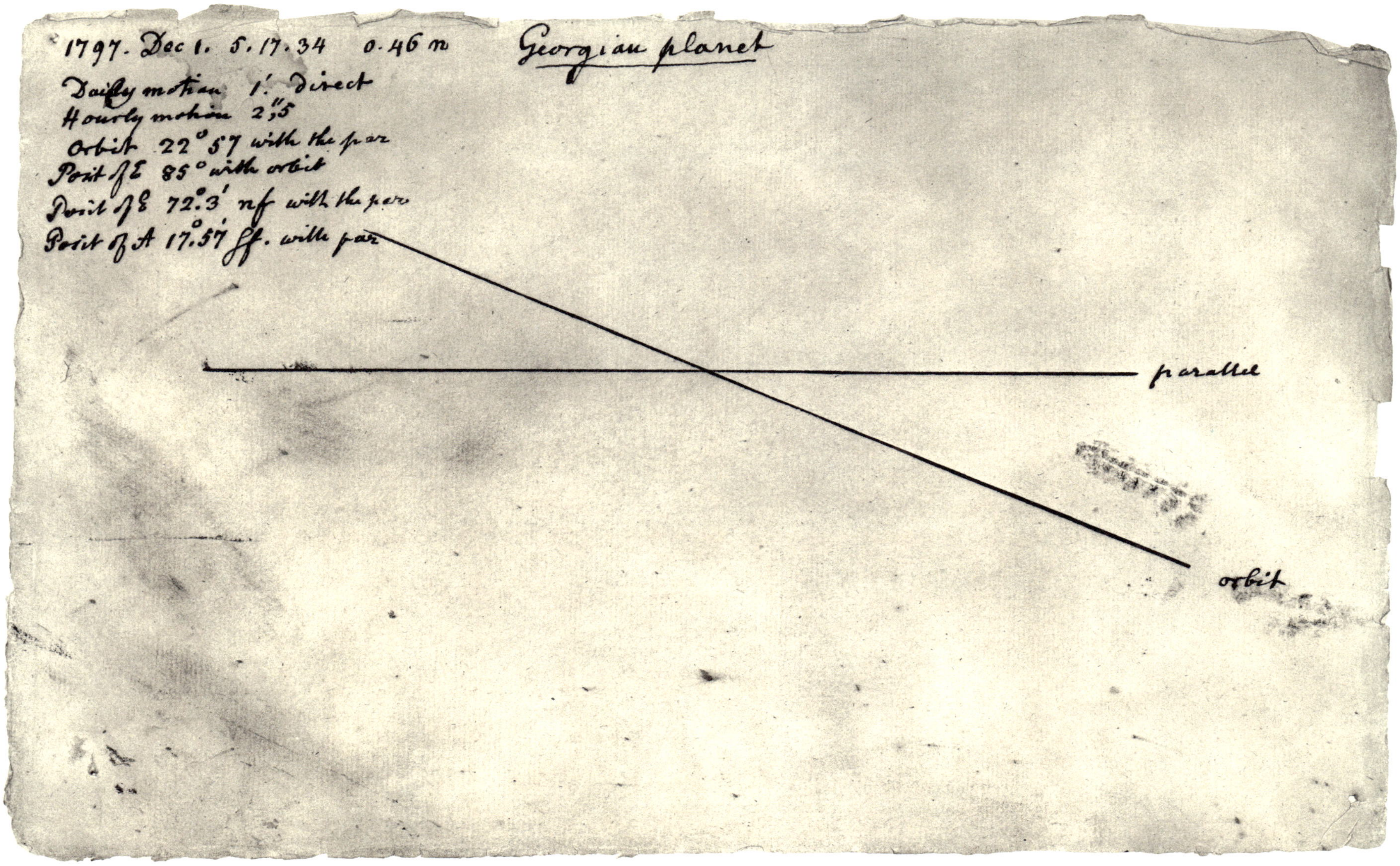

OBSERVATION OF URANUS BY ITS DISCOVERER, SIR WILLIAM HERSCHEL 8½ × 13⅜ inches
Transferred from the Astronomical Library

The History of Science

WHEN Harrison D. Horblit, H 1933, published *One Hundred Books Famous in Science* (1964), it was found that the Harvard libraries already possessed 106 of the titles he described—an agreeable paradox explained by the fact that, counting alternates, the Horblit list actually contains 130 books. All but a handful had been acquired by the University practically when they were issued, in aid of the regular work of Harvard scientists.

But retrospective collecting has also been taking place. Even before the Department of the History of Science was established, the library was not only beginning to respond to the demands of scholars but attempting to anticipate them. Friends with similar interests have come forward, giving material aid and also exhorting to greater efforts: Mr. Horblit himself, for example, and David P. Wheatland, H 1922, who presented among other things a run of Robert Boyle that brings Harvard holdings very near completeness.

Music

MUSIC has been an official part of the Harvard curriculum since 1873, when John Knowles Paine was appointed Assistant Professor of Music, to become full professor two years later. It comes as no surprise to find the working manuscripts of most of Paine's own compositions in the Houghton Library.

No subject better illustrates the interlocking of the university's numerous library units. Music is divided among the Isham Library in the Memorial Church, the Eda Kuhn Loeb Library in the Music Department, and several other collections; the Houghton Library is entrusted with most of the manuscripts and rare editions. Neither accident nor bureaucratic whim dictates this division, which results instead from careful planning to place materials where they will be best cared for and most readily available for use.

All aspects of music are represented, but the principal focus is on theoretical and historical studies.

WILLIAM BYRD: MANUSCRIPT PART-BOOK [CA. 1603]
Acquired in 1927 with the Elkan Naumburg Fund

MVSICA SIMPLEX.

Kyrie eleyson. Kyrie eleyson. Kyrie eleyson.

CHriste eleyson. Christe eleyson. .ij.

Kyrie eleyson. Kyrie eley-son. Kyrie eleyson.

MVSICA SIMPLEX. A

NICOLAS FORMÉ: *MUSICA SIMPLEX QUATUOR VOCUM*, 1638
Given in 1955 by Mrs. Henry S. Grew

The Theatre Collection

THE Harvard Theatre Collection, one of the most comprehensive in its field in any library, has been built up almost entirely during the present century. In 1915 George Pierce Baker, H 1869, persuaded his classmate Robert Gould Shaw to found the Collection, the Corporation to accept its foundation, and the library administration to devote suitable rooms to its housing and display. In 1949 the Collection moved into the Houghton Library, where in 1952 its permanent display rooms, a memorial to Edward Sheldon, H 1908, were opened.

Robert Gould Shaw's enormous personal library formed the nucleus of the Collection, and it was very nearly doubled by the bequest in 1917 of the truly remarkable library of Evert Jansen Wendell, H 1882. Other benefactions came from Frank E. Chase, H 1876, Daniel Payne Griswold, H 1887, and Winthrop Ames, H 1895. Together, these gifts shaped the Collection and pointed the course it still follows today.

Primarily a collection on stage history, it is particularly but by no means exclusively strong in the English and American theatre. It contains more than two million playbills; nearly 100,000 prints; a quarter of a million photographic portraits; a vast file of sheet music; more than 2,500 promptbooks; and countless letters, manuscripts, drawings for scene designs and costumes, together with many other kinds of theatrical materials. A particular specialty is the ballet, greatly enriched by the magnificent collection of George Chaffée. One room is devoted to the life and works of Edward Sheldon, who had his first hit on Broadway while still a student in the famous 47 Workshop, and whose family established the display rooms in his memory.

ROBERT EDMOND JONES, H 1910: DESIGN FOR *RICHARD III*, 1918   6¼ × 9⅞ inches
Given by Lee Simonson, H 1909

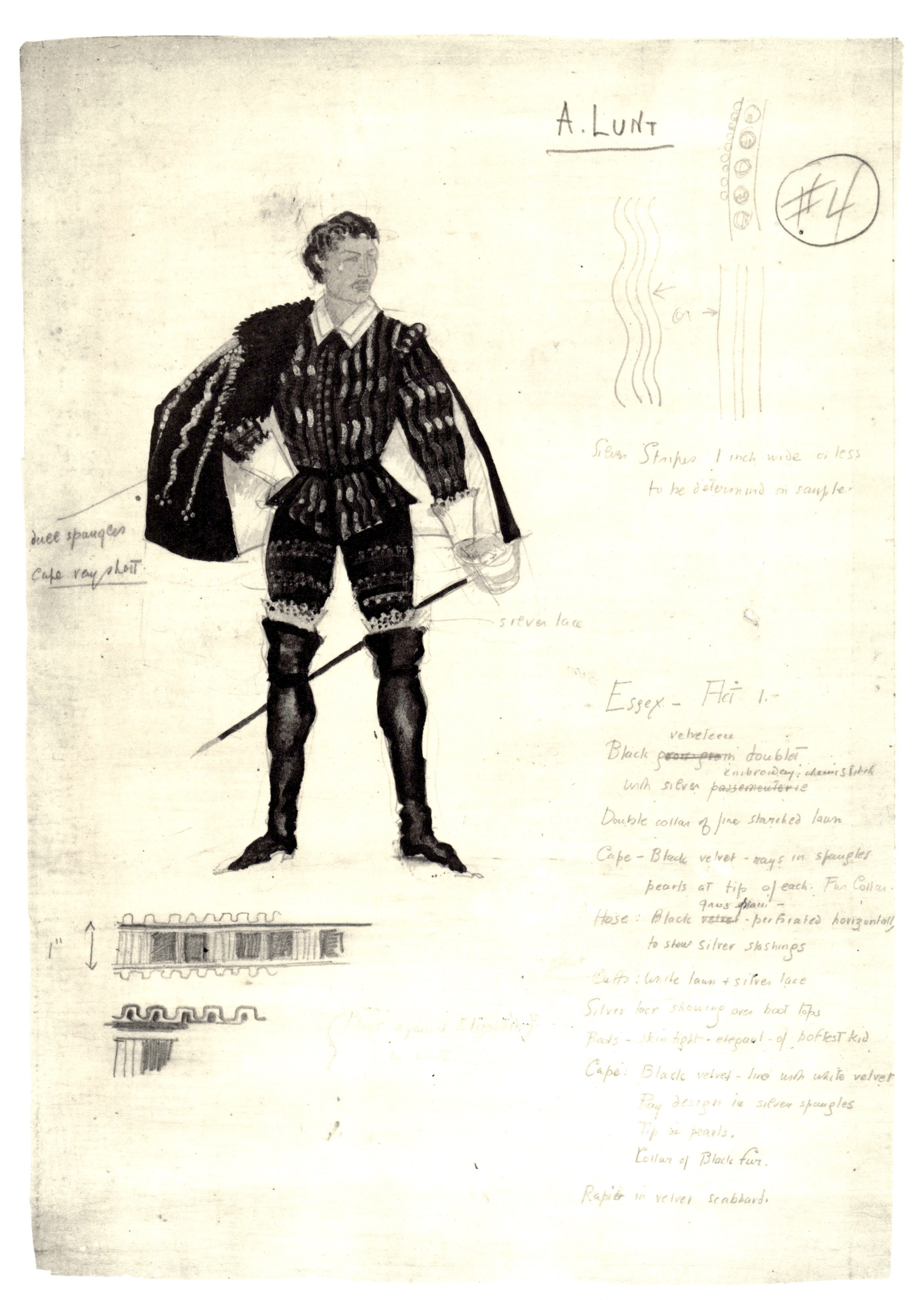

LEE SIMONSON, H 1909: DESIGN FOR *ELIZABETH THE QUEEN*, 1930   13⅝ × 9⅝ inches
Given in 1964 by the artist, through Orville K. Larson, in memory of Dr. William B. Van Lennep, H 1929

165

Andriæ

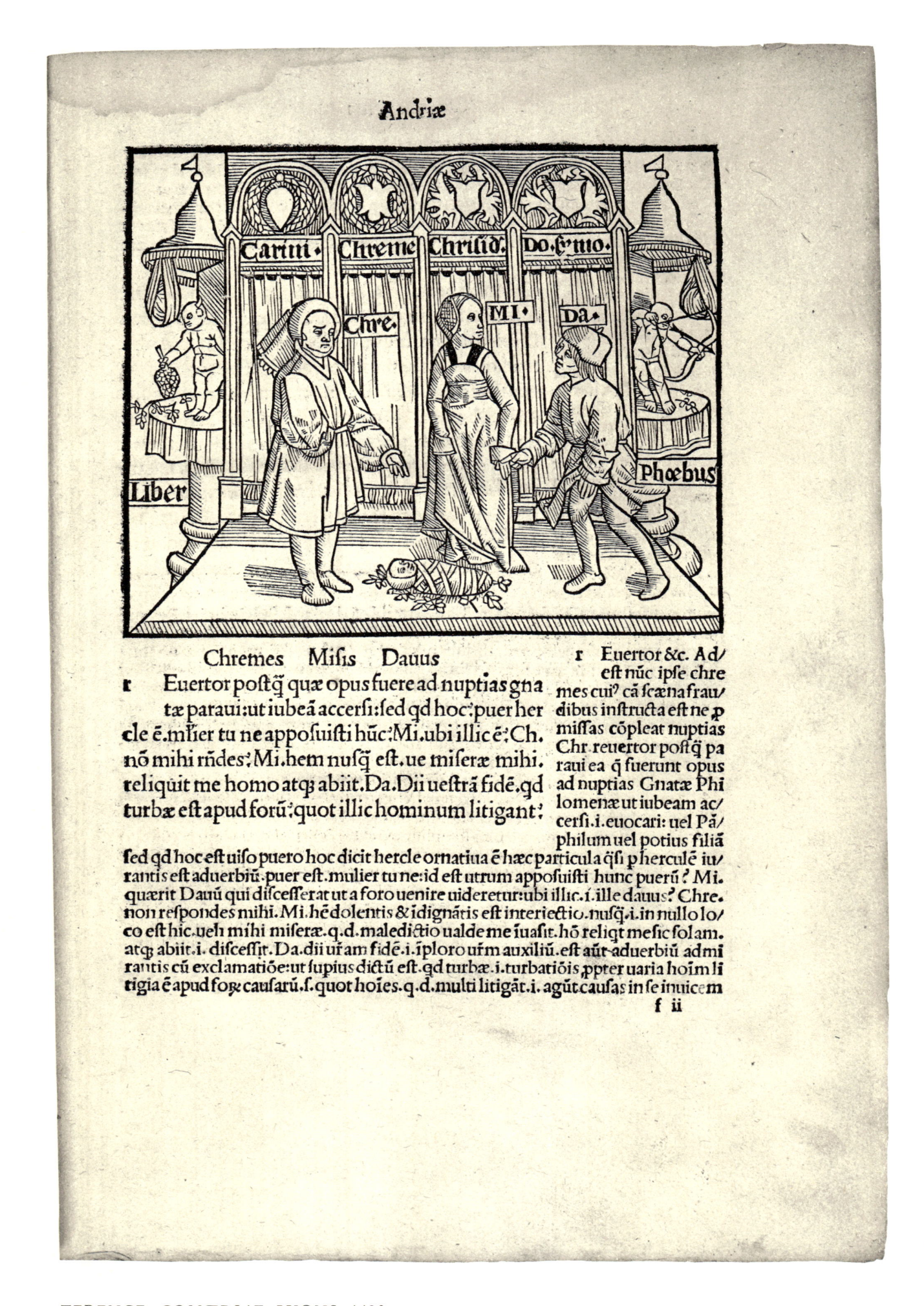

Chremes Misis Dauus

r Euertor postq̃ quę opus fuere ad nuptias gnatę paraui:ut iubeā accersi:sed qd hoc:puer hercle ē.mlier tu ne apposuisti hūc:Mi.ubi illic ē:Ch. nō mihi rn̄des:Mi.hem nusq̃ est.ue miserę mihi. reliquit me homo atq̃ abiit.Da.Dii uestrā fidē.qd turbę est apud forū:quot illic hominum litigant:

r Euertor &c. Adest nūc ipse chremes cui° cā scæna fraudibus instructa est ne p missas cōpleat nuptias Chr.reuertor postq̃ paraui ea q̃ fuerunt opus ad nuptias Gnatæ Philomenū ut iubeam accersi.i.euocari:uel Pāphilum uel potius filiā

sed qd hoc est uiso puero hoc dicit hercle ornatiua ē hæc particula q̃si p herculē iurantis est aduerbiū.puer est.mulier tu ne:id est utrum apposuisti hunc puerū? Mi. quærit Dauū qui discesserat ut a foro uenire uideretur:ubi illic.i.ille dauus? Chre. non respondes mihi.Mi.hē dolentis & idignātis est interiectio.nusq̃.i.in nullo loco est hic.ueh mihi miseræ.q.d.maledictio ualde me iuasit.hō reliqt me sic solam. atq̃ abiit.i.discessit.Da.dii ur̄am fidē.i.iploro ur̄m auxiliū.est aūt aduerbiū admirantis cū exclamatiōe:ut supius dictū est.qd turbæ.i.turbatiōis.ppter uaria hoīm litigia ē apud forū.causarū.s.quot hoīes.q.d.multi litigāt.i.agūt causas in se inuicem

f ii

TERENCE: *COMŒDIAE*, LYONS, 1493
The first printed book with plates of theatrical performances
Acquired in 1958 with the F. E. Chase Fund

166

THOMAS GOFFE'S AUTOGRAPH PARTBOOK FOR POLYPRAGMATICUS IN *PHILOSOPHASTER*
[1617?] 5⅞ × 7¾ inches
Given in 1960 by John F. Fleming

ROBERT BURTON: AUTOGRAPH MS. OF *PHILOSOPHASTER*, 1617 7½ × 10⅝ inches
From the collection of William Augustus White, H 1863, given in 1941 by Harold T. White, H 1897, and Mrs. Hugh D. Marshall

The Theatre Collection 167

CONTEMPORARY BINDING ON KILLIGREW'S *CLARASILLA*
Acquired in 1946, the gift of Friends of the Library

Act. 1:

Enter King Appius, Selucus and Attendants

King. Selucus, you know the soule of our designe
Lies in the speedie and silent execution of
the plot: Lett vs not presume in security,
Till wee fall in our owne; But goe, and when
y'haue beguirt the place, giue vs notice, that
with our charge, they may at once feare and feele
their danger, and by vs bee cloth'd in ruine,
Ere they know whose Livery they weare. — *Exit Selucus*
This, if Fortune bee a God, and ioyne with
Justice, and with her strength will assist,
Our Industry, must bee: For, where Justice
Strikes, in what corner of the Earth can
Victory hide her selfe, and that youthfull
Hand not find her.

App: I should blush at this, if there needed more
Arguments to confirme, I shall bee Victorious,
Then the Reward proposed. For had the Gods
Intended the farr-fam'd Clarasillas vertues
A reward for treason, They would then have
Left her vertue such a Guard, whose power
hath stood amongst Traytors, when yours
fell vpon the Faith that bore it.

King. You oblige me Sr. And this sweetnes makes mee
Beg, you will bee pleas'd to let mee once agen
Call to your Memory some perticulars of that
Tedious story, my miserie made mee account
To you. This Traytor Siluander, haveinge
by my Loue gain'd an Interest, and by mee
Clim'd over the heads of all his fellowes,
In the strength of his trust, grew too
powerfull with mee, and in a battaile, where
my cause only strucke, gott the day.

THOMAS KILLIGREW: AUTOGRAPH MS. OF *CLARASILLA*, 1639
Acquired in 1946, the gift of Friends of the Library

THE EARLIEST ENGLISH PLAYBILL [CA. 1655]
Given in 1915 by Robert Gould Shaw, H 1869

PLAYBILL FOR SALEM, MASSACHUSETTS [1799]   19⅝ × 11¾ inches
Given in 1914 by Professor James Hardy Ropes, H 1889

Last Night

Of performing this Season,

THEATRE

WASHINGTON HALL,

On *Friday* Evening, June 14th, will be performed the celebrated Comedy, of

THE

Spoiled Child

LITTLE PICKEL (THE SPOILED CHILD) with Songs,	Miss WESTRAY.
TAG (THE AUTHOR)	Mr. MUNTO.
JOHN	Mr. MOORE,
AND OLD PICKEL	Mr. SIMPSON,
MARIA	Mrs. GRAUPNER.
AND Miss PICKEL,	Mrs. SIMPSON.

End of the Comedy, The Celebrated Patriotic Song, written by THOMAS PAINE Esq. A. M. Called the,

Green Mountain Farmer,

or, Adams, Washington & Liberty, by Mr. Munto.

After which the Comic Song, of MEG OF WAPPING, or the WIFE OF SEVEN HUSBANDS, by Mr. SIMPSON.

To Conclude with a favorite Song by Mrs. Graupner.

TO WHICH WILL BE ADDED,

The Musical Drama of the

Waterman,

OR FIRST OF AUGUST,

TOM TUG, (THE WATERMAN)	Mr. MUNTO.
BUNDLE,	Mr. MOORE.
AND ROBIN (THE MACARONI GARDNER)	Mr. SIMPSON.
Mrs. BUNDLE,	Mrs. SIMPSON.
AND WILHALMINA,	Mrs. GRAUPNER,

☞ TICKETS TO BE HAD AT DOCTOR STEARNS's, COVERLY's PRINTING OFFICE, AND OF Mr. SIMPSON, AT DOCTOR BACON'S, Essex-Street.——BOXES. 4/6. PIT, 3/.—CHILDREN NOT EXCEEDING TEN YEARS HALF PRICE.

☞ DOORS TO BE OPEN AT HALF PAST SEVEN, AND PERFORMANCE TO BEGIN AT EIGHT O'CLOCK.

GIOVANNI BATTISTA CORIOLANO: *TEATRO DEL TORNEO*, 1628

ALFONSO PARIGI & STEFANO DELLA BELLA: *LA NOZZE DEGLI DEI*, 1637
Acquired with the F. E. Chase Fund

The Theatre Collection 173

JACOB DE GHEYN: MASKED ACTORS, 1629
Given in 1963 by friends in memory of Dr. William B. Van Lennep, H 1929

JULES BOUVIER: LITHOGRAPH, *LE PAS DES DÉESSES*, 1846   21½ × 17 inches
  Bequeathed in 1917 by Evert Jansen Wendell, H 1882

ROMANESQUE BINDING ON MANUSCRIPT OF *LEVITICUS GLOSSATUS* (SAEC. XIII)
One of the finest surviving examples
Given in 1955 by Philip Hofer, H 1921, in honor of William A. Jackson

Printing and Graphic Arts

NEARLY thirty years ago Philip Hofer, H 1921, founded the Department of Printing and Graphic Arts, and he has served as its curator ever since. So far as is recorded, no major library had hitherto established a collection specifically to gather, teach, and show all aspects of the 'Arts of the Book.'

Before 1938 the Harvard Library had few fine illustrated books, very few medieval illuminated manuscripts, and practically no oriental picture scrolls and books. The department now contains about 15,000 volumes and is strong in all these fields, but particularly in the first, with probably the principal collection in this country for the sixteenth, seventeenth, and nineteenth centuries. Its strength in the eighteenth century is growing, with perhaps the leading American collection of Italian illustrated books, and it has made a late but determined start in twentieth century printing and illustration.

The collections cover all areas of pictorial interest, including science and travel, fiction, the classics, and other conventional and unconventional subjects. The calligraphic manuscripts and writing books, both western and eastern, exhibit a variety and depth probably unrivaled elsewhere in America. Printers' type specimen books are present in great strength, thanks largely to William Bentinck-Smith, H 1937, who added his collection to that of the curator. Drawings for book illustration are represented in some quantity, and there is a smaller but important group of bindings. The printed and decorated book papers gathered by Rosamund Bowditch Loring form the nucleus of another large collection. A small group of inscriptions of all periods on stone, silver, vellum, wood, and other materials displays the art of letter design. Many of the modern examples were commissioned for the library by the curator. The reference library on the Arts of the Book numbers over five thousand books and pamphlets, and many of them are special and annotated copies.

A publication program makes the riches of the department available to students everywhere. The first catalogue based on its holdings, two volumes recording the French sixteenth century illustrated books, was compiled by Miss Ruth Mortimer of the department's staff, and published by the Belknap Press of the Harvard University Press in 1964. Two more catalogues of even larger dimensions are in preparation, covering Italian illustrated books of the sixteenth and eighteenth centuries. In 1951 Mr. Hofer published the first general book about European baroque illustration, and in 1961 the Assistant Curator, Miss Eleanor M. Garvey, in consultation with the curator, compiled an authoritative catalogue of an exhibition of modern European and American illustration, *The Artist and the Book: 1860–1960*, published jointly with the Boston Museum of Fine Arts and now in its second edition.

The pages that follow, the longest individual section in this book, may serve to demonstrate the dazzling variety of the collections in Printing and Graphic Arts.

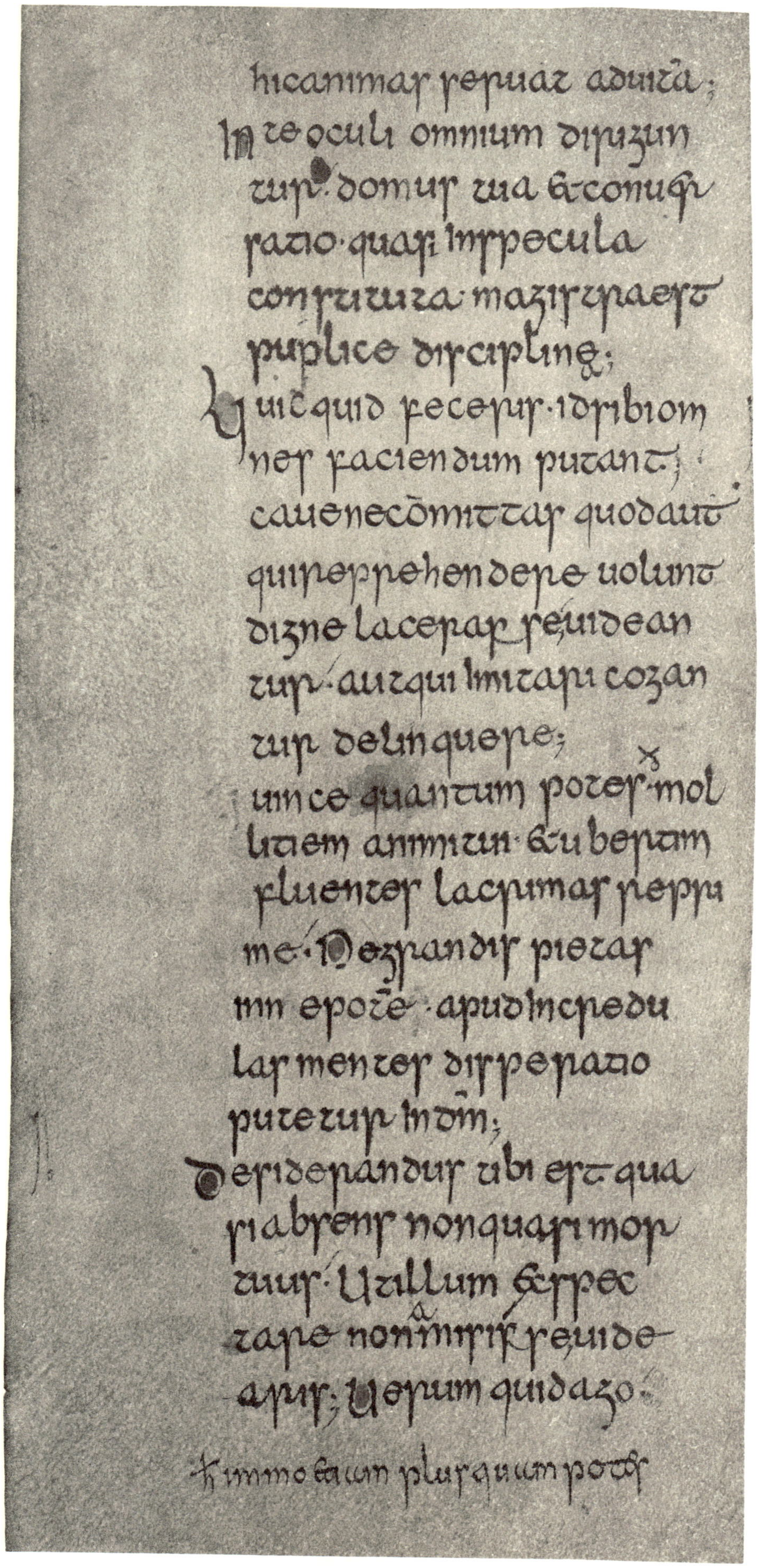

MANUSCRIPT FRAGMENT OF ST. JEROME:
EPISTULA AD HELIODORUM (SAEC. VIII) 12 × 5½ inches
   Acquired in 1946 with the Hofer Fund

MANUSCRIPT SACRAMENTARY,
NORTH ITALY (SAEC. XI) 9 × 5⅛ inches
   Acquired in 1955 with the Hofer Fund

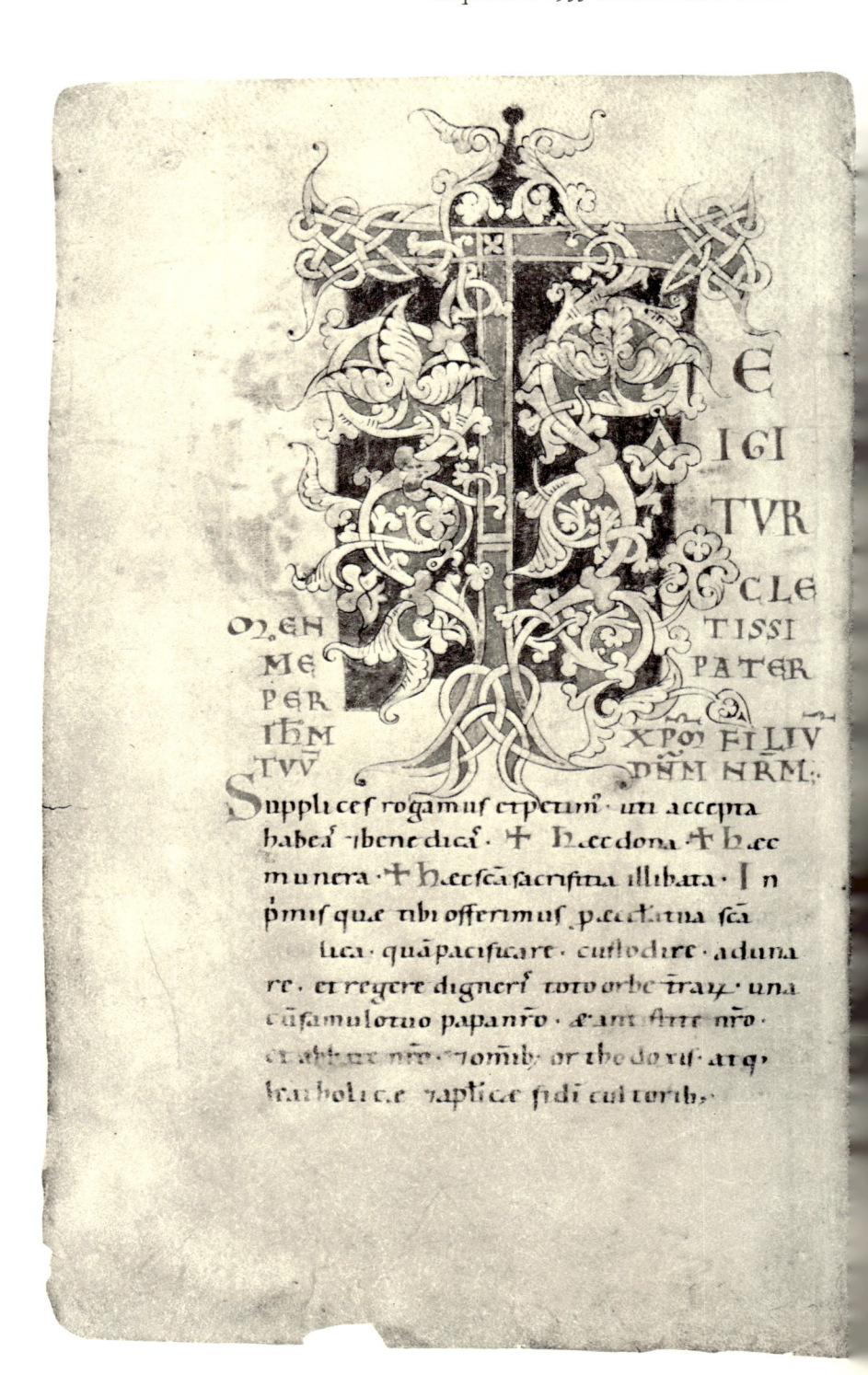

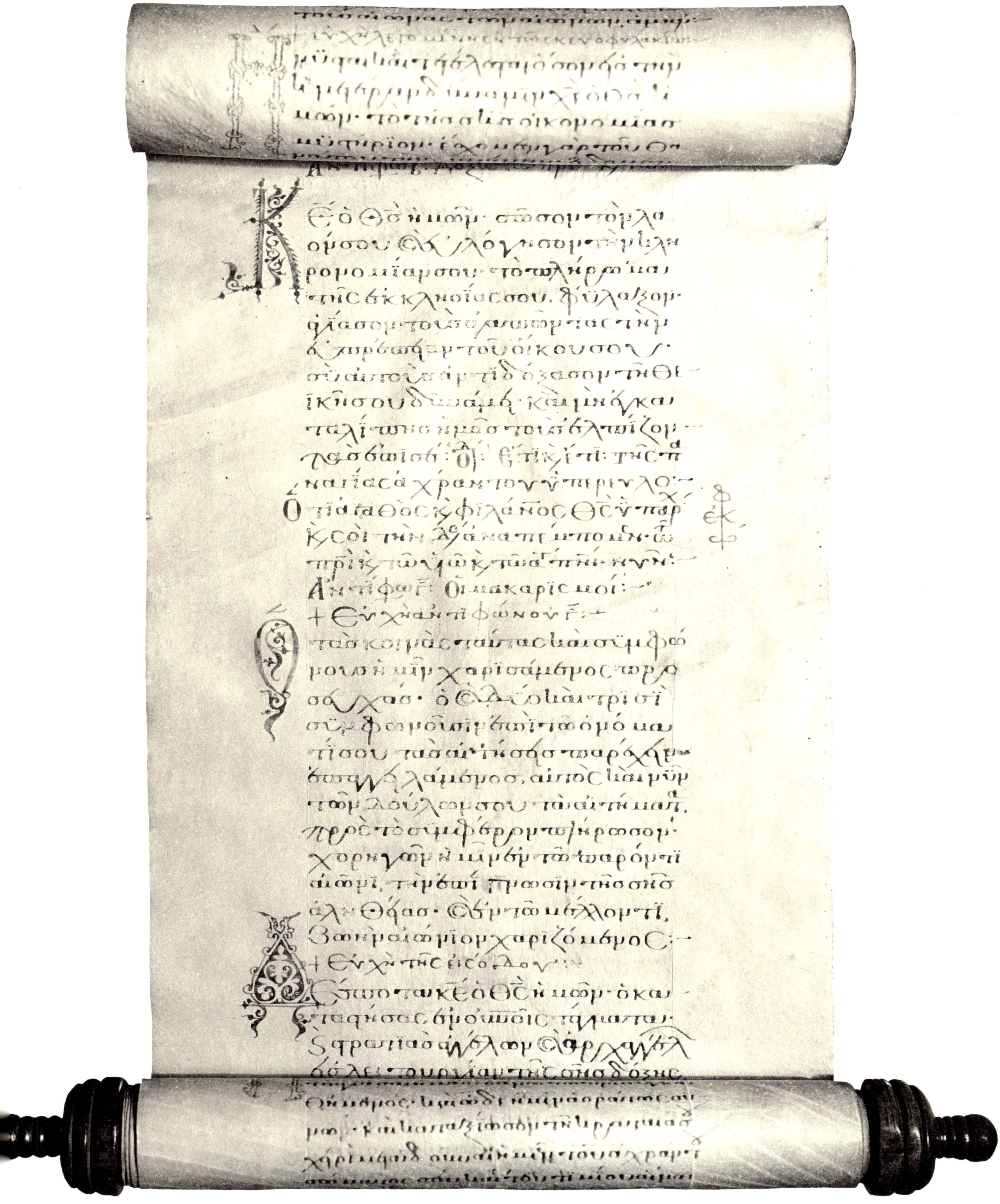

MANUSCRIPT OF THE LITURGY OF ST. BASIL THE GREAT (SAEC. XI)   12 × 8¾ inches
Acquired in 1955 with the Hofer Fund

Printing and Graphic Arts   179

APOCALYPSE BLOCK BOOK, GERMANY [CA. 1465]
One of the few complete block books in this country
Acquired in 1948 with the Hofer Fund

MELUSINE, STRASSBURG: PREUSS [CA. 1480]
   Given in 1950 by Philip and Frances Hofer

NEAPOLITAN GILT BINDING ON MANUSCRIPT OF LEONARDO ARETINO:
DE PRIMO BELLO PUNICO (SAEC. XV)
One of the earliest gold-tooled European bindings
  Given in 1952 by Imrie de Vegh

De crismandis in fronte pueris

Pontifex pueros in fronte crismare
uolens paratus est amictu, stola plu-
uiali albi coloris & mitra. premit-
tit ad monitiones prout dicet. in t. de in-
sitandis pueris. deinde loto prius & tersio
pollice docent manus. cosinandis genu-
a flectentibus. & iunctis ante pectus manibus.
stans mitra deposita. iunctis similiter an-
pectus manibus dicat.

**PIRI-
TUS
SANC-
TUS SUP-
VENI**

THE CALDERINI PONTIFICAL
 Northern Italy, ca. 1380, for Andrea Calderini,
 Bishop of Ceneda in the Veneto
 Given in 1943 by Philip Hofer, H 1921

14½ × 10½ inches

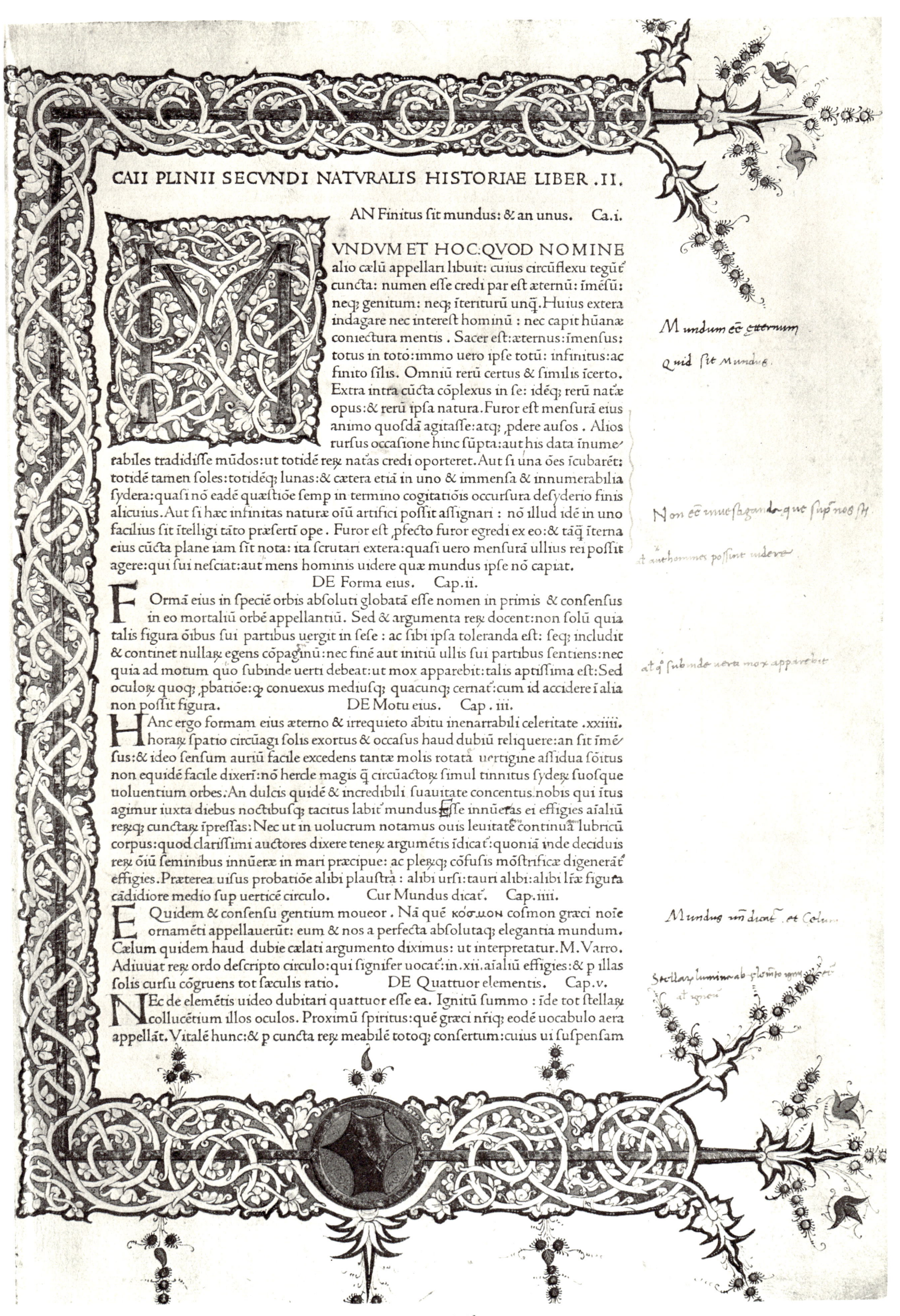

CAII PLINII SECVNDI NATVRALIS HISTORIAE LIBER .II.

AN Finitus sit mundus: & an unus. Ca.i.

VNDVM ET HOC, QVOD NOMINE alio cælū appellari libuit: cuius circūflexu tegūt cuncta: numen esse credi par est æternū: ímēsū: neq; genitum: neq; íteriturū unq̄. Huius extera indagare nec interest hominū: nec capit hūanæ coniectura mentis. Sacer est: æternus: imensus: totus in toto: immo uero ipse totū: infinitus: ac finito silis. Omniū rerū certus & similis icerto. Extra intra cūcta cōplexus in se: idéq; rerū natæ opus: & rerū ipsa natura. Furor est mensurā eius animo quosdā agitasse: atq; pdere ausos. Alios rursus occasione hinc sūpta: aut his data inumerabiles tradidisse mūdos: ut totidē rerū natās credi oporteret. Aut si una ōes icubarēt: totidē tamen soles: totidéq; lunas: & cætera etiā in uno & immensa & innumerabilia sydera: quasi nō eadē quæstiōe semp in termino cogitatiōis occursura desyderio finis alicuius. Aut si hæc infinitas naturæ oīū artifici possit assignari: nō illud idē in uno facilius sit ītelligi tāto præsertī ope. Furor est, pfecto furor egredi ex eo: & tāq̄ īterna eius cūcta plane iam sit nota: ita scrutari extera: quasi uero mensurā ullius rei possit agere: qui sui nesciat: aut mens hominis uidere quæ mundus ipse nō capiat.

DE Forma eius. Cap. ii.

Formā eius in specie orbis absoluti globatā esse nomen in primis & consensus in eo mortaliū orbē appellantiū. Sed & argumenta rerū docent: non solū quia talis figura ōibus sui partibus uergit in sese: ac sibi ipsa toleranda est: seq; includit & continet nullarū egens cōpaginū: nec fine aut initio ullis sui partibus sentiens: nec quia ad motum quo subinde uerti debeat: ut mox apparebit: talis aptissima est: Sed oculorū quoq; pbatiōe: q̄ conuexus mediusq; quacunq; cernat: cum id accidere ī alia non possit figura. DE Motu eius. Cap . iii.

Hanc ergo formam eius æterno & irrequieto ābitu inenarrabili celeritate .xxiiii. horarū spatio circūagi solis exortus & occasus haud dubiū reliquere: an sit īmēsus: & ideo sensum auriū facile excedens tantæ molis rotatā uertigine assidua sōitus non equidē facile dixerī: nō hercle magis q̄ circuactorū simul tinnitus sydex suosque uoluentium orbes. An dulcis quidē & incredibili suauitate concentus nobis qui itus agimur iuxta diebus noctibusq; tacitus labit mundus esse innūeras ei effigies aīaliū rerūq; cunctarū ipressas: Nec ut in uolucrum notamus ouis leuitatē continuā lubricū corpus: quod clarissimi auctores dixere tenerū argumētis īdicāt: quoniā inde deciduis rerū oīū seminibus innūeræ in mari præcipue: ac plerūq; cōfusis mōstrificæ digenerāt effigies. Præterea uisus probatiōe alibi plaustra: alibi ursi: tauri alibi: alibi lrā figura cādidiore medio sup uertice circulo. Cur Mundus dicat. Cap.iiii.

Equidem & consensu gentium moueor. Nā quē κόσμον cosmon græci noīe ornamēti appellauerūt: eum & nos a perfecta absolutaq; elegantia mundum. Cælum quidem haud dubie cælati argumento diximus: ut interpretatur M. Varro. Adiuuat rerū ordo descripto circulo: qui signifer uocat: in .xii. aīaliū effigies: & p illas solis cursu cōgruens tot sæculis ratio. DE Quattuor elementis. Cap.v.

Nec de elemētis uideo dubitari quattuor esse ea. Ignitū summo: īde tot stellarū collucētium illos oculos. Proximū spiritus: quē græci nřiq; eodē uocabulo aera appellāt. Vitalē hunc: & p cuncta rerū meabilē totoq; consertum: cuius ui suspensam

PLINY: *HISTORIA NATURALIS* [VENICE: NICOLAS JENSON, 1472]
15½ × 11 inches   Given in 1949 by Philip Hofer, H 1921

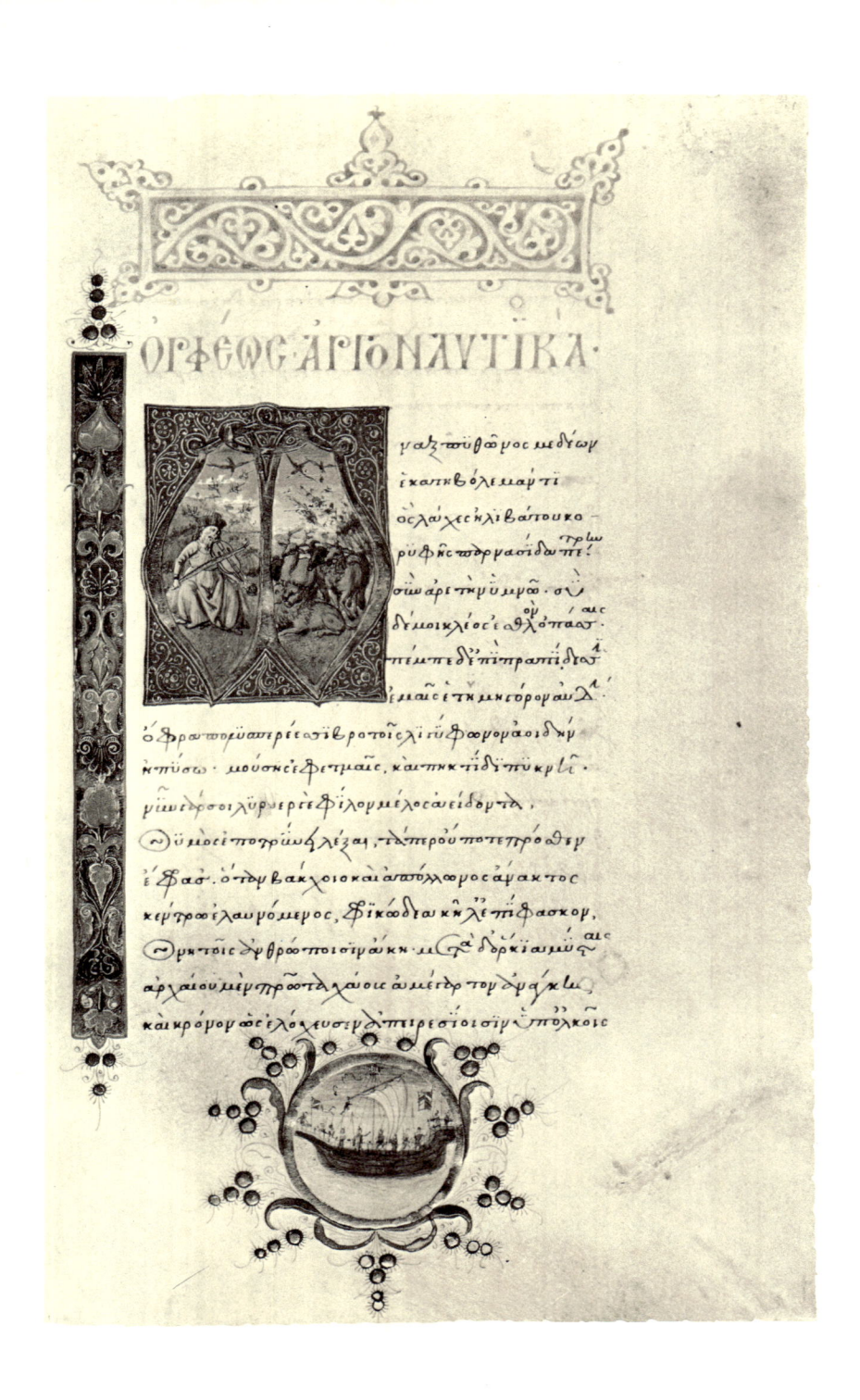

MANUSCRIPT OF GREEK POETS,
ITALY [CA. 1490]   8½ × 5½ inches
Written by Joannes Rhosos
Given in 1948 by Philip Hofer, H 1921,
in honor of Mrs. Frederick Winslow

*EL CONTRASTO DI CARNESCIALE &
LA QUARESIMA* [FLORENCE, 1495?]   7½ × 5½ inches
One of the rarest Florentine incunabula
Acquired in 1956 with the Hofer Fund

184

Io sono il gran capitano della morte
Che tengo le chiaue de tutte le porte

ℂ Chi uuol ditâta gloria pôter dire
La doue sta latrinita gioconda
diuotamente a dio si uol seruire
& del peccato far lanima monda
uuol esser dextro & saper contradire
al diauol che lanima non confonda
ciascun mintenda cô sôma memoria
per bono exempio diroue una istoria

ℂ Dice lhuomo uiuo
O Iesu Christo tu che mi mostrasti
la morte in uista e non inuisione
ancor piu bella gratia mi donasti
chauesti dil tuo seruo compassione
cô il tuo sancto sangue il ricôprasti
pero ti prego dio di passione
donami gratia con perfecta stima
che cioche intesi ui dimetta in rima

a

CONTRASTO DEL VIVO E DEL MORTO
[FLORENCE, 1495?] 7¾ × 5½ inches
Acquired in 1956 with the Hofer Fund

Hor dunque fugi sua giostra uiolente
Che le anime con lui stan mal contente

AESOPUS MORALISATUS [VERONA, 1479] 8 × 5⅜ inches
The only known copy on vellum
Acquired in 1956 with the Hofer Fund

Printing and Graphic Arts   185

USATGES DE BARCELONA E CONSTITUTIONS DE CATALUÑA [BARCELONA, 1495]
Given in 1921 by John B. Stetson, Jr., H 1906

THE HOURS OF JUANA LA LOCA
   Flanders, ca. 1500
   The two volumes of this manuscript were once owned by William Augustus White, H 1863;
   one was presented in 1958 in memory of Mr. White and his daughter Frances White Emerson,
   by Harold T. White, H 1897, Donald Moffat, H 1916, and Mrs. Jon Wiig;
   the other was deposited in 1966 by Mrs. Adrian van Sinderen.

HOURS WRITTEN BY BARTOLOMEO SAN VITO
   Northern Italy, ca. 1500, possibly for Isabella d'Este Gonzaga,
   Marchioness of Mantua
   Given in 1966 by Philip Hofer, H 1921

Memoria de sancta barbara

INCIPIUNT SEPT
EM PSALMI PENI
TENTIALES Antiphona
Ne reminiscaris. PSALMUS
OMINE NE IN FU
RORE TUO ARGUAS
ME NEQUE IN IRA

JOHANNES MAUBURNUS: *ROSETUM EXERCITIORUM SPIRITUALIUM ET SACRUM MEDITATIONUM*,
ZWOLLE, 1494
  Given in 1942 by Philip Hofer, H 1921

MISSAL, USAGE OF PRAGUE [LEIPZIG, 1522]
Woodcut attributed to Matthias Grünewald
Acquired in 1959 with the Hofer Fund

LUCAN, IN FRENCH [PARIS, 1500] 13⅝ × 9½ inches
Given in 1951 by Philip Hofer, H 1921

Printing and Graphic Arts 189

BREVIARY, USAGE OF PADUA, VENICE, 1517 13⅞ × 9⅜ inches
Given in 1941 by Philip Hofer, H 1921

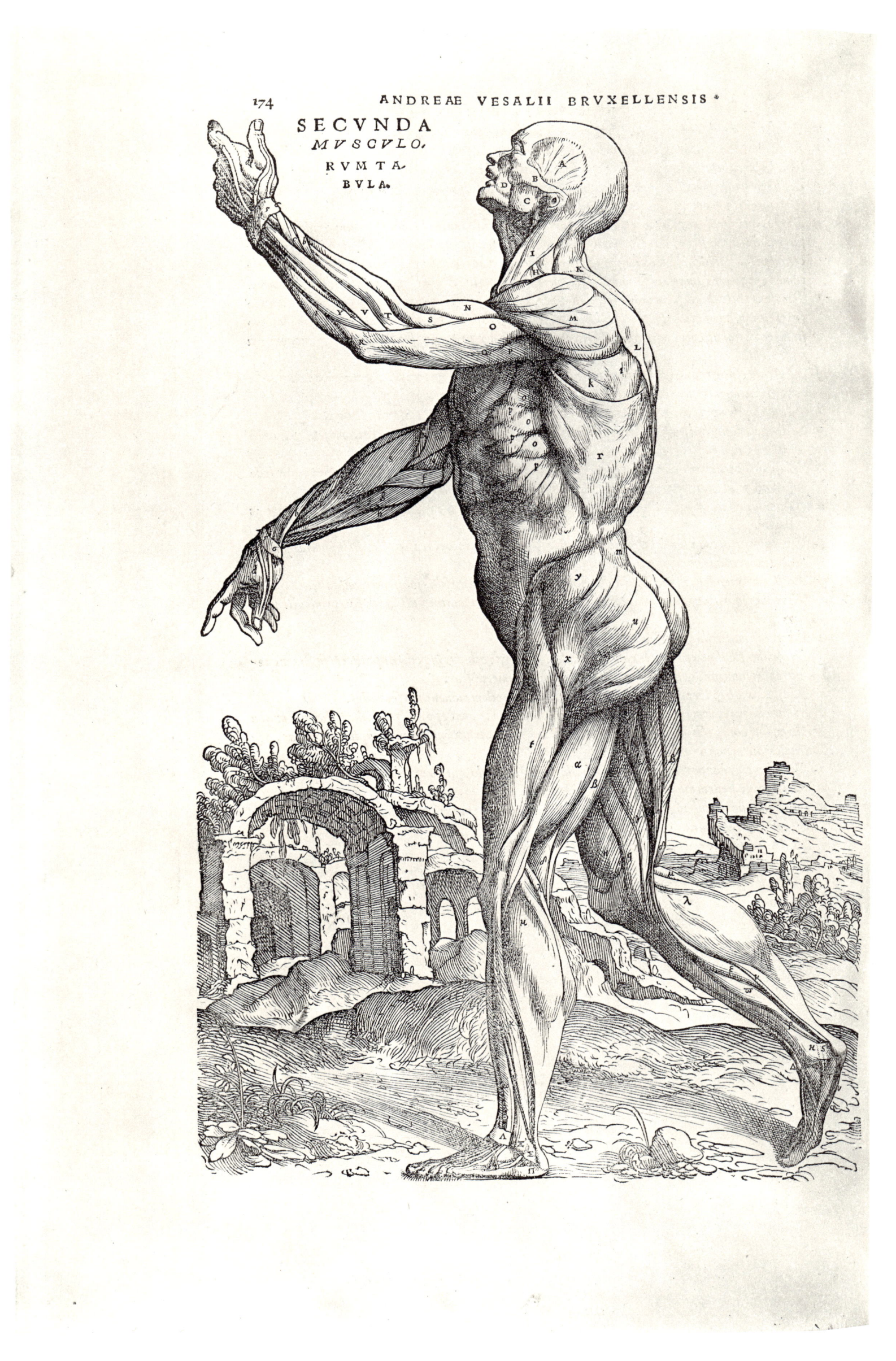

ANDREAS VESALIUS: *DE HUMANI CORPORIS FABRICA*, BASEL, 1543   16⅝ × 11½ inches
The first scientific work on anatomy
    Given in 1939 by Philip Hofer, H 1921, in memory of Sumner Mead Roberts, H 1921

Printing and Graphic Arts   191

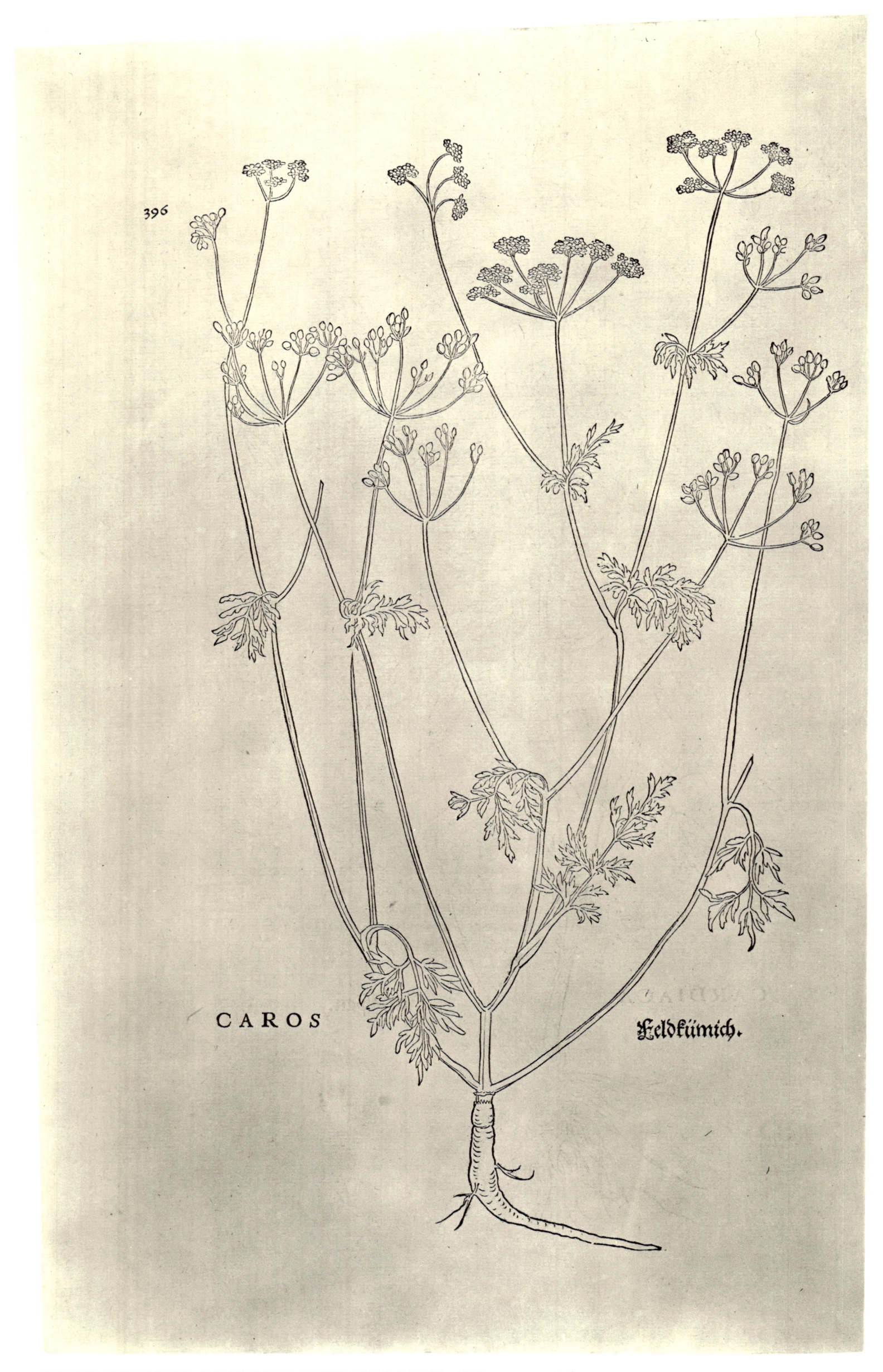

LEONHARD FUCHS: *DE HISTORIA STIRPIUM*, BASEL, 1542   14¾ × 9¾ inches
The most important herbal of the period
Given in 1941 by Philip Hofer, H 1921

JEAN PÈLERIN, CALLED VIATOR: *DE ARTIFICIALI PERSPECTIVA*, TOUL, 1505
The first published work on perspective
   Given in 1957 by Philip Hofer, H 1921

SIGMUND HERBERSTEIN: *RERUM MOSCOVITICARUM COMENTARII*, VIENNA, 1549
One of the earliest printed books on Russia
Given in 1941 by Philip Hofer, H 1921

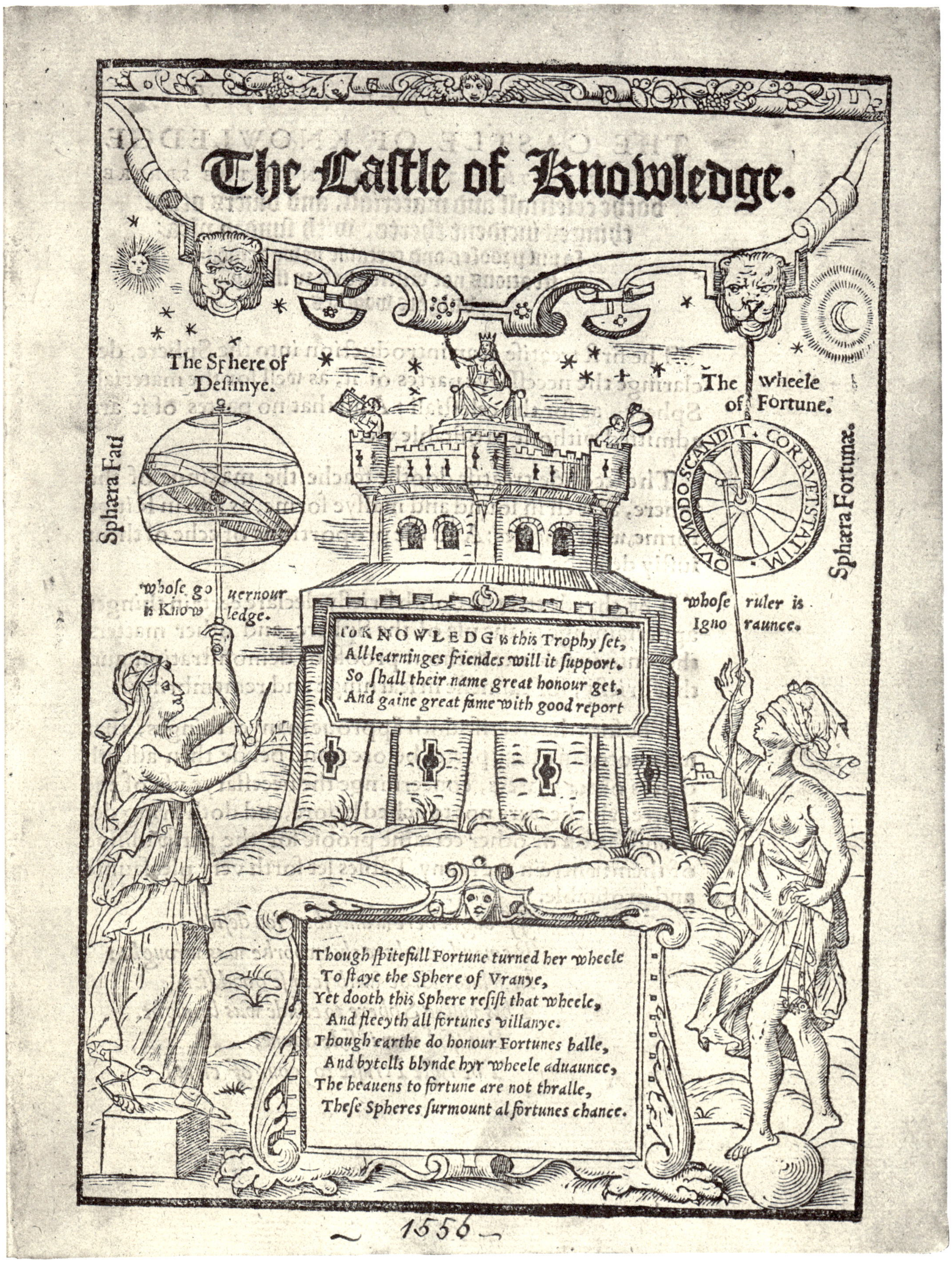

ROBERT RECORDE: *THE CASTLE OF KNOWLEDGE*, LONDON, 1556 (S.T.C. 20796)
Given in 1941 by Philip Hofer, H 1921

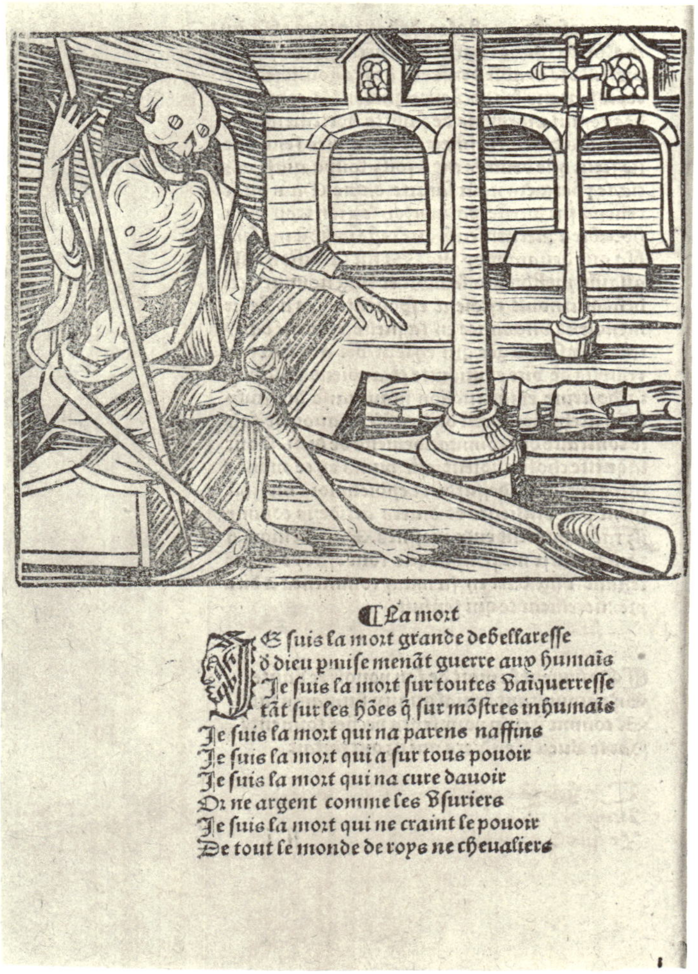

ROBERT GOBIN: *LES LOUPS RAVISSANS*,
PARIS [CA. 1505]   7 × 5 inches
   Given in 1961 by Philip Hofer, H 1921

ARISTOTLE: *DE ANIMA* [CRACOW, 1513]   8¼ × 5½ inches
   Given in 1941 by Philip Hofer, H 1921

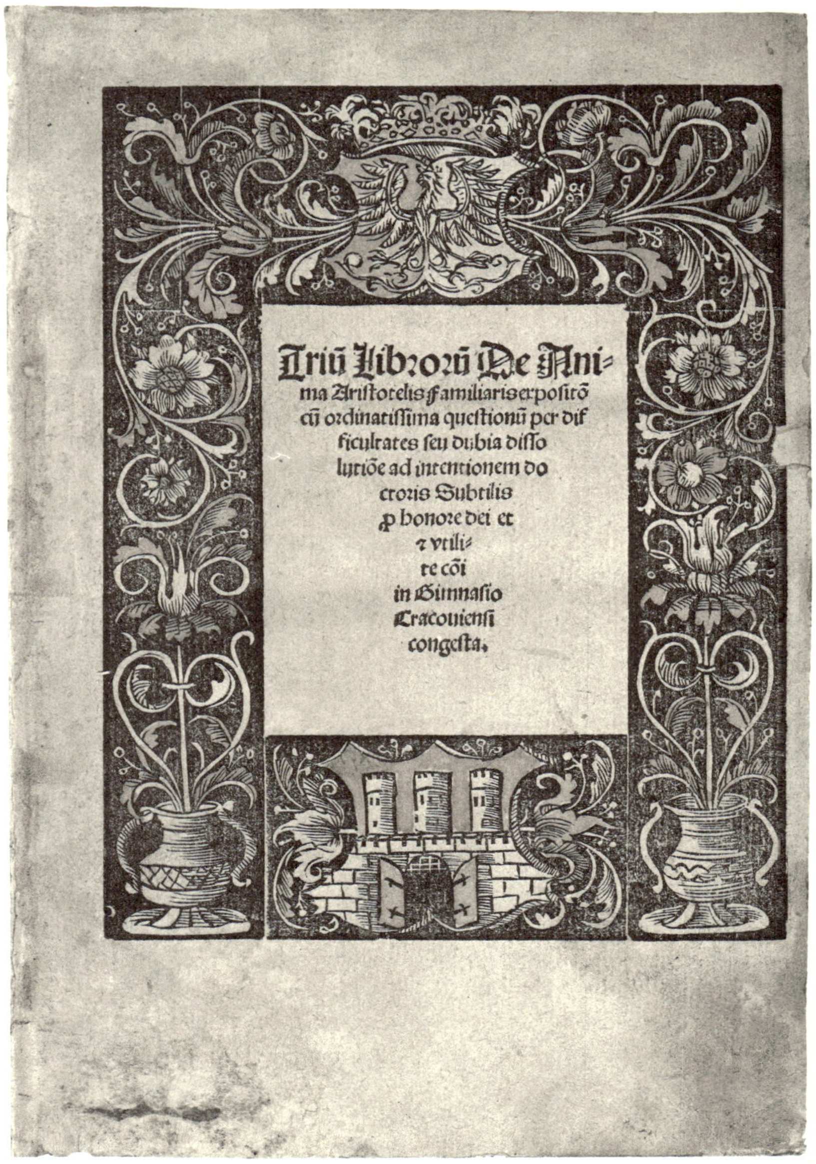

BINDING FOR FRANCIS I ON *HORAE VIRGINIS MARIAE*, PARIS,
GEOFFROY TORY, 1527   8½ × 6⅛ inches   The dedication copy
   Given in 1961 by Philip Hofer, H 1921

HORAE VIRGINIS MARIAE, PARIS, S. DE COLINES
FOR G. TORY, 1525   7⅝ × 4⅞ inches
Illuminated copy, possibly bound for the Emperor Charles V
   Given in 1961 by Philip Hofer, H 1921

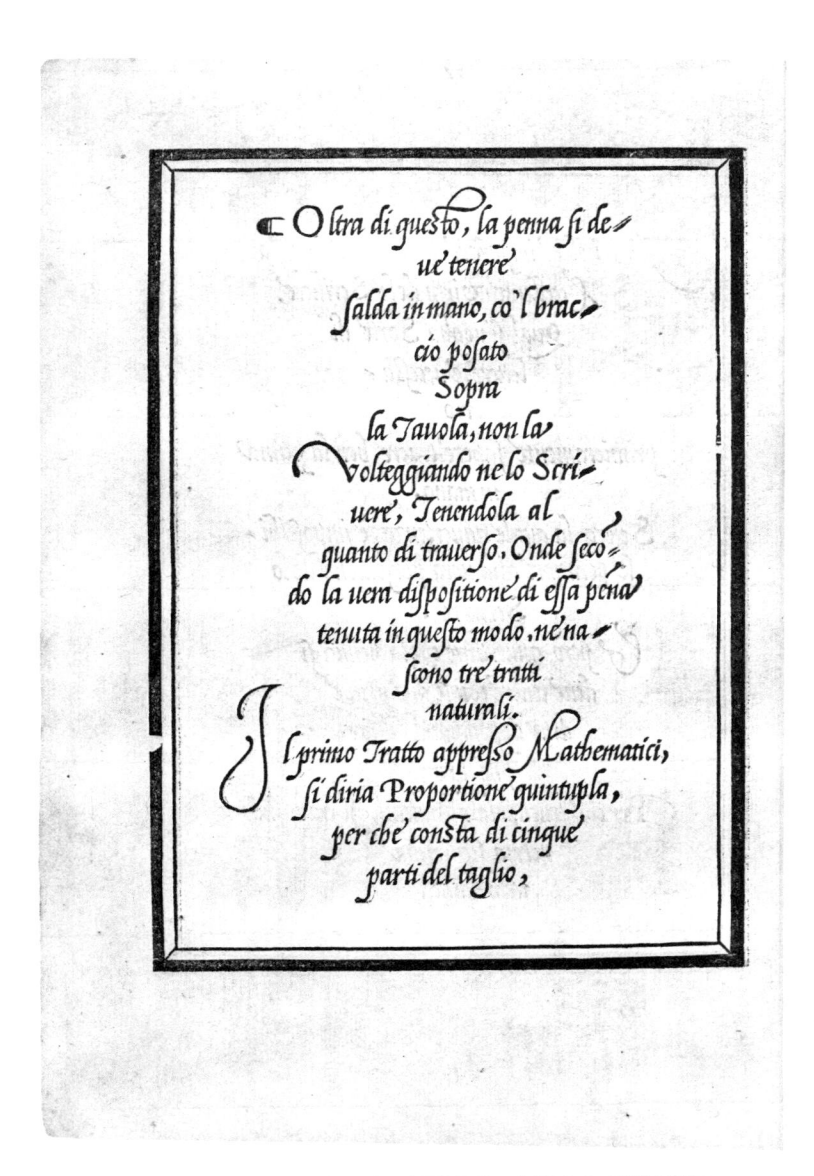

GIOVANNI BATTISTA PALATINO: *LIBRO NUOVO D'IMPARE A SCRIVERE* [ROME, 1540]   7¾ × 5⅛ inches
Given in 1945 by Philip Hofer, H 1921

ANDRÉ DE RESENDE: *DE VERBORUM CONIUGATIONE COMMENTARIUS*, LISBON [1540]   7¼ × 5¼ inches
Given in 1951 by Philip Hofer, H 1921

SEBASTIAN MÜNSTER: *COMPOSITIO HOROLOGIORUM*, BASEL, 1531   7⅜ × 5¾ inches   Woodcuts designed by Hans Holbein
Given in 1939 by Philip Hofer, H 1921

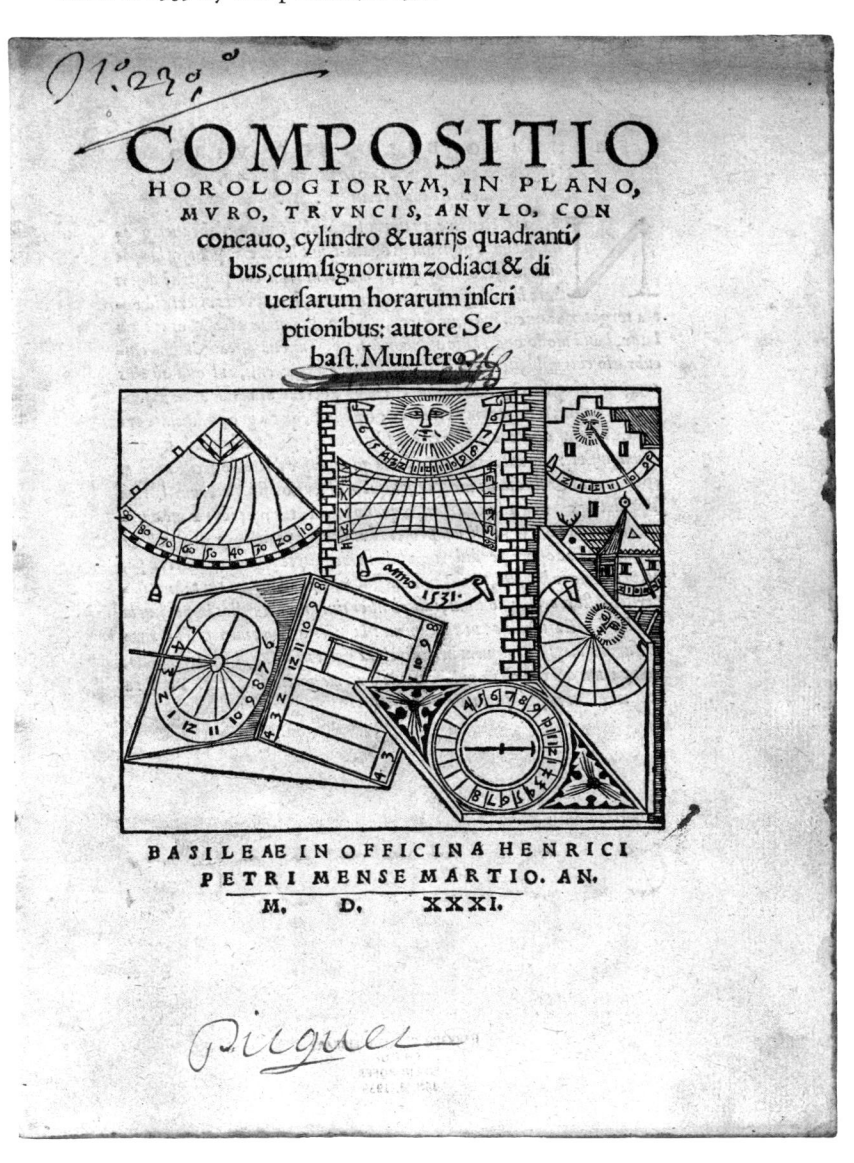

CARMINA APPOSITA PASQUILLO, ROME, 1513   7¾ × 5⅜ inches
Given in 1941 by Philip Hofer, H 1921

Printing and Graphic Arts   197

JACQUES ANDROUET DU CERCEAU: *LE SECOND VOLUME DES PLUS EXCELLENTS BASTIMENTS DE FRANCE*, PARIS, 1579
  Acquired in 1950 with the Degrand Fund

SEBASTIANO SERLIO:
EXTRAORDINARIO LIBRO DI ARCHITETTURA,
VENICE, 1560   13¾ × 9¾ inches
Given in 1941 by Philip Hofer, H 1921

IL TERZO LIBRO
DI SABASTIANO SERLIO BOLO-
GNESE, NELQVAL SI FIGVRANO, E DESCRIVONO LE
ANTIQVITA DI ROMA, E LE ALTRE CHE SONO
IN ITALIA, E FVORI D'ITALIA

Con noue additioni, come ne la Tauola appare.

· ROMA QVANTA FVIT IPSA RVINA DOCET

IN VINEGIA CON PRIVILEGII.

Printing and Graphic Arts 199

BINDING FOR QUEEN CHRISTINA OF SWEDEN ON NICOLAS ANTONIO: *BIBLIOTHECA HISPANA*, 1672; ITALY (SAEC. XVII) 14¼ × 9¾ inches
Acquired in 1950 with the Hofer Fund

MARY, QUEEN OF SCOTS
Portrait ascribed to François Clouet, d. 1572
Given in 1947 by Philip Hofer, H 1921

la royne d'escosse

le roi francoys secom

FRANÇOIS II OF FRANCE
   Portrait ascribed to François Clouet, d. 1572
   Given in 1947 by Philip Hofer, H 1921

CASPER GEVARTIUS: *POMPA INTROITUS FERDINANDI AUSTRIACI*, ANTWERP, 1641   20 × 17½ inches
Title page designed by Peter Paul Rubens
Given in 1966 by Philip Hofer, H 1921

ATHENAEUS NAUCRATITA: *LES QUINZE LIVRES*,
PARIS, 1680   9⅞ × 6¾ inches
Engraved portrait by Robert Nanteuil
Acquired in 1962 with the Hofer Fund

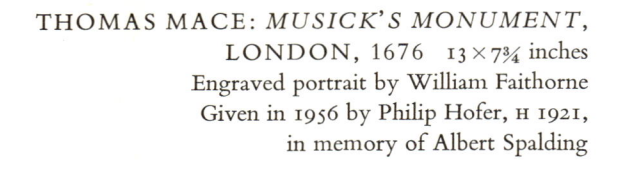

THOMAS MACE: *MUSICK'S MONUMENT*,
LONDON, 1676   13 × 7¾ inches
Engraved portrait by William Faithorne
Given in 1956 by Philip Hofer, H 1921,
in memory of Albert Spalding

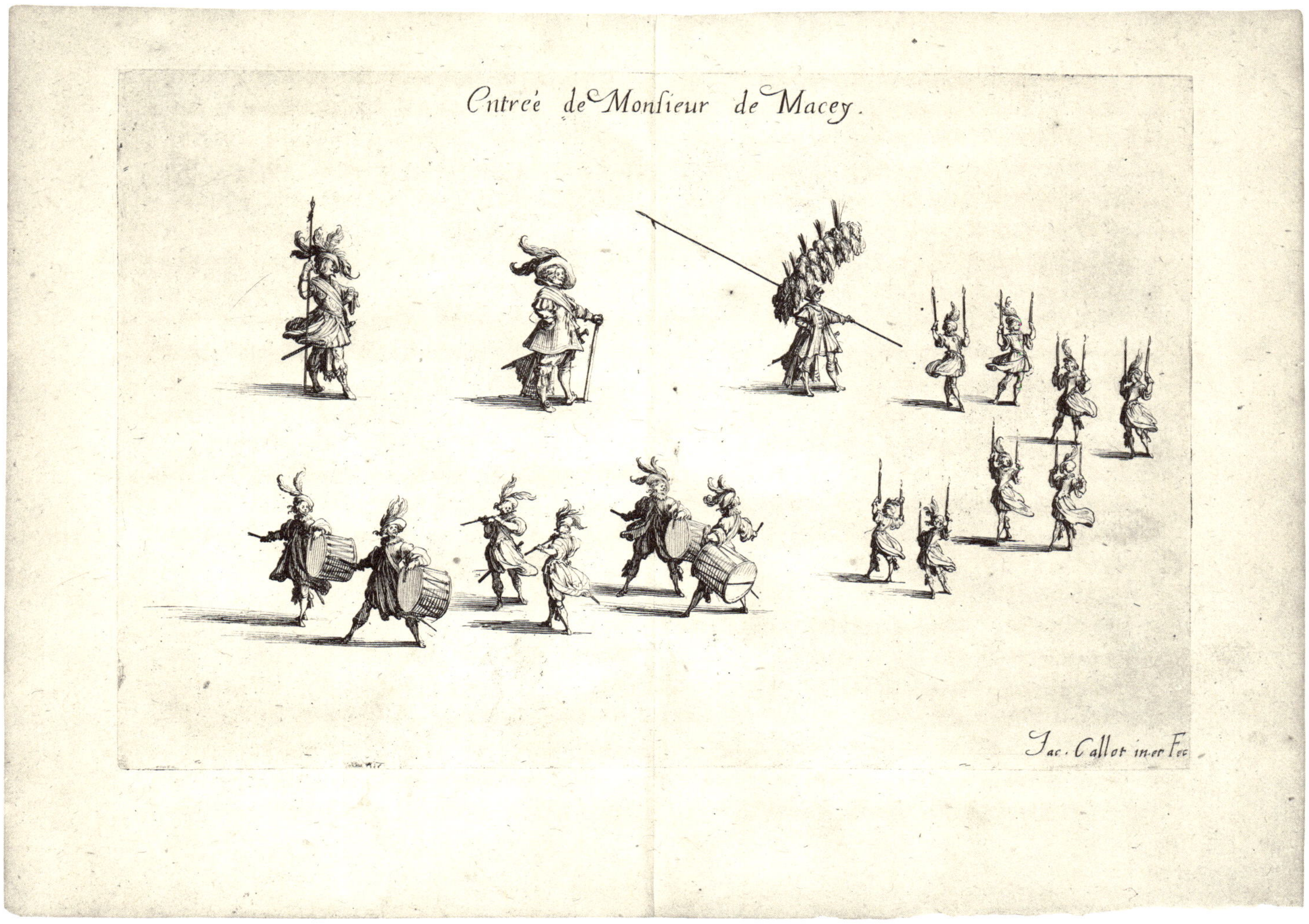

HENRY HUMBERT: *COMBAT À LA BARRIÈRE*, NANCY, 1627   7⅝ × 10⅝ inches
Engravings by Jacques Callot
    Given in 1947 by Philip Hofer, H 1921

COMMENCEMENS DE L'HIDROGRAPHIE, MANUSCRIPT, FRANCE [CA. 1630]   6⅜ × 13⅜ inches
    Acquired in 1946 with the Hofer Fund

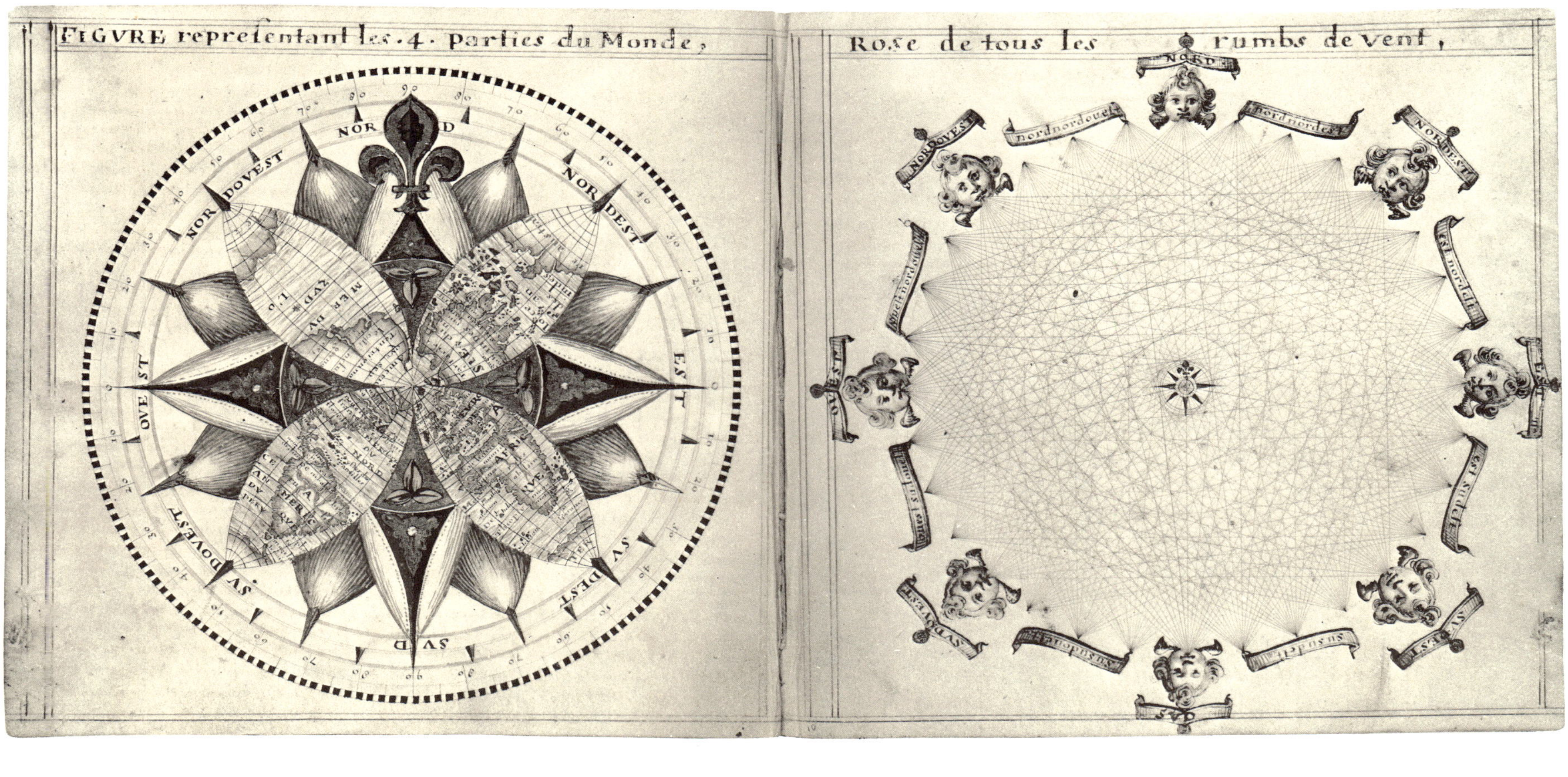

Printing and Graphic Arts   203

ROLAND FRÉART DE CHAMBRAY: *PARALLÈLE DE L'ARCHITECTURE ANTIQUE AVEC LA MODERNE*, MS.,
[FRANCE, CA. 1650]
Acquired in 1951 with the Degrand Fund

FERNANDO DE LA TORRE FARFAN: *FIESTAS DE LA SANTA IGLESI[A]
DE SEVILLA*, SEVILLE, 1671   17¼ × 10⅞ inch[es]
Acquired in 1962 with the Hofer Fun[d]

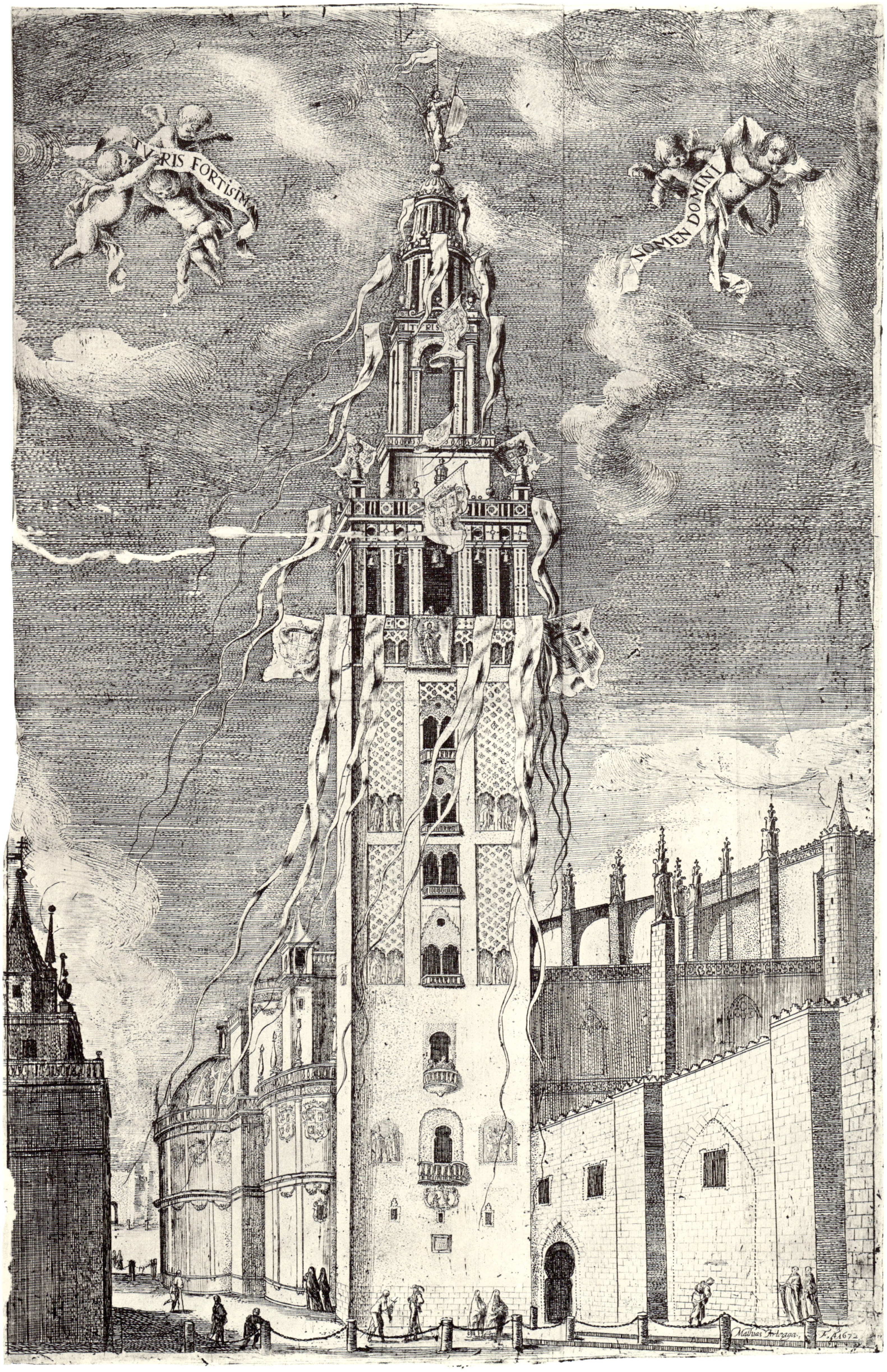
TVRIS FORTISIM
NOMEN DOMINI

PTOLEMY: *GEOGRAPHIAE LIBRI OCTO*, FRANKFURT, 1605 16¾ × 20 inches
Given in 1941 by Philip Hofer, H 1921

OLAF RUDBECK: *ATLAND ELLER MANHEIM*, UPSALA, 1675-1679, 3 VOLS. AND ATLAS
15¾ × 12¼ inches   Given in 1941 by Philip Hofer, H 1921

JOHANN BAYER: *URANOMETRIA*, AUGSBURG, 1603   14 × 9⅞ inches
Given in 1941 by Philip Hofer, H 1921

GIOVANNI BATTISTA FERRARI: *HESPERIDES*, ROME, 1646   14¾ × 9½ inches
Title-page designed by Pietro da Cortona
Given in 1942 by Philip Hofer, H 1921

Printing and Graphic Arts   209

FRANCIS BACON: *INSTAURATIO MAGNA*, LONDON, 1620 (S.T.C. 1163)
 Given in 1941 by Philip Hofer, H 1921

DE MAGNETE, LIB. III.

CAP. XII.
Quomodò verticitas exiſtit in ferro quouis excocto magnete non excito.

Actenùs naturales & ingenitas cauſas, & acquiſitas per lapidem potentias declarauimus: Nunc verò & in excocto ferro lapide non excito, magneticarum virtutum cauſæ rimandæ ſunt. Admirabiles nobis magnes & ferrum promunt & oſtendunt ſubtilitates. Demonſtratum eſt anteà ſæpiùs, ferrum lapide non excitum in ſeptentiones ferri & meridiem; ſed & habere verticitatem, id eſt proprias & ſingulares polares diſtinctiones, quemadmodùm magnes, aut ferrum magnete attritum. Iſtud quidem nobis mirum & incredibile primùm videbatur: Ferri metallum ex vena in fornace excoquitur, effluit ex fornace, & in magnã maſſam indureſcit, maſſa illa diuiditur in magnis officinis, & in bacilla ferrea extenditur, ex quibus fabri rurſus plurima componunt inſtrumenta, & ferramenta neceſſaria. Ita variè elaboratur & in plurimas ſimilitudines eadem maſſa transformatur. Quid eſt igitur illud quod

conſeruat

WILLIAM GILBERT: *DE MAGNETE*, LONDON, 1600 (S.T.C. 11883)
Given in 1941 by Philip Hofer, H 1921

JOHN STALKER: *A TREATISE OF JAPANING & VARNISHING*, OXFORD, 1688   14⅝ × 8⅞ inches
Given in 1939 by Philip Hofer, H 1921

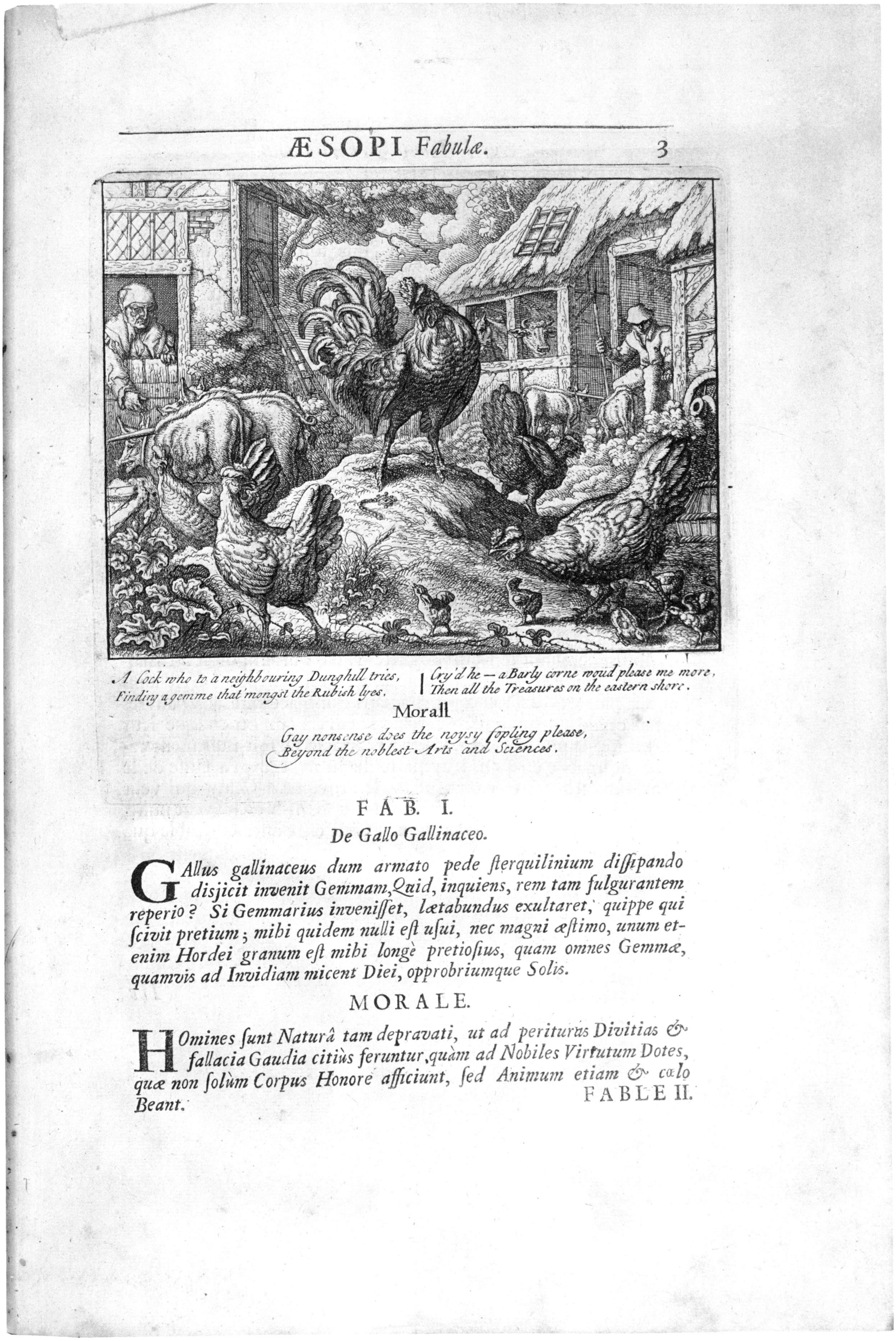

ÆSOPI *Fabulæ.* 3

*A Cock who to a neighbouring Dunghill tries,
Finding a gemme that 'mongst the Rubish lyes.* | *Cry'd he — a Barly corne woud please me more,
Then all the Treasures on the eastern shore.*

Morall
*Gay nonsense does the noysy fopling please,
Beyond the noblest Arts and Sciences.*

FAB. I.
De Gallo Gallinaceo.

Gallus gallinaceus dum armato pede sterquilinium dissipando disjicit invenit Gemmam, Quid, inquiens, rem tam fulgurantem reperio? Si Gemmarius invenisset, lætabundus exultaret, quippe qui scivit pretium; mihi quidem nulli est usui, nec magni æstimo, unum etenim Hordei granum est mihi longè pretiosius, quam omnes Gemmæ, quamvis ad Invidiam micent Diei, opprobriumque Solis.

MORALE.

Homines sunt Naturâ tam depravati, ut ad perituras Divitias & fallacia Gaudia citiùs feruntur, quàm ad Nobiles Virtutum Dotes, quæ non solùm Corpus Honore afficiunt, sed Animum etiam & cœlo Beant.

FABLE II.

AESOP'S FABLES, LONDON, 1687   14⅜ × 9⅛ inches   Engravings by Francis Barlow
Given in 1941 by Philip Hofer, H 1921

INDICE DE CARATTERI NELLA STAMPERIA VATICANA,
ROME, 1628   7⅜ × 5¼ inches
Only known example printed on satin;
probably the dedication copy
Given in 1962 by William Bentinck-Smith, H 1937

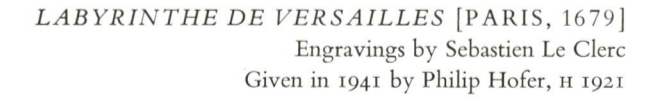

LABYRINTHE DE VERSAILLES [PARIS, 1679]
Engravings by Sebastien Le Clerc
Given in 1941 by Philip Hofer, H 1921

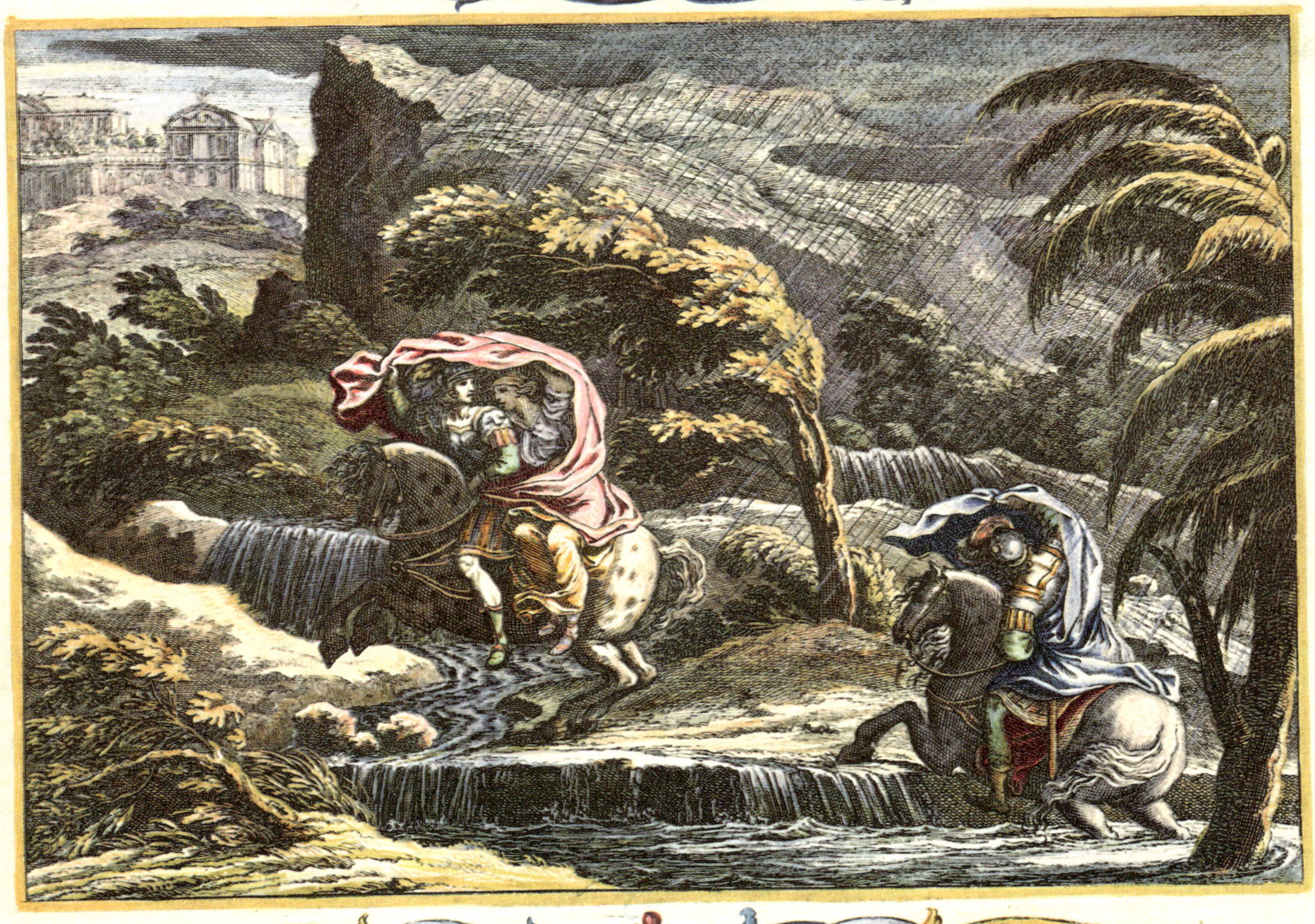

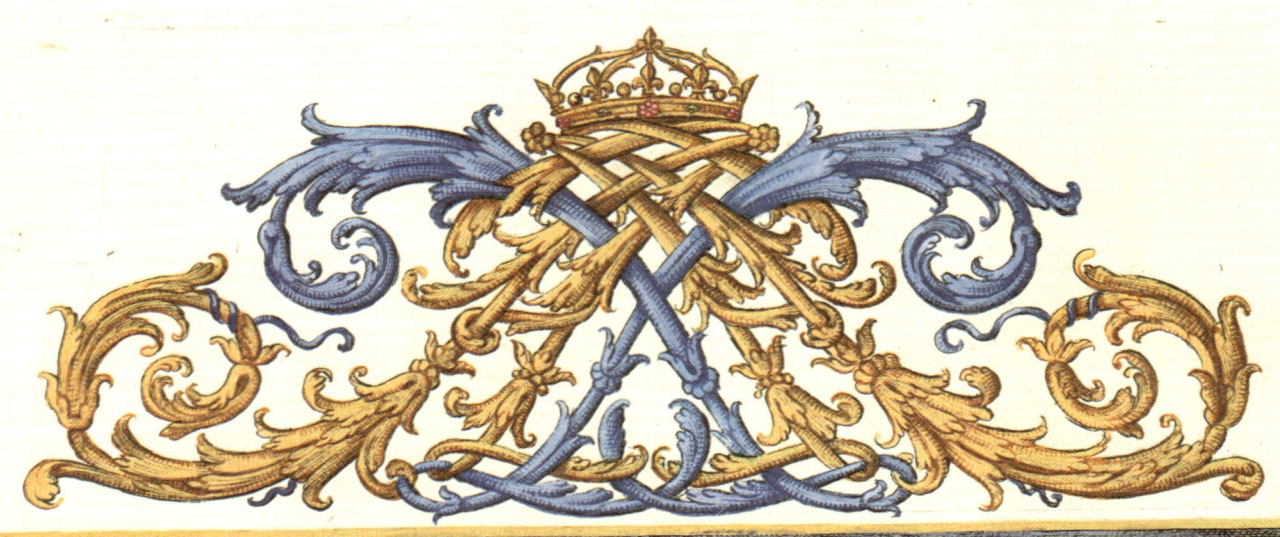

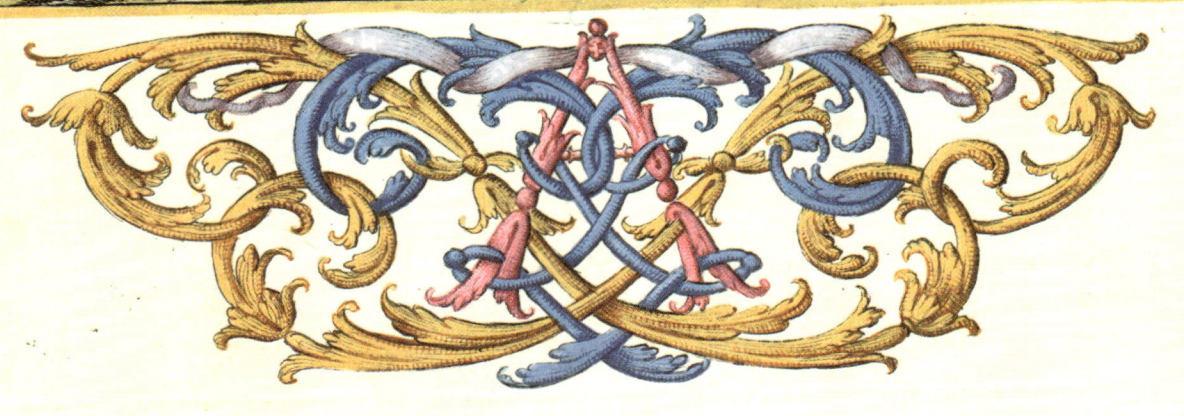

JEAN DESMARETS DE ST. SORLIN: *CLOVIS OU LA FRANCE CHRESTIENNE*, PARIS, 1657
  The royal dedication copy, specially illuminated and bound for Louis XIV
  Given in 1966 by Philip Hofer, H 1921

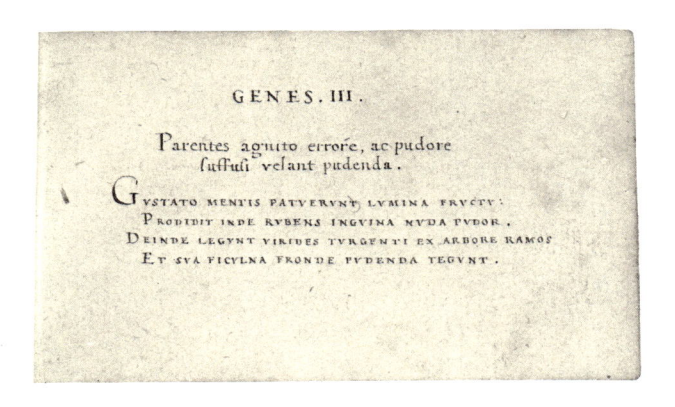

ESTHER INGLIS KELLO:
ARGUMENTA SINGULORUM CAPITUM GENESEOS,
MANUSCRIPT, LONDON, 1606
Bequeathed in 1874 by Charles Sumner, H 1830

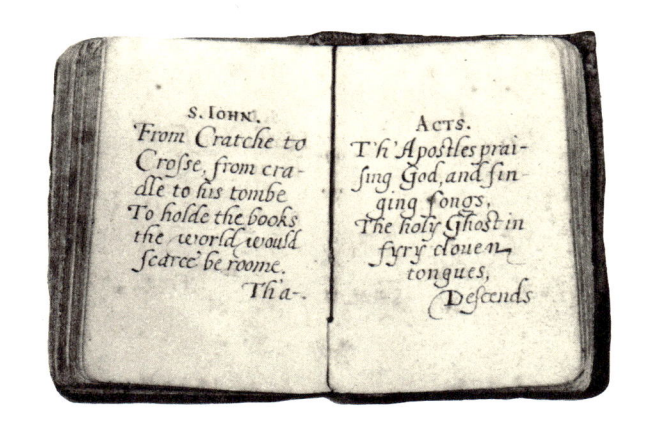

JOHN TAYLOR, *VERBUM SEMPITERNUM,*
MANUSCRIPT [ENGLAND, SAEC. XVII]
Written by Esther Inglis Kello
Acquired in 1949 with money from the sale of duplicates

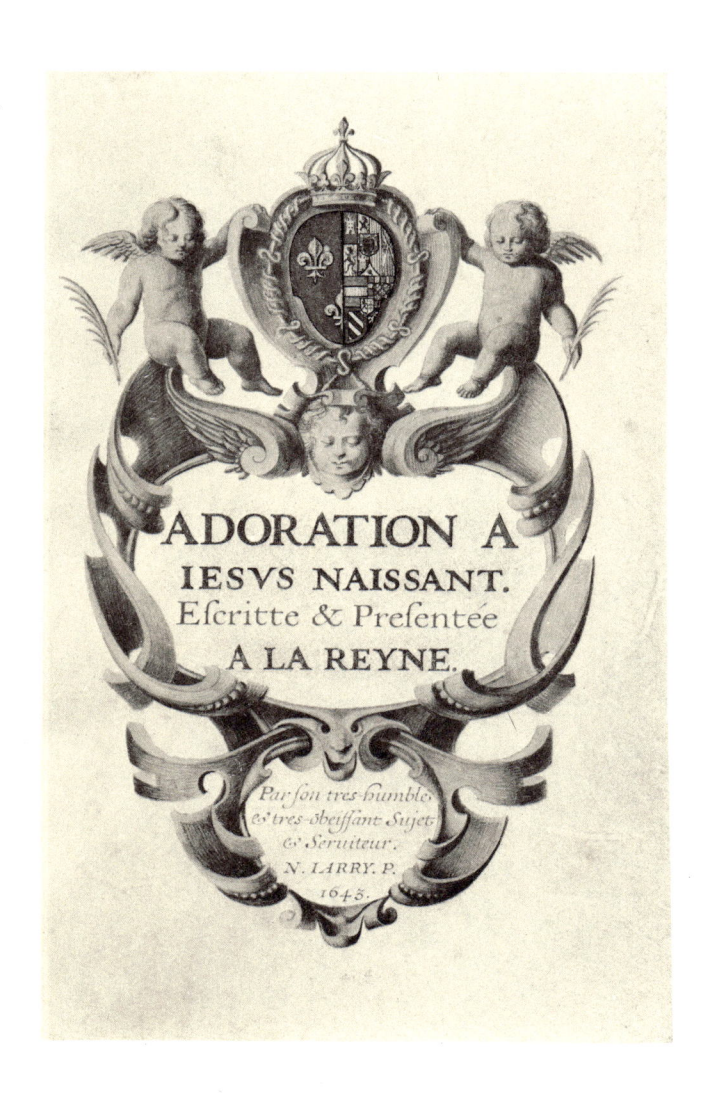

ADORATION À JESUS, MS., FRANCE, 1643
Written by Nicolas Jarry for Anne of Austria
Given in 1957 by Susan Dwight Bliss

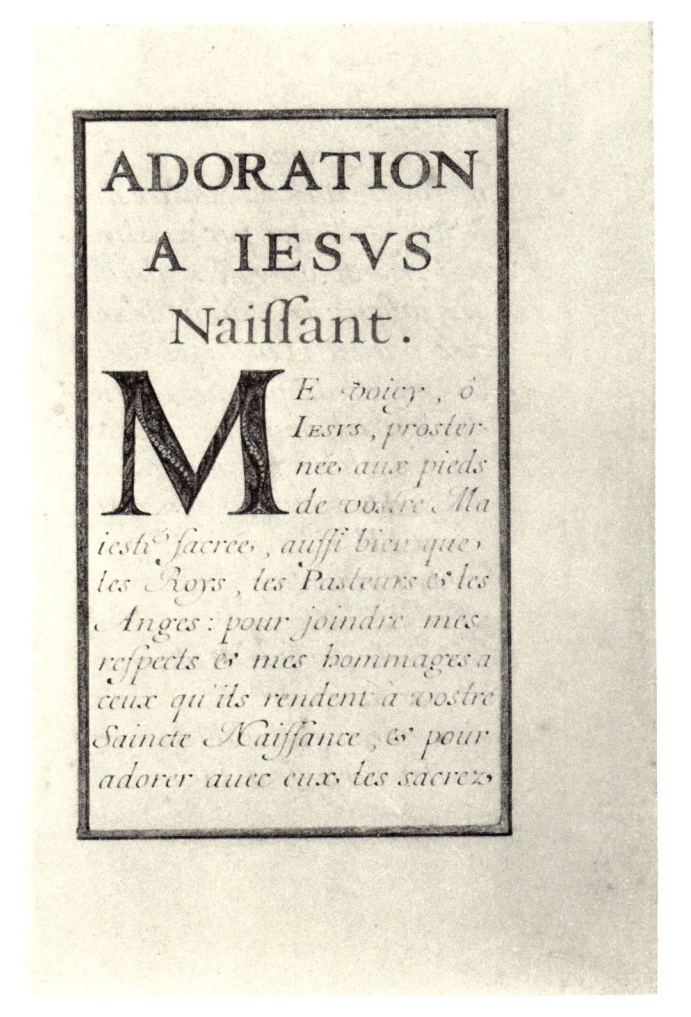

Printing and Graphic Arts 215

GIUSEPPE GALLI DA BIBIENA: DRAWING BOOK, ITALY, 1739–1745   Acquired in 1956 with the Hofer Fund

HUBERT FRANÇOIS BOURGUIGNON, KNOWN AS GRAVELOT:
DRAWING FOR GAY'S *FABLES*, LONDON, 1738   8¼ × 4 inches
One of a set of twelve Gravelot drawings for this publication
Acquired in 1955 with the Hofer Fund

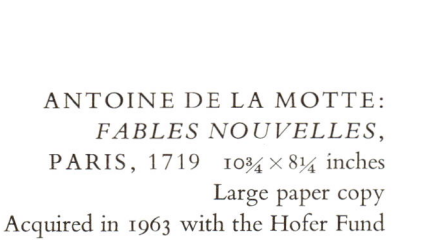

ANTOINE DE LA MOTTE:
FABLES NOUVELLES,
PARIS, 1719   10¾ × 8¼ inches
Large paper copy
Acquired in 1963 with the Hofer Fund

BINDING FOR GEORGE III ON ROBERT ADAM: *RUINS OF THE PALACE OF THE EMPEROR DIOCLETIAN AT SPALATRO*, LONDON, 1764   21¼ × 15⅛ inches
Binding designed by the author-artist-architect   Acquired in 1955 with the Amy Lowell Fund

GIOVANNI BATTISTA PIRANESI: *LE MAGNIFICENZE DI ROMA*, ROME, 1751   19¼ × 12⅜ inches
Acquired in 1965 with the Osgood Hooker Fund

Printing and Graphic Arts

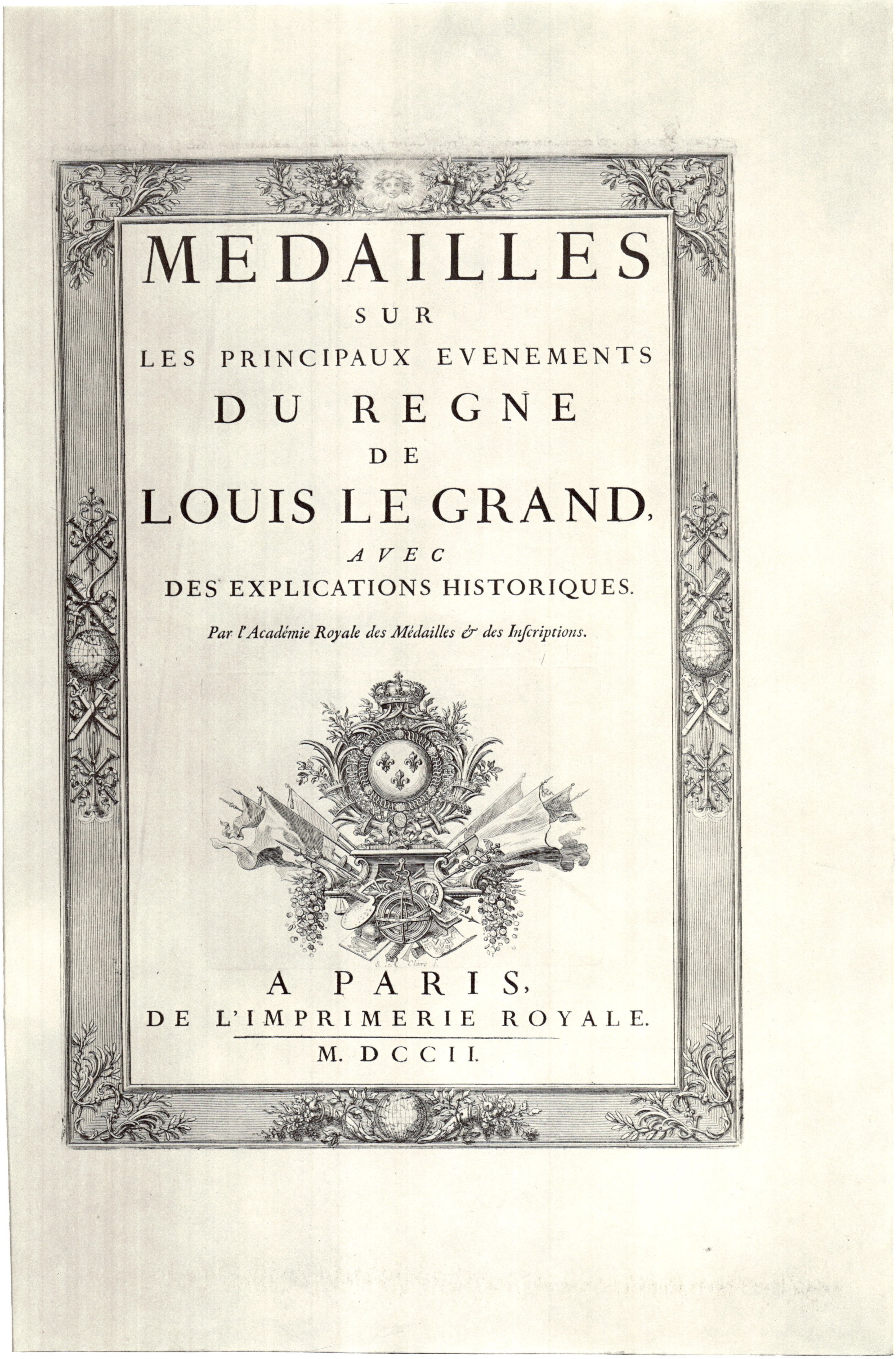

MEDAILLES
SUR
LES PRINCIPAUX EVENEMENTS
DU REGNE
DE
LOUIS LE GRAND,
AVEC
DES EXPLICATIONS HISTORIQUES.

Par l'Académie Royale des Médailles & des Inscriptions.

A PARIS,
DE L'IMPRIMERIE ROYALE.
M. DCCII.

MEDAILLES SUR LES PRINCIPAUX EVENEMENTS DU REGNE DE LOUIS LE GRAND, PARIS, 1702   17¼ × 11 inches
Presentation copy   Given in 1938 by Philip Hofer, H 1921

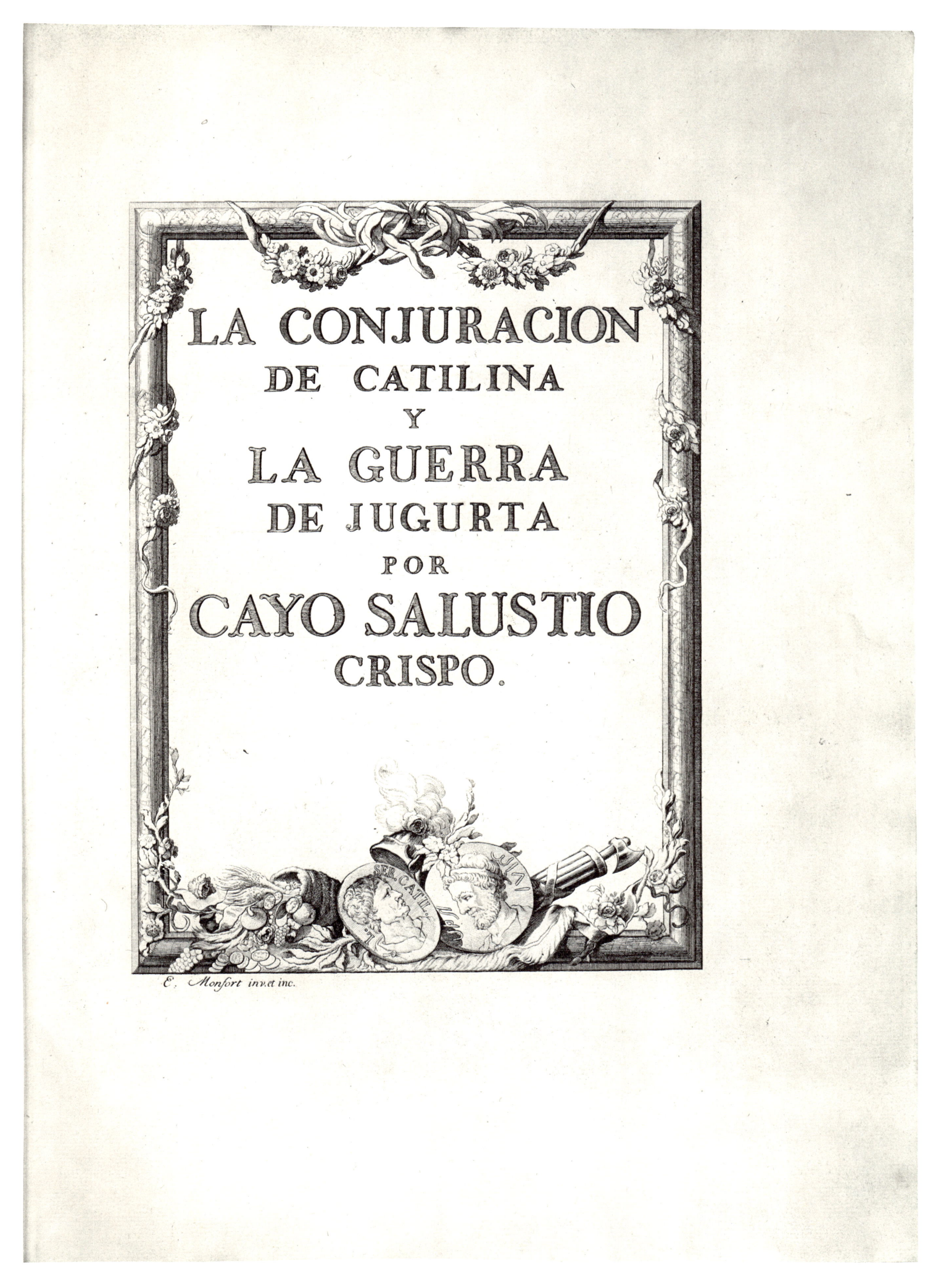

SALLUST: *LA CONJURACION DE CATILINA*, MADRID, 1772   13⅝ × 9⅝ inches
Given in 1929 by Philip Hofer, H 1921

RELAZIONE.

Negozianti di Parma affrettaronsi anch' essi a segnalare il loro giubilo, e la viva loro gratitudine. Memori, e penetrati da quanto l'augusto Padre del R. Infante aveva operato a favor loro, andavano raccogliendo di giorno in giorno nuovi frutti della bontà, e saggia provvidenza del Principe. Protezione, eccitamento, moltiplicati soccorsi, e quanti vantaggi possono procacciare al commercio un Governo illuminato, e benefiche Leggi, godeanli tutti a quel grado che la natura medesima dello Stato ad essi prescrivea. Avevano già veduto scaturire, e vedevano ora sempre più diffondersi le sorgenti della loro prosperità.

Chiesero, ed ottennero la permissione di render solenni i sentimenti della divota, e

RELATION.

LES négocians de Parme s'empresserent de même à signaler leur joie & leur vive reconnoissance. Pénétrés de ce que l'auguste pere de l'Infant avoit fait en leur faveur, ils recueilloient chaque jour de nouveaux fruits de la bonté & de la sagesse du Prince. Protection, encouragement, secours multipliés, tous les avantages qu'un gouvernement éclairé, des lois bienfaisantes, peuvent procurer au commerce, ils les éprouvoient autant que le permettoit la nature même de l'état. Ils avoient vu naître, ils voyoient s'étendre de plus en plus les sources de leur prospérité.

Ils demanderent & obtinrent la permission de faire éclater leurs sentimens

DESCRIZIONE DELLE FESTE PER LE NOZZE DI L'INFANTE DON FERDINANDO COLLA
REALE ARCHIDUCHESSA MARIA AMALIA, PARMA, STAMPERIA REALE (G. B. BODONI), 1769   21⅝ × 15½ inches
A royal presentation copy   Given in 1941 by Philip Hofer, H 1921

ARGOMENTO.

Fugge Erminia e un pastor l'accoglie; intanto
Tancredi invan di lei cercando, il piede
Pon ne' lacci d'Armida: il fero vanto
D'Argante riprovar Raimondo ha fede:
Però difeso da custode santo
Seco entra in campo: Belzebù, che vede
Ch'al Pagan male il folle ardir riesce,
Per lui salvar guerra e procelle mesce.

CANTO SETTIMO.

I.

INTANTO Erminia infra l'ombrose
    piante
D'antica selva dal cavallo è scorta:
Nè più governa il fren la man
    tremante;
E mezza quasi par tra viva e morta.
Per tante strade si raggira e tante
Il corridor, ch'in sua balìa la porta;
Ch'alfin dagli occhi altrui pur si dilegua,
Ed è soverchio omai ch'altri la segua.

(77)

TORQUATO TASSO: *GERUSALEMME LIBERATA*, VENICE, 1745   17⅝ × 12⅛ inches
Engravings after Giovanni Battista Piazzetta   Given in 1941 by Philip Hofer, H 1921

JOSEPH EMANUEL FISCHER VON ERLACH: *ENTWURFF EINER HISTORISCHEN ARCHITECTUR*, VIENNA,

YUAN-MING-YUAN: EUROPEAN BUILDINGS AND GARDENS DESIGNED BY THE JESUITS
FOR THE EMPEROR'S SUMMER PALACE AT PEKING [N.P., CA. 1783] 20½ × 34½ inches
Acquired in 1956 with the Amy Lowell and Hofer Funds

CORNELIUS NOZEMAN: *NEDERLANDSCHE VOGELEN*, AMSTERDAM, 1770 20¾ × 13¾ inches
Given in 1942 by Philip Hofer, H 1921

FLORA ROSSICA,

EDITA

IUSSU ET AUSPICIIS

AUGUSTISSIMÆ ROSSORUM

IMPERATRICIS

CATHARINÆ II

MAGNÆ, PIÆ, FELICIS, PATRIÆ MATRIS.

PETROPOLI,
MDCCLXXXIV.

PETER SIMON PALLAS: *FLORA ROSSICA*, ST. PETERSBURG, 1784   18 × 11 inches
Given ca. 1810 by John Quincy Adams, H 1787

Printing and Graphic Arts   227

GEORGE STUBBS: *THE ANATOMY OF THE HORSE*, LONDON, 1766   15 × 18¾ inches
Acquired in 1942 with the Hofer Fund

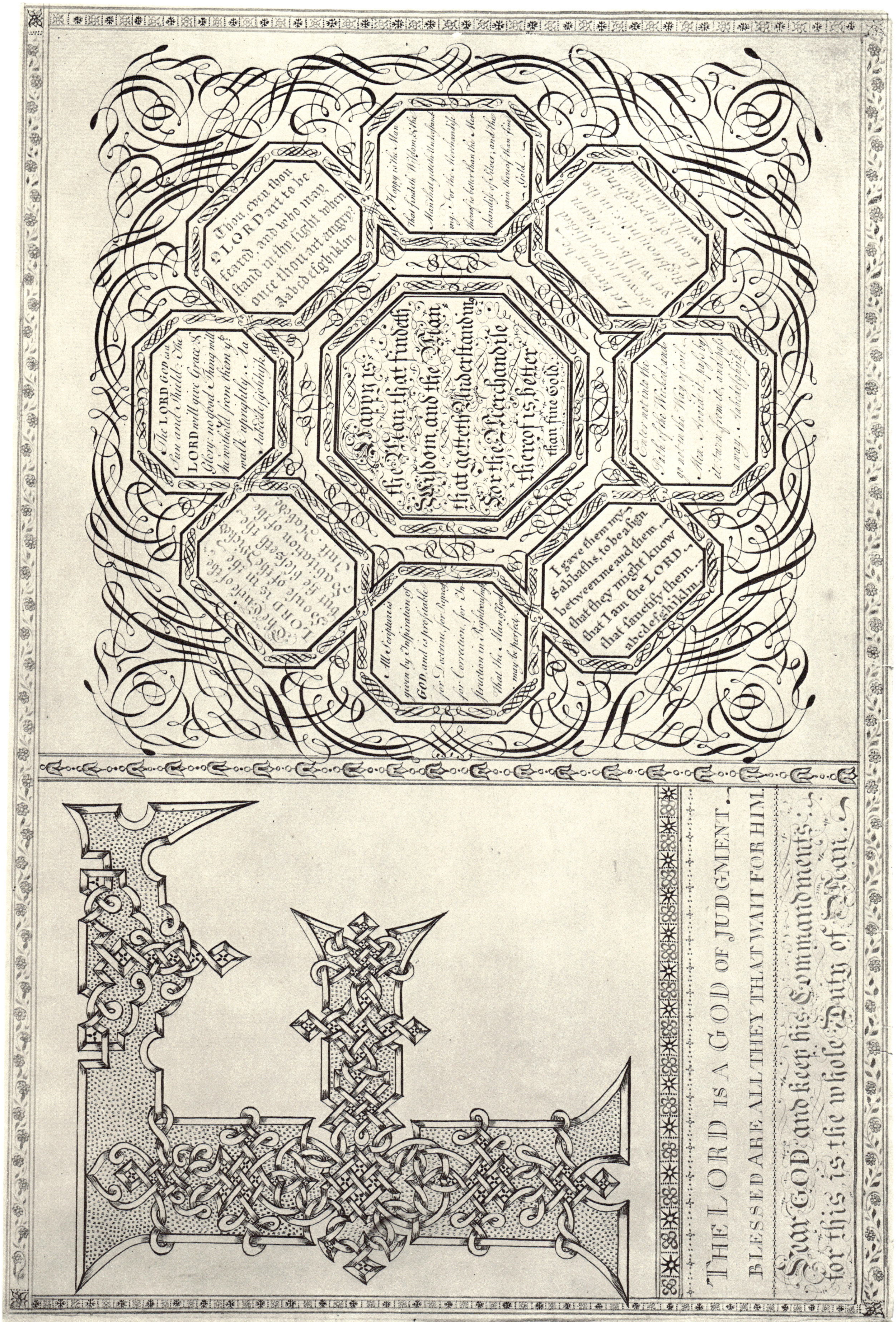

ABIAH HOLBROOK: *THE WRITING-MASTER'S AMUSEMENT*, MS, BOSTON, 1767 10¼ × 15¾ inches
Bequeathed in 1794 by Mrs. Rebecca Holbrook

Printing and Graphic Arts 229

JOHN MILTON: *PARADISE LOST*, LONDON, 1827   14½ × 10⅜ inches   Engravings by John Martin
Given in 1942 by Philip Hofer, H 1921

WILLIAM BLAKE: *EUROPE, A PROPHECY*, LAMBETH, 1794
 Given in 1963 by Mrs. Harold T. White

Printing and Graphic Arts 231

FRANÇOIS LEVAILLANT: *HISTOIRE NATURELLE DES OISEAUX DE PARADIS*, PARIS, 1806   23 × 16½ inches
Acquired in 1942 with the Hofer Fund

Anamenia Coriacea

Peint par P. J. Redouté.   Gravé par L. J. Allais.

E. P. VENTENAT: *JARDIN DE MALMAISON*, PARIS, 1803   21 × 13½ inches   Plate designed by Pierre-Joseph Redouté
Given in 1942 by Philip Hofer, H 1921

Printing and Graphic Arts   233

DESCRIPTION DE L'EGYPTE PUBLIÉ PAR LES ORDRES DE SA MAJESTÉ NAPOLEON LE GRAND, PARIS, 1809
24 × 17⅝ inches   Given in 1963 by Philip Hofer, H 1921

THE SANCTUARY OF THE GREAT TEMPLE OF ABOO-SIMBEL, NUBIA.

The adytum of the Temple, which terminates the great excavation at Aboo-Simbel, and is seen only in the gloom of its profundity in the larger drawing of the Interior, is a chamber which measures, from the door of the sanctuary to the wall behind the figures, twelve feet three inches, and in width twenty-three feet seven inches. In this cella are four sitting statues; three of them the Theban triad of deities, the fourth is Remeses, who is here admitted to a seat among them.

Roberts says that the statues in the sanctuary have been painted of various colours; before them is an altar cut, like the figures themselves, out of the solid rock; it is squared on the sides, and formed like a truncated pyramid, the top of it is broken. On the sides of the wall, about two feet in advance of the altar, are the marks of grooves, with holes for fastenings for a screen, probably of open-work and metal, to prevent too near an approach of the worshippers, if they were ever allowed to proceed so far. The sandstone is soft in which these statues are hewn. The statue on the left has an ornament reaching from his chin down nearly to his feet; the second has a head-dress like the tutulus, or palm-branch; the third wears a sort of helmet; and the last is the hawk-headed deity. This is said to be the oldest of the Nubian or the Egyptian Temples: if the arts were thus advanced at so remote a period as the construction of this Temple, what has become of those that preceded it? for such excellence could only have sprung from progressive improvement.

Wilkinson's Egypt and Thebes.   Roberts's Journal.

WILLIAM BROCKEDON: *EGYPT & NUBIA, FROM DRAWINGS MADE ON THE SPOT BY DAVID ROBERTS,*
LONDON, 1846–1849, 3 VOLS.   24 × 16¼ inches   Acquired in 1963 with the Hofer Fund

Printing and Graphic Arts   235

ACTUALITÉS

UN CAUCHEMAR DE M. DE BISMARK.
— Merci !...

Du reste, il n'est à peu près occupé qu'à juger des gens qui paraissent peu disposés à sauver la France (par bonheur on n'aura pas besoin d'eux pour cela).

C'est tous les jours à la 6ᵉ et à la 7ᵉ chambre un défilé de prussophiles que l'on condamne à deux, trois, quatre et jusqu'à huit mois de prison, suivant leurs antécédens judiciaires (et bon nombre d'entre eux, disons-le, en ont d'assez complets).

Il est juste de dire que nous voyons des Prussiens partout. Jeudi dernier, j'ai rencontré un prêtre conduit au poste par deux sergens de ville et escorté d'une foule de gens parmi lesquels étaient ceux qui l'avaient fait arrêter. J'ai eu la curiosité de demander à l'un de ceux-ci ce qu'était ce prêtre. — « Monsieur, me dit-il, c'est un espion prussien déguisé comme vous voyez. — Ah !... Et comment avec vous découvert cela ? — Comment ?... mais, monsieur, devant une affiche qu'il lisait en même temps que nous, et qui mentionnait nos avantages... Alors le faux prêtre avait l'air de dire que tout ça n'était peut-être pas grand chose ; que les Prussiens n'étaient pas encore vaincus..., enfin un tas de choses de ce genre-là. »

Je quittai ce brave homme, convaincu jusqu'à preuve contraire qu'il avait fait arrêter tout simplement un disciple de saint Thomas.

∴

Un prussophile ou du moins prétendu tel, puisqu'il était traduit devant la 7ᵉ chambre correctionnelle, s'est tiré d'affaire par une explication qu'envierait l'avocat le plus retors, si elle n'est pas l'expression de la vérité.

Le 16, il se mêlait à la conversation de deux personnes arrêtées à parler de la guerre, et il disait : « Ce sont les gens qui ont voté *oui*, comme vous, qui ont amené les Prussiens en France ; ce n'est pas à Commercy que je voudrais les voir, c'est à Paris ! »

M. LE PRÉSIDENT. — Reconnaissez-vous avoir dit que vous voudriez voir les Prussiens à Paris ?

GARNIER. — Parfaitement, monsieur le président, et je le dis encore : Je voudrais les voir à Paris, parce qu'il n'en sortirait pas un seul vivant ; j'ai ajouté ça. Si on ne l'a pas entendu, ce n'est pas ma faute.

Cette explication est accueillie par l'auditoire avec un éclat de rire qui entraine les juges eux-mêmes. Le tribunal avait ri, il était désarmé. Notre homme a donc été acquitté ; mais, si ce n'est pas un bon Français, c'est un joli roublard.

∴

Par contre, la même chambre a assez mal traité, à la même audience, un marchand de vins-logeur, nommé Timerch, dont j'ignore la nationalité, mais dont le nom vous a un petit parfum allemand ! On en mangerait.

Ce marchand de vins logeur était signalé à la police comme recevant chez lui quantité de Prussiens qui, par leurs propos, leurs menaces et leurs fanfaronnades, étaient devenus la terreur du voisinage, lorsque, le 15 août, on l'arrêta au moment où il criait avec persistance : Vive la Prusse ?

Il en a eu pour son année de prison.

∴

Et dire que j'ai vu l'autre jour devant la justice un gaillard qui pourrait manger tous les Prussiens à lui tout seul ; seulement, comme il faudrait les lui faire cuire, on fera bien de se débarrasser d'eux par un autre moyen.

Cette réalité du Bouffe-la-Balle de *la Chatte blanche* est un pauvre diable nommé Bellon aux trois quarts aveugle et atteint d'un diabète faméliques sans exemple. Il lui faut par jour soixante-six livres d'alimens solides et soixante-six litres d'eau. De telle sorte qu'il est obligé d'aller quémander à la porte des casernes les restes des soldats ; or, à l'heure qu'il est, les casernes étant vides, je me demande de quoi vit ce nouveau Gargantua.

Pourchassé par tout le monde pour sa voracité, ce malheureux voit partout des persécuteurs ; de là une voie de fait qu'il avait commise sur la personne d'une femme qui ne le connaissait pas du tout.

Le tribunal, ayant égard à sa triste position, ne l'a condamné qu'à seize francs d'amende.

Seize francs *d'amandes* feraient mieux son affaire.

JULES MOINAUX.

HONORÉ DAUMIER: *UN CAUCHEMAR DE M. DE BISMARK*, LITHOGRAPH FROM *LE CHARIVARI*, PARIS, AUGUST 22, 1870   16½ × 11½ inches   From a complete set of the periodical   Acquired in 1931 with the Degrand Fund

.... De temps en temps j'aime à voir le vieux Père,
Et je me garde bien de lui rompre en visière.........

JOHANN WOLFGANG VON GOETHE: *FAUST*, PARIS, 1828   16½ × 10⅞ inches
Lithographs by Eugène Delacroix   Given in 1941 by Philip Hofer, H 1921

EDWARD LEAR: DRAWING, *ULYSSES' ISLAND*
One of more than 3,500 drawings by Lear at Harvard
Given in 1945 by William B. Osgood Field

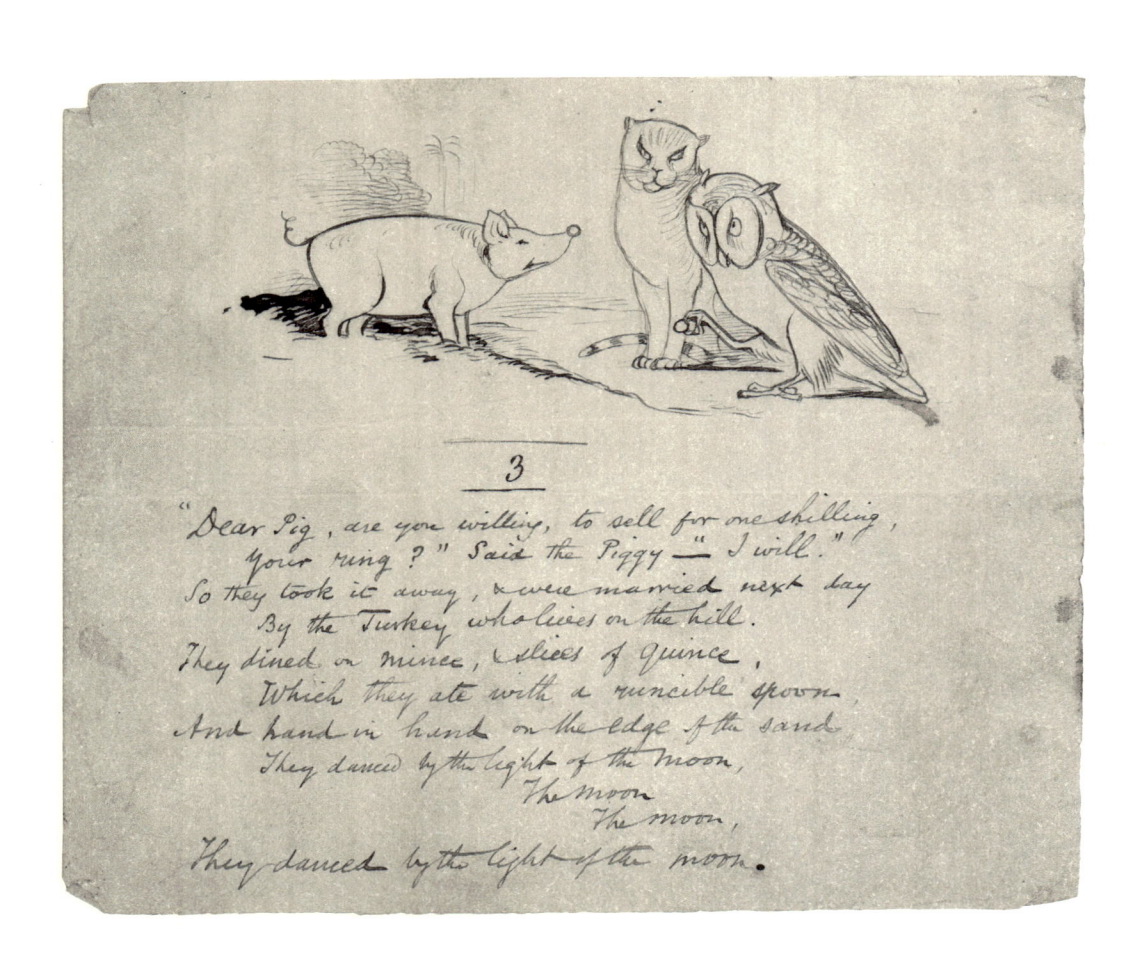

EDWARD LEAR: DRAWING, *SELF-PORTRAIT*
Acquired in 1963 with the Bemis Fund

EDWARD LEAR: DRAWING, *THE OWL AND THE PUSSY CAT*
Given in 1941 by Philip Hofer, H 1921

JULES RENARD: *HISTOIRES NATURELLES*, PARIS, 1899
Lithographs by Henri de Toulouse-Lautrec
Given in 1954 by Philip Hofer, H 1921

ODILON REDON, LITHOGRAPH FOR STÉPHANE MALLARMÉ: *JAMAIS UN COUP DE DÉS N'ABOLIRA LE HASARD* [PARIS, 1897] 13¾ × 12 inches
Unpublished work of which the typography was designed by Mallarmé
Given in 1961 by Mrs. Gardiner Fiske and Philip Hofer, H 1921

les autres tissoient du poil de chèvre ou faisoient des collets à prendre les oiseaux. Le soin qu'il falloit lors avoir des bœufs, étoit de leur donner de la paille à manger en la bouverie, aux chèvres et brebis de la feuillée en la bergerie, aux pourceaux de la faîne et du gland en la porcherie.

151

LONGUS: *DAPHNIS ET CHLOÉ*, PARIS, AMBROISE VOLLARD, 1902
Lithographs by Pierre Bonnard
Given in 1961 by Philip Hofer, H 1921

MAX JACOB:
LE SIÈGE DE JÉRUSALEM, PARIS,
HENRY KAHNWEILER, 1914   6⅜ × 4¼ inches
Etchings by Pablo Picasso;
his second illustrated book
Given in 1961 by Philip Hofer, H 1921

GUILLAUME APOLLINAIRE:
L'ENCHANTEUR POURRISSANT, PARIS,
HENRY KAHNWEILER, 1909   10½ × 8 inches
The first woodcuts by André Derain
to appear in a book
Transferred in 1958 from the Fogg Art Museum

TRISTAN TZARA: *VINGT-CINQ POÈMES*,
ZURICH [1918] 7¾ × 5⅝ inches
Woodcuts by Hans Arp
Acquired in 1951 with the library of Karl Viëtor

WASSILY KANDINSKY AND FRANZ MARC, ED.:
DER BLAUE REITER, 2ND ED., MUNICH, 1914
11⅜ × 8⅝ inches
Cover design by Kandinsky
Given in 1939 by Philip Hofer, H 1921

Printing and Graphic Arts 243

ANDRÉ SUARÈS: *PASSION*, PARIS, AMBROISE VOLLARD, 1938 17¼ × 13¼ inches
Color etchings by Georges Rouault
Given in 1961 by Philip Hofer, H 1921

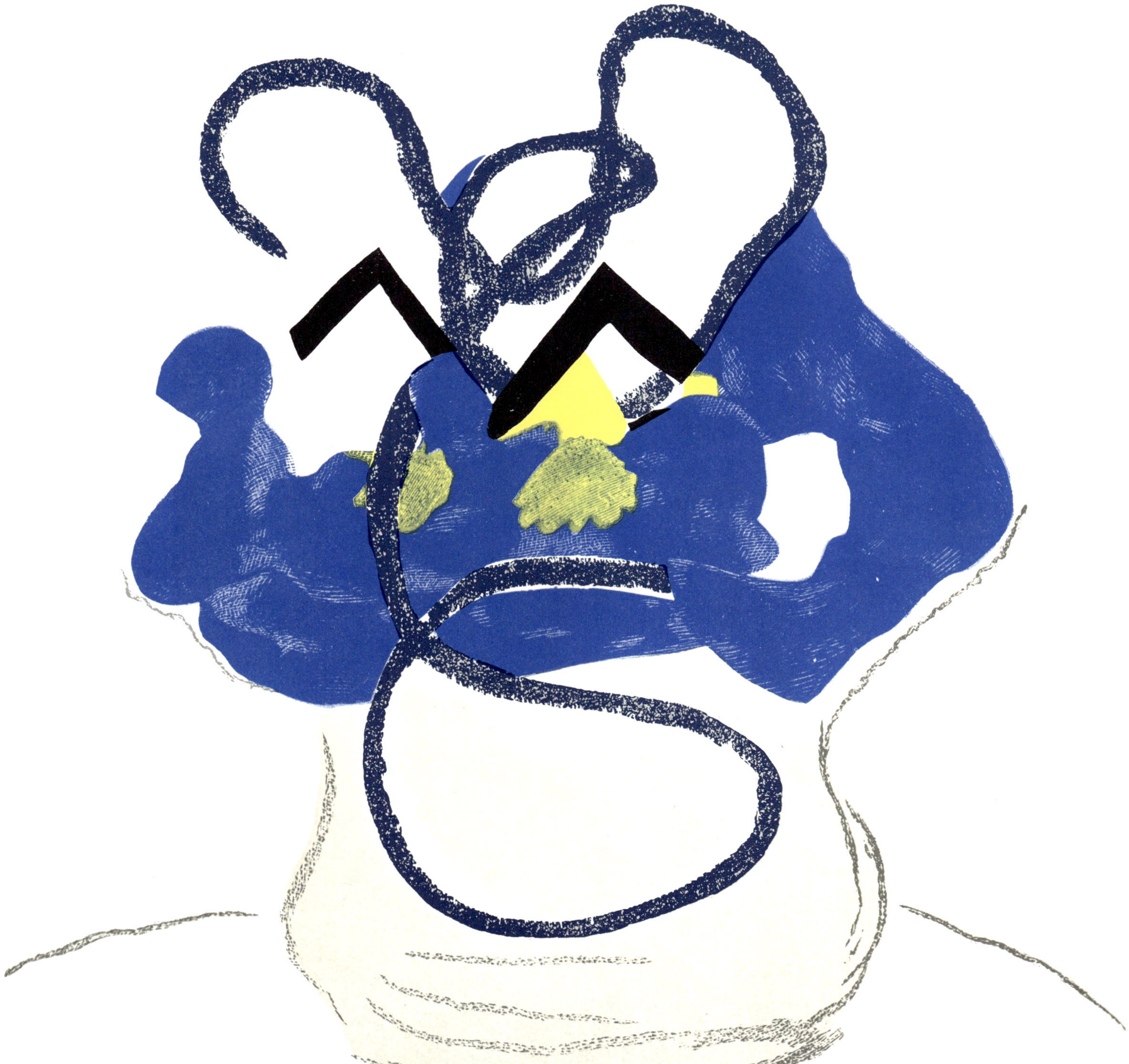

GUILLAUME APOLLINAIRE: *SI JE MOURAIS LA-BAS*, PARIS, 1962
　Illustrated by the author's friend Georges Braque to
　commemorate his own eightieth birthday
　Given in 1965 by Philip Hofer, H 1921

18½ × 14¼ inches

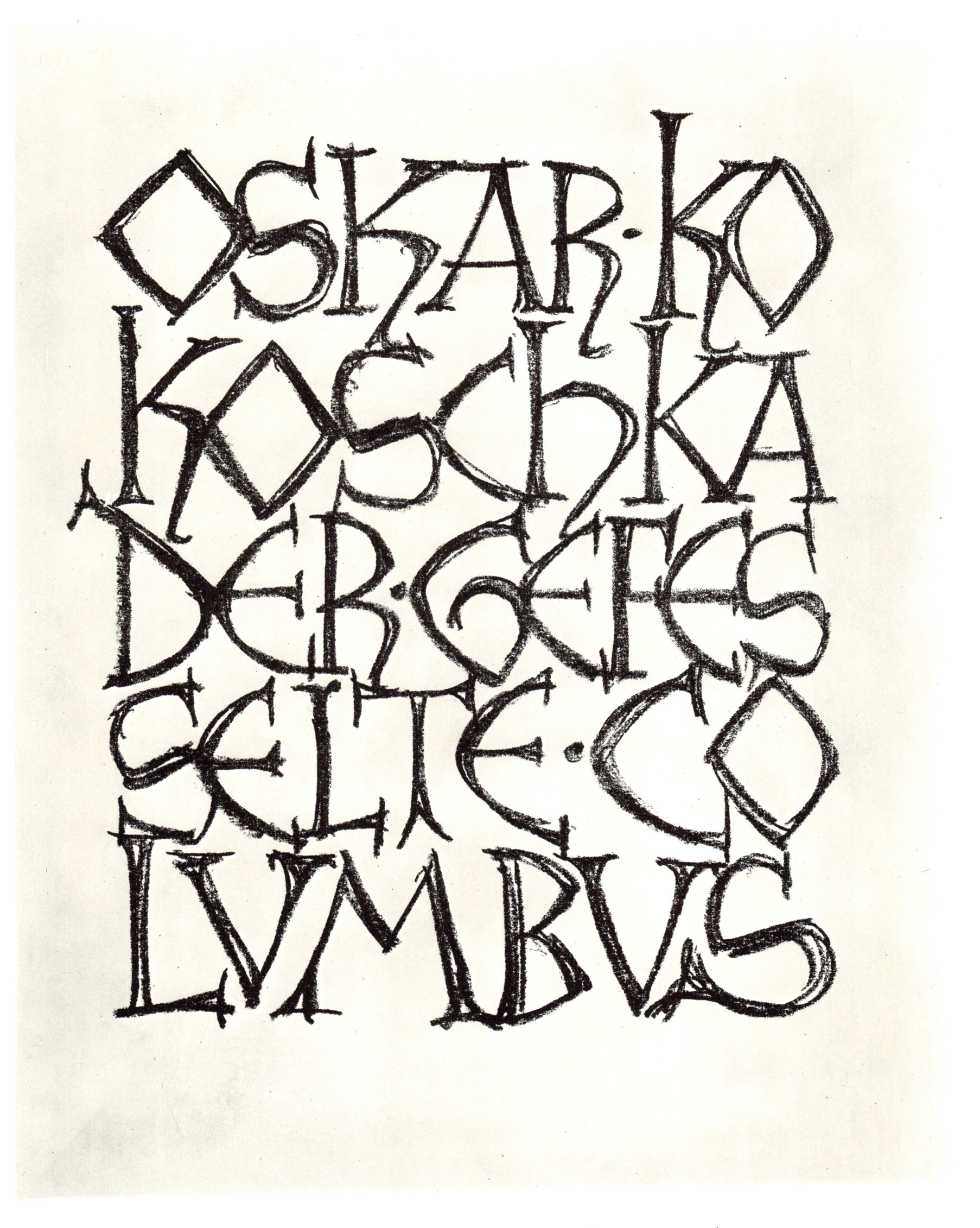

OSKAR KOKOSCHKA: *DER GEFESSELTE COLUMBUS* [BERLIN] 1921   19½ × 15¼ inches
Lettering by E. R. Weiss
  Given in 1961 by Philip Hofer, H 1921

Printing and Graphic Arts   245

MICHEL LEIRIS: *BAGATELLES VÉGÉTALES*,
PARIS, 1956   9¼ × 7⅛ inches
Color etchings by Joan Miró
Given in 1961 by Philip Hofer

VIRGIL: *GEORGICA*,
WEIMAR, CRANACH PRESSE, 1926
13 × 10 inches
Woodcuts by Aristide Maillol
Given in 1927 by Friends of the Library

TITYRUS
O Meliboee deus nobis haec otia fecit.
namque erit ille mihi semper deus, illius aram
saepe tener nostris ab ovilibus imbuet agnus.
ille meas errare boves, ut cernis, et ipsum
ludere quae vellem calamo permisit agresti.
MELIBOEUS
Non equidem invideo, miror magis: undique totis
usque adeo turbatur agris. en ipse capellas
protinus aeger ago; hanc etiam vix Tityre duco.
hic inter densas corylos modo namque gemellos
spem gregis—a—silice in nuda conixa reliquit.
saepe malum hoc nobis, si mens non laeva fuisset,
de caelo tactas memini praedicere quercus.
sed tamen iste deus qui sit da Tityre nobis.
TITYRUS
Vrbem quam dicunt Romam Meliboee putavi

6

246

LEONARD BASKIN: *HORNED BEETLES & OTHER INSECTS*, NORTHAMPTON, 1958   5 × 7 inches
Acquired in 1958 with the Hofer Fund

RENÉ CHAR: *RETOUR AMONT*,
PARIS, 1965   9½ × 7 inches
Etchings by Alberto Giacometti
Acquired in 1966 with the Hofer Fund

Printing and Graphic Arts

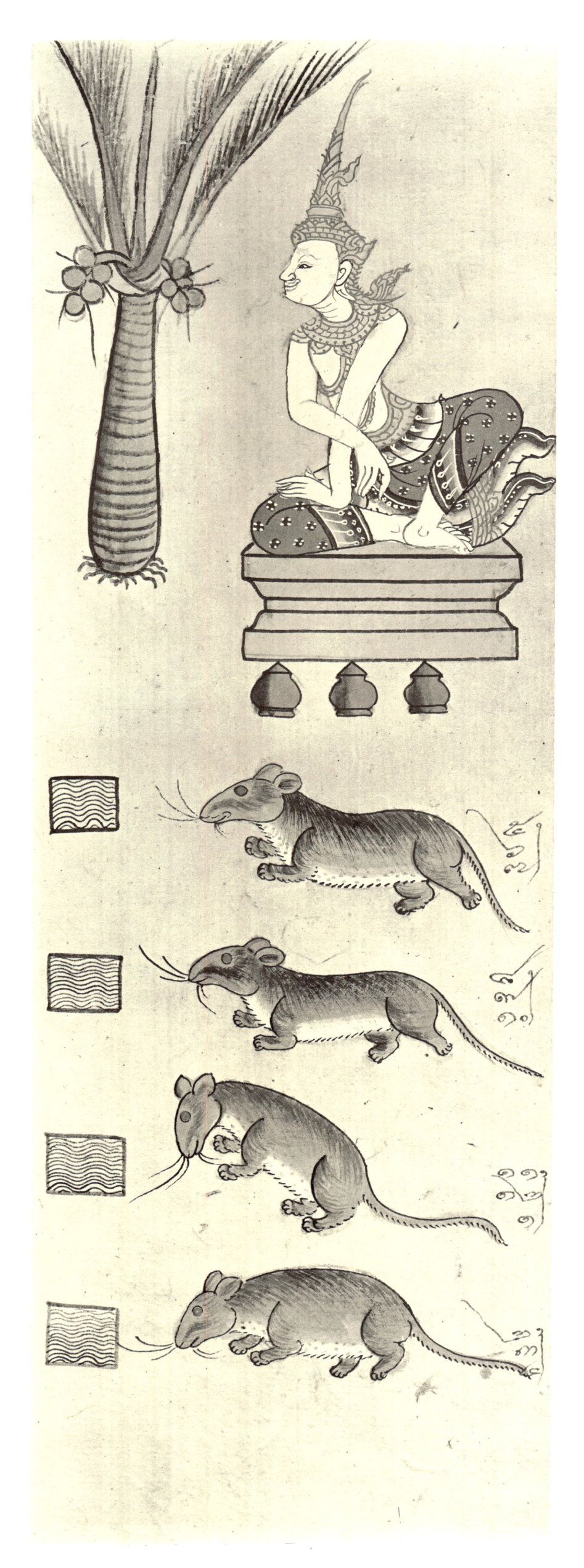

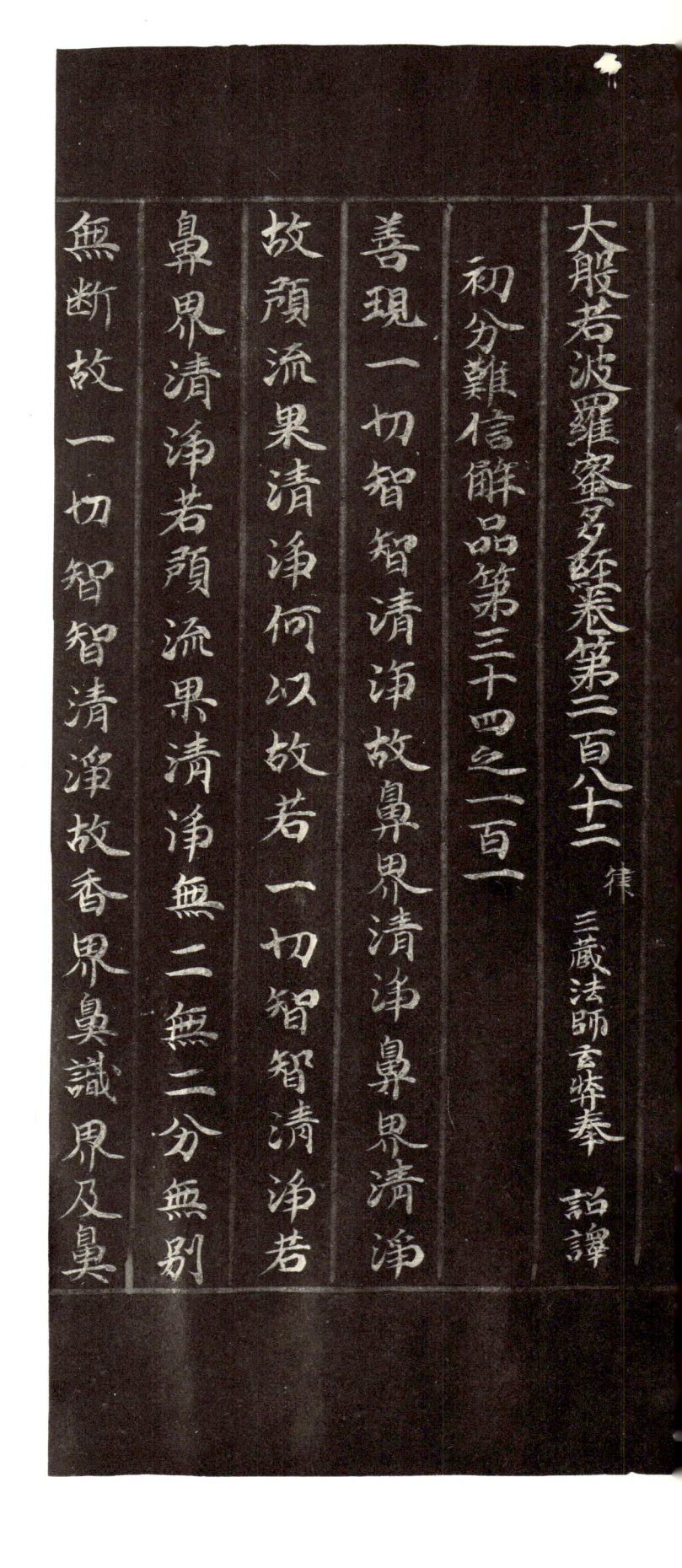

THAI MS.: A TREATISE ON FORTUNE-TELLING
(SAEC. XIX)   14¼ × 4⅞ inches
Given in 1944 by M. A. DeWolfe Howe, H 1887

JAPANESE MS.: BUDDHIST SUTRA (SAEC. XII) 10 × 12 inches
Acquired in 1955 with the Hofer Fund

Printing and Graphic Arts

Index

Adam, Robert, 218
Adams, Henry, 109
Addison, Joseph, 56
Aeschylus, 109
Aesop, 185, 213
Aiken, Conrad, 114
Alamanni, Luigi, 154
Alcott, Louisa May, 104
Aldrich, Thomas Bailey, 112
Aldus Manutius, 21
Allestree, Richard, 42
Amerbach, Bruno, 32
Anacreon, 43
Anderson, Maxwell, 165
Androuet du Cerceau, Jacques, 198
Anne, of Austria, 215
Antonio, Nicolas, 200
Apocalypse, 180
Apollinaire, Guillaume, 242, following 244
Aretino, *see* Leonardo Aretino
Ariosto, Ludovico, 156
Aristotle, 196
Arnim, Achim von, 136
Arp, Hans, 243
Athenaeus Naucratita, 202
Auden, Wystan Hugh, 71
Audubon, John James, 97
Augustine, St., 12, 36, 37

Bacon, Sir Francis, 210
Balzac, Honoré de, 149
Barcelona, *Usatges*, 186
Barlow, Francis, 213
Barrie, Sir James M., 70
Bartolomeo San Vito, following 186
Bartolomeus filius Andreae Maççonis, scribe, 15
Baskin, Leonard, 247
Baudelaire, Charles, 150
Baudouin, Nicolas, 159
Bayer, Johann, 208

Beerbohm, Sir Max, 70
Beethoven, Ludwig van, 88
Benn, Gottfried, 140
Benson, John Howard, xv, 250
Berardi, M., 150
Berçeure, Pierre, 39
Bernstein, Aline, 119
Bibiena, Giuseppe Galli da, 216
Bible, English, following 42, 48; French, 42; Greek, 10; Latin, 14, 176, 180
Biencourt, 121
Binding, Bury St. Edmunds, 36; by Robert Adam, 218; by Padeloup, 42; by Queen's Binder B, 42; by Roger Payne, 43; repaired by Payne, following 42; English 17th century, following 42, 168; for Queen Christina of Sweden, 200; for John Evelyn, 54; for François I of France, 196; for George III of England, 218; for Jean Grolier, 43; for Thomas Hollis, 4; for Abp. William Laud, 45; Neapolitan gilt, 182; Powdered gold, 44; Romanesque, 176
Blake, William, following 62, 231
Blaue Reiter, 243
Block book, 180
Boccaccio, Giovanni, 38, 40
Bodenstein von Carlstadt, Andreas, 29
Bodleian Library, Curators, 16
Bonnard, Pierre, 241
Book of Common Prayer, following 42
Boswell, James, 58, 84
Bourguignon, Hubert François, *see* Gravelot
Bouvier, Jules, 175
Brahe, Tycho, 160
Braque, Georges, following 244
Brentano, Clemens, 136
Breviary, usage of Padua, 190
Brockedon, William, 235
Brontë, Charlotte, 86
Brontë, Patrick Branwell, 86
Browning, Elizabeth Barrett, 67

Browning, Robert, 87
Bruno, Giordano, 48
Buchan, David Stewart Erskine, Earl of, 63
Büchner, Georg, 137
Bullard, Otis A., 116
Bulstrode, Cecilia, 82
Burnet, Bishop Gilbert, 52
Burns, Robert, 63
Burton, Robert, 167
Byrd, William, 162

Calderini *Pontifical*, following 182
Callot, Jacques, 137, 203
Calvin, Jean, 30
Camoës, Luis de, 158
Camus, Albert, 153
Cardoinus, Camillus, 51
Carlyle, Thomas, 7
Carmina apposita Pasquillo, 197
Carroll, Lewis, 76–79
Casanova, Jacques, 157
Cervantes Saavedra, Miguel de, 159
Chamisso, Adelbert von, 136
Char, René, 247
Charivari, 236
Chase, Owen, 106
Chaucer, Geoffrey, 9
Chevalier, Étienne, 38
Cipriani, Giovanni Battista, 55
Clouet, François, following 200
Coleridge, Samuel Taylor, 64, 134
Collins, Wilkie, 66
Columbus, Christopher, 16
Comberford, Nicholas, 24
Commencemens de l'hidrographie, 203
Communist Manifesto, 128
Compagnie des cent associés, 121
Conrad, Joseph, 70
Constant de Rebecque, Benjamin, 149
Contrasto del vivo e del morto, 185
Contrasto di carnesciale & la quaresima, 184
Coriolano, Giovanni Battista, 172
Corneille, Pierre, 147
Cortona, Pietro da, 209
Cranch, Christopher Pearse, 103
Cummings, Edward Estlin, 115

Dante, 15
Daumier, Honoré, 236
De Buz *Hours*, following 38
Declaration of Independence, 95
Delacroix, Eugène, 237

Della Bella, Stefano, 173
Derain, André, 242
Desbordes-Valmore, Marceline, 149
Description de l'Egypte, 234
Descrizione delle feste, 222
Desmarets de St. Sorlin, Jean, following 214
Dickens, Charles, 66
Dickinson, Emily, 116, 117
Dodgson, Charles Lutwidge, 76–79
Donne, John, 54
Dorat, C. J., 41
Dostoevskii, Fedor, 127
Downame, John, 2
Dryden, John, 50
Duma decree, 128

Eadmer, 13
Eck, Johann, 31
Eisen, Charles, 41
Eliot, Andrew, 4
Eliot, George, 87
Eliot, John, 90
Eliot, Thomas Stearns, 113
Emerson, Ellen, 104
Emerson, Lidian, 104
Emerson, Ralph Waldo, 102, 103, 104
Engels, Friedrich, 128
Erasmus, 32, 33
Evelyn, John, 54

Faithorne, William, 202
Farfan, Fernando de la Torre, 205
Farnsworth, C. B., 108
Federov, Ivan, 125
Ferrari, Giovanni Battista, 209
Fischer von Erlach, Joseph Emanuel, 224
Flaubert, Gustave, 152
Fore-edge painting, following 42
Formé, Nicolas, 163
Foscolo, Ugo, 157
Foster, John, 100
François I, of France, 196, following 200
Fréart de Chambray, Roland, 204
Frost, Robert, 112
Fuchs, Leonhard, 192

Garnett, Edward, 80
Garrard, George, 82
Gay, John, 58, 217
George, Stefan, 140
Gevartius, Casper, 201
Gheyn, Jacob de, 174

Giacometti, Alberto, 247
Gilbert, William, 211
Gobin, Robert, 196
Göschen, Georg Joachim, 131
Goethe, Johann Wolfgang von, 6, 59, 130, 237
Goffe, Thomas, 167
Goldsmith, Oliver, 59
Goncourt, Edmond de, 151
Gottsched, Johann Christoph, 132
Gravelot, 217
Gray, Thomas, 59
Gregorius Nyssenus, 11
Grolier, Jean, 43
Grünewald, Matthias, 188

Hale, Nathan, 64
Hamann, Johann Georg, 132
Hamilton, Alexander, 96
Hancock, John, 94
Hardenberg, Friedrich von, 131, 133
Harman, Thomas, 47
Harvard, John, 1, 2
Harvard College, 1, 3
Hawthorne, Nathaniel, 107
Hegel, Georg Wilhelm Friedrich, 135
Heine, Heinrich, 142, 143
Henry VIII, of England, 28
Herberstein, Sigmund, 194
Herbert, George, 53
Herschel, Sir William, 161
Hölderlin, Friedrich, 136
Hoffmann, E. T. A., 137
Hofmannsthal, Hugo von, 139
Holbrook, Abiah, 229
Hollis, Thomas, 4, 5, 55
Holmes, Oliver Wendell, 105, 108
Home, Francis, 4
Homer, 17
Horace, 8
Hours, De Buz, following 38; usage of Rome, following 186; Juana la Loca, following 186; Tory, 196
Howells, William Dean, 105
Hugo, Victor, 149
Humbert, Henry, 203
Hutten, Ulrich, 31
Huysmans, Joris Karl, 150

Igor' Tale, 124
Imitatio Christi, 19
Incunabula, identified by numbers in Goff's census: A-148, 185; C-761, 16; C-873, 185; C-874, 184; E-101, 32; H-300, 17; I-4, 19; L-70, 20; M-376, 187; M-479, 181; M-880, 35; P-371, 155; P-788, 183; S-5, 34; T-91, 166; U-78, 186; W-69, 18.
Inglis, Esther, 215
Ingolstadt world-map, 22

Jacob, Max, 242
James I, of England, 53
James, Henry, 105, 111
James, William, 110
Japanese MS., 248, 249
Jarry, Nicolas, 215
Jerome, St., 178
Johnson, Samuel, 58, 84
Johnston, Thomas, 120
Jones, Robert Edmond, 164
Jonson, Ben, 83
Joyce, James, 71
Juana la Loca, *Hours*, following 186

Kafka, Franz, 140
Kandinsky, Wassily, 243
Keats, John, 72–75
Kello, *see* Inglis
Killigrew, Thomas, 168, 169
Kipling, Rudyard, 67
Kirchenordnung, Wittenberg, 29
Klinger, Friedrich Maximilian von, 132
Kokoschka, Oskar, 245

Labyrinthe de Versailles, 214
La Fontaine, Jean de, 82
Lamb, Charles, 85
La Motte, Antoine de, 217
Latini, Brunetto, 20
Laud, Archbishop William, 45
Lautrec, Henri de Toulouse, 239
Lawrence, T. E., 80, 81
Lear, Edward, 238
Le Clerc, Sebastien, 214
Lee, Arthur, 94
Leech, John, 66
Leicester, Robert Dudley, Earl of, 49
Leiris, Michel, 246
Leonardo Aretino, 182
Leopardi, Giacomo, 157
Lescarbot, Marc, 121
Lessing, Gotthold Ephraim, 133
Levaillant, François, 232
Lincoln, Abraham, 99
Linné, Carl, 59

Liturgy of St. Basil the Great, 179
Livy, 39
Locke, John, 55
London, city of, 46
Longfellow, Henry Wadsworth, 104, 105, 109
Longus, 241
Louis XIV, of France, following 214
Lowell, James Russell, 104, 105, 108
Lucan, 189
Lunt, Alfred, 165
Luther, Martin, 26, 28

Mace, Thomas, 202
Madison, James, 96
Maillol, Aristide, 246
Mallarmé, Stéphane, 240
Mann, Thomas, 141
Manuscripts, pre-1600, 8–15, 21, 27, 32, 37–40, 49, 154, 156, 178, 179, following 182, 184, following 186
Maps, 22–25, 203, 206
Marc, Franz, 243
Martin, John, 230
Marx, Karl, 128
Mary, Queen of Scots, following 200
Masefield, John, 70
Mather, Cotton, 101
Mather, Richard, 100
Mauburnus, Johannes, 187
Maupassant, Guy de, 150
Mayhew, Jonathan, 4
Médailles de Louis le Grand, 220
Melanchthon, Philipp, 27, 29
Melusine, 181
Melville, Herman, 106
Mercator, Gerardus, 23
Merck, Johann Heinrich, 59
Milton, John, 51, following 62, 230
Minute Men, 92
Miró, Joan, 246
Missal, 188
Molière, 147
Monroe, James, 93
Montaigne, Michel de, 146
Moreau, J. B., 147
Musil, Robert, 140
Münster, Sebastian, 197
Musaeus, 35

Nanteuil, Robert, 202
Napoléon I, 234
Nicolay, John G., 99

Norton, Charles Eliot, 105
Novalis, *see* Hardenberg
Nozeman, Cornelius, 226

Orpheus, 184
Ovid, 43

Padeloup, 42
Palatino, Giovanni Battista, 197
Pallas, Peter Simon, 227
Parigi, Alfonso, 173
Payne, Roger, following 42, 43
Pèlerin, Jean, 193
Pelham, Peter, 101
Percy, Bishop Thomas, 62
Petrarch, 155
Piazzetta, Giovanni Battista, 223
Picasso, Pablo, 242
Piozzi, Hester Lynch Salusbury Thrale, 58, 84
Pirandello, Luigi, 157
Piranesi, Giovanni Battista, 219
Playbill, English, 170; Salem, Mass., 171
Pliny, 183
Poe, Edgar Allan, 108
Pontifical (the Calderini Pontifical), following 182
Pope, Alexander, 57
Pound, Ezra, 113
Premierfait, Laurent de, 38
Ptolemy, 206
Pushkin, Aleksandr, 124, 126

Quebec, 120

Racine, Jean, 147
Radishchev, A. N., 124
Râle, Sebastien, 91
Randolph, Peyton, 96
Recorde, Robert, 195
Redon, Odilon, 240
Renard, Jules, 239
Resende, André de, 197
Rhosos, Joannes, 184
Richelieu, Armand Jean du Plessis, Cardinal de, 121
Rilke, Rainer Maria, 144, 145
Roberts, David, 235
Robinson, Edwin Arlington, 112
Rochester, John Wilmot, Earl of, 52
Rohan atelier, following 38
Ronsard, Pierre, 146
Rosset, François de, 159

Rouault, Georges, 244
Rousseau, Jean-Jacques, 148
Roxbury Latin School, 90
Rubens, Peter Paul, 201
Rudbeck, Olaf, 207
Ruzicka, Rudolph, end-papers and seal on binding
Ruzicka, Veronica, end-papers

Sabellico, 34
Sacramentary, 178
Sallust, 221
Schiller, Friedrich, 134
Schlegel, August Wilhelm, 133
Schopenhauer, Arthur, 138
Ségur, Louis Philippe de, 7
Serlio, Sebastiano, 199
Servetus, Michael, 30
Shakespeare, William, 47, 133, 164
Shaw, George Bernard, 68
Shelley, Percy Bysshe, 65
Shestakov, A., 25
Short-title Catalogue books: 1163, 210; 2328.5, 48; 3935, 48; 3936, 48; 3937, 48; 3938, 48; 3940, 48; 7137, 2; 10498, 33; 11883, 211; 12787, 47; 16473.9, 46; 20796, 195; 22292, 47
Simonson, Lee, 165
Smart, Christopher, 60, 61
Smith, Dorothy, 54
Smith, Samuel Francis, 98
Southey, Robert, 64
Sparks, Jared, 96
Spenser, Edmund, 72
Stalker, John, 212
Stifter, Adalbert, 137
Strada, Jacobus de, 44
Stubbs, George, 228
Suarès, André, 244
Sutra, 248, 249

Tasso, Torquato, 156, 223
Taylor, John, 215
Tenniel, Sir John, 77
Tennyson, Alfred, Baron, 67
Terence, 166

Thackeray, William Makepeace, 66
Thai MS., 248
Theophrastus, 21
Thomas à Kempis, 19
Thoreau, Henry David, 104, 109
Tieck, Ludwig, 133
Trotsky, Leon, 129
Tycho Brahe, *see* Brahe
Tzara, Tristan, 243

Vatican, type-specimen, 214
Ventenat, E. P., 233
Verlaine, Paul, 150
Very, Jones, 108
Vesalius, Andreas, 191
Viëtor, Karl, 14
Virgil, 54, 246
Voltaire, 148

Wagner, Richard, 138
Walpole, Horace, 59
Walton, Izaak, 54
Ward, Artemas, 94
Washington, George, 93, 96
Watts, Isaac, 6
Weiss, E. R., 245
White, Francis, 45
Whitman, Walt, 89
Whitney, Geoffrey, 49
Whittier, John Greenleaf, 109
Wieland, Christoph Martin, 132
Wittenberg *Kirchenordnung*, 29
Wolfe, James, 122, 123
Wolfe, Thomas, 118, 119
Wolfe, Walter, 122, 123
Wolfram von Eschenbach, 18
Woodhouse, Richard, 73
Wordsworth, William, 65

Yeats, William Butler, 69
Yuan-Ming-Yuan, 225

Zola, Émile, 150
Zunz, Leopold, 143
Zwingli, Ulrich, 31

The staff of the Houghton Library combined
to select the illustrations and to suggest the text
of this book. Roderick Stinehour designed its
format & typography, and the type was com-
posed at The Stinehour Press under the super-
vision of C. Freeman Keith. E. Harold Hugo
was responsible for the photography, except
for the pictures on pages xv, 23, 250, & facing
page 43, which were taken by Barney Burstein.
The book was printed under Mr. Hugo's direction at The Meriden Gravure Company with
the supervisory assistance of William J. Glick.
Robert Wessmann directed the binding
at the J. F. Tapley Company.

The expenses of publishing this volume
have been assumed by a friend of
the Houghton Library.

673